The Damned and the Dead

The Damned and the Dead

The Eastern Front through the Eyes
of Soviet and Russian Novelists

Frank Ellis

University Press of Kansas

Published by the University Press of Kansas (Lawrence, Kansas 66045), which was organized by the Kansas Board of Regents and is operated and funded by Emporia State University, Fort Hays State University, Kansas State University, Pittsburg State University, the University of Kansas, and Wichita State University

Library of Congress Cataloging-in-Publication Data

Ellis, Frank, 1953-

    The damned and the dead : the Eastern Front through the eyes of Soviet and Russian novelists / Frank Ellis.

        p.   cm. — (Modern war studies)

    Includes bibliographical references and index.

    ISBN 978-0-7006-1784-5 (cloth : acid-free paper)

    1. Russian literature—20th century—History and criticism.

    2. Russian fiction—20th century—History and criticism.

    3. World War, 1939-1945—Literature and the war.

    4. War in literature.

    5. Novelists, Russian—20th century—Biography.

    6. Veterans—Soviet Union—Biography.

    7. World War, 1939-1945—Personal narratives, Soviet.

    8. World War, 1939-1945—Campaigns—Eastern Front.

    9. Soviet Union. Raboche-Krest'ianskaia Krasnaia Armiia—History. 10. Stalin, Joseph, 1879-1953.   I. Title.

    PG3026.W3E455 2011

    891.73'44093584054217—dc22   2011002809

British Library Cataloguing-in-Publication Data is available.

Printed in the United States of America

10 9 8 7 6 5 4 3 2 1

The paper used in this publication is recycled and contains 30 percent postconsumer waste. It is acid free and meets the minimum requirements of the American National Standard for Permanence of Paper for Printed Library Materials Z39.48-1992.

Mothers, mothers! Why have we resigned ourselves to savage human memory and reconciled ourselves to violence and death? Greater than the rest of us and more courageously do you suffer in your primeval loneliness and in your holy and animal longing for your children. One cannot purge oneself by suffering for a thousand years and hope for a miracle. There is no God! No faith! Death reigns over this world. Mothers, on whom can we hope?
—Viktor Astaf'ev, *The Shepherd and the Shepherdess*

All people stand guilty before a mother who has lost her son in war and throughout mankind's history they have tried in vain to justify themselves in her eyes.
—Vasilii Grossman, *Life and Fate*

When the battles in the forest which surrounded our Berlin suburb were over, many dead were lying around, both Russians and Germans. We buried them, and I was struck by something. We found identity tags on the Germans, but there was no information on the Russians as to who they were. And while we put them into the ground I thought about the Russian women who were waiting for these lads, about the women who would never be able to find out where they had met their end. Now, Russia no longer seemed to me to be that fairy-tale land of childhood, or the land of a cruel dictator. For me it had been transformed into a land of great mourning, into a land of sobbing mothers.
—Gabrielle Leech-Ansprach, *My Meetings with Russians*

CONTENTS

PREFACE

We are orphans and fatherless, our mothers are as widows.
—Lamentations 5:3

Isolated Soviet and Russian war novels have been studied, and some have been translated, but no Western scholar has yet devoted a monograph entirely to Soviet and Russian war literature based on the experiences of World War II (the Great Patriotic War, Velikaia Otechestvennaia voina). Such a monograph is long overdue, and that is the aim I set myself in writing *The Damned and the Dead: The Eastern Front through the Eyes of Soviet and Russian Novelists*.

Given the astonishing amount of material in the public domain, the lack of interest is difficult to explain. One practical reason may simply be that most of the literature is available only in Russian. Or it may have something to do with the perception, even among Slavists, that Soviet war literature is hopelessly boring and scarcely worth reading. True, there are Soviet novels that deserve this assessment, but by no means all do. Some of the best Soviet war literature—the work of the Belorussian writer Vasil' Bykov, for example—is superb. Even the avowedly conformist novels that seek to rehabilitate Stalin in the 1970s cannot be dismissed out of hand. It would be a mistake to believe that all literature that attacks Stalin and the Soviet state is, ipso facto, good and that anything that praises Stalin and party is bad.

The amount of published literature in Russia that is devoted to the war is enormous. Some of the authors studied here will be familiar to Slavists for writing on themes other than the war—Viktor Astaf'ev, for example; others, I suspect, will not. I have tried to cover a spectrum of writing, ranging from works that during the Soviet period were recognized by Soviet critics as ideologically dubious and completely unpublishable to novels that were considered less ideologically threatening. I also offer a detailed study of two neo-Stalinist war novels.

Censorship was a major obstacle when writing about the war, or indeed about anything deemed to be remotely threatening to the Soviet regime's view of the world. Anatolii Kuznetsov's novel about life under German occupation, *Babii IAr* (1966), was severely mauled, as was Viktor

Astaf'ev's *Pastukh i Pastushka: Sovremennaia pastoral'* (The Shepherd and Shepherdess: A Modern Pastoral, 1971). Vasilii Grossman's two major Stalingrad novels both suffered as well. *Za pravoe delo* (For a Just Cause, 1952) was subjected to a severe battering by the censors and their stooges in the Union of Writers. Soon after it was serialized in *Novyi mir* at the end of 1952, Grossman was caught up in the wave of anti-Semitism that accompanied the so-called Doctors' Plot and subjected to ferocious criticism. Having survived this onslaught, Grossman then watched as the KGB "arrested" the manuscript of *Zhizn' i sud'ba* (Life and Fate, 1988).

Authorized translations were another method of attack deployed by the censors. Vasil' Bykov's works suffered from this technique, and given that I have confined my study in chapter 3 to the Russian-language versions of Bykov's works, the author's counterideological thrust will at times be much weaker than that in the original texts, which were written in Belorussian. Although Bykov is not a Russian, the case for including his works in any study of Soviet-Russian war literature is overwhelming. The case has been well made by Lazar' Lazarev:

> Not merely because he translated nearly all his own work himself, or to be more precise, rewrote them in Russian, and several of them first appeared in Russian publications (he was a regular writer for *Novyi mir* when the journal was run by Tvardovskii, circumstances that partly account for the malicious persecution of several of his stories by semiofficial critics). The main thing, as it happened, was that his books became an organic and integral part of Russian literature, which must not be divorced from the literary process.[1]

Appendixes A and B are translations of two orders, respectively, Order № 270 (16 August 1941) and Order № 227 (28 July 1942), which were issued by Stalin. The full text of these two orders was first published in 1988. Both orders deal with vital and recurring themes in Soviet/Russian war literature—desertion, executions, and morale—and I thought it would be useful to include full translations because they provide a historical frame of reference for the many authors discussed, especially Astaf'ev, Bykov, But, Grossman, and Vladimov. Appendix C is a translation of another important historical document, which deals with, among other things, the themes of desertion and filtration: the statute founding the Soviet counterintelligence agency SMERSH, confirmed by Stalin on 21 April 1943. The Russian original document was declassified only in 2003.

While working on another war-related project in the Bundesarchiv-Militärarchiv in Freiburg-im-Breisgau, I came across a lot of material that is directly relevant for some parts of this study (mainly chapters 5 and 6). A full list of cited archive material is included in the bibliography of primary sources. Given that it is an analysis of declassified NKVD documents that were first published in 2000, chapter 6 is something of an anomaly when compared with the other chapters, which deal exclusively with war litera-ture. The point of including this chapter is that it provides a historical and well-documented context for one of the main battles on the Eastern front, thus supplementing the works of literature. It also raises some interesting questions about what I shall call Grossman's patriotic thesis, which I dis-cuss in detail in chapter 6.

Some of the experiences and incidents reflected in Soviet and Russian war literature will be immediately recognizable to anyone who has read some of the better-known Western war novels or who may have personal experience of war, cold, hunger, fear, and exhaustion. Others are peculiar to the Soviet experience of war—the scale of executions at Stalingrad, for example—and strike the Western reader as bizarre, incomprehensible, or scarcely believable. I have tried in this book to bring out the common expe-riences as well as examining the peculiarities of Russia at war, as reflected in literature. One huge difference that separates the Western attitude to, and interest in, the war, from the Russian obsession with the Great Patri-otic War is the scale of suffering; the devastation; and the sheer number of casualties, killed and wounded. As Solzhenitsyn reminds us, only "a rare Russian village welcomed back its men."[2] Then there is the psychological legacy and the grief that are only now being overcome. Time is the great healer, but this process has taken a very long time. And with recovery comes a certain indifference toward the past, especially on the part of younger generations.

In writing this book, I am sensible of the fact that I am dealing with a great nation's past and memories—a past and memories that, if not treated with respect and handled carefully, can cause great pain to the living. It is most certainly not my intention to give offense to Russians, though perhaps it is unavoidable. Even as an Englishman, I am conscious of an obligation to the life and work of Alexander Solzhenitsyn, Vasilii Grossman, Viktor Astaf'ev, and Vasil' Bykov, an obligation that I have tried to honor to the best of my ability. I salute the bravery of all Soviet soldiers—especially the partisans who often died alone and unseen, defending the Soviet Union and fighting for what they believed would be a better nation after the war—but equally, I lament the terrible loss of life and the courage wasted in defending Stalin's regime. Russians fought and won only to be cruelly betrayed after 1945. This is one of the most painful outcomes of the Great Patriotic War.

I would like to thank the following people for their advice and assistance: the late Professor John Erickson, University of Edinburgh; Professor David Gillespie, University of Bath; Mr. Martin Dewhirst; Chris Donnelly, Senior Fellow, Defence Academy of the United Kingdom, and coeditor of the *Journal of Slavic Military Studies*; Dr. Bernhard Chiari of the Militärgeschichtliches Forschungsamt, Potsdam; and Ms. Karin Sidow, Universität der Künste Berlin. I am especially indebted to Mr. Martin Dewhirst, Honorary Research Fellow, Department of Slavonic Studies, University of Glasgow, for the time he expended in reading the manuscript and for his encyclopedic knowledge of all things Soviet and Russian. I would also like to express my profound gratitude to the Leverhulme Trust for awarding me a two-year Research Fellowship, which allowed me to complete this book. I would also like to thank Dr. Robert Sansam of the Computing Support Staff at the University of Leeds for his assistance in solving a number of software problems and Ms. Maureen Pinder and Mr. Richard Davies of the Brotherton Library, University of Leeds, for their assistance in tracking down various sources.

Transliteration conforms to that used by the Library of Congress, with some exceptions, most notably "Alexander" instead of "Aleksandr." According to the Library of Congress, "SMERSh" is the correct transliteration. I prefer "SMERSH": It looks, appropriately, more sinister. Because the overwhelming majority of novels discussed in this book were written during the Soviet period, and those that were not written during the Soviet period still pertain to it, I use "Belorussia" and "Belorussian" instead of the current usages "Belarus" and "Belarusian." Unless otherwise stated or indicated, all translations from all languages are mine. All errors and interpretations contained in this book are mine alone.

Readers of this book will be familiar with the unforgettable opening scenes of Stephen Spielberg's *Saving Private Ryan* (1998), in which U.S. infantry are cut down on Omaha Beach. More shocking still, I would suggest, is the scene in which the priest makes another visit to Mrs. Ryan's farmhouse to tell her that the war has taken yet another son. Those who know their Russian films will recall Mrs. Ryan's counterpart in *Ballada o soldate*

(Ballad of a Soldier, 1959), who grieves for a son who will never come home. Mothers pay a terrible price in war, and in the literature on which this book is based, the presence of the grieving, weeping mother never seemed far away. I dedicate this book to all the Soviet Union's mothers, Mrs. Ryan's kindred and wounded spirits whose sons, husbands, and brothers did not come home from that dreadful war. Lord knows, you were so strong, you endured so much, you waited, and then you wept bitter tears of love. God bless you.

Frank Ellis
Ampleforth, North Yorkshire, England

The Damned and the Dead

1 The Sword and the Pen: An Overview of War Literature

Blessed be the Lord my strength, which teacheth my hands to war, and my fingers to fight.
—Psalms 144:1

This chapter begins with a brief discussion of the relationship between art and war and then provides an overview of the way writers—from Thucydides to Ernst Jünger—have responded to the war experience, with reference to some of the main theorists of war. Based on the work of writers, soldiers, and philosophers, I identify five specific responses to war: pacifism, Remarquism, heroic pragmatism, the just war, and Jüngerism. These five responses provide a basis for interpreting the war experience as recorded in Soviet and Russian literature. I discuss general developments in Soviet and Russian war literature between 1941 through glasnost and beyond, examining some of the problems caused by censorship and Marxism-Leninism.

War and Art

Some years ago during one of my solo peregrinations across the mountainous desert of Nevada, I stopped to refill my water bottle from a small creek that flowed behind a large rock. As I knelt down I noticed pictures— images of sticklike humans chasing deerlike creatures—that had been scratched or carved on the rock's surface. My discovery of these startling petroglyphs in the vast, trackless wilderness was pure chance, a rare and exciting moment when a lone modern met his ancestors and was reminded of their harsh struggle for survival in an unforgiving world. Perhaps, I speculated, the artist had taken water from the same creek.

These two events—the hunt and the depiction of the hunt—are a reminder that the relationship between the hunt (a precursor of the more organized violence directed at human rivals that we call war) and art is an ancient one. Art and war have been joined together from the moment when hominids first decorated their bodies with ochre, possibly as long as 100,000 years ago, and then started to record the hunt in caves or on rock, or to pass on the history of the tribe and its deeds orally and eventually in writing. War (the deed) is to art (reflection and creation) as the moment is to memory. One of the earliest, and certainly one of the greatest, syntheses of praxis and reflection is *The History of the Peloponnesian War* (ca. 440–404 B.C.). Now, Thucydides was not solely adding to the foundations of the study of history laid by Herodotus; he was also building a memorial to himself and to the Greece he had served. Like that ancient rock-carving artist who depicted the hunt, he aspired to immortality. "My work," in the words of his famous introduction, "is not a piece of writing designed to meet the taste of an immediate public, but was done to last forever."

Art's capacity to function as a medium by which the memory of a person's deeds is perpetuated may help to explain the primeval relationship between art and war. Not to be remembered is somehow to have died in vain, one's deeds forgotten. Is this not the author's hidden fear recorded on the memorial to the men of Thermopylae? "Go, tell the Spartans, thou that passest by / That here, obedient to their laws, we lie." Or, much closer to my heart as an Englishman, we might recall the inscription on the Kohima Memorial to the British and Indian soldiers who fell in Burma in World War II: "When you go home / Tell them of us and say / For your tomorrow / We gave our today." More recently, in an excellent account of U.S. Marine training and subsequent active service in Afghanistan and Iraq, Nathaniel Fick reinforces the point about duty, death, and memory: "Past deeds are a young Marine's source of pride, inspiration to face danger, and reassurance that death in battle isn't consignment to oblivion. His buddies and all future Marines will keep the faith."[1] Cenotaph Corner in London; the memorial commemorating the raising of Old Glory on Iwo Jima's Mount Suribachi by five U.S. marines and a navy corpsman, which stands in Washington, D.C.; and the monument to the fallen in Volgograd (Stalingrad) all make the same point: The sacrifice of the dead imposes an obligation on the living to remember. In Russia after 1991 this obligation led to the compilation of the *Knigi pamiati* (The Books of Remembrance).[2] Equally important—and this is where memory becomes a battlefield—is the fact that no nation has a monopoly on glorious deeds. As Georgii Vladimov reminds us in *General i ego armiia* (The General and His Army, 1994), "Who has a memory, has glory and oblivion."[3]

The oblivion of which Vladimov warns shows itself in two ways. First, we see it as part of the deliberate and systematic attempt in former totalitarian communist states to destroy certain memories, to render certain individuals unpeople, to censor all levels of intellectual endeavour. Mikhail Bulgakov's defiant assertion that the censor's work is in vain because, as he famously put it in *Master i Margarita* (Master and Margarita, 1966–1967), "manuscripts don't burn"[4] is comforting but not always supported by experience. The reality, as John Stuart Mill reminds us, is somewhat harsher:

"The dictum that truth always triumphs over persecution is one of those pleasant falsehoods which men repeat after one another till they pass into commonplace, but which all experience refutes. History teems with instances of truth put down by persecution."[5] Second, a willingness to ignore the less noble and darker episodes in their histories may be found in all nations. Remembering the dead, a worthy, honorable, and perhaps psychologically necessary undertaking for the living, brings with it the obligation to be honest with the past and ourselves. Among British memories of World War II are the devastating defeat inflicted on the British Expeditionary Force in France as well as the great victory over the Luftwaffe in the summer of 1940. In the Far East the humiliating collapse of Singapore in 1942 and William Slim's final victory over the Japanese in Burma in 1945 are the low and high points, respectively, for British arms. In 1945 an exhausted Vasilii Grossman, pondering the four years of war with Nazi Germany, recognized the connection between the shame and the glory: "He who has not tasted the grief of the summer of 1941 will not understand in the depths of his being the happiness of our victory."[6] Grossman is surely right. What must he have thought—he who had gone through the entire war, from the disastrous summer of 1941 through Stalingrad, Ukraine, and the liberation of Treblinka to victory—as he surveyed the rubble of Berlin? Grossman echoes here the thoughts of the great German general, Helmuth von Moltke the senior, who believed that to earn the laurels of greatness a general must have known defeat as well as victory. The same is perhaps true of a nation.

War literature, like any other artistic endeavor, can be ephemeral and lack originality. In Germany the success of Erich Maria Remarque's *Im Westen nichts Neues* (*All Quiet on the Western Front*, 1929) spawned a host of imitators, very few of which are read these days. The same fate may well await some of the sensationalist memoirs of former Special Air Service soldiers— much of it more war pornography than war literature—that were published in the 1990s. At its best, however, war literature offers profound insights into man as soldier and into the deeds, glorious and shameful, of individuals and nations. *The History of the Peloponnesian War*, the Russian chronicles *Voina i mir* (*War and Peace*, 1865–1869), and *The Naked and the Dead* (1948) represent a small sample of humankind's accumulated knowledge, insight, and even wisdom on the subject. In its more serious manifestations war literature is, I believe, preeminently the literature of remembrance, sometimes an expression of reverence for the fallen. In the Soviet era, the harder the screws of censorship bore down on writers, the more tenaciously some of them resisted.

The Five Ways of the Warrior

War literature, the evolution of modern war (the inventions of gunpowder and firearms and greater understanding of ballistics), and the academic study of war are interrelated, arising in fact from a common source, namely the technological and scientific revolutions that gathered momentum beginning in the fifteenth century. War literature and the whole range of responses to war found in memoirs, novels, poetry, and monographs are epiphenomena of an industrialized society. Certainly we have accounts of war before the advent of mass literacy and printing presses, but nothing on the same scale. The volume and diversity of literary responses to war (World War I, for example) are also consequences of universal conscription, itself a concomitant of industrialized nation-states. In World War I, huge numbers of men were exposed to war, and a significant number—more than in any previous war—wrote about it afterward. Likewise, there was a pressing need, arising from the changes in armaments and weaponry that occurred especially rapidly in the period between the American Revolutionary War and the Franco-Prussian War, to formulate new strategic and tactical doctrines. Carl von Clausewitz in writing his study of war attempts to do just that.

In the light of these interrelationships, twentieth-century war literature and the study of the *Kriegserlebnis* (war experience) can be better understood if the student of war literature has at least some familiarity with war's theorists as well as its artists. I am not concerned here with the problems of grand strategy and logistics. Rather, I am interested in the apparent contrast between the attempt to comprehend war rationally, on the one hand, and the complex of emotional and psychological responses to war, on the other, which is the proper domain of war literature. These two different approaches are not separate and mutually incompatible. Thus, *War and Peace* is manifestly an attempt by its author to combine a personal experience of the battlefield—what would later become known in Soviet war literature and criticism as *okopnaia pravda* (the truth of the trenches)—with a strategic view of war. One consequence is Tolstoy's sustained attack on the figure of Napoleon as a man and on his reputation as one of history's great captains. Whether one agrees with the substance of Tolstoy's attacks on Napoleon is not important. What is important is the synthesis he was trying to achieve.

With two very different ends in mind, Ivan Stadniuk's neo-Stalinist war novel *Voina* (War, 1970–1980) and Vasilii Grossman's two Stalingrad novels, *Za pravoe delo* (For a Just Cause, 1952) and *Zhizn' i sud'ba* (Life and Fate, 1988) attempt something similar. Grossman, for example, having shown that Tolstoy's arguments on encirclement had been made redundant, demonstrates an acute understanding of the psychological implications of an army's being encircled: "An encircled army, deprived of its mobility, loses more than its military-technical advantages. Soldiers and officers of encircled armies are extruded, as it were from the world of modern civilization into the world of the past."[7] The gradual physical and psychological decay of the German 6th Army inside the *Kessel*, as recorded in the army's own documents, supports Grossman.

The voluminous literature on all aspects of war—historical studies, novels, and treatises—makes it possible to draw some general conclusions and to isolate some of the moral, philosophical, and sociopsychological problems of war. The works of Sun Tzu, Thucydides, Augustine, Thomas Aquinas, Niccolò Machiavelli, Hugo Grotius, Carl von Clausewitz, Baron Henri de Jomini, Quincy Wright, and Basil Liddell Hart occupy a special place in the study of war but are not the sole preserve of the professional soldier or historian. These authors add insight to the study of war literature that has, I believe, been overlooked. Some examples from this huge body of writing can illustrate the point. Von Clausewitz's "friction in war" is not merely an explanation of what happens when simple military operations are carried out. It is also a brilliantly concise and apposite metaphor for what we find in many Soviet and Russian war novels: the friction of ideas; the antitheses of duty and cowardice, treachery and loyalty, commissars and officers. Likewise, when Wright notes that "people are influenced to support war by language and symbols rather than by events and conditions," he offers one reason why war literature in the Soviet Union was such an ideologically charged subject—and, incidentally, reinforces the connection between art and war.[8] In Vladimir But's *Orel—reshka* (Heads—Tails, 1995), as we shall see in Chapter 7, the unraveling of the Soviet plan of attack, with its catastrophic consequences, provides powerful confirmation of von Moltke's simple truth that no plan survives contact with the enemy.

The account of the *Kriegserlebnis* that an author lays before us is informed both by his own reaction to war and by the ethos of war that is dominant in a particular nation-state. German war literature offers a striking example. Von Clausewitz, Heinrich von Treitschke, Friedrich Nietzsche, and Max

Scheler contributed substantially to a social-educational ethos that enno-
bled the way of the warrior. In the person and work of Ernst Jünger, we find
its apotheosis. Comparing the various accounts of the Kriegserlebnis, with
due regard for some of the theoretical studies of war, one can formulate
discrete categories or frameworks for interpreting war literature. Remarque and Jünger suggest two. What Soviet critics called Remarquism has
much in common with certain shades of pacifism. What I shall call
Jüngerism owes more to Sparta or to that distinct stratum of biological nationalism that was influential at the end of the nineteenth century and in the
early twentieth century and was by no means confined to Germany. To Remarquism and Jüngerism one can add pacifism, heroic pragmatism, and
the concept of the just war.[9] Taken together, pacifism, Remarquism, heroic
pragmatism, the concept of the just war, and Jüngerism both reflect the
changing ethos of war and incorporate certain recurring responses to the
age-old summons. I do not claim that these categories are exhaustive, but
they provide some way of managing the material that is both plausible and,
importantly, consistent with observed behavior. In the following sections I
extract and summarize some of the main points of each category.

Pacifism

In Ping Fa (The Art of War, ca. 400–320 B.C.), Sun Tzu conceives of war—its
planning, prevention, and prosecution—as being organically linked to the
entire process of a state's activity. War, he writes, "is a matter of life and
death, a road either to safety or to ruin."[10] Or, in the words of that universally
famous dictum, "War is nothing but the continuation of policy with other
means."[11] Weakness invites aggression, and rulers must study war and be
prepared because war determines the state's survival. War is a brute fact of
humankind's existence. This is the central message, from Sun Tzu to Niccolò
Machiavelli's Arte Della Guerra (The Art of War, 1521) and von Clausewitz.

Pacifism, defined by Brock as "an unconditional renunciation of war by
the individual," and other expressions of nonviolent resistance, from the
beatitudes to Tolstoy and Gandhi, have a long history, yet theoretically and
practically they have not led to a cessation of war.[12] Jünger identifies two
types of pacifism: one based on idealism, the other repelled by blood.
Jünger admires the idealist: "He is a soldier of the idea. He has courage. It
follows that he must be respected."[13] At a national level pacifism, however
much one might respect certain aspects of it, can be disastrous. Overcome
by the horrors of war, pacifists retreat from any practical measures to limit

and to prevent war, thus encouraging the aggressor. It was this realization, among other things, that prompted Reinhold Niebuhr to reject 1930s pacifism, the incunabula of which are to be found in his *Moral Man and Immoral Society* (1932). The aggressive expansion of Nazi Germany in the 1930s was demonstrably assisted by a British policy of appeasement. A more recent manifestation of appeasement was the attempt made by movements such as the Campaign for Nuclear Disarmament (CND) to secure Britain's unilateral nuclear disarmament in the mid-1980s. As Niebuhr recognized, political morality, in order to work, must be informed both by moralists and by political realists.

Pacifism (unilateral disarmament) fails this test because history teaches us that abstinence from violence is not universally reciprocated. Taken to its logical conclusion, pacifism is an act of extreme self-denial because even when threatened with extinction, the pacifist refuses to defend himself and, perhaps more importantly, those who rely on him for protection. This extreme view was summed up by Bertrand Russell in the debates over nuclear disarmament in the 1950s when he argued "better red than dead." In one of his first interviews with the British Broadcasting Corporation (BBC) following his expulsion from the Soviet Union in 1974, Solzhenitsyn singled out Russell's stance as an example of what he regarded as the West's moral cowardice in the face of Soviet aggression: "In this horrible expression of Bertrand Russell there is an absence of all moral criteria. Looked at from a short distance these words allow one to manoeuvre and continue to enjoy life. But from a long-term point of view it will undoubtedly destroy those people who think like that. It is a terrible thought."[14]

Remarquism

Repeatedly deployed as evidence of the folly and senselessness of war, *All Quiet on the Western Front* is probably the world's best-known antiwar novel. The central paradox arising from Remarque's novel is that, despite the undoubted horrors of war, the author and his generation do not throw down their rifles and mutiny but continue to fight and kill. This paradox reveals something about the nature of pacifism and war itself: The biological and cultural predisposition to war, amply confirmed by history, is more powerful than the call to love one's neighbor. Remarque's soldiers curse the war yet do their duty. War highlights a divided self: A rationalist, individualist rejection of war based on the not unreasonable desire for survival and the view that war is madness clash with the primeval lure of comradeship and collectively inflicted violence. One of the better-known incidents in the novel demonstrates the tension between homicidal impulse and a common humanity. Paul, Remarque's central character, repeatedly stabs a French soldier who seeks safety from shellfire in the same crater in no-man's-land. As his fear and aggression subside, the German surveys his handiwork and then tries to save the Frenchman's life. Humankind, Remarque suggests, is powerless to resist the call of war. Wars must take their course, and man, to use the title of Willi Heinrich's novel, is "the willing flesh," or perhaps the reluctant flesh.

Of Remarque's novel Andrew Rutherford has quite correctly argued that "the emphasis on degradation, demoralisation and futility, and the repudiation of any conception of the heroic, were immensely influential, establishing in effect a new norm of war literature."[15] After Remarque there could be no heroism, just fatalism; no moral and physical endurance, just apathy—all causes were equally futile. Remarque's novel and, to a lesser extent, Henri Barbusse's Le Feu: Journal d'une escouade (Fire: Journal of a Section, 1918) and Ludwig Renn's Krieg (War, 1928) did for twentieth-century pacifism what Rachel Carson's Silent Spring (1962) did for the green movement.

Heroic Pragmatism

The British resolve to confront Adolf Hitler was a different type than that which welcomed the declaration of war in 1914. There was no euphoria, just a quiet determination to see the war against Hitler through to the end. This practical, stoical approach to war finds its best reflection in British novels about the war at sea. In Alistair Maclean's HMS Ulysses (1955) we find none of the pessimism of Wilfred Owen, Siegfried Sassoon, and Richard Aldington, who are much closer to Remarque. The enemy, as Nicholas Monsarrat indicated, is as much the cruel sea itself as the German wolf packs and their long-range bombers. Maclean introduces another dimension: the arctic. The men of HMS Ulysses are fighting a war of which even the admiralty's strategists have no real understanding. With the crew of HMS Ulysses near to breaking point, the ship's doctor explains to a skeptical representative of the admiralty, sent to investigate a mutiny: "'Isolation' implies a cutting off, a detachment from the world, and your implication was partly true. But—and this, sir, is the point—there are more worlds than one. The northern seas, the Arctic, the black-out route to Russia—these are another world, a world utterly distinct from yours. It is a world, sir, of which you cannot possibly have any conception. In effect, you are completely isolated from our world" (emphasis in the original).[16]

Maclean's sailors are not the soldiers who grew up in the belle époque and welcomed the outbreak of World War I as the start of a great adventure, only to become disillusioned. On the contrary, memories of World War I were fresh. War is exhaustion, fear, and cold, the destroyer of families; yet there is a job to be done, as Richard Vallery, the reluctant, dedicated professional and truly inspiring captain of HMS Ulysses, realizes:

> He hated it because he was a deeply religious man, because it grieved him to see in mankind the wild beasts of the primeval jungle, because he thought the cross of life was already burden enough without the gratuitous infliction of the mental and physical agony of war, and, above all, because he saw war all too clearly as the wild and insensate folly it was, as a madness of the mind that settled nothing, proved nothing—except the old, old truth that God was on the side of the big battalions.
>
> But some things he had to do, and Vallery had clearly seen that this war had to be his also.[17]

"Some things he had to do" is, I believe, an accurate reflection of the general British attitude toward World War II. War is an ugly, dirty business, but when there is evil abroad the good shall be permitted no rest. Vallery is obliged to serve, dying of exhaustion. Vallery's volunteering for service, despite his profound moral misgivings about war, implies that there are times when the cause is just; that inaction in the face of evil is itself unjust—which, as Edmund Burke reminds us, leads to the triumph of evil. Articulated here is the essence of Niebuhr's rejection of Christian pacifism in the 1930s.

The British response to war, at least in 1939, was a heroically pragmatic compromise between pacifism and Jüngerism. Although not a celebration of war, HMS Ulysses is nevertheless a celebration of the British way of making war (at a particular moment in British history): the story of reluctant and bloodied amateurs who become hardened professionals by necessity because they want to finish the war and get home. Heroism is forced on the crew. Recent definitions of war as an "epidemic of trauma"[18] or a "uniquely horrible activity"[19] are much closer to the war depicted in HMS Ulysses. Von Clausewitz fails, as perhaps he must do, to convey any idea of what takes place when two enemy patrols encounter one another in no-man's-land at night, or what it is like to be on the receiving end of artillery fire. Maclean shows some of the horror of the war at sea, adding flesh to von Clausewitz's bloodless formulation.

The Just War Tradition

Three ideas are central to the just war tradition, *jus ad bellum* (the right to make war): that the cause be just, that there exists a properly constituted authority to wage war, and that the war do no more harm than good. Once the battle is joined, *jus in bello* (the law of war) and questions of discrimination and proportionality come to the fore.[20]

Whatever the conceptual failings of the just war tradition, especially when concerning religion or the criticism that such war is merely a self-serving institution to hide aggressive ambitions, the fact that states recognize the need to argue *ab initio* the case for war reflects a measure of compromise between Thrasymachus's rule of the fist and the rule of law: that war is not lawlessness. In the modern era the seminal work is Hugo Grotius's *De Jure belli ac pacis* (*The Law of War and Peace*, 1625), yet Christian thought has an exceptionally strong tradition of justifying war even when it might seem superfluous to do so. It is indeed remarkable, as James Johnson points out, that even as Rome was about to be "overwhelmed by invaders from the North, [Augustine] found it necessary to *justify* Christian participation in their defence."[21] When the Mongols entered the Russian lands, their policy was one of conquest and securing tribute. For them—as for the ancient Assyrians, one of the most aggressive peoples of the ancient world, who expressed themselves almost entirely through war—justness was equated with winning, so winning was vindication enough. Jünger, whose attitude toward war seems much closer to that of the Assyrians than to that of Augustine and the drafters of the Geneva Convention, nevertheless feels able to summon God to his cause: "War," he argues, "is always something holy, God's judgement over two ideas."[22]

Class and race add new dimensions to the just war tradition in the twentieth century, though both are not unique to the modern world. In Thucydides' account of what befell Corcyra in book 3 of *The History of the Peloponnesian War* there is evidence of class war, and Plato's conception of *The Republic* (ca. 370 B.C.) owed something to the author's desire to avoid the same. Precedents for genocide, or something close to it, can also be found in the Bible. When "Mordecai bowed not, nor did him reverence," Haman sought the destruction of the Jews (Esther 3:5).

Railways and industrialization made it possible for Stalin and Hitler to kill on a scale that would have been inconceivable in the ancient world. Murder on this scale was not, however, simply a matter of technology. Ideologies of class and race war that are peculiar to the modern world provided the justification. The rise of modern capitalism, according to Marx, created two classes: exploiters and the exploited. In the ensuing class struggle the ownership of the means of production would pass to the exploited class. Such, according to Marx, would be the inevitable resolution of history. Soviet ideologists incorporated Marx's teachings into a special Soviet version of the just war (*spravedlivaia voina*): "Just wars have progressive aims,"[23] which is to say that wars waged by socialist states to further socialist goals were inherently just—or "progressive"—whereas wars waged by capitalist states were not progressive and thus unjust. If the interests of the working class were threatened by either internal or external enemies, then all measures were justified. Extermination of the class enemy was the obligation that history imposed on the Communist Party. Class war was a just war. So, according to the Nazis, was the war waged for the protection of the race. In Soviet literature Grossman's *Life and Fate* is the most searching examination of both Nazi race war and Soviet class war. It is one of Grossman's many achievements in *Life and Fate* that he manages to convey something of the human catastrophe of race and class war and the totalitarian collusion that linked National Socialist Germany and the Soviet Union.

Jüngerism

"Whatever questions and ideas have moved the world," wrote Ernst Jünger, "it was always the battlefield which decided the issue. All freedom, all greatness and all culture may well have been born in the idea and in peace but only by means of war were they preserved, spread or lost."[24] Whether Jünger's view will be rendered redundant in the centuries ahead remains uncertain. Thus far in the trajectory of humankind's history Jünger's point is unassailable.

Frequently reviled as a Nazi supporter or accorded grudging admiration at a safe distance, Jünger and his work are not nearly as well known as Remarque and his writings. In a series of diaries and essays published after World War I—*In Stahlgewittern* (In Steel and Thunder, 1920), "Der Kampf als inneres Erlebnis" (Combat as an Inner Experience, 1922), *Das Wäldchen 125: Eine Chronik aus den Grabenkämpfen 1918* (Copse 125: A Chronicle from the Trench Battles 1918, 1925), and *Feuer und Blut* (Fire and Blood, 1925)—Jünger reveals a view of war that is an exceptionally powerful challenge to twentieth-century pacifism and the pessimism of Remarque.[25] War, argues Jünger, is the eternal law that humankind cannot escape. Pacifism is based on a dangerous illusion.

Whereas Remarque is broken by his experiences in the trenches, Jünger experiences *Erneuerung* (renewal), even rebirth. His attitude toward war is stated with absolute clarity in the introduction to *Combat as an Inner Experience*. War is the inescapable and ineluctable prime mover in man's universe: "War, the father of all things, is also ours. It has hammered, chiselled and tempered us and made us what we are. . . . It has bred us to struggle, and warriors we will remain as long as we are."[26] "War, the father of all things" can be first attributed to Heraclitus, being later embodied in Nietzsche's eternal recurrence.[27] Yet Jünger's views on war are not the passively absorbed thoughts of others. They represent the profound reflections of an outstanding, highly decorated, professional soldier, arguably the finest infantry officer on any side in World War I, who endured, observed, and recorded war at its worst. Jünger is the supreme theoretician and practitioner of trench warfare. The essential components in his view of war are biological and ontological. Civilization is a shallow veneer. The long years of prosperity leading up to the outbreak of World War I fooled people into thinking that humankind had conquered its savage past. Luxury, argues Jünger in an echo of Juvenal, weakens man's moral and physical sinews:

> Up to now so we have lived and we were proud of it. As the sons of a time intoxicated with matter it seemed to us that progress was perfection, the machine the key to our godlike nature, the telescope and microscope the instruments of knowledge. However, beneath the ever more brilliantly polished exterior, beneath all the robes with which we had decorated ourselves, we remained as naked and as brutal as the dwellers of the woods and the steppe.
>
> This revealed itself as the war tore Europe's community to pieces, as we marched towards the age-old decision behind banners and symbols, which for so long many had ridiculed in disbelief. There in an orgy of intoxication man made up for everything that had been lost. There his instincts for so long blocked by society and its laws once again became the one and holy thing, the final reason. And everything that the mind had perfected in the course of hundreds of years merely served to raise the power of the fist to something immeasurable.[28]

The soldiers—Jünger refers to them as *Landsknechte* after the corps of German pikemen used against the Swiss in the sixteenth century—who survive the front are a new breed distinct from, and superior to, their civilian counterparts. In fact, the barrier between the two is insurmountable. The *Landsknechte* have far more in common with the enemy. They have confronted fear, even terror. They have evolved a new psychology, or rather, Jünger would have us believe, have rediscovered their past. They are both *Urmensch* (primeval man) and *Übermensch* (superman): "They were conquerors, adapted to war in its most terrible form . . . the most acute concentration of body, intelligence, will and senses."[29]

Jünger's war is a release, an escape from the enervating comfort and security of bourgeois life. Like the saints and great artists, the warrior can know that moment of ecstasy (*Ekstase*): "This is intoxication above all forms of intoxication, an unleashing which ruptures all ties. It is a frenzy without care and limits which can be compared only with the forces of nature. In such a state man is like the howling storm, the raging sea and roaring thunder. Then he is one with the universe. He surges towards death's dark gates like a bullet to the target."[30]

Here and elsewhere in Jünger's work we see that the bigger picture is not significant. War is pursued for its own sake, and what matters is not what the soldier fights for but how he fights.[31] Emphasis is on "the inner experience": To fight is to know; to fight is to experience knowledge forbidden to all but the elect.

The fictional Captain Richard Vallery in HMS *Ulysses* and Leutnant Ernst Jünger would, one suspects, have recognized and admired one another's warrior virtues instantly. Yet they would remain implacable enemies. Jünger's outstanding qualities as soldier and thinker should not blind us to the fact that his real enemy is the liberal-bourgeois society that Vallery seeks to protect. Though Jünger's uniform conveys the impression that in some way he is a defender of order and an opponent of barbarism, his legitimation of killing and destruction has something in common with the revolutionary, nihilist fanatics who inhabit the pages of Dostoyevsky's novels.

Pacifism, Remarquism, heroic pragmatism, and the just war tradition recognize in varying degrees that war is a bad, even an evil thing, that however just the cause, humankind is tainted. They reflect the view of José Ortega y Gasset in *Le Rebelión de las Masas* (The Revolt of the Masses, 1930) that "civilization is nothing else than the attempt to reduce force to being the *ultima ratio*."[32] Jünger's glorification of the warrior and violence is quite distinct from the other four categories. Jünger assists those, be they on the left or the right, who, in the words of Ortega y Gasset, proclaim "violence as *prima ratio*, or strictly as *unica ratio*."[33]

War Literature and World War II

The war literature of the belligerent nations of World War II reflects both the universal experience of war and the peculiarities of the individual nations themselves. Norman Mailer's *The Naked and the Dead* (1948) and James Jones's *The Thin Red Line* (1962), both of which deal with the U.S. war in the Pacific, are concerned, like many war novels, with two conflicts: that between the protagonist and the enemy, in this case the Japanese, and an internal one in which values of decency, typically represented by junior officers with a liberal education, are ridiculed and stamped on by ruthless noncommissioned officers and senior officers. British war literature offers an exceptionally rich and diverse record of the war experience: war in the air, at sea, in the desert, and in the jungle; humor; and captivity and escape. Paul Brickhill's biography of Douglas Bader, Victoria Cross (VC), *Reach for the Sky* (1954); Len Deighton's *Bomber* (1970); and *Enemy Coast Ahead* (1946) by Guy Gibson, VC (Gibson led the raid against the Ruhr dams in 1943) capture the various aspects of the air war. For the war at sea Nicholas Monsarrat's *The Cruel Sea* (1951); Roger Hill's *Destroyer Captain* (1975); and Alistair Maclean's *HMS Ulysses*, discussed earlier in this chapter, are essential reading. For the soldier's war Evelyn Waugh's somewhat bleak and, in places, very funny *Sword of Honour* (1952–1961) gives an account of British incompetence and muddling through. As a morale booster for the shell-shocked reader, the picaresque antics and adventures of Spike Milligan, as recorded in *Adolf Hitler: My Part in His Downfall* (1971) and similar titles, are wonderfully uplifting and in their own way a fine tribute to the men of the British 8th Army. France's war, whatever contribution the French resistance made, is overshadowed by collaboration and the Vichy regime.

In German war literature there is a definite stratum of writing that has attempted to derive some measure of heroism, even virtue, from the German fight against the overwhelming superiority of the Allies. This theme is especially true of the literature dedicated to the Eastern front, as in, for example, Heinrich Gerlach's Stalingrad novel, *Die verratene Armee* (The Betrayed Army, 1957), and *Das geduldige Fleisch* (The Willing Flesh, 1955) by Willi Heinrich (discussed later in this chapter). A pariah after 1945, Ernst Jünger enjoyed something of a revival in Germany in the 1980s, though one suspects that many Germans find him an embarrassment. At the other extreme of atonement—or, rather, lack thereof—is Japan. Although it has abandoned any form of militarism, Japan has nevertheless not subjected itself to anything like the protracted soul-searching of post-1945 Germany. Despite themes of heroic resistance in the work of some writers, Germany, pursuing its policy of *Vergangenheitsbewältigung*, has made heroic efforts to confront the Nazi past. In the case of Japan we must look hard to find any trace of the spirit of national atonement that characterizes Germany. An outstanding Italian novel is Eugenio Corti's epic *Il Cavallo rosso* (The Red Horse, 1983), which, in the author's restless quest to grasp the nature of war and the twin catastrophes of Soviet Communism and National Socialism, bears comparison with Viktor Astaf'ev's *Prokliaty i ubity* (The Damned and the Dead, 1992–1994) and Grossman's *Life and Fate*.

Soviet War Literature

Most Soviet war literature deals with two wars. The first began on 22 June 1941 when the German Army invaded the Soviet Union, ending the uneasy truce between the two totalitarian states. This war ended on 9 May 1945. Strictly speaking, the second war began as soon as Lenin introduced Soviet censorship, although for the sake of the study of war literature we might take its first shots to have been fired in 1941. It entered its terminal phase with Gorbachev's policy of glasnost, which led to the formal abolition of censorship on 1 August 1990 and ended, finally, in 1991 with the collapse of the Soviet Union.

A study of Soviet war literature must deal with both wars: the first because so many important historical events and campaigns—the summer rout of 1941, the Battle of Stalingrad, and partisan warfare, to name three—feature in the literature, and an intimate knowledge of these campaigns is essential; the second because the course of Soviet war literature from 1941 to 1991 documents a bitter struggle between writers and the Communist Party. The survivors of the Great Patriotic War—the former war correspondents and *frontoviki* (frontline soldiers) who wanted to start coming to terms with Russia's catastrophe, to remember the dead, or merely to leave a record of their own experiences—now confronted an invigorated enemy.

In the Soviet Union the party and the literary establishment, the apparatus of censorship, and when necessary the secret police sought to impose a view of the German-Soviet war that was as far as possible congenial to Marxism-Leninism. The desired themes were mass heroism, unflinching resistance, the total evil of the Nazis (or fascists, as Soviet propaganda dubbed them), the monolithic unity of party and people, Allied timidity and the extent to which the Western Allies could or could not be trusted, the war of liberation, and Stalin. The problem for the party was that Soviet war literature not only looked to the Soviet past for themes that were relevant to the war, especially collectivization and the purges, but also dealt with highly sensitive issues thrown up by the war itself. The capture of General Andrei Andreyevich Vlasov and his subsequent collaboration with the Germans is an excellent example. War literature was simply too important to be just about the war.

One of the things that made the war such a sensitive issue in Russia comes across very clearly in the hostile reception to Viktor Astaf'ev's novel *The Damned and the Dead*. V. Zelenkov (a veteran of the war whom we shall have occasion to encounter again in Chapter 7), who bitterly resented what Astaf'ev had written, nevertheless makes the essential point that any Soviet or Russian novel about the Great Patriotic War is also a foray into history. "*The Damned and the Dead*," he writes, "is not a work of satire but one of realism, moreover one that is historical, for a novel about the Great Patriotic War cannot but be historical even if there are only invented characters in it. Astaf'ev imbues his characters with the psychology of contemporary people of a definite understanding, and throughout the course of the whole work declares his current views."[34] We might also heed the caveat of another Russian critic, writing in 1995 to mark the fiftieth anniversary of the war's end:

> In an argument the war is the trump card of the more or less main
> adherents of the socialist idea and the anticommunists of various
> degrees. Therefore the conception of the Great Patriotic War that is
> being defended, which has as its aim the objective search for the
> truth about wartime, goes beyond the framework of strictly military
> events, reducing to its sphere of analysis a whole raft of historical
> material touching upon the foreign policy of the Soviet government,
> collectivization, industrialisation, the personality of Stalin, Zhukov
> and other military leaders.[35]

Other, nonideological factors explain the obsessive determination of Russian writers to fight for the past. Faced with the possibility of extermination at the hands of a cruel invader, the survivors feel a deep, primeval need to remember and to pay homage to their fallen heroes. Viktor Astaf'ev's epitaph to a lone Russian soldier in *Pastukh i Pastushka: Sovremennaia pastoral'* (The Shepherd and the Shepherdess: A Modern Pastoral, 1971) has a crucial relevance for understanding the theme of remembrance in Soviet Russian war literature. A grief-stricken woman finds the grave of the soldier she loved and lost during the war: "She untied her shawl and pressed her face to the grave.—Why dost thou lie alone in the middle of Russia? And she asked nothing more. She thought. She remembered."[36]

With their repeated emphasis on the superb equipment and professionalism of their armed forces, Soviet prewar propagandists undoubtedly helped to make the shock of the German invasion in 1941 all the greater. Nikolai Shpanov's *Pervyi udar: Povest' o budushchei voine* (The First Blow: The Story of the Future War, 1939), a fictional account of a future war with Germany, is a salutary and noteworthy example of the dangers of such inflationary expectations. By a quirk of fate the manuscript went to press on 31 May 1939, a mere two and a half months before Stalin and Hitler concluded their squalid Non-aggression Pact, which provided for the dismembering of Poland, among other things, and introduced a temporary lull in the ferocious propaganda war between the two states. The pact, the low point in a low decade, shattered once and for all the myth (popular in the 1930s) that only the Soviet Union could save Europe from Hitler.

Shpanov helps to sustain this myth of salvation. *The First Blow* is a mixture of war story, science fiction, and ideological fantasy. Judging from the many references to the political landscape of the late 1930s, Shpanov and, one assumes, some of his party sponsors considered such a war unavoidable and imminent. Nor does Shpanov appear to harbor illusions about the nature of this imminent war: "The war will be terrible. One of fire, steel, chemistry and electricity."[37]

The background to Shpanov's war owes much to Soviet propagandists' explanations of World War I, which they called the "imperialist war" and described as a scramble for colonies and raw materials. In Shpanov's scenario, Germany seizes the Portuguese Gold Coast and then concludes a deal on the allocation of colonies with Britain. Italy and Germany make territorial demands of France. German mobilization follows. According to Shpanov, the working classes in France, Britain, and Germany long to be liberated from the yoke of capitalism and look to the Soviet Union—and, of course, to Stalin—for hope. This is the basis of the just war, indicated in Shpanov's epigraph, a quotation from Lenin. Just wars, according to Lenin, are those that liberate people from slavery, which naturally means the unbearable yoke of capitalism; the Soviet Union, which, in the words of one Soviet pilot, represents "the most unusual, the most astonishing and the most beautiful thing that history has ever known,"[38] is obliged to wage this just war on behalf of the world's oppressed. Undeterred by the Soviet state's official policy of atheism, Shpanov declares that "the war against fascism will be a holy war."[39]

The First Blow abounds in hostages to fortune and some excruciating inconsistencies. As the states of Europe move toward war, the French are warned about making any deals with Germany: "To prepare any deal with Fascist Germany is more shameful and dreadful than ever before"[40] (one assumes that Vyacheslav Mikhaylovich Molotov and Stalin did not read Shpanov's novel). The focus on the Soviet military repeatedly suggests extreme awareness of the danger presented by Germany and a determination to defeat it. The very idea that the Soviet Union would be caught out by a surprise German attack is, Shpanov argues, quite preposterous. Shpanov's argument that treaties in modern war count for very little is another portent of Stalin's failures two years later. Though treaties appear to be tools of peacetime diplomacy, they are in fact tools of war: "And if even now after the terrible experiences of the last war, nations decorate themselves with a badge of noble humanity, then the looming war will change all this into a scrap of torn paper."[41] The torn paper is perhaps an allusion to Neville Chamberlain's return from Munich in 1938 after signing the agreement that marked the abandonment of Czechoslovakia by Britain and France and in another unwitting irony anticipates Hitler tearing up his pact with Stalin. The book views the 1930s as a new age of cynical, utterly ruthless diplomacy, though perhaps that is too harsh a judgment. The attitude toward pacts and treaties during the civil war in Corcyra, revealed by Thucydides in book 3 of The History of the Peloponnesian War, instructs us that the ancient world was just as cynical and opportunistic as Hitler and Stalin. No matter—the inexorable move toward total war imposes its own terms. The Western democracies, and especially Hitler, are simply not to be trusted. The Soviet Union, Shpanov assures his reader, is well aware of Albion's perfidy and Hitler's duplicity. Forewarned, the Soviet Union is forearmed. Stalin is like the witch in Macbeth: By the pricking of his thumbs, he knows something wicked his way comes.

The detail of military operations provided in The First Blow creates the impression that the Soviet Union is at the forefront of technical and tactical innovation (there is no mention of the purges). The heroes and heroines are Komosomol pilots—Stalin's falcons—who are setting new altitude and speed records and sports parachutists who serve in the airborne units.

Pride of place goes to the long-range bomber force, whose strategic goal is the total destruction of Germany's military-industrial complex situated in Nuremberg.

Comparing Shpanov's fictional war with what actually happened in World War II yields some uncannily accurate predictions, though none favorable to the Soviet Union. Shpanov correctly identifies the effectiveness of airborne troops and long-range bombers as well as the need for initiative and professionalism, yet very little of these requirements and qualities were to be found on the Soviet side. The Soviet Union may have devoted a great deal of time to training airborne troops, but it was the Germans who first used them to devastating effect. During World War II long-range bombing was a monopoly of British and U.S. forces. One interesting and prophetic feature of Shpanov's war is the Soviet attack on Nuremberg, the aim being to destroy the dams that provide electricity for the factories. During the night of 16–17 May 1943, Royal Air Force Lancaster bombers, led by Wing Commander Guy Gibson, who won a VC for his part in the raid, attacked the Möhne, Eder, and Sorpe dams. Again, in a complete reversal of actual official Soviet attitudes and behavior in World War II, Shpanov assures us that the Soviet forces make every attempt to save lives, both of their own men and of German civilians. He also points to certain failures inherent in the German forces: "The very first hours of the war exposed the reality of the social shortcomings in the enemy's army, which in peace time were covered up by harsh discipline."[42] Quite unintentionally Shpanov comments on the state of the Red Army in that real future war, not its superbly trained and well-led adversary.

For all its Soviet baggage and propaganda, The First Blow belongs to a well-established genre in which authors speculate about the nature of future wars and conflicts. In Britain, before the outbreak of World War I, any number of novels and short stories were dedicated to variations on the theme of war between Britain and Germany. The Riddle of the Sands: A Record of Secret Service (1903) by Erskine Childers and The Invasion of 1910 (1906) by William Le Queux are two of the better-known English-language exemplars. Written by August Niemann, Der Weltkrieg: Deutsche Träume (The World War: German Dreams, 1904) was a highly successful German response to what many Germans believed was a deliberate targeting of Germany by the British press before and after the war. In fact, the German threat, real or imagined, was something of an obsession for the mass-circulation Daily Mail, founded by Lord Northcliffe. Le Queux's novel was serialized in the Daily

Mail, and in order to counter claims that he had helped to incite the war, Northcliffe ordered that the anti-German articles published in the *Daily Mail* before the outbreak of war in 1914 be reissued as a pamphlet—*Scaremongerings from the Daily Mail 1886–1914: The Paper That Foretold the War* (1914)—to show how prescient the *Daily Mail* had been. Since the end of World War I there have been many additions to the future-war genre: for example, Hector Bywater's *The Great Pacific War* (1925), an account of a Japanese surprise attack on Pearl Harbor, and at the height of the Cold War General Sir John Hackett's *The Third World War* (1978), which examines the likely outcome of a war between the North Atlantic Treaty Organization (NATO) and the Warsaw Pact countries in August 1985. In terms of military erudition, these two books, especially Hackett's, are in a different league from Shpanov's ode to Stalin. What makes *The First Blow* of special interest is that so much of the author's fantasy—the view that technically and tactically the Red Army was the most advanced in the world—was accepted at all levels of Soviet society.

Despite the best efforts of the party and censors, the thematic range of Soviet war literature could not be restricted to a narrow, party-approved spectrum. Nor, as the decades passed, was the party able to maintain or impose an ideologically correct interpretation of, say, Stalin's reign and the purges. Discussion of the purges could not avoid the role of the Narodnyi komissariat vnutrennikh del (NKVD) and the Special Sections, which enforced the provisions of Orders № 270 and 227 by interrogating soldiers suspected of desertion and carrying out executions. The tension between soldiers and commissars could not be ignored; nor, later in the war, could the role of Smert' shpionam (SMERSH) operatives. The summer routs of 1941 and 1942 were obviously linked to Stalin. Why were the Germans so successful, and to what extent was Stalin to blame? Attitudes toward Germans and German culture posed something of a problem for Soviet propagandists and writers, especially with the assertion of a specifically Russian nationalism after the Battle of Stalingrad. And how should Soviet writers react to the Holocaust and the fact that too many Soviet citizens became Hitler's willing executioners? With Vlasov's defection, a whole series of questions were raised: collaboration and the sheer numbers of Soviet soldiers who deserted, life under German occupation, and the way the Soviet Union treated its soldiers who had been prisoners of the Germans. For every one of these themes there was an orthodox position and what one might term a dissenting one—sometimes several.

Conspicuously absent from Soviet war literature until very recently were accounts of life in German captivity. Humor is rare. Of Jüngerism there is no trace. Accounts of escape from and fortitude in both German and Japanese captivity feature prominently in British war literature: Escape attempts from Colditz have long been celebrated as an example of British prisoners of war outwitting the Germans. Four outstanding accounts of life in Japanese captivity should be mentioned: James Clavell's *King Rat* (1962), Jim Bradley's *Towards the Setting Sun: Escape from the Thailand-Burma Railway, 1943* (1982), Eric Lomax's *The Railwayman* (1996), and Arthur Godman's *The Will to Survive: Three and a Half Years as a Prisoner of the Japanese* (2002). Regarding the theme of escape in film, one must acknowledge the inspirational and morally uplifting *Un Condamné à Mort s'est échappé où Le vent souffle ou il veut* (A Man Escaped, or the Wind Bloweth Where It Listeth, 1956), directed by Robert Bresson.

The contrast between Soviet and Western attitudes toward prisoners of war can be seen in the fate of two successful escape attempts from the Soviet concentration camp system, both of which became the basis of best sellers. Written by Slavomir Rawicz, a former Polish army officer who was sentenced by the NKVD to twenty-five years in a labor camp, *The Long Walk* (1956) recounts an astonishing escape from Siberia across the Gobi Desert and over the Himalayas to India, where Rawicz enlists in the British Army. The second account is Josef Martin Bauer's *So Weit wie die Füße tragen* (As Far as My Feet Will Take Me, 1955). Bauer was a German army officer who was captured in 1942 and, instead of being repatriated at the war's end, was sentenced to twenty-five years of hard labor. Bauer escaped in 1949 and made his way along the edge of Lake Baikal until he eventually crossed into Iran, returning to Munich in December 1952. The closest examples of escape in Soviet war literature are the attempts by Soviet units to break out of German encirclement, though should they make it back to Soviet lines the soldiers could expect to be viewed with extreme suspicion, not to be commended for their resourcefulness. One example of escape from German captivity can be cited, though what happened to this soldier on his return is not recorded: "I was a prisoner of the Germans for 7 months and crossed the whole Ukraine on foot, through all the cities of Belorussia, from near Vitebsk to Kharkov and back to our side on the 12th May 1942."[43]

A number of British novels and memoirs are notable for humor, most obviously those of Spike Milligan; there are also some excellent humorous asides in Evelyn Waugh's and Arthur Godman's books and in Wilfred

Thesiger's autobiography, *The Life of My Choice* (1987). The nature of the Russo-German war almost certainly precludes anything remotely comparable, though two examples of humor and the military can be found in Vladimir Voinovich's *Zhizn' i neobychainye prikliucheniia soldata Ivana Chonkina* (The Life and Extraordinary Adventures of the Soldier Ivan Chonkin, 1975) and his more recently published *Monumental'naia propaganda* (Monumental Propaganda, 2001).

Viewing Jüngerism as in part an acute reaction to rising levels of prosperity and security, which then leads to a neoprimitive cult of glorifying violence, may explain the absence of any similar cult of war in Soviet war literature. Life in Russia has always been hard and violent. There are, however, resonances of military adventurism. Russia, as Solzhenitsyn shows in *August 1914*, was not immune to the patriotic fervor that swept through the rest of Europe.

Much closer to Jünger are some of the themes in Isaac Babel's Civil War classic *Konarmiia* (Red Cavalry, 1926). The Cossacks are violent and predatory and live for war and plunder. Jünger, writing of the Mongols and other steppe raiders, could easily be writing of the Cossacks: "They behaved as was consistent with their being. For them, killing was their moral code, as loving-thy-neighbour was for Christians. They were wild conquerors."[44] Babel's own failure to become one with the Cossack warriors highlights, I believe, the fundamental flaw in Jüngerism. Jünger's pitiless analysis of war is its great strength and weakness. The Cossacks do not rationalize their behavior. They are what they are: They kill; therefore they exist. They are outside civilization and unfettered by its conventions. Reason is not their master. Jünger's rational analysis of savagery invalidates any attempt by him to engage in such savagery or to justify it because from the moment he identifies the lure of violence, he has the option not to pursue it. The will to violence is also the will to act in other, conscious ways. The product of a comfortable childhood, Jünger, like Babel, can claim no innocence. "Innocence once lost," as Sir Karl Popper reminds us, "cannot be regained, and an artificially arrested closed society, or a cultivated tribalism, cannot equal the genuine article."[45] Jünger cannot act in the manner of a Cossack or steppe raider because he is not one. War did not choose Jünger, overwhelming him in inexplicable, existential calamity: Jünger chose war.[46]

Now, Grossman and Astaf'ev would agree with Jünger that technical and scientific progress have not weakened humankind's capacity for violence. In

both *For a Just Cause* and *Life and Fate*, their depictions of the battle of Stalingrad, for all the justness of the Russian national cause, frequently evoke some
of the same dark images that we encounter in Jünger. In the opening chapter
of *The Shepherd and the Shepherdess*, appropriately titled "battle," Astaf'ev casts
the battle as a manifestation of something primeval and demonic:

> In a burning rage, the one armed with a crowbar was terrible. His
> shadow rushed about, appearing and disappearing, and he himself,
> like a denizen from the underworld, would flare up, then darken and
> disappear. He howled wildly, showing his teeth, and it seemed that
> he was covered in thick hair and the crowbar was no longer a
> crowbar but a club of oak, torn out at the roots, and he had long
> hands with claws. . . . He exuded cold and blackness, some ancient
> demon. Behind him blazed a torch, suggesting the reflected light of
> those firestorms from out of which this monster had emerged and
> risen from its knees and come to our own time with the unchanged
> visage of the caveman.[47]

What separates Grossman and Astaf'ev from Jünger is that although
they fully recognize the demonic in humankind and its capacity for evil, and
deplore the consequences, they, like Richard Vallery, recognize that some
wars have to be fought. Grossman's and Astaf'ev's soldiers do not seek war:
It is thrust upon them. They must do or die. Jünger's relativism, apparent in
his argument that the Christian call to love one's neighbor is no better or
worse than the cult of the steppe raider, absolves the Nazis of any wrongdoing and demeans the Russian struggle for national survival. Not all struggles are of equal merit. If they were, and if the essence of being a Nazi were
to use all possible technical means to exterminate people deemed to be in-
ferior, then there can exist no moral or judicial basis for condemning Hitler. The distinction between perpetrator and victim disappears, and we are
beyond good and evil.

If we look back at the period from 1941 to 1991, certain publications appear significant for the way in which they challenge the party view of the
war, encouraging and opening the way for others to excavate hitherto untouched themes. Viktor Nekrasov's *V okopakh Stalingrada* (In the Trenches of
Stalingrad, 1946) and Emmanuil Kazakevich's *Zvezda* (Star, 1946) are highly
untypical for the period immediately after the end of the war. Another remarkable book for the time was Grossman's *For a Just Cause*. By the end of
the 1950s, IUrii Bondarev—*Batal'ony prosiat ognia* (The Battalions Request

Fire Support, 1957) and *Poslednie zalpy* (The Final Salvoes, 1959)—and Grigorii Baklanov—*IUzhnee glavnogo udara* (South of the Main Blow, 1958) and *Piad' zemli* (A Piece of Ground, 1959)—had published a series of utterly convincing accounts of their particular wars. By the mid-1960s, really controversial themes were being addressed and established themes were being treated anew. Baklanov's *Mertvye sramu ne imut* (The Dead Feel No Shame, 1961) and *Iiul' 41 goda* (July 1941, 1965), Viktor Astaf'ev's *The Shepherd and the Shepherdess*, and Anatolii Kuznetsov's *Babii IAr* (1966) are major contributions. Baklanov, Bondarev, Vasil' Bykov, and to a certain extent Konstantin Simonov[48] helped to undermine the Stalinist view of war by giving the Soviet reader unvarnished accounts of cowardice, incompetence, and heroism. Other writers sought to convey the same message by understating horrors. We see this tendency in Bulat Okudzhava's *Bud' zdorov, shkoliar* (Take Care, Schoolboy, 1961), Konstantin Vorob'ev's *Ubity pod Moskvoi* (Killed at Moscow, 1963), and Viktor Kurochkin's *Na voine kak na voine* (In War as in War, 1965).

Take Care, Schoolboy is the most explicitly Remarquist account of war in Soviet Russian literature. Okudzhava's own epigraph—"These are not adventures. They are about how I fought. How people wanted to kill me, but I was lucky"[49]—appears to be a deliberate echo of Remarque's in *All Quiet on the Western Front*: "This book is intended neither as an accusation nor as a confession. It merely attempts to tell the story of a generation which was destroyed by war even if it escaped the grenades." Okudzhava's soldier hero, or rather antihero, is bewildered and overwhelmed by what he experiences at the front. He has no sense of taking part in a historic struggle against any fascist invader. He survives the war but does not understand how he managed it or whom he should thank. The narrative's simple, apparently artless observations render the soldier's experiences all the more horrifying. Is it right, Okudzhava asks, that young soldiers, barely out of school, should be sacrificed in such a cruel war?

Killed at Moscow gives some idea of the desperate nature of the defense of Moscow in the winter of 1941. Students, untrained and inadequately equipped (some are unarmed, and they lack entrenching tools) are thrown into battle against the Germans. Encircled, the survivors must fight their way back to their own lines. Vorob'ev strikes a far more depressing note than does Alexander Bek in *Volokolamskoe shosse* (The Volokolamsk Highway, 1943), a novel that also deals with the defense of Moscow. The chain of command seems to have broken down in the chaos of battle. The bigger picture is not clear, and the presence of the NKVD checking for deserters just behind the front line suggests that Soviet morale is somewhat fragile. Nevertheless, the students submit to the war, their optimism—or rather that of the survivor—giving way to a sense of grim determination.[50]

Kurochkin chronicles the highs and lows in the life of the crew of a self-propelled gun as it moves to the front to engage the Germans. In an echo of Okudzhava, we see war initially as a series of challenges to the material well-being of the crew: the need to secure food, warmth, and sleep and to avoid being noticed by one's superiors, all of which the crew manages with varying degrees of success. Unusually for a Soviet Russian war story, there are elements of farce and comedy that would not have been out of place in Spike Milligan's adventures. The gun-crew commander, Lieutenant Maleshkin, is commander in name only. His immediate superior delights in tormenting him, and his crew adopts an attitude of benign tolerance, disobeying his orders. Maleshkin dreams of heroic deeds yet never seems to secure moral ascendancy over his crew. He is too much one of them, a young man thrust into war who, like the others, learns the hard way. In the cramped space of a self-propelled gun, formal military discipline counts for very little. The contradictions between youthful fantasies of glory and the often banal realities of war or even military life are one of a number of parallels with *Take Care, Schoolboy*. Yet the Remarquist label would not be accurate. In Maleshkin's transition from being the butt of his crew's and superiors' jokes to his eventual emergence as a leader in battle, Kurochkin offers insights into the nature of heroism and leadership that are all the more convincing for being stripped of party rhetoric about mass heroism. Maleshkin's fears and insecurities are those of all young men at war, on whatever side they fight. Maleshkin gets his chance to prove himself: In an attack, he destroys two German tanks and is nominated for the award of Hero of the Soviet Union. After the battle, enjoying his moment of personal triumph, Maleshkin is killed by a stray shell. We are reminded of the title, which in the French original, cited by one of the crew, underlines the cruel vagaries of war: À la guerre comme à la guerre.[51]

The party fought back. Terrified by the possibility that Grossman's *Life and Fate*, already denounced by one journal as anti-Soviet, would be published abroad, the State Security Committee (KGB) simply arrested the manuscript in 1961. Anatolii Kuznetsov's *Babii IAr*, an account of life under German occupation, was heavily censored before publication (the author defected to the West in 1968, after publication of the book in the Soviet

Union). Yet the masterful novels and stories of Vasil' Bykov were still being published—just barely in the case of *Mertvym ne bol'no* (The Dead Feel No Pain, 1966)—and over a remarkable thirty-year period the author continued his relentless and cunning assault on Soviet censorship and the party's organized lying and omissions about the war.[52]

The party also kept historians on a tight leash. In 1941, 22 *iiunia* (1941, 22 June, 1965) Aleksandr Nekrich examined what Soviet historians referred to as the *nachal'nyi period* (the initial phase) of the war. Nekrich's conclusions about Soviet readiness were devastating. He identified multiple failures by intelligence agencies and pointed out that Stalin's reaction to warnings received from Churchill that a German attack was imminent had disastrous consequences: "Assuming that Churchill was trying to outwit him, Stalin tried to outwit Churchill. But Stalin ended up outwitting himself, to the detriment of the Soviet people, the state, and the Communist Party of the Soviet Union."[53] Stalin had not actually needed warnings from Churchill. Well before the first German tanks crossed the border, any responsible military leader should have drawn the obvious conclusions from what was taking place in the border region. Armed confrontations between Soviet border guards and German spies, sabotage groups, and recconnaissance patrols were not isolated incidents. Beginning in April and May 1941, German intelligence started to deploy highly qualified agents who had passed through training schools in Stettin, Berlin, Königsberg, and Vienna.[54] German attempts to infiltrate across the Soviet border and Soviet attempts to counter the threat have all the characteristics of a full-blown border war. German losses in killed and wounded in this secret war alone amounted to about 1,300.[55] On 13 June 1941, nine days before Hitler finally abandoned the pretence of nonaggression, TASS, the Soviet news agency—perhaps mindful of the rumors circulating among diplomatic circles at home and abroad—issued what was to become one of its most notorious communiqués, flatly denying any suggestion of a rift in Soviet-German relations. Nekrich leaves us in no doubt that this communiqué had an utterly demoralizing effect on the Red Army. Many writers, among them Grigorii Baklanov, Konstantin Simonov, and Ivan Stadniuk, have pondered the significance of the communiqué in their novels, as we shall see in later chapters.

Nekrich's book sold well in the Soviet Union. It also attracted a great deal of attention in the West, which probably hurt the author as much as anything else. Nekrich was summoned to appear before various party committees and defend his conclusions despite the fact that the book had been subjected to prior censorship. By the time final approval for publication was granted, six institutions—Glavlit (the common name for the Soviet censorship), the military censors, the special military censor of Soviet Military Intelligence (GRU), the KGB, the Ministry of Foreign Affairs, and the science section of the party's Central Committee—had examined the manuscript and passed comment.[56] In one hearing before the party's Komitet partiinogo Kontrolia (Control Committee), Nekrich was asked what he regarded as most important: political expediency or historical truth.[57] The central theme in the accusations leveled at Nekrich was that he had "lost his sense of party spirit [partiinost']. There is no place for him in the party."[58] Nekrich was duly expelled, the official reason being "for premeditated distortion in the book 1941, 22 June of the policy of the Communist Party and the Soviet government on the eve, and in the initial period, of the Great Patriotic War, which was exploited by foreign, reactionary propaganda for anti-Soviet purposes."[59]

As a counterargument to those put forward by Nekrich and, it must be said, by the overwhelming majority of historians with whose work I am familiar, I must mention Ledokol: Kto nachal vtoruiu mirovuiu voinu? (The Icebreaker: Who Started the Second World War?, 1992). The author, writing under the pen name Viktor Suvorov, is a former Soviet military intelligence officer, Vladimir Rezun, who defected to Britain in 1978. His sensational thesis is that Stalin had been preparing to attack Hitler and that Hitler's invasion in June 1941 was a preemptive strike. Soviet leaders, according to Suvorov, regarded Hitler as the "Icebreaker of the Revolution." The hope was that Hitler, by waging war against the rest of Western Europe, would create the instability and chaos necessary for the Soviet Union to invade Western Europe while posing as a liberator. The Icebreaker does not strike me as a book that can be dismissed out of hand. It contains weaknesses and inconsistencies, but Suvorov has clearly done a great deal of research and raises questions for which there are no easy answers. One of his themes is the development of airborne and glider troops by the Soviet military during the 1930s, a major theme that is also explored in Shpanov's The First Blow. Glider and parachute troops are the preeminent assault troops. Why, asks Suvorov in chapter 12, did Stalin need so many, in all ten airborne corps?

Having earlier summarized Remarquism, I must now attempt a more detailed discussion because during the 1960s, All Quiet on the Western Front posed a number of problems for Soviet critics that emerged as major issues in Soviet war literature. Soviet critics welcomed what they saw as Remarque's exposure of a bloody imperialist war and the sacrifice of the working class to further the interests of German capitalists. Yet Remarque's emphasis on fatalism, resignation to duty, and a total absence of any class consciousness in his soldiers lent no support to the view that World War I had been waged for purely economic aims. An orthodox view was that Remarquism was alien to any reading of the Soviet Union's war. In fact, Remarquism covered a multitude of sins—from ignoring Stalin to highlighting any Soviet failures to promoting alienation and despair, or simply posing the "incorrect" questions.

On the other side of the ideological divide, National Socialist propagandists attacked Remarque for his deeply pessimistic account of war, which was hostile to the military-patriotic ethos demanded by Hitler and Goebbels. Manuscripts, unfortunately, do burn. On 10 May 1933, Nazi student fanatics, the progeny of Dostoyevsky's devils and the parents of Mao's Red Guards, proclaimed and executed their *Feuerspruch*, literally "the verdict by fire." On that shameful day, *All Quiet on the Western Front*, together with works by other famous German writers, among them Stefan Zweig and Heinrich Mann, that were deemed to be corrupting German youth were publicly burned.

One particular aspect of Remarque's account of World War I that made it highly suspect in the eyes of Soviet orthodoxy was the attention paid to battlefield hospitals and casualty clearing stations:

> One cannot grasp the fact that attached to these torn bodies there can be human faces in which life takes its normal course. And this is just a single military hospital, a single outpost. There are hundreds of thousands of these in Germany, hundreds of thousands in France, and hundreds of thousands in Russia. How senseless everything is that has been written, done, and thought when such things are possible! Everything must be a lie and meaningless if thousands of years of culture could not prevent even once these streams of blood from being shed and these torture chambers from existing in their hundreds of thousands. Only a military hospital shows what war is about.[60]

In the 1930s, the major ordeal with Nazi Germany still to come, the Soviet literary and military establishments asserted that the psyche of Soviet soldiers was quite distinct from that of soldiers in capitalist states and that, therefore, the criteria used to assess, say, Remarque and Sassoon were

inapplicable to any assessment of Soviet war literature. The work of Baklanov; Okudzhava; Kazakevich; Bykov; and in the 1980s a series of powerful
stories by Anatolii Genatulin—*Ataka* (The Attack, 1982), *Sto shagov na voine*
(A Hundred Steps in War, 1983), and *Tunnel'* (The Tunnel, 1987)—did not
support that view; hence party fears about a convergence of recorded experiences between Remarque and Soviet writers.

In his insightful study of heroic virtue in British war literature, Andrew
Rutherford draws conclusions that have some relevance for Soviet Russian
war literature generally and Remarquism specifically. For example, Rutherford notes that there is a general bias that assumes that only antiwar poetry
is any good. There is also a conspicuous failure to reckon with the limita-
tions of the genre. The poem, as Rutherford points out, "could quintessen-
talize an emotion or perception, and in doing so it often achieved effects of
great intensity; but it could not by its very nature deal with the totality of war
experience."[61]

Poetry—or prose for that matter—that in any way admires the heroic
deed is somehow suspicious or not worthy of serious consideration (see
Jünger). The debunking of the heroic deed—Rutherford cites the work of
the revisionist biographer Lytton Strachey—leads to a situation in which
"vices are, in some unexamined sense, more real than virtues—that vanity,
hypocrisy and self-deception, for example, somehow constitute a truer reality than altruism, self-sacrifice and heroism, *even when these are known to
have existed.*"[62] This is the point that some of the more balanced Soviet critics
of Remarque and Remarquism were making in their arguments with Soviet
writers. One must allow for the ideological assumptions of Soviet critics,
but they, or at least some of them, could reasonably argue—as have British
critics of Owen and Sassoon—that the picture of the war experience found
in, say, *Take Care, Schoolboy* does not account for the bravery and self-
sacrifice without which the Germans would not have been defeated. Had
Soviet critics been prepared to concede that Okudzhava was honestly reflecting one personal view of war and deserved to be heard, then the arguments over Remarquism would not have been so fraught with danger or so
virulent. But then they would not have been Soviet critics.

The determination of writers such as Baklanov, Genatulin, Okudzhava,
and Nekrasov to relate their war as they saw it, not through the lens of
Marxism-Leninism but deliberately highlighting the darker sides, would
seem to imitate the earlier approach of the British war poets, who, according
to Rutherford, adopted a polemical stance "as a corrective to the falsities of

traditional war poetry, journalistic rhetoric, official propaganda and civilian ignorance; but this very polemical intention, while sharpening the focus of their poetic vision, also narrowed its scope by restricting their conception of the truth that must be told."[63] Certainly there is no question that Baklanov and the others were trying to overcome party propaganda and lies. However, their real crime as far as the party was concerned was not that they in any way narrowed or restricted the truth of the war. Quite the reverse: They were attempting to widen and deepen the portrayal of the war, to go into forbidden territory, to rescue the truth from the party and the censors. The work of Baklanov, Bondarev, and Genatulin clearly views the war against the Germans as a holy war, a just war, but they also write of cowardice and incompetence. The good and the brave do not always triumph.

Accusations of Remarquism were quite deliberately intended to intimidate writers who probed too far. Assessing British war literature, Rutherford could just as well have been speaking of the stance of Baklanov and his fellow dissenters and what they were trying to achieve: "Much of the finest literature of the war transcends the simplicities of protest to acknowledge a far greater complexity of response to disturbingly complex experience, and . . . much of it also reasserts an heroic ideal, stripped of romantic glamour certainly, but redefined convincingly in terms of grim courage and endurance in the face of almost unbearable suffering and horror."[64]

The impact of *All Quiet on the Western Front* is all the more powerful for concentrating on the fate of a small group of soldiers. Whereas in Remarque's novel this focus serves to uncover the grim, the banal, and the brutal, in later German novels about the eastern front in World War II, the Remarquist focus on small groups and the fate of individual, often heroic soldiers serves to hide the big picture and the wider complicity of Germans in Nazi crimes. It is here, one feels, that Soviet critics, by concentrating too much on World War I, have missed an opportunity to make some useful observations. Willi Heinrich's novel *The Willing Flesh* is a case in point. Set immediately after the fall of Stalingrad, *The Willing Flesh* concentrates on the fate of one platoon led by the consummate military professional Sergeant Steiner. Steiner is no Nazi, yet—and this is important for Heinrich's story—he is a loyal German who serves in the war out of a sense of duty. A great deal of the narrative is based on the hostility between Stransky, the new battalion commander and well-connected Junker, and Steiner. This personal hatred is the device by means of which Heinrich tackles certain German themes: the role of the Junker class (Prussian landed aristocracy) in the army and meritocracy and connections in the army (and by implication civilian life in Germany as well).

With the war lost, German officers consider why the men still fight so well. "They're fighting," argues Major Vogel, the veteran battalion commander, "for nothing but their naked lives, for their bedeviled, unfortunate flesh."[65] "Heroism," argues Captain Kiesel, the regimental adjutant, "begins where the meaninglessness of the sacrifice becomes the last, the only message the dead can leave behind."[66] All such talk is of course tantamount to treason as far as Stransky is concerned. In some ways, the response of Stransky—the Junker, the believer in Hitler—is more honest than those of Vogel and Kiesel. When Vogel says that German soldiers are no longer fighting for world freedom or the West, he deliberately ignores the central themes of Hitler's war in the East: *Drang nach Osten, Endlösung, Lebensraum,* and *Untermenschen.* German soldiers were emphatically not fighting for "world freedom" or the ideas embodied in the political concept of the West. Quite the reverse: Weimar Germany, the nation's first attempt at democracy, was despised and undermined by both the left and the right. *Drang nach Osten* was far more than a physical move toward the East. It was the repudiation of Western liberal democracy and the glorification of the *Staat.* Vogel's reasons are designed to rewrite history, showing the German army as being engaged in a struggle to save the West—a disgraceful appropriation of the West—while attacking the very ideals on which the West is based. That the Soviet Union was far more murderous in its pursuit of class war in no way strengthens Vogel's case. Kiesel is probably right that the fundamental decency of the soldier's desire to stand by his fellows accounts for the resolve of the German army after so many reverses. His claim, however, that the flesh has been baited with so-called ideals is not entirely convincing. The implication that ideals are false, that the unscrupulous manipulate them for power, is nothing new, but in implying that all ideals deserve to be prefaced with "so-called," Kiesel argues that *all* ideals are somehow suspect. In so doing, he undermines what he regards as the soldier's sole claim to self-respect, namely, his refusal to abandon his comrades. He attacks the "so-called" ideals of Hitler's Germany—though he avoids citing these ideals—only to assert the ideal of *Kameradschaft.* Is the ideal of *Kameradschaft* above reproach when the ideals of rapine and conquest are now, in the face of defeat, somehow suspect? And how is heroism possible if the sacrifice is meaningless? Kiesel's position is relativist and not far removed from Jünger's.

Well before the German defeat at Stalingrad, the Nazis had appropriated the theme of *Kameradschaft*. It was a central plank in Nazi propaganda aimed at the military, the brownshirts, veterans' organizations such as the Stahlhelm, and the Hitler Youth. While *Kameradschaft* was an essential ingredient of German military prowess, as the heterogeneous Western Allies and the Soviet Union repeatedly discovered, it was a strength that could be turned against the army as the situation on all fronts deteriorated. Criticism of military leadership could now easily be cited as disloyalty, as a violation of the sacred code of *Kameradschaft*, as undermining Goebbels's call for total war—and so the army would fight on and obey orders. To the very end of its existence, the intensively nurtured claims of *Kameradschaft* remained one of the Wehrmacht's great strengths. At the same time, it functioned as a narcotic, legitimizing blind instinct when some rational appraisal was required. The outcomes at Moscow in 1941 and Stalingrad in 1942–1943 reveal both its strength and its weakness.

For the officer class, *Kameradschaft* is replaced by duty. Realizing that the division is lost, Brandt, the weary, hardheaded divisional commander, seems unable to comprehend what Germany has done: "We could scarcely expect anything else, and we have done our duty. You and I and all of us. But we undertook to do too much, and that is our misfortune."[67] Brandt's appeal to duty is unconvincing. Why is the German army in Russia? Who is responsible? What about the duty of the German officers? To whom or to what do they discharge their duty? And at what stage does the call of duty (for officers) and *Kameradschaft* (for soldiers) merely serve to hide the enormity of Germany's crimes and the complicity therein of the German army? Heinrich provides no answers to these questions.

Memory can be suppressed, possibly destroyed. But the censors and the KGB are not the sole enemies. The past can also fade or be rendered irrelevant, or even inspire indifference among those who were not there. Or it can be misunderstood. Is the literature of a terrible war only for the survivors, or can it say something to subsequent generations? Vasil' Bykov goes to the heart of the matter in *Kar'er* (The Quarry, 1986), a short novel published on the eve of glasnost. Ageev, a former partisan, excavates a quarry in search of the remains of the woman whom he loved, who was executed by the Germans. Ageev's son is perplexed by his father's quest. Why, he wonders, is this necessary after all this time?

It's possible that you won't understand. Because you're of a generation a long way from that time. No, it's not a question of the depth of knowledge. We know loads about the war. But about the atmosphere of the time, that finer point that can't be grasped by logic. You feel it on your skin. Your blood. Your life. That's not been given to you. Moreover, perhaps it's not necessary that it be given to you. You have yours. And as far as the war is concerned, then maybe you have sufficient understanding that you get from the mass media. There everything is all neat and logical, simple, and even beautiful. Especially when all the guns, all in a neat line, are blasting away at the enemy.

And: "In order to know something properly, you've go to get into this 'something' up to your ears. Like a science or art. Or when this 'something' becomes your fate. But not as a topic of brief interest or even worse of passing curiosity."[68]

In 2000, Georgii Vladimov expressed another fear, namely, that the skepticism and irony shown toward the Afghan and Chechen wars, both disastrously prosecuted by the Soviet Union and the Russian Federation, respectively, may affect the way in which the Great Patriotic War is perceived. One consequence, he believes, is the creation of an atmosphere receptive to books such as The Icebreaker.[69]

Conclusion

If, as far as war literature is concerned, the publication of Grossman's Life and Fate in 1988 marks the high point of glasnost, then the honors of the first post-Soviet decade belong to Viktor Astaf'ev, who throughout the 1990s published a series of war novels and memoirs. To The Shepherd and the Shepherdess, already noted, Astaf'ev added the apocalyptic and remarkable novel The Damned and the Dead, which won him a whole series of literary prizes. This was followed by Tak khochetsia zhit' (I Really Want to Live, 1995), Oberton (Overtone, 1996), and Veselyi soldat (The Cheerful Soldier, 1998), all of which bring different and important insights to the war. Either as a consequence of a dreadful, terrible conflict or a reflection of the artistic resourcefulness of Soviet and now Russian writers, the Great Patriotic War has a capacity continually to generate new insights and new additions to the genre. Take Vasil' Bykov, whose work will be examined in chapter 3; far from standing down from his post in 1991, Bykov continued to write on the war theme. *Stuzha* (The Great Freeze, 1993) is classic Bykov. In *Boloto* (The Swamp, 2001) he adds yet another twist to his accounts of partisan warfare, of which he is the absolute master of the genre. In *The General and His Army*, Georgii Vladimov turns to the life and fate of Andrei Vlasov, breaking one of the few taboos left over from the Soviet period. And in another variation of the role of the NKVD and blocking detachments, Vladimir But's *Heads—Tails* was published in 1995 and recognized by Bykov as a major contribution.

By far the best literature on this theme has been written by writers who, for various reasons, were hostile to the Soviet state. One possibility is that a new generation of writers or some lone pen unconnected with the Soviet past will revisit the Great Patriotic War and try to remove the patriotic label from Astaf'ev, Grossman, Bykov, and Solzhenitsyn. So far the attempt has failed. Would such a novel be possible? Would it be possible to write truthfully about Stalin and the war and still produce something to rival *Life and Fate* or *The Damned and the Dead*? Whatever the outcome, can we really be certain, even now, so many years after the end of the war, that Russian writers have had the last word?

Time will tell. Meanwhile, in the next chapter I consider a selection of stories written by some of the early dissenters.

2 Return from the Front: The Veterans Dissent

There is the generation which grew up in war, and the generation which grew up in the rear. You fought, we studied. These are two different generations, even though the gap in years is hardly anything.
—IUrii Bondarev, *Silence*

One of the anomalies of Soviet censorship was that accounts of the war that did not gloss over the darker sides were published even while Stalin was alive. However, the real stimulus to dissent came in 1956 with Nikita Khrushchev's partial denunciation of Stalin. After that, former junior officers and war correspondents started to publish stories based on their frontline experiences. Some of these authors—for example, Grigorii Baklanov, IUrii Bondarev, and especially Vasil' Bykov—offered a range of challenges to what one might term the Stalinist view of the war. In this chapter, I examine a selection of works by Emmanuil Kazakevich, Grigorii Baklanov, and IUrii Bondarev.

Introduction

The aesthetic barrenness and emotional sterility of much Soviet war literature stem in part from the heavy layer of ideological baggage that prevented authors not just from confronting some of the darker sides of humankind at war but from admitting that *Homo sovieticus* enjoyed no immunity from fear, terrifying loneliness, cowardice, and selfishness while, of course, being capable of astonishing sacrifice, endurance, and bravery. Their failure to confront human weakness in war suggests, implausibly, that Soviet soldiers did not experience these emotions on the battlefield. Indeed, could they exist when so many Soviet commentators routinely wrote of mass heroism?

One way in which the work of Baklanov, Bondarev, Kazakevich, and others like them makes such an important break with Soviet orthodoxy is that the war they portray and the way their soldiers behave under the pressures of war is recognizably more consistent with the norms (and extremes) of human behavior than with the enforced myths of the party and its censors. These authors recognize that although soldiers are part of a large army, they experience war in small groups. War at the sharp end is very personal, and it is in small groups of soldiers, such as scouts, Soviet soldiers trying to escape German encirclement in the summer of 1941, and the isolated gun crew desperately clinging to the beachhead, that we get as true a picture of war's horrors as we are likely to get secondhand.

Two early examples are Emmanuil Kazakevich's *Star* and *Dvoe v stepi* (Two Men on the Steppe, 1948), both of which offer, among other things, less than flattering insights into the workings of military tribunals. IUrii Bondarev (*The Final Salvoes* and *The Battalions Request Fire Support*) and Grigorii Baklanov (*South of the Main Blow*, *A Piece of Ground*, *The Dead Feel No Shame*, and *July 1941*), who were prominent in the glasnost debates of the 1980s—though by this time in their careers often on opposite sides politically—continued the trend of small-group actions with hefty doses of frontline realism.

Emmanuil Kazakevich

During the war, Kazakevich served in a reconnaissance section and was decorated for snatching a German for interrogation purposes, referred to in Russian as *iazyk* (literally "tongue"). Kazakevich finished the war as head of reconnaissance at army headquarters, and his firsthand knowledge and personal experience are clearly evident throughout *Star*. The result is a thoroughly convincing story based on a highly specialized military skill.

Star (1946)

A short, convincing story with a gradual buildup to the moment when Travkin and his men cross the German lines to meet their fate, *Star* conveys some of the violent uncertainties of war and humankind's response to them. Kazakevich's soldiers readily take life but also meet their own deaths with fortitude. Anticipating Western films such as *The Keep* (1983) and *Dog Soldiers* (2002), allusions to the supernatural add a highly unusual dimension to a Soviet war story. On a deeper, nonmilitary level, the hinted existence of dark, malevolent forces somehow controlling the fate of these soldiers implies that man does not manage war but is manipulated by it.

The patrol's mission, code name Star, is to reconnoiter the extent of a German military buildup that is thought to be the prelude to a major German assault. The scouts are participants in the ancient military task of acquiring knowledge of the enemy's intentions by stealth and guile, first studied and elucidated as a basic principle in *The Art of War*. In the words of Sun Tzu: "What enables the wise sovereign and the good general to strike and conquer, and achieve things beyond the reach of ordinary men is foreknowledge. Now this foreknowledge cannot be elicited from spirits;

it cannot be obtained inductively from experience, nor by any deductive calculation. Knowledge of the enemy's dispositions can only be obtained from other men."[1]

Two things make Star particularly absorbing and unusual when compared to the run-of-the-mill Soviet war story. First is the timing of publication, at the start of Andrei Zhdanov's postwar purge, the Zhdanovshchina. At a time of an almost rabid xenophobia and anti-Western propaganda, Star is, for a Soviet war story, remarkably free of set-piece ideological rants. In fact, as Don Piper has pointed out, Star and Two Men on the Steppe "verge upon dissidence."[2] Second, an atmosphere of unremitting menace envelops the patrol. Terrain, the local population, the Soviet military police (references to which Soviet readers would have taken as an allusion to something more sinister, such as SMERSH or the NKVD or even Stalin's Russia itself), and elemental or even supernatural forces all seem to be conspiring against the scouts. Well before Lieutenant Travkin's patrol is discovered and hunted down by the Germans, Kazakevich suggests that it is doomed. The atmosphere of menace is ubiquitous, and it is this, as much as the author's expertly deployed knowledge, that makes Star special.

Consider the introductory paragraph, the description of the forest as the author sets the tactical scene: "As the division advanced, it penetrated ever more deeply into boundless forests. With their roads churned up by the war, then washed away by the spring rains, these vast forest expanses had accomplished something that neither German tanks, nor the German air force, nor even the bandit gangs that rampaged through these parts had managed to do: They had engulfed the division."[3] Here and elsewhere in Star, Kazakevich depicts nature as hostile or indifferent to Russians and Germans alike.

The bandit gangs to which Kazakevich refers are one of many indications that the Soviet army may not be welcome in the forests of Ukraine, or indeed in Ukraine itself, which bore the full brunt of Stalin's Terror-Famine. In the 1960s and 1970s, Bykov frequently exploited the legacy of collectivization to complicate the question of collaboration in his accounts of partisan warfare. Writing in 1946, Kazakevich has to proceed with caution. Nevertheless, he manages to convey an impression that something is amiss. In one scene, which in the 1960s became something of a cliché in spaghetti Westerns, Kazakevich implies that Travkin's men are not exactly received with open arms as they enter a village that has been abandoned by the Germans after nearly three years under German occupation: "From a huge cross, at least three times the size of a man, the crucified form of Christ gazed down on the soldiers. The streets were empty, and only the barking of dogs in the yards and the barely perceptible movement of the homespun canvas curtains in the windows indicated that people, fearful of gangs of bandits, were carefully watching the soldiers as they passed through the village."[4]

The book contains several strong hints that loyalties among Ukrainians are divided: Some of the armed groups, the red partisans, living in the forests are loyal to Moscow; others are hostile to Soviet power and the return of the Red Army after three years of German occupation. The presence of the large cross as the men enter the village is an astonishingly flagrant affront to the atheism sponsored by the Soviet state. The image of Christ gazing down on Red Army soldiers arouses any number of interpretations: compassion, solidarity with the oppressed, forgiveness, and even reproach for waging war. The image poses a direct question to the Red Army: Do you come as saviors or with retribution in your hearts? The image also suggests something about the nature of war and the nature of suffering: Both are timeless, part of humankind's lot, at least in this world. The cross would certainly have been removed during the Soviet campaigns to eradicate religion. Religion was a source of comfort to believers, a non-Soviet source of allegiance that had to be crushed. The years under German occupation saw a rebirth of religious expression—encouraged no doubt by the Germans for their own purposes—and with it a hardening of anti-Soviet sentiments.

The very nature of the scouts' work is stealth and secrecy, and here, too, the supernatural element comes into play. The scout departing on his mission is no ordinary soldier. He is about to enter a world in which the rules that guide conventional war no longer apply. Kazakevich reveals some of the mystery of this ancient and arcane art: "He is able to do without all articulated speech, confining himself to imitations of birdcalls in order to pass signals to his comrades. He merges with the fields, the forests, the gullies. He becomes the spirit of these places, an alert and dangerous spirit, who in the depths of his soul cares for one thing only: the mission. So begins the age-old game in which there are only are two protagonists: man and death."[5]

As the scouts cross the German lines, they are, it seems, crossing over into hell, a sense reinforced by Kazakevich's use of the Old Testament term *kromeshnaia temnota*, "the outer darkness." To a half-awake and frightened German, the Soviet patrol inspires terror: "The utterly strange appearance of these green shadows and, perhaps, the vague silhouette of their figures in the morning mist, gave the German an impression of something completely unreal and magical. Not for one moment did he think that these were Russians. Nor did he link this apparition in any way at all with thoughts of the enemy. Frightened, he just muttered to himself, 'Green ghosts.'"[6]

One relatively minor event acquires dramatic significance for the patrol's fate. Two horses borrowed by the patrol are not returned to their owners. One of the scouts, Mamochkin, against the orders of Travkin, decides to retain them and allow another peasant to use them in return for food. This act initiates a military investigation in response to complaints from the peasants, which, regardless of the patrol's mission, is pursued with zeal. Now, there is something not quite right about the appropriation of the horses and what appears to be a routine investigation. The situation hints at the ubiquitous presence of the NKVD and SMERSH. Are the scouts suspected of having established contact with the bandits, which would be of the greatest interest to SMERSH? Is this, one wonders, the real reason for the investigator's attention? Does he really care about missing horses? It may not be significant, but the term *sledovatel'* (investigator) was standard among SMERSH officers.

More interestingly, the appropriation of the horses seems to initiate some form of supernatural retribution. Indeed, the guilty soldier realizes that he has brought a curse upon himself. As the Germans start to close in on the patrol, the superstitious soldier confesses to his commander that he failed to return the horses. He has, it is suggested, violated the unwritten laws of hospitality and thus brought retribution down upon himself and the patrol (an echo perhaps of Samuel Coleridge's *The Ancient Mariner*, 1798 and 1817).

Two Men on the Steppe (1948)

In *Two Men on the Steppe*, Kazakevich explores the psychological isolation that faces the soldier awaiting execution. Whereas in battle the soldier is sustained by the fellowship in which all are exposed to fear and danger, the soldier—especially the Soviet soldier—who faces execution is legally defenseless, alone and despised.

The plot develops on the basis of an entirely plausible battlefield incident. Contact with a division has been lost, and Ogarkov, a young and inexperienced officer, is given the task of making his way to the division and reporting back. However, in the confusion caused by the rapid German advance, he cannot locate the unit, and his mission ends in failure. Despite the obvious mitigating factors, he is taken before a military tribunal and sentenced to death. Here, as in *Star*, Kazakevich reflects on the nature of Soviet justice. Under the circumstances, the punishment appears disproportionately harsh. It also appears senseless at a time when the Red Army needs every able-bodied man. One suspects that Kazakevich intends the arbitrary and indifferent manner of the tribunal to bring the reader to this conclusion. This intent is also strongly implied by the testimony of Siniaev, another officer who was given a task similar to Ogarkov's and who is called as a witness. He says Ogarkov lost his nerve, though he has no knowledge regarding what happened after they parted company: So much for a fair hearing. It is, too, a mockery of Ogarkov's belief: "This is the Soviet Union, where every person has the right to be heard."[7]

Another prisoner in the condemned cell is openly hostile to the Soviet regime. A Baptist, he has deserted from the army and been condemned to execution. The Baptist seems to accept the tribunal's verdict as confirmation that the Soviets are as bad as the Germans, whereas Ogarkov maintains his faith in the Soviet system despite the unjust verdict. A less obvious point that emerges is that the Baptist can face the possibility of his death with a certain equilibrium and even calmness of mind, which is impossible for Ogarkov.

A German attack prevents the sentence from being carried out. Escorted by his guard, Ogarkov marches eastward to rejoin the main Soviet armies. Dzhurabaev, the guard, is a harsh and unthinking supernumerary. He is like a well-trained sheepdog. His inflexibility and harassment of Ogarkov as they travel across the steppe remind us of the tribunal itself, relentless, rigid, and unjust:

> Toward evening, when the sun was behind them, Ogarkov saw Dzhurabaev's shadow beside him. Ogarkov soon felt a profound antipathy, almost hatred, toward that shadow. Not toward Dzhurabaev, but above all toward the shadow. To Dzhurabaev himself, Ogarkov nurtured no enmity. The guard was doing his job. But his shadow, wide, short, and not receding for one step, as if it was firmly attached, threw Ogarkov into a powerless state of exasperation, and he tried not to look at it at all.[8]

In the chaos of the retreat, circumstances allow Ogarkov to demonstrate to Dzhurabaev that he is not a coward. Joining the scattered remnants of other retreating soldiers, Ogarkov distinguishes himself in battle, and

Dzhurabaev's grip gradually weakens. By the time of Dzhurabaev's death at the Don crossing, the relationship between the two men is no longer that of guard and prisoner but of comrades who have shared the perils of battle. Dzhurabaev's death and the all-too-obvious intentions of a recently widowed woman are a temptation and an opportunity for Ogarkov. Here Kazakevich tries to answer, or inadvertently raises, the question of why citizens who were treated so horrendously by the Soviet system remained loyal. Why does Ogarkov not reject the Soviet state, as does the Baptist? Even though Ogarkov is aware that he has not been treated fairly, he wants to return to the fold: "He would act like a son of his country ready to die by its hand because he was unable to live as a person guilty and rejected by it."[9] Ogarkov's desire to prove his innocence makes sense, but his acknowledgment that he is guilty seems implausible. Implausible and duplicitous most certainly is the reaction of Siniaev, whom Ogarkov meets after his return. At first Siniaev does not recognize Ogarkov; then recognition dawns, reflected in his face (Siniaev izmenilsia v litse).[10] The verb izmenit'sia, "to change/to betray," returns us to the tribunal hearing. Had Siniaev not been so quick to assume cowardice—for which he had no evidence—and unduly influenced the tribunal, the verdict would not have gone as it did. With Ogarkov's case being reconsidered and the expectation that he will be reprieved, the knowledge that Siniaev and others have "accused the tribunal of callousness and formalism"[11] is no comfort at all. Siniaev's behavior is hypocritical and inconsistent with his earlier evidence. This anodyne ending might have satisfied the censors, but it offers an abysmal picture of Soviet military justice as more like Russian roulette than rational appraisal.

Grigorii Baklanov

Grigorii Baklanov began his military career as a forward observer in the 307th artillery regiment on the Northwestern Front. After being badly wounded in the battle for Zaporozhe, he returned to service and took part in the capture of Vienna. He ended the war with the rank of lieutenant in charge of the reconnaissance section of an artillery battalion. The fate of artillery units features in two of Baklanov's early stories, *South of the Main Blow* and *The Dead Feel No Shame*.

South of the Main Blow (1958)

Set in Hungary in the winter of 1943–1944, *South of the Main Blow* portrays the desperate attempts of a Soviet artillery battery to stem a German tank attack. The story exploits the psychological conflict arising between the immediate dangers facing a small unit under attack by superior enemy forces and the bigger strategic picture of which the soldiers are unaware. Loss of life in war is unavoidable—sometimes unforgivable when soldiers are incompetently led and badly prepared, as in the terrible summer of 1941—but sometimes it is necessary if bigger goals are to be achieved. One of the harsher facts of war that Baklanov confronts is that strategic success sometimes demands tactical sacrifices. Indeed, even at the tactical level soldiers have to die so that objectives can be taken. Baklanov also confronts, as he will again in later works, the themes of encirclement, cowardice, duty, comradeship, and the psychological barriers between frontline and rear-echelon troops.

Comradeship is a pervasive theme in Baklanov's war stories, mitigating some of the horrors and privations of frontline service. On a purely practical level, it serves as the device that binds men together in danger to make an effective unit. This effect is clearly underlined by the early return of the battery commander, Captain Belichenko, from hospital. Rather than be discharged from the army, he voluntarily returns to the front because comradeship is more important than the relative comfort of the rear and the hospital. Comradeship also inspires self-discipline. Thus, the newly arrived Lieutenant Nazarov is acutely aware that he must not fail or be seen to fail: "Nazarov was not terrified by the battle itself but by the fact that in the battle he would suddenly turn out to be a coward and that everyone would see it and think, 'The best thing would be for him to be killed immediately,' he thought heatedly."[12]

A staple of Soviet propaganda was that the rear echelons and the soldiers at the front were united in the struggle against the German invaders. This assumption ignores, however, the fact that there is a psychological difference between the soldiers at the front and those in the rear that is found in all armies. We see this difference in the hospital. There is the type of soldier represented by Belichenko and that represented by a major in the supply troops. The major advises Belichenko to make sure that he has all the necessary paperwork relating to his wound and time in hospital. "After the war," he warns, "every bit of paper will be necessary, and you will be able to prove anything."[13] This may have been good advice in the world of Soviet bureaucracy, but it shows that not all soldiers dedicated themselves to the cause of victory. The war will soon be over, and the major has his eye on the postwar period. Belichenko refuses to be discharged from the army and returns to the front to deal with unfinished business. Now he realizes why he hated this major during his time in the hospital: The two men live in two different worlds, in two different armies.

The dichotomy of *tylovik* and *frontovik* is present even in the attitudes of soldiers in the same unit: Some are in headquarters set back immediately behind the lines—clerks and cooks, for example—whereas others are situated in forward positions, manning guns and trenches. Baklanov provides two examples that illustrate the problem. Two soldiers, Sergeant Major (*starshina*) Ponomarev and Dolgovushin, take some food up to the front. Meanwhile, the Germans have broken through into the Soviet rear. The two men encounter Germans, and in the exchange of fire Ponomarev is wounded and captured. When he returns to his unit, Dolgovushin lies about what happened, claiming that he tried to drag Ponomarev's body away. He is believed, and Ponomarev will never be able to bear witness against him because he is executed by the Germans. Dolgovushin's behavior is set against that of a headquarters clerk, Leont'ev, who is sent with one of the scouts to deliver orders and conducts himself well in his baptism of fire.

As in *The Dead Feel No Shame*, the theme of *okruzhenie* (encirclement) in *South of the Main Blow* is pervasive, giving rise to endless conflicts and even serving as a plot multiplier. Occupying a piece of high ground, the Soviet artillerymen are surrounded. The commander, Bogachev, must consider whether to withdraw:

> Bogachev was very familiar with that sly feeling that troubles one
> on every occasion in battle if you have to make the decision
> yourself: to retreat or to remain? But he had fought through the
> war; he had not retreated once, had attacked, been in encirclement.
> He could not but fail to understand that while he held the height,
> another height, or a third one, then the Germans' hands were tied.
> And he held the height.[14]

Bogachev's apparently straightforward thoughts go to the heart of a permanent dilemma facing Soviet commanders at all levels. However rational the decision to retreat and however solid the military necessity, retreat always comes with the suspicion of desertion. It is noteworthy that the Russian word for sly—*lukavyi*—is also one of a number of words for the devil. In the Red Army, decisions to withdraw or stay put are fraught with moral or perhaps ideological temptation. If a higher military authority gives the order, then the junior commander is absolved of any responsibility. However, if the junior commander has to make the decision, the risk that he will be investigated for desertion or dereliction of duty will always enter into his calculus of decision-making. Such considerations cannot promote effective command.

Belichenko, the battery commander, is well aware of the sacrifices that he has to make in order to stop the Germans: "War! As is well known: there is no war without blood."[15] In Baklanov's fiction, the lieutenants are, to allude to the title of another work by the same author, forever nineteen years old. These boys pay a heavy price. Hardheaded professional though he now is after so many battles, Belichenko is not indifferent to their fate:

> Belichenko walked and thought about the fate of these lieutenants. Tomorrow on the outskirts of this unfamiliar Hungarian town, a long, long way from their homes, they faced their first battle. And everything that they had lived through up till then, everything that they had experienced and read, everything that they had been taught, everything about which they had dreamed, all this was a preparation for tomorrow morning. . . . Belichenko did not know what would become of them. But no matter what happened, no matter how short and difficult their fate was, he believed that wars would pass, battles would rage, and people would envy their fate.[16]

The problem is that he can pass on only so much of his experience. Each new wave of recruits must learn—and die—the hard way. We might see Belichenko's gift of a captured German pistol to a newly arrived lieutenant as a symbolic transfer of knowledge and experience on the eve of battle. The lack of experience is cruelly exposed. German tanks tempt Soviet guns to open fire, and the Soviet guns are then destroyed. Desperate pleas are made to Belichenko to assist the guns under fire. He refuses because he knows that opening fire on the German tanks will betray his carefully camouflaged positions to the enemy, who will then avoid the trap that has been set for them:

> Were he to open fire, the tanks would discover his camouflaged battery and would bombard it from afar from their advantageous positions, just as they had his neighboring battery. He was responsible for soldiers' lives, but these people averted their gaze when he looked at them as if he was a person who had done

something terrible. Well, people are not obliged to love their commander, but they must submit to his will.[17]

Belichenko's dilemma is not unlike that faced by the destroyer captains in Nicholas Monsarrat's The Cruel Sea and Alistair Maclean's HMS Ulysses: Do they stop to pick up survivors of U-boat attacks, thus exposing the destroyers and their crews to danger, or do they sail on? Belichenko's determined refusal to assist the other battery hints at the problem in the title, namely, that Soviet units are being sacrificed south of the main blow in order to secure success elsewhere. As Belichenko will sacrifice the neighboring battery in order to achieve greater success later and to protect men under his command, so he must reckon with the possibility that his unit will also be sacrificed. Yet another incident presses home the idea that soldiers must sacrifice themselves so that others may achieve their mission. In view of advancing tanks, a Soviet soldier sets hay alight so that the German tanks will be illuminated for the artillery. There is no escape, and he, knowing this, uses soldiers' letters to start the fire.

The sacrifices that so many of Baklanov's soldiers are called upon to make highlight a special type of raw courage, the sort demonstrated by Bogachev, the scout, and soldiers, unnamed, found dead at their posts who died alone, their deeds unseen by their comrades. We are reminded of Dolgovushin's behavior. It seems that the chaos of war favors neither the unseen fainthearted nor the unseen brave-hearted. In the aftermath of a battle, Orlov, one of Belichenko's soldiers, comes across an abandoned antitank gun. The gunner, having fired his weapon at the tank, escapes. Nearby reposes a machine gunner's crushed body. Both men have done their duty. One survives to fight again; the other dies at his post. Orlov admires the bravery of the lone machine gunner and approves of the antitank gunner's decision to escape. Courage and initiative are required, a lesson, Baklanov suggests, that the Red Army has been somewhat slow to learn. Yet even at this stage of the war, possibly because soldiers know the end is near, there are manifestations of mass panic and desertion. It is to Baklanov's credit that he does not shirk this theme. Soviet infantry abandon their positions, exposing the artillery to risk: "The wind clearly carried the revving and roaring of tank engines, and the soldiers listened for a while. Out of the dark the infantry started running away in ones and twos. Several looked back while they were running, firing somewhere above and behind, and then ran on further, passing by the battery."[18]

The sacrifice/cowardice theme is explicitly linked with the summer disaster of 1941 and the way that Soviet soldiers behaved in encirclement. Belichenko unexpectedly meets a Sergeant Arkhipov with whom he evaded capture in 1941. The link is both historical and moral. If the Red Army of 1944–1945 is better able to deal with the Germans, that is in part due to the sacrifices made earlier in the war: "The experience acquired at the cost of life in 1941 had transferred to them. They were finishing what had been started by others."[19] And at the very end of the story, with the German infantry closing in, Arkhipov makes the final sacrifice, buying time for Belichenko to make his escape. These recollections of 1941 prepare the way for the full-blown account given in July 1941.

The Dead Feel No Shame (1961)

Set somewhere on the Eastern front in the winter of 1943–1944, The Dead Feel No Shame begins with the interception and decoding of a German radio message that reveals an imminent tank attack. A depleted Soviet artillery battalion (divizion) is deployed to meet the threat with the aim of gaining time for a counterattack. In the course of the battle, the exemplary unit commander, Major Ushakov, is killed and the battery scattered. Under the leadership of Captain Vasich, the unit political officer (zampolit), the survivors break out of temporary German encirclement and return to the Soviet lines. Whereas Vasich manifests the highest possible standards of military leadership, the chief of staff, Captain Ishchenko, abandons the battlefield in blind panic at a crucial moment. Later reunited with Vasich's group, Ishchenko escapes punishment because none of the witnesses to his cowardice have survived. Baklanov manages to pack in a great deal into a short work, examining the themes of okruzhenie (encirclement), cowardice, dereliction of duty, and Soviet military justice.

Most of the plot lines in The Dead Feel No Shame are based on the occupational hazard of okruzhenie. The theme first emerges when a group under the command of Vasich is conducting a reconnaissance as part of the unit's deployment. In an incident that is also mentioned in South of the Main Blow, one of the scouts, Mostovoi, recalls being caught by some Germans in the summer of 1941: "In 1941 we escaped from encirclement in the area of Khomutovka. Have you heard of Khomutovka? Anyway, encirclement is encirclement."[20] Stopping at a farmhouse in search of food, Mostovoi and others are captured by the Germans. One of the Germans lets them go, and they make it back to Soviet lines. Upon their return, their account of the escape is interpreted by one Soviet officer as an attempt to undermine morale, and they are arrested. The fact that they were released by the Germans is a direct challenge to the view endlessly propagated in Soviet media that all Germans are sadistic monsters. The apparently casual manner in which this episode emerges—it is offered to the reader as just another fortuitous mishap in the summer of 1941—is misleading because this sort of incident goes, in fact, to the heart of one of the most controversial themes in Soviet-Russian war literature. Mostovoi's view that encirclement is something that just happens would be accepted by professional military officers but would not be shared by the operatives of the Special Sections of the NKVD, who were predisposed to see plots and sabotage where frequently there were none. For example, Mostovoi would have been subjected to interrogation upon his return to Soviet lines. The fact that he had been captured and then released by the Germans would instantly have aroused suspicion not only that he had collaborated with the Germans but worse, that he had been recruited by them to spy on his own side.

In view of the fact that he had earlier been arrested and interrogated, one would think that in the Soviet scheme of things the smart move would be never to mention this incident again and to consider himself lucky that he escaped any punishment. In their present circumstances, raising this matter in the presence of Vasich, the political officer, betrays a certain naïveté, even recklessness. Unfazed, unaware, or simply indifferent, however, Mostovoi pushes the matter further: "Well, commissar, you tell me. The war will finish, of course. And in the worldwide scale of things, the matter is clear; who is right, and who is guilty, who should be dealt with. But one man, even this German who let us go? What do you reckon? Will it be possible to examine everyone after the war? Everyone!"[21] That Mostovoi addresses Vasich as "commissar" may not be entirely irrelevant or innocent. The institution of commissars was abolished in October 1942. *Zampolit* Vasich may be, but Mostovoi's use of "commissar" suggests that although the title has changed, the function still sets Vasich apart from soldiers. Mostovoi's points are precisely the comments that Vasich is duty-bound to counter with either threats of arrest or argument. His counterarguments about the threat posed by Hitler are true enough yet lack conviction. Again, regardless of the obvious ideological perils and potential accusations of undermining morale and engaging in anti-Soviet propaganda, Mostovoi defends the German who let him go: "What you say is correct. but there's something else one can't just ignore—said Mostovoi.—Here I stand alive, but I could long ago have been rotting in concentration camps. The Germans are not all the same, and one individual must not have to answer for another."[22]

The real target in the exchanges between Mostovoi and Vasich is not the Germans but the way in which innocent Soviet soldiers are treated by their own counterintelligence agencies when they return to Soviet lines. When Mostovoi points out that but for the German who let him go he would be rotting in some concentration camp, he indirectly draws attention to the fate of many Soviet soldiers and civilians. In the tried and tested manner of Aesop, Baklanov is inviting Soviet readers to recall all the stories they have heard, even their own personal experiences, of soldiers and civilians who were relentlessly interrogated by the Special Sections and, later, SMERSH and the many who ended up in labor camps or were sent to penal battalions. Nor is it entirely clear, despite Mostovoi's claims, who in the grand scheme of things is right and who is guilty. Where does the Soviet-German Non-aggression Pact belong in the scale of right and wrong? Moreover, Mostovoi's question—Will it be possible to examine everyone after the war?—points to the sheer scale of SMERSH interrogations and filtration, which did not end in 1945.

When he meets Vasich's group, Ishchenko betrays himself by his hysterical reactions to Vasich's reasonable questions about his absence and behavior. At this point, Vasich starts to suspect that Ishchenko indeed abandoned his men. Ishchenko tries to camouflage his failings by attacking the original orders: "To send a weakened artillery battalion to be crushed under tank tracks, without any reconnaissance, without any attempt to find out what was going on or to clarify the situation! They stuffed the hole with us, like an embrasure being blocked with a body! Who will answer for that? They ran all over us! People were crushed by tanks."[23]

Ishchenko protests too much, yet despite his obvious cowardice and failure of duty, he has a point. The remnants of the unit were sacrificed in order to win time for a larger-scale counterattack. Baklanov's response to Ishchenko seems to be articulated by Vasich, who, grudgingly mindful that Ishchenko may be right about the manner in which the battalion was deployed, nevertheless articulates the view, which would not have disgraced the pages of Clausewitz's masterpiece, that "others pay in blood for those who spare themselves in battle: That is the law of war."[24]

Neither the regimental commander, Lieutenant Colonel Stetsenko, nor the SMERSH captain can make a case against Ishchenko (Vasich is killed in the breakout, and the regimental commander is well aware that the artillery was indeed sacrificed to disrupt the German attack, as Ishchenko asserted). Having survived the interrogation, Ishchenko meets the other survivors, ordinary soldiers, who believe that he has been interrogated on their behalf. The comradely warmth extended to him, a parody of the genuine warmth that existed between Major Ushakov and the regimental commander, leaves a sour taste. Here we should recall Mostovoi's words that "one individual must not have to answer for another." In other words, collective punishment is unjust. Will suspicion fall on the other soldiers who escaped, not just Ishchenko? Will they be deemed by SMERSH to have colluded with Ishchenko? In the Soviet ideological universe, these are real possibilities. Yet Stetsenko has no doubt that Ishchenko is guilty. His thoughts on the fate of the artillery battalion suggest that Baklanov's title refers both to Vasich and Ushakov (the honorable dead) and to Ishchenko (the morally dead): "Glory lives on after death: Even death cannot wipe away a coward's shame."[25] The dead who have done their duty feel no shame, and their memory will not be tainted, whereas those, such as Ishchenko, who have betrayed their comrades and survived at the expense of others are the morally dead, doomed to suffer perdition.

The title of this work is derived from the apothegm first attributed to Chilon of Sparta and more widely known in its Latin translation, de mortuis nil nisi bonum, "of the dead nothing but good" or "do not speak evil of the dead." Stetsenko's moral assessment of Vasich and Ishchenko suggests a variation on the title: Vasich's sense of duty and Ishchenko's cowardice speak for themselves. In fact, Baklanov poses something of a challenge to the ancient view that no ill shall be spoken of the dead. His earlier work, South of the Main Blow, is dedicated to his two brothers, IUrii Fridman and IUrii Zelkind, who were killed in the war. The act of remembrance is clearly selective: It differentiates between those who made the ultimate sacrifice — in the Soviet lexicon, "those who died the death of the brave" — and those who did not. Are works of this kind to be dedicated to cowards and deserters? Given that remembrance of the honorable dead is actively pursued by all societies that engage in war, can there be any harsher judgment uttered against the dishonorable dead than that they are sentenced to oblivion, or should the silence be broken so that their names are accompanied by curses and imprecations? All are not equal in death.

Like Mostovoi's experiences, Ishchenko's obvious cowardice and dereliction of duty seem to be a device used by Baklanov to examine the theme of punishment in greater detail. For example, the fact that Ishchenko is clearly guilty of desertion yet has apparently escaped any punishment represents a miscarriage of Soviet military justice. Ishchenko's case is, of course, just one among many, but if the guilty escape punishment, what about those who are punished even though they are innocent of any wrongdoing? There is no question regarding Ishchenko's guilt, but how many Soviet soldiers and officers found themselves in similar circumstances—cut off and encircled in the chaos of battle—and carried out their duty only to be arrested and punished on returning to Soviet lines? These, I suggest, are the real and massive miscarriages of Soviet military justice toward which Baklanov nudges the reader. Mostovoi's experiences in the summer of 1941 are the obvious example of what can happen—and did happen on a very large scale.

Additional detail concerning the arbitrary nature of Soviet ideologically based justice is revealed when Ishchenko ponders the fact that on their return to Soviet lines, Vasich's account is likely to be accepted: "And he'll be believed—thought Ishchenko—one word and a person's life could be struck off."[26] Immediately after these gloomy thoughts, Ishchenko recalls his slow, laborious career progress in the 1930s. He appears to be driven by a streak of envy toward his more talented peers. Baklanov hints that Ishchenko's promotion to the rank of captain was not based solely on professional military criteria, that he may have been a beneficiary of the 1937 purges of the Red Army, that he has a talent for denouncing others. Initially ridiculed by his more talented colleagues, he nonetheless finds himself promoted. If any person can appreciate the fact that "one word and a person's life could be struck off," it is Ishchenko. It falls to Vasich, the former commissar who is now the political officer—an irony in view of the role of such political functionaries in the purges of the Red Army—to realize the consequences:

> Vasich was suddenly struck by a thought: There he is, this
> Ishchenko, wearing the uniform, protected by his rank and making
> demands of others. Behind every word of his, behind every order
> given to a subordinate, an order that's never discussed, stands the
> entire army, its entire moral authority, the glory of the living and the
> dead. He gives his orders in their name. At that moment their power
> is in his hands. And there he is reduced to his essence, naked with
> fear. And the authority and lives of others have been entrusted to
> such a person! And Vasich coldly and firmly thought about it for a
> bit: "If we get out of this, he's going before a court."[27]

Baklanov is indicting not just Ishchenko's incompetence and cowardice but the purges that led to the mass culling of many talented officers at all levels in the Red Army, creating gaps that had to be filled. Vasich, brave and resourceful, also indicts the political class of ideological functionaries to which he belongs. In 1937, they, like many army officers, remained silent when innocent men were arrested and executed. The consequences were devastating for the Red Army and the Soviet Union. In *The Dead Feel No Shame*, this theme is merely alluded to. It would be examined in much greater detail in *July 1941*.

July 1941 (1965)

Even allowing for what was published in the glasnost years and beyond, Baklanov's *July 1941* remains one of the outstanding accounts in Soviet and Russian war literature of the 1941 summer retreat. Far harsher and more abrasive than anything else written by Baklanov in the early part of his career, *July 1941* must have been a shock to Soviet readers. It is disaster in concentrated form. The author shows the consequences of the total tactical surprise achieved by the Germans: The Soviet air force is largely destroyed on the ground (and Soviet reinforcements meet a similar fate long before they get anywhere near the front); Soviet formations, large and small, are bypassed by the German armored columns and doomed either to captivity, with all that meant for a Soviet soldier, or destruction; other units and small groups set out on the grueling march eastward, attempting to cross the German lines, only to be regarded as somehow tainted. Henceforth the mark of *okruzhenie*, all too often and unjustly a euphemism for a lack of fighting spirit or worse, remained with them.

Not all is gloom—there is sporadic opposition, as for example in General Shcherbatov—but the overall picture is one of chaos: poor organization, lack of preparation, and paralysis. Equally unflattering for Soviet arms and the state are Baklanov's various explanations of the disasters. Many of these ideas have now been well established, but in the Soviet Union in 1965 challenging the official view was fraught with danger, as we have seen by what befell Nekrich's book *1941, 22 June*. Though Baklanov's novel escaped such a fate, *July 1941* touched unavoidably upon Stalin, which meant the effects of the military purges, the Non-aggression Pact, and the failures of Soviet intelligence.

Baklanov's portrayal of the impact of the purges on Soviet military performance is, remarkably, not shared by Vasil' Bykov. In a long article written in 1995 to mark the fiftieth anniversary of the war's end, Bykov questions whether the purges really made any difference:

There exists a widely disseminated myth that the failures of the first
period of the war were caused, among other things, by the
repressions of the senior command stratum of the Red Army on the
eve of war. It goes without saying that the repressions were an evil in
all respects. But not all officers were repressed; the most experienced
ones remained and headed the army. And the first months of the war
showed the complete inability of the former command staff to resist
a well-equipped European army, which the Wehrmacht was. Very
soon, other commanders who had recently been occupying less
important duties in the regiments, brigades, and divisions quite
rightly took up positions of responsibility. It was precisely these men
who taught their superiors how to fight in the new conditions, and,
no matter how strange it sounds, Stalin on the basis of this
experience learned something as well.[28]

This is a highly idiosyncratic view from a writer of Bykov's caliber and
one that flies in the face of a great deal of evidence. In Soviet Russian literature there are multiple examples of officers who are frightened to make
militarily correct decisions for fear of incurring suspicion of cowardice or
desertion. Nearly all such cases indicate a fear of showing initiative, one of
the more serious legacies of the purges. Bykov expects us to believe that the
much-publicized judicial murder of senior Soviet officers and the arrests of
thousands of middle-ranking officers, majors and colonels, did not affect
the discharge of professional military duties when all the evidence—anec-
dotal, biographical, historical, and empirical—leaves little doubt that the
purges did just that. The execution of thousands of officers, among whom
were some talented commanders, was bad enough; almost as bad was the
psychological damage done to the survivors. Showing initiative, expressing
one's own ideas, and leading—all the things that an officer in a modern
army should do—became dangerous, so officers blindly obeyed orders.
Some of Bykov's own stories—The Dead Feel No Pain and Dozhit' do rassveta
(To Live until Dawn, 1972)—offer clear support for the view that the purges
and the state of mind they induced, which survived long after 1937–1938,
exerted a debilitating effect on command and control. And in Bykov's partisan cycle of stories, for example, Sotnikov (1970), Obelisk (The Obelisk,
1972), and Volch'ia staia (The Wolf Pack, 1974), the disastrous performance
of the Red Army in the summer of 1941 is shown to have left its mark on the
characters. It would be unusual, to say the least, if one could not make a

link between what Bykov acknowledges as "the catastrophic failures of the initial period of the war"[29] and the purges.

In many ways the title of Baklanov's novel is a misnomer. Though the author is concerned with portraying the German invasion in the summer of 1941, he is as much interested in the party's war against the Red Army in 1937. If we want to understand what went so horribly wrong in 1941, we must, implies Baklanov, return to the purges that undermined the Red Army in many ways. Two officers provide the bridge between 1937 and the summer of 1941: One is the thoroughly professional army officer, General Shcherbatov; the other is Major Shalaev, the head of the Special Section, who, like many of that ilk, is obsessed with unmasking traitors.

One obvious consequence of 1937 was that many officers who were untouched were promoted to fill the vacancies left by their executed and arrested colleagues. Shcherbatov's superior, Sorokin, is one such beneficiary, as is the front commander, Lapshin. There is no suggestion that Sorokin has advanced his career through the use of the *donos* (denunciation). Rather, he is shown as the sort of mediocre timeserver who keeps his head down, a type found in all armies. A clue to his military abilities is provided by his reaction to the German invasion: "This was all so inconceivable, nothing like what he believed and knew."[30] Promoted beyond his abilities, Sorokin is a dangerous liability in the age of mobile warfare.

Shcherbatov remembers the purges with a sense of personal shame. Why did he and so many others fail to challenge the absurd claims and confessions made at the time? One incident typical of the psychological intimidation used to isolate individual officers involves a Colonel Masenko being singled out at a party meeting and accused of having links to Trotskyite groups, a deadly accusation in 1937. Desperate to deflect attention from himself, Masenko implicates Shcherbatov. What the party achieves is not the unmasking of "enemies of the people" but the destruction of the spirit of professional, military autonomy, the esprit de corps without which an army cannot function. The same is true for the civilian population, which is atomized by the purges. "Vigilance" and the need to unmask alleged "enemies of the people," so prevalent in 1937, are conspicuously absent in 1941, when vigilance concerning the ambitions of a real enemy of the people might have made some difference.

Even Shcherbatov seems vulnerable to the paranoia of 1937. During a conversation with Emel'ianov, a colleague, he consciously parrots the party line, not because he believes it but because it is prudent to do so: "And suddenly he realized: He was not speaking to Emel'ianov or even himself . . . he was speaking like this because somebody might be listening to them; he was speaking in the presence of the phone."[31] For his part, uninhibited by the phone, Emel'ianov identifies the Stalin cult with the Age of the Lie:

> It's terrible that we ourselves helped to strengthen the blind faith in him, and now we are powerless before that faith. Holy truth looks like a terrible lie if it doesn't fit in with people's current ideas. Can you imagine what would happen were there some person who told the whole country about what was going on and about Stalin over the radio? From the very beginning, even someone who was wavering would believe that there were enemies everywhere and would believe everything. And any harshness would be justified. The real danger is that the effects of massive events are not felt immediately. People suffer much later.[32]

In the months leading up to the German invasion, the implications of the fact that "holy truth looks like a terrible lie" are obvious. Three weeks before the start of the war, the evidence of the Germans' hostile intent is overwhelming: German artillery pieces are being put into place right on the border; rumors of war are circulating among the civilian population, which is stockpiling essential commodities; even German deserters warn of an attack. The commander of the border troops says that when he reports this to his superiors, he is told that "our main task is not to succumb to any provocation."[33] Shcherbatov ponders the official reluctance to face what is happening: "What is this, a firm conviction that there will be no war in the next few months, or complete ignorance of the situation? But even firm conviction, even this cannot justify such a terrible risk, which puts the country on the edge of catastrophe." "The more one thought about it, the more inexplicable, the more inconceivable, every fact seemed."[34] Shcherbatov tries to raise the issue of preparedness and German intentions with Lapshin, the front commander. Predictably, Lapshin, who later accepts the infamous TASS communiqué at face value, accuses Shcherbatov of giving in to "defeatist sentiments."[35] Shcherbatov, confirming Emel'ianov's observation made during the purges, lays the blame on the purges and the moral and psychological weakening of the army and political leadership: "The events that were unleashed and set in train long ago were now developing with all their inevitable consequences, consequences that at the beginning could not have been foreseen but were now leading to catastrophe."[36]

Shalaev (in Russian the name appropriately suggests a whole range of negative qualities, from the verb *shalet'*, to go crazy, to *shalopai*, a good-for-nothing) is the dangerous, fanatical, and envious residue of 1937. He despises individuals who think critically and any manifestation of skepticism. The disaster that threatens to overwhelm the Soviet Union is, he is certain, caused by traitors and cowards:

> Shalaev was not stunned by the failures of the first days of the war. But he was struck by the scale of treachery that was revealed. How other than by treachery was it possible to explain the rout and retreat of our army, the strength of which he knew? . . . And only words such as "treason" and "treachery," only those words could immediately explain everything. The fact that after all the work done in the country, after so many trials of traitors of the Motherland, there was still treason, and indeed on such a scale, this undoubtedly confirmed the main thing that Shalaev had known before: that little, far too little of it had been eradicated before the war; that we had not managed to eradicate all of them. Here and there the roots had not been torn out, and look, they stuck their heads up to meet the Germans like mushrooms after rain.[37]

At Shcherbatov's headquarters, Shalaev wastes no time in spreading unsubstantiated rumors, namely, that Korotkov, a senior commander, was killed while trying to desert to the Germans. In a nice reversal of roles that must have warmed the hearts of some of Baklanov's readers, Shcherbatov orders Shalaev to shut up or face a charge of spreading panic. Even more gratifying for those with memories of rough NKVD justice meted out to Soviet soldiers is Shalaev's comeuppance. Intercepted by a group of soldiers whom he initially takes to be German saboteurs, Shalaev goes for his pistol. The soldiers are not Germans but Soviet troops, and Shalaev's reaction when they stop him hardens the suspicion that he was trying to desert to the Germans. Perhaps at this juncture his earlier words to Shcherbatov concerning the purges return to him: "Better to neutralize ten innocent men than allow one enemy to get away. Even a hundred innocent men."[38]

The determined refusal by too many senior officers to acknowledge the impending German invasion—a sort of hysterical faith in Stalin—contaminates the minds of the civilian population. As in the purges, individuals innocent of any wrongdoing are accused of helping the enemy. In a gruesome incident, a village teacher suspected of signaling German bombers is dragged away to be lynched, a latter-day witch burning. Baklanov shows that such hysteria is not solely, possibly not even principally, attributable to rumors of German spies and fifth columnists but is a legacy of the prewar campaigns to unmask "enemies of the people" and of the "holy fury"[39] whipped up by the party. Such panic and hysteria manifestly assist the Germans, another unforeseen consequence of the purges. Among the innocents are those who are only too willing to help the Germans. Even the super-"vigilant" Shalaev is shocked by the depth of hatred and contempt expressed by one individual toward the Soviet state, though the shock may be due to his encountering a real enemy for the first time instead of a party caricature. Here perhaps is yet another consequence of the 1930s: Campaigns against fictional enemies, with all the accompanying brutality and injustice, created real enemies with legitimate grievances.

The blame for the purges and for the damage done to the military rests with the party. Yet there are hints of criticism directed at the military. At the very least, Baklanov poses some awkward questions: Why do professional soldiers with impeccable military records from the Civil War and other conflicts fail to resist the NKVD? Why do officers stand by as their comrades, men with whom they have risked their lives, are publicly slandered? Why the deafening silence when false accusations start to fly?

Baklanov suggests two answers. First is the nature of the military itself. Public attacks by the party lie outside the training and experience of soldiers. The psychological strain of resisting such pressure is made all the more difficult by the absence of any dissenting tradition. Second, the purges exerted a corrosive effect on loyalty and comradeship. Brovalskii, one of Baklanov's more competent commanders, recalls the fate of his brother, who is arrested because his chief of staff signs a document under pressure. More importantly for understanding the lack of resistance to the purge, the warrant for his arrest is signed by a famous military commander, "in his own time a hero but now executed as an enemy of the people."[40] This unnamed senior commander had a chance to prevent the arrest yet did nothing, and his behavior explains a great deal about why the military colluded with their attackers:

> But he did not realize that in signing my sentence, he had already signed his own. So it was. If people, turning away in silence, sacrifice one victim, then they in so doing confirm the right to deal with each one of them in the future. Everything begins with one person. That

one is important: the first. If people think it worthwhile to turn away from him, silently confirming the lawlessness, then all of them can be denied any rights in the future. What is difficult to do with one is easy to do with thousands in the future.[41]

This is the very essence of Pastor Martin Niemöller's own experience in Nazi Germany: Silence in the face of tyranny spurs the tyrant to ever greater acts of evil.

Adult timidity is often contrasted with the spontaneous courage of children. At the height of the purges, it is the schoolchildren, Shcherbatov's son and his school friends, who question whether the NKVD is doing the right thing and make fun of the politically correct censorship. As the teacher is being dragged away, it is not Shalaev who attempts to save him—his instincts are with the mob—but the teacher's son, who somehow shames the hysterical, frightened villagers. Shalaev's conspicuous failure to intercede for the teacher is in striking contrast to the way Brovalskii behaves in German captivity. The Germans are tormenting an exhausted Soviet prisoner, and Brovalskii demands that the sadism stop, for the humiliation inflicted on the Soviet soldier is "his shame, his pain."[42]

This experience of genuine professional solidarity is what was missing during the purges and is now being slowly rekindled by German brutality and the harsh realities of war. If the summer of 1941 was in large part due to what happened in 1937, then much of what followed later in the war—the slow restoration of Soviet military performance, albeit at a dreadful cost—was tempered in the retreat. Echoing a theme pervasive in Baklanov's war stories, Shcherbatov realizes that "in this war the blood spilled by the dead was a call to the living."[43]

IUrii Bondarev
The Battalions Request Fire Support (1957)

Deception in war is the art of misleading and confusing the enemy so that he acts in ways that further one's objectives. In order for the enemy to be deceived, it is necessary that the deception be credible both as a potential threat and in execution. It is not sufficient to convince the enemy alone; one's own troops must believe that what is demanded of them is militarily worthwhile and, the normal dangers and hazards of war notwithstanding, that their commanders will deploy them with due regard for their welfare. The Battalions Request Fire Support is highly controversial because it suggests

that there may be some substance to the frequently repeated accusation that
Stalin and senior Red Army commanders were indifferent to the lives of
their soldiers; that Soviet victories were achieved at the price of too much
blood. Based on the themes of ends and means and the conflicts that arise
from them, *The Battalions Request Fire Support*, with the crossing of a major
water obstacle as a pivotal part of the plot, anticipates Vladimir But's much
harsher treatment of the same themes in *Heads—Tails.*

The Battalions Request Fire Support is set in the autumn of 1943. The Red
Army is planning to force the river Dnieper, one of a number of major
water obstacles that had to be crossed as the Germans were pushed back.
The rivers were natural and formidable defensive lines, the crossing of
which required careful planning and execution. The Soviet plan of attack is
based on a strategic deception: By attacking one point on the far bank, the
Soviet battalions lead the Germans into believing that it is the main crossing point. At a vital moment in the battle, when they are surrounded by the
Germans, the Soviet battalions are denied the necessary artillery support,
promised before the operation, because the main assault is to be made
elsewhere. The Soviet troops are in fact sacrificed by their own side in
order to ensure the bigger operational prize of crossing the river and securing a major foothold.

Bondarev examines the theme of deception from the viewpoints of the Soviet divisional commander, the hardheaded Colonel Iverzev, and one of the
survivors of the doomed assault, Captain Ermakov. The final confrontation
between the two men is finely balanced. Initially, our sympathies are with Ermakov and the battalions that appear to have been callously abandoned to die
for no good cause. It is only after the meeting, during which Ermakov is
threatened with a tribunal for insubordination, that we start to see the problem from Iverzev's point of view. His reasons for behaving the way he did are
brutally clear and underline what to the frontline soldier seems to be the cruel
indifference to his plight shown by what used to be known in the British army
as "brass hats" (or, more colorfully, in the U.S. army as "REMFs," rear-
echelon motherfuckers). Iverzev has been ordered by the army commander to
redeploy his division immediately to another beachhead to the north. Iverzev
knows full well what the consequences of this order will be: "either supporting fire for the division in the Dneprov area or artillery fire easing the fate of
the battalions. There was no other way out. . . . The battalions are to fight to
the death relying on their own weapons."[44] When Colonel Guliaev, the regimental commander, asks how the battalions are to survive without artillery

fire, Iverzev's response is brutal: "What are you on about, Colonel? For God's sake, how long have you been in the army?"[45]

This problem is found in all armies: the tactical and strategic calculus of gain and loss needed to secure objectives and thus win the war. Don Piper's judgment that Iverzev "is a careerist, willing to sacrifice men for the sake of success,"[46] misses the point. Battles are not won without sacrifices, and senior commanders have to make them. The careerist label also suggests cowardice, which is hardly true of Iverzev, who, during another crossing, when the battalion's attack stalls, leads from the front. After the battle, he orders that Ermakov be included in the list of officers to be decorated. Iverzev is no vindictive apparatchik. For all his outrage when he discovers that the battalion was sacrificed, Ermakov himself is quite ready to lie in order to achieve his own military objectives. As the position on the beachhead becomes perilous, he tells the dwindling group of survivors that the division has launched its attack. When asked by another officer why he has lied, Ermakov explains, "If the battalion is to perish, then it can do so believing."[47]

The themes of truth, lying, and sacrifice reappear in a minor incident, but one that is clearly related to the main plot. Honest regarding the nature of military realities, Bondarev is less than clear-cut on the reasons why some Russians are fighting for Vlasov and the Germans. The Vlasov theme, hinted at earlier by the suspicious questions posed by strange Russian speakers trying to elicit information about the Soviet position, reemerges in the capture of a Russian-speaking soldier in German uniform. After a cursory interrogation, he is executed. Among the traitor's personal belongings is a letter from his wife, which, despite Ermakov's best efforts to harden his heart, arouses some sympathy toward the unknown widow: "He handed the papers to Orlov, trying to suppress any feelings of pity toward this Katia, a complete stranger to him, who would never know the whole merciless truth about who had just died."[48]

Bondarev ignores the fact that the wife's letter will make it possible for the NKVD to track her down. Eventually she will learn—because the NKVD will tell her—that her husband was a traitor, a member of Vlasov's army. Henceforth she will be regarded with profound suspicion by the NKVD. Worse still, under the provisions of Order № 270, she is likely to be denied even some of the most basic state support, which, as a widow with a child, she will desperately need.

At the time when Bondarev was writing this story, the Soviet people still did not know the "whole merciless truth" about the war. Here, surely, is a veiled demand to tell the truth, however merciless. For example, why were Russians fighting in German uniform against the Soviet state? What drove them, rightly or wrongly, to such desperate behavior? The incident reveals the common Russian view that Russians who served with Vlasov forfeited the right to be considered Russians: They were somehow unpersons, fit only for execution and an unmarked grave. If, as Ermakov believes, the widow will never know the "whole merciless truth," then neither will the men who have been sacrificed on the beachhead, the soldiers who believed Ermakov's holy lie that help was on its way. Both the widow, surely innocent of any wrongdoing, and the soldiers are victims of the war.

If soldiers can be fed the heroic lie so that their morale can be sustained, what about the nation during and after the war? Is lying about or hiding the "whole merciless truth" of the Great Patriotic War justified? Or is the "whole merciless truth" essential for a nation's revival so that the wounds can be healed when the guns have fallen silent?

The Final Salvoes (1959)

The action in The Final Salvoes takes place on the edge of the Carpathian Mountains on the border with Czechoslovakia. The war—as suggested by the title—is moving toward its end. Yet the German army is still fighting well and with added desperation. Hemmed in by mountains, the Germans must break through the Soviet positions if they are to escape. A Soviet artillery unit bars the way, and so the stage is set for a decisive battle: Soviet artillery versus German tanks. Even though the war has been won, Soviet troops are expected to make sacrifices until the final German defeat. The moral and professional dilemmas of military command and the loneliness of command are the novel's central themes. Whereas in The Battalions Request Fire Support, Iverzev's physical and psychological detachment from the smaller units under his command somewhat ease the burdens of decision-making, Captain Novikov, the battery commander in The Final Salvoes, is located on the front line. Like Ermakov, his obvious counterpart in The Battalions Request Fire Support, Novikov experiences a degree of intimacy and familiarity with his men (and the female medic) that complicates the exercise of command.

Novikov's code of leadership and command is summed up in his reflections on the value of human life in war. Having just dispatched one of his signalers to repair a broken line, a dangerous task on the front line, he muses, "A man's life in war was of great value to him when that life did not seek to be saved at the expense of others."[49] Such a code means sacrifice in order to achieve military goals. Moreover, and as far as Novikov is concerned, this code imposes an especially strict burden on the officers. One of Novikov's gun commanders, Lieutenant Ovchinnikov, is ordered to place his guns in front of the likely German advance. During the battle, the Soviet infantry abandon their positions, and, fearing that the gun positions will be overrun, Ovchinnikov abandons his surviving gun. On the face of it, this is a clear-cut example of desertion under fire. Much worse, Ovchinnikov leaves some of his wounded to their fate. Perhaps aware that he momentarily succumbed to fear, Ovchinnikov runs back to the gun in an attempt to redeem himself. Captured by the Germans and interrogated by a Russian working for the enemy, Ovchinnikov refuses to answer any questions and is shot. So, unknown to Novikov, Ovchinnikov's honor is restored even though the evidence suggests desertion.

This incident goes to the heart of the themes of ends and means. As the battle progresses, and with the knowledge that Ovchinnikov's wounded survivors have been cut off, Novikov's men cannot understand why he does not give the order to rescue the gun crew. His concerns are purely tactical: If the gun crew is evacuated, the rescuing force will be seen by the Germans, who will push all the harder to break out. The Germans are deceived by his keeping the Soviet gun crew where it is, even if the suffering of the gun crew is prolonged. Based on his own harsh experience of war, Novikov justifies his decision: "At times a move toward doing something good, the striving immediately to put a stop to the sufferings of a few people, leads to losses for which there is no justification. As far back as two years ago, I would have thought differently."[50] What then is the difference between Ovchinnikov's abandonment of the gun and men and Novikov's exploitation of the same wounded in order to deceive the Germans? Presumably the answer we expect is that Ovchinnikov violates the written and unwritten codes of his command in order to save himself, whereas Novikov exploits the same men in order to deceive the enemy for the greater military good. If they die believing, then all well and good; if they realize that they are going to be sacrificed and abandon their positions, then they will meet a less than glorious end in front of the firing squad. Novikov's willingness to use false words and deeds to deceive his own men flies in the face of the way he reacts to what the medics say to the dying: "Novikov could not stand the false words that the nurses spoke to the dying."[51] Furthermore, in the post-1945 climate, we might see this as an allusion to the party-sponsored lies about the war: The truth is needed, however harsh. Or are lies needed in peacetime as well?

As in *The Battalions Request Fire Support*, there is an absence of any discussion of why Russians are assisting the Germans. Ovchinnikov's accusation, which he hurls at his Russian interrogator—"You betrayed the Motherland for three cigarettes"[52]—overlooks many of the justified grievances that turned Soviet citizens against the Soviet state. The discovery of women's underwear, French chocolate, and wine in a building that has been hastily abandoned—almost certainly a brothel for German officers, though euphemistically referred to by Bondarev as a "health resort"—implies that local women have been willing to provide sexual favors to the hated German occupiers. Collaboration is not isolated: It is an inevitable by-product of war and occupation. Life, or whatever one can salvage, goes on. In fact, the discovery of this brothel highlights a minor yet persistent theme in *The Battalions Request Fire Support*, *The Final Salvoes*, and *Goriachii sneg* (Hot Snow) that German soldiers are obsessed with pornography and that in some unspecified way this obsession is a direct consequence of Nazi ideology. One assumes that when Soviet soldiers seized German bunkers and found pornographic magazines and pictures, they cast them away in disgust, washed their hands, and turned to a good propaganda piece in *Pravda*.

Conclusion

Kazakevich, Baklanov, and Bondarev are not consciously engaging in ideological debunking, though it is an unavoidable consequence of their writing and how it appeared to the critics. Their works do not insult the memory of the fallen, nor do they besmirch "the just cause." Their writing confirms that people's attitudes toward truth and lies tend to be complicated. The incidents revealed in their stories likely were not surprising revelations to a generation that had been through the war.

Take, for example, the theme of *okruzhenie*. The mere use of the word would instantly have alerted Soviet readers of *The Dead Feel No Shame* and *July 1941* to potential ideological controversy. It is a fair bet that some of Baklanov's readers had themselves been encircled during the war, so they would have grasped the point immediately. So many Russian writers obsessively highlight this theme because many Soviet soldiers suffered cruel injustices on getting back to their own lines. The Special Sections of the NKVD, and later SMERSH, did not accept the fact that soldiers had been encircled as an occupational hazard of fast-moving warfare. Instead they regarded such experiences as a consequence of cowardice, desertion, or even an attempt by the Germans to recruit Soviet soldiers as spies and then send them back across the lines. Western readers of Baklanov, Bondarev, and other writers cannot fail to note the role played by encirclement in Soviet-Russian war literature as a driver of the plot and conflict. Without the knowledge of how the NKVD regarded encirclement, the obsessive references to encirclement and breaking out appear as overstated and tiresome. With the knowledge of the provisions of Orders № 270 and 227, the picture changes dramatically, and the reader understands what these writers are trying to achieve.

Soldiers may experience the war in platoons, companies, and battalions, but each man approaches the moment of truth in his own way. This is not to say that the dissenters were always right, but in order to arrive at a more honest understanding of the war, more in tune with what people lived through and recognized themselves as having lived through, the dissenting view could not be completely excluded. Here was the real danger posed by Baklanov and his contemporaries to the Soviet status quo: the assertion of authorial independence, a refusal to accept that the party and its institutions represented the last word on human experience either in war or in peace.

In the next chapter I examine the work of a writer who throughout his career mounted one of the most determined challenges posed by any author to the party-sponsored orthodoxy concerning the Great Patriotic War.

3 Traitors, Wolves, and Infernal Cold: The War Stories of Vasil' Bykov

But cruel are the times when we are traitors.
—*Macbeth*, Act IV, Scene 2

Vasil' Bykov devoted virtually all of his fiction to the Great Patriotic War. Whether in the conventional setting of the Soviet army or in the author's favored context, partisan warfare and life under German occupation in Belorussia (Belarus), Bykov's stories are a pitiless analysis of human behavior under duress. In this respect, Bykov has much in common with Dostoyevsky. This chapter offers an examination of some of Bykov's major works and his huge contribution to Soviet Russian war literature.

Introduction

Born in 1924, Vasil' Bykov, who died on 22 June 2003, belongs to the generation of young officers who came of age during the war, of whom so much was expected and who suffered such disproportionately high losses. In the 1950s, Bykov's peers—Grigorii Baklanov, IUrii Bondarev, and Vladimir Bogomolov, to name some of the better known—started to make substantial contributions to Soviet Russian war literature and to enjoy deservedly high reputations. However, Bykov, a native of Belorussia, has carved out such an important place for himself in Soviet Russian war literature over the past fifty years that he has eclipsed his accomplished comrades. So great indeed are Bykov's mastery of his themes, his acute understanding of human behavior in the laboratory of war, his technical virtuosity, and a relentless determination to recover the truth—or at least some of it—that even the preeminence of Viktor Astaf'ev and Vasilii Grossman cannot be taken for granted.

War is a state of extremes, and Bykov is interested above all in human behavior in extreme states. To quote Lazar' Lazarev:

> In the process of defining the structure of ideas and ethics of Vasil' Bykov's works, critics have called them moral experiment stories. In actual fact the author places his protagonists in such conditions that the pressure of unfavorable circumstances achieves its highest

critical point. This allows him to expose the maximum potential—
negative or positive—of their personal opportunities. Under the
pressures of normal conditions, it is impossible to uncover these
inner spiritual reserves or hidden fissures.[1]

From the standpoint of Soviet officialdom, all of Bykov's themes, to which
he returned throughout his career, were highly sensitive and brought harsh
criticism down on the author for his unyielding stand. Loyalty figures prominently in nearly every work. Within the context of the conventional Soviet
unit, Bykov explores loyalty to one's comrades and the willingness (or otherwise) of soldiers to make the necessary sacrifices for their nation's cause. In
the murky world of partisan warfare, where families are frequently divided
between violent opposition to the German occupation and the need to reach
some kind of accommodation with the invaders in order to survive the war,
the theme becomes complicated by personal vendettas that often have nothing to do with the occupation. Central for Belorussians under German occupation was the legitimacy of claims on their loyalty to Soviet power, especially
with the memory of collectivization. The NKVD and SMERSH units that followed hard on the heels of the Red Army in 1944 had no doubt that anything
other than active resistance to the German occupation amounted to collaboration. The mere fact of having lived for nearly three and half years under German occupation invited suspicion, created a presumption of guilt. Not a
Marxist or a believer in crude reductionist explanations of human behavior,
Bykov nevertheless recognized that people do not always behave as we might
expect them to, especially in war. Those who appear strong and confident
often turn out to be morally suspect and weak. On the other hand, the apparently weak show strength of character and resilience in adversity, and the
physically courageous in Bykov's work are often capable of moral vacillation
and indecision. Often attractive, physically strong, socially adept, and intelligent, traitors in Bykov's stories are never what they first appear. Collaboration in all its forms—and they are many—is of central concern for Bykov and
is explored profoundly and comprehensively. It follows that the theme of the
enemy can hardly be straightforward. Compared with the traitors on one's
own side and the attentions of the NKVD and SMERSH, the Germans can be
seen in an almost neutral light. Bykov's use of weather and landscape also invites close scrutiny and suggests comparison with Jack London's The White Silence (1899), The Call of the Wild (1903), or White Fang (1905). Weather, sometimes hostile, even malevolent, is another enemy with which the soldier or

partisan must contend. Bykov's weather descriptions also provide key insights into characters' motives and hint at certain outcomes in the narrative. Amid the treachery, suffering, and despair of the war, cold temperatures and snow remind the reader that weather is cruelly indifferent to the vulnerability of men at war, or even that war itself is just another natural hazard periodically overwhelming humankind, reminding us, like disease, of our mortality.

Bykov's stories rely on one of two backgrounds: a small Soviet army subunit—a patrol, a platoon, or an artillery battery—cut off from the larger formation and having to fight its own war, or small groups of partisans or individuals fighting the Germans, and frequently among themselves, in German-occupied Belorussia. Typical of this first category would be *Tret'ia raketa* (The Third Flare, 1962), *Frontovaia stranitsa* (A Page from the Front, 1963), *Zapadnia* (The Snare, 1964), *Mertvym ne bol'no* (The Dead Feel No Pain, 1966), *Dozhit' do rassveta* (To Live until Dawn, 1972), and *Ego batal'on* (His Battalion, 1976). The second setting for Bykov's stories makes up a collection that would more than guarantee the author's reputation on its own. To this category belong *Kruglianskii most* (The Kruglianskii Bridge, 1969), *Sotnikov* (1970), *Obelisk* (The Obelisk, 1972), *Volch'ia staia* (The Wolf Pack, 1974), *Poiti i ne vernut'sia* (To Set off and Not Return, 1978), *Znak bedy* (The Sign of Misfortune, 1983), *Kar'er* (The Quarry, 1986), *Stuzha* (The Great Freeze, 1993), and *Boloto* (The Swamp, 2001).

The Dead Feel No Pain (1966)

The Dead Feel No Pain is one of Bykov's finest war stories; in it the author pays tribute to the young officers who died in such large numbers. The work's most controversial theme is the role of the Special Sections and SMERSH and the endemic suspicion of these organizations' operatives toward frontline soldiers, which, as Bykov demonstrates, frequently led to punitive measures being taken against innocent men. Through his portrayal of this uniquely Soviet problem, Bykov highlights the bitter contemporary struggle to come to terms with the Stalinist past and its legacy. At the time *The Dead Feel No Pain* was published—1966, the year of the show trial of the writers Yuli Daniel' and Andrei Siniavskii for having published anti-Soviet material—writing on such a theme was a dangerous undertaking.

It is 9 May 1965, the Victory Day holiday, and Lieutenant Vasilevich is waiting at a barrier. A stranger tries to jump the queue. His face looks familiar. Vasilevich reflects that the man might be a certain Sakhno, who once caused him and his comrades much misery. As he follows the stranger into the crowd, painful memories return to haunt him: "A thread connecting events long past begins to unwind in my agitated memory. I already know that the past can't be simply broken off, that it can't be drowned in vodka and forgotten. It remains in the heart because—it is me."[2]

Even though the military action of *The Dead Feel No Pain* is set in January 1944, Bykov refers frequently to the disastrous Soviet retreat of 1941. The Germans have as good as lost the war, yet they are still a force to be reckoned with, and Soviet military competence even at this late stage in the war, Bykov implies, leaves much to be desired. When Soviet forces are caught in a German tank attack, their countermeasures are ineffective. There is even evidence of the same panic that was a feature of the 1941 summer retreat. In the critical situation, a sergeant major takes command and manages to extricate the wounded from immediate danger. When ordered to explain why he left his position, he asks pointedly, "Where were you earlier, comrade colonel?"[3] The sergeant major's defiance is entirely justified. As Vasilevich realizes, the colonel is trying to deflect attention from his own failures by attacking his subordinates, one of the behavioral legacies of the purges. The sergeant major's questioning of the colonel's bravery and competence, and thus his fitness to exercise command, makes the point that rank alone cannot confer respect and trust in one's leadership. These responses must be earned. And where rank has accrued solely through bureaucratic procedures, the result is failure on the battlefield. Bykov's numerous references to 1941 make it clear that the Red Army has still not fully absorbed the lessons of that fateful summer.

Though it was not formed until April 1943, SMERSH and, by association, the NKVD constitute the element of coercive and inflexible bureaucracy that also evokes the desperate measures of 1941. Sakhno's sole interest is the question of security, which is defined by the changing requirements of the NKVD and SMERSH. He has no interest in whether soldiers are competently led. Should they, however, driven to despair, decide to disobey some absurd order, then that is a matter for him to investigate. It is Sakhno's detachment from the Red Army's military problems and his involvement in exposing real or imagined traitors that equip him to deal pitilessly with his work. The question that Bykov examines is whether Sakhno assists or impedes the war effort.

Even in January 1944, Soviet soldiers are still viewed by the NKVD and SMERSH as being predisposed to desertion. Another company in Vasilevich's unit, under the command of Lieutenant Krotov, has spent the night in the same village as the Germans. The Germans managed to leave before anything could be done—indeed, before anyone was aware that they were there—and Krotov and his men are suspected of having been prepared to desert to the Germans, or of having allowed the enemy to escape. As an interim punishment pending investigation, Krotov is removed from his post and ordered to escort some German prisoners to the rear with Vasilevich and Sakhno's clerk, Shashok. Along the way, the clerk deserts them, and in an exchange of fire with the Germans Krotov is killed.

After this episode, Vasilevich is subjected to a grueling interrogation by Sakhno, who is not at all bothered by the clerk's return. The interrogation is designed to secure a signed document from Vasilevich stating that Krotov did not die fighting the Germans but rather that he deserted to the Germans, thus justifying the decision to remove him from his post. Vasilevich is struck by Shashok's notebook: "The notebook is a captured one, there is no doubt about that, but I involuntarily maintain my glance on that emblem, and something inside me arouses a still as yet unrealized protest."[4] Later Vasilevich admits that he cannot avert his eyes from the "fascist eagle on the cover."[5] Bykov is hinting that the term "fascist," a standard though inaccurate term of abuse in Soviet propaganda, is not applicable solely to the Germans. Very little seems to separate the mentality, methods, and approaches of the Gestapo from those of the NKVD and SMERSH. Sakhno believes that one's own are potentially a greater threat than the enemy, and his methods and psychology are consistent with that outlook. This theme is stressed indirectly in the closing of the distance between Vasilevich and one of the German prisoners. Once the initial shock of capture has worn off, captive and captor start to reach a common understanding based on the immediate needs of food, warmth, and shelter. Sakhno is an enemy to them both.

Sakhno's harsh treatment of Red Army officers and men who must make decisions in the heat of battle and then justify the actions they took in fast-moving battlefield conditions over which they exercise little or no control, and his insistence on sticking to the rule book regardless of events are at odds with his own behavior on the front line. Ghostlike, he appears as if from nowhere in moments of relative safety while manifesting a miraculous ethereality in moments of danger. And when he and Vasilevich are captured by the Germans, he shows that he has something in common with all those Red Army soldiers who were captured in 1941, selflessly denying himself the obligatory bullet in the head.

Bykov emphasizes Sakhno's elusiveness, even a demonic aspect, on a number of occasions. Just after the wounded are rescued by a tank, "Sakhno disappeared";[6] then "Sakhno appeared";[7] and later "and here between the tanks, Sakhno appeared from somewhere."[8] As Vasilevich and IUrka, a fellow officer, ponder the next move, we see Sakhno in the shadows, watching and waiting: "Well, of course Captain Sakhno is here as well. In a dark corner. From there he is barely visible. He can probably see everything."[9] In a particularly telling image Sakhno is identified with one of Bykov's favorite themes, extreme cold (stuzha): "Legs wide apart, Sakhno stood in the doorway like an unyielding block, his pistol pointing in the direction of the hut. A bitter cold [moroznaia stuzha] piled in through the open door."[10]

In the process of transporting the wounded, Vasilevich and his men are attacked by German tanks. After the attack, Sakhno reappears. A sergeant major attacks the incompetent army leadership, and Sakhno, unusually, remains silent. His silence does not imply any support; it is a manifestation of complete indifference to military problems. Such problems are for the Red Army. This essential lack of interest and obsession with the prerogatives of SMERSH can be seen in the death of Katia, the medic. Sakhno forces Vasilevich and his troops to cross a minefield. Katia's death—both of her legs are blown off—has enormous shock effect in the story. The reactions of Vasilevich and Sakhno to her death are what we would expect from each man. For Vasilevich, Katia's death raises questions about the role of women in war and the nature of the society that sends them to die:

> Katia's death devastates me. How many have already perished before my eyes, those I knew and the unknown, but I have never before felt anything like this. Maybe because they were men and soldiers. Death in war is a very simple thing. But why did this girl have to die? Who sent her off to war, and for what? Could she have requested this? But what did she know about war? And she's dead, torn to pieces by some chance mine, and there is nothing we could do to help her. And what is this all for? Do we not have enough men? At the front, in the rear, in the country as a whole? For every ten in the chain, there are a good hundred in the rear. And what men, strong, educated, who know the score. So why do we send girls to their death?[11]

Sakhno's reaction betrays his profession and the enormous gulf that separates him from the frontovik. There is no sympathy, no remorse that this young woman died because of his decision to cross a minefield. His search of her body for documents defiles her, stripping her of any dignity. His sole comment on Katia is that she was the mistress of the battalion commander. With that dismissive reference, Sakhno completes her defilement, reducing the brave, self-sacrificing nurse to a mutilated harlot. To the extent that Vasilevich identifies Katia as exemplifying something holy and unsullied, as someone who inspires hope and love, that idea too is trampled underfoot by Sakhno.

In the postwar part of *The Dead Feel No Pain*, Vasilevich tracks down the man who jumped the queue and confronts him in a restaurant. It turns out that he is not Sakhno. However, in his attitudes toward the past and the present, and especially his wartime service, Gorbatiuk is a Sakhno clone. We learn that he is a major in the reserve, a legal consultant, and that during the war he served on military tribunals. Sakhno's ultimate fate is not important: He lives on in Gorbatiuk.

Gorbatiuk's wartime service was in an arena that would have brought him into contact with Sakhno's colleagues, and Vasilevich's revelations about Sakhno do not arouse any disapproval in him. On the contrary, citing Stalin, Gorbatiuk approves: "I'll tell you something based on my own experience. In the war there was a regime where soldiers were more afraid of their commanders than of the Germans. . . . Such a commander has everything: The task gets done, and there are medals for him too."[12] This comment is an explicit link with the incompetent colonel and with Sakhno. Gorbatiuk boasts of the inversion of roles and priorities in the army. Thus, he notes that even though he was a captain, the colonel in charge of the regiment would salute him first. He believes that this gesture indicates respect and honor and moreover is his due. Regarding his tribunal service, he shows no evidence of remorse: "You're probably thinking: A tribunal—that means an outright violation of the law? These days it's fashionable to think so. It's fashionable to rehabilitate. It's fashionable to heap everything on the judges. And nobody bothers to consider: In whose name did they do all this? They resolved crimes, went without food and sleep, visited the front line, came under bombardment. On behalf of what?"[13] Gorbatiuk defends the mass arrests in 1937 and regards the party as the final arbiter of truth and falsehood: "Such was the line. What was not right the party has corrected."[14] Gorbatiuk's self-justification marks him as a neo-Stalinist and draws attention to the various currents in Soviet society in the 1960s that were contesting and reevaluating, or even reasserting, the legitimacy of the

Stalinist era. Gorbatiuk's presence suggests that nothing has changed. On the other hand, there are cracks in the edifice, signs that the postwar generation will not allow itself to be intimidated, expressed perhaps in the motif "No need to be afraid, those times have passed"[15] and the fracas in the restaurant caused by a group of young diners—whose fathers died in the war—who publicly insult Gorbatiuk.

In the contemporary part of the novel, Bykov conspicuously raises the historical profile of Belorussia, which he rightly feels has been ignored and marginalized to serve the Soviet project. The war memorial built "according to the pompous canons of its time"[16] has little relevance for Belorussians: "It is a tall memorial decorated with precious items that were presented to the marshals, to the generalissimo, and to the Romanian King Michael. As far as Belorussia is concerned, it has a merely symbolic function."[17] Gorbatiuk's attitude to Belorussia—dismissive and contemptuous—is another obvious fault line between him and Vasilevich and arouses the latter's ire:

> You bastard! What do you know about this republic? Couldn't you find a place in a hotel? All the pastries gone? But have you heard anything about the half a million strong army of partisans in this republic? Do you know anything about Belorussia's tens of thousands of Oradours and Lidices? What about the two million or so victims? What about the fact that even today this republic has still not reached the prewar level of population?[18]

At a time when the Soviet state's functionaries were still vehemently denying any responsibility for the series of massacres in and around Katyn, instead blaming the Nazis, and when the KGB's campaign against "nationalist elements" was being stepped up, these were powerful and provocative sentiments guaranteed to single out the author.

The official silence about the ravages of the German occupation (and much else besides) does, of course, undermine the pomp of the Victory Day parade, the optimistic claim made by the schoolgirl that "nobody has been forgotten; nothing will be forgotten."[19] Vasilevich is much closer to the real picture—one of officially sponsored pomp and deliberate ignorance—when he argues that for the bulk of today's generation, the war is "an abstraction, like the freezing over of Europe, like the New Stone Age."[20] To emphasize the quite deliberate, official "forgetting" of the past, Bykov inserts another bitter memory. Mingling with the crowd, Vasilevich encounters a group of veterans, one of whom admits that he was the commander of a penal company:

> What are you looking at? You condemn us? Well, do you condemn us? Twelve times two hundred, just think. And where are they? Six feet under. And you think they were criminals? To hell with that! They escaped from captivity. They didn't stay put for the whole war. So there you are. Who are among the heroes today? The Brest fortress and so on? I buried four from the Brest fortress on Sandomirskii. So there! Then they didn't ask how you were captured but why you didn't shoot yourself! Got it?[21]

The truth of the war—how it was, how the veterans experienced it—is a crucial part of this story. Yet the demand for the truth appears to be selective. For example, Vasilevich does not tell IUrka's mother the full story about her son's death. She was told that he fell while destroying German tanks, not that he lost hope and shot himself. "After that," Vasilevich asks, "can I tell her the full truth about your death?"[22] His failure to tell her the whole truth, his choice to gloss over things, is what the Soviet state has been doing since 1945 with regard to the war. In 1966, this concept is, among other things, an attack on the consequences of censorship. However, the problem of the truth about the war goes somewhat deeper. Vasilevich's silence, out of fear that he might damage the mother's image of her son, reminds us that truth is not something that can be used exclusively against our opponents. (In *The Dead Feel No Pain*, these are the Soviet state and its representatives.) It may be gratifying to expose the historical lies and deliberate falsifications of the state and its functionaries. Yet at a personal level, truth can be far more devastating to the individual than the knowledge that Stalin lied about Bukharin and Tukhachevsky during the Great Terror. Can we always blame the state? Are we not, even if only on a small scale, sometimes culpable ourselves? We, the living, need the lies: The dead feel no pain.

Sotnikov (1970)

Two partisans, Sotnikov and Rybak, are sent by their commander to forage for food. During the course of their expedition, they encounter members of the local population, some of whom are not sympathetic to the partisans. After a series of episodes in which Bykov explores themes of loyalty and collaboration, the two men are captured by the Polizai and handed over to the Germans for interrogation. Wounded and suffering from bronchitis, Sotnikov resists the interrogation and is hanged. At the eleventh hour, Rybak decides to opt for survival at any cost and throws in his lot with the Germans, becoming a member of the Polizai.

Sotnikov is a former artillery officer whose regiment was overwhelmed in the first summer of the war. In a recollection of the summer retreat, Sotnikov implies failure on the part of the Soviet high command: "Unfortunately, that ill-fated battle once again bore witness to the immutable but not infrequently ignored fact that mastery of the lessons of the previous war involves not only the strength but also the weakness of an army."[23] In the face of powerful and overwhelming odds, men like Sotnikov did their duty. Sotnikov's name, suggesting a Cossack leader (a *sotnik*), is entirely appropriate. Captured by the Germans, he manages to escape and joins a partisan band, where, despite his officer's rank, he serves as an ordinary partisan. Sotnikov's sense of duty, whether to his partisan group, the Soviet Union, his fellow soldiers, or even the abstract notion of duty itself, is perhaps his most dominant characteristic. As his prime motivating factor, it is apparent from the very beginning of the story. In spite of a debilitating attack of bronchitis, the cause of much later trouble, Sotnikov volunteers to accompany Rybak in the search for food. To Rybak, who is puzzled by Sotnikov's gesture, Sotnikov replies, "I couldn't refuse what the others had refused."[24] In other words, somebody has to go. The fact that Rybak finds this sense of duty perplexing, even alien, is important for what emerges later.

Bykov suggests on several occasions that the key to understanding the differing attitudes to what is proper, what constitutes duty, in the two partisans can be found in their prewar lives and even childhoods. By the standards of Soviet society in the 1930s, Sotnikov enjoyed a privileged upbringing. His father has a distinguished Civil War record. He himself completed a teacher's training course and before joining the partisans was a battalion commander in the artillery. Certainly a gulf exists between the two men in terms of educational attainment and status. Rybak, we learn, is barely literate; we receive the impression that he nurtures a vague grievance against life in general, that in some unspecified way he feels cheated. As the work progresses, Sotnikov gradually and imperceptibly emerges as the focal point for Rybak's frustrated grievances and envy. There are hints that Rybak sees a kind of existential justice in Sotnikov's being struck down with illness, that it somehow assuages his sense that life has dealt him a bad hand—even that he derives pleasure from Sotnikov's physical weakness because it renders

Sotnikov dependent on him. Social differences may count for nothing in this bleak landscape, yet the innate moral differences between the two are increasingly accentuated as their situation becomes worse.

Incidents from the men's childhood help to explain crucial differences between them. Just before he decides to join the German-controlled Polizai, conscious that he is standing on the edge of "a precipice,"[25] Rybak recalls a time when he was traveling along a winding road, one he had traveled many times, when unexpectedly something happened with the reins and he lost control of the horse and wagon. Instead of acting decisively to turn the front of the wagon, he jumped off, and the horse and wagon with two girls on board tipped over into the ravine. Rybak's response to this incident highlights his capacity for self-deception. After the event he admits to himself that he behaved badly but immediately tries to justify what he did by implying mitigating circumstances: "But it is still uncertain what would have happened had he remained. Perhaps he would have fallen under the wagon and been killed. Many years had passed since that time; right up to now he still had no idea about how to behave correctly."[26] Again, his claim that this incident somehow corrupted his moral compass is not entirely satisfactory. In the sequence of events leading up to their capture, Sotnikov is wounded. Rybak returns for him when he could easily have disappeared into the night. For Rybak, who has always had to live by his wits, concepts such as duty, loyalty, and honor are flexible, pragmatic, and subject to interpretation in the light of changed circumstances. His approach is almost Brechtian: "Erst kommt das Fressen, dann kommt die Moral" (First you fill your face, then comes morality).[27] He returns for Sotnikov because Sotnikov would have returned for him.

Captivity is, of course, the new set of circumstances. Captured, they are no longer partisans, and they are free, Rybak believes, to argue their case before their own consciences and to negotiate the best deal they can with their German captors. If the price of survival is to renounce the partisans and wear the uniform of the Polizai, then so be it. As far as Rybak is concerned, their arrest had rendered the contract between him and Sotnikov and the rest of the partisans null and void: "Now the most terrible thing for Rybak was that barrel. It decided everything. With a sideways glance, but keeping his eyes fixed on it, Rybak raised his hands. So far there was no burst of fire; his end had been delayed. That was the main thing. For him nothing else meant anything."[28]

Under interrogation, Rybak pointedly denies firing any shots, thus incriminating Sotnikov. Even before his interrogation, Rybak is developing a rationale for treachery: "Having lapsed into these thoughts, he suddenly sat up, startled by something unexpected—alongside the straw a rustling sound could be heard, and something living and soft moved over his boot. In the corner the *starosta* [elder], showing his disgust, moved his leg: Rats, curse them!—and at that moment Rybak caught sight of a rat under the wall."[29] Bykov's pun on the verb *predat'sia*—to lapse into reverie/to go over to the enemy—and the sudden appearance of rats evokes something Dostoyevskyian, perhaps the tortured dreams and rationalizing of Raskolnikov as he contemplates murder. Indeed, Bykov emphasizes Rybak's "crossing the threshold" of the interrogator's office as if he has crossed a moral threshold and is about to commit a crime. After the interrogation, the process of rationalizing his treachery accelerates. It would, Rybak argues, be best for all concerned were Sotnikov to die:

> Of course, he understood the whole inhumanity of this revelation, but no matter what he thought, he invariably [*neizmenno*] returned to the idea that it would be for the best. For him, Rybak, and indeed for Sotnikov himself, who, after all that had happened, was more or less indifferent as to whether he lived or not. But Rybak could perhaps get himself out of this and then get even with these bastards for Sotnikov's life and for his own sufferings as well. He had no intention of giving away any partisan secrets to them at all, and even less intention of joining the Polizai, though he understood that to get out of that one would not be easy. However, it was important for him to win time; everything else depended on that, on how many days he could secure so as to hold out.[30]

It is in captivity that Bykov's aside, made when Sotnikov was wounded, carries its greatest weight: "As always at a moment of the greatest danger, each person worried about himself, took his own fate into his hands."[31]

Rybak's eventual treachery is adumbrated by Bykov in his usage of specific words and verbs, and even in weather descriptions well before his interrogation. Consider the following passage describing the terrain, which appears early in the work, just after Sotnikov and Rybak have set out on their mission: "The same ghostly black expanse stretched in every direction—the gray field, snow, the murkiness, with its multitude of elusive shadowy transitions and spots. And nowhere was there even a sign of light or movement. Silent and lifeless, the earth had hidden itself."[32] Within the context of *Sotnikov*, this weather digression amounts to more than just a powerful description of the sort of terrain in which the partisans must operate. It can also be seen as a metaphor of the struggle itself, in which loyalties to causes are subject to change and yesterday's friend and comrade is tomorrow's enemy. Thus, when Bykov writes of "elusive shadowy transitions and spots," he also describes the changing allegiances of partisan warfare, where decisions to trust people are based more on gut feelings than on rational evaluation; where the features in the moral landscape are, like the winter landscape, vague and elusive; where clarity is not always possible. This suggestion is implicit in the dual meanings of the Russian words "transition" (*perekhod*), as in crossing over to the enemy, and "spots" (*piatna*), which suggests "stains" or "blots" on one's conscience. Again, today's comrade, if conditions change, can become tomorrow's enemy. This is the "knife edge"[33] along which Sotnikov and Rybak move, the fine line between loyalty and treachery. Or is the individual partisan concerned more with permanent interests than with permanent friends and allegiances? Is genuine comradeship possible under such conditions? Treacherous thoughts and changing loyalties are also indicated by Bykov's frequent use of the verb *izmeniat'* and the adjective *izmenchivyi*. These words indicate not merely physical change but also treason and betrayal. Later in the story, with Sotnikov wounded, Rybak considers whether to leave him and return to his unit: Rybak hears the exchange of fire in which Sotnikov is wounded and speculates that something might have changed (*izmenilos'*).[34]

On balance, Bykov tends to be sympathetic toward people who through no fault of their own have been abandoned by the Red Army and must make the best of things under German occupation—or, as in the case of Moroz in *The Obelisk*, show that there are other ways of resisting the Germans. An encounter with an old couple—the husband is the German-appointed *starosta*—reveals Bykov's sympathy and the differences between Sotnikov and Rybak on how to deal with the old man. Rybak does himself no favors in this encounter, noisily and angrily accusing the old man of collaborating with the Germans. In view of what comes later, Rybak condemns himself: "Rybak felt no respect for this person; his general observations and reasons did not interest Rybak at all. The fact of his serving the Germans decided everything for Rybak."[35] Yet the old man does not allow himself to be intimidated. In a reproach aimed at Sotnikov, the regular soldier, the old man points out that had the Red Army done its job, the Germans would not be there. Moreover, when accused by Rybak of being an enemy of the Russians, the man pointedly replies that he is not an enemy of his own people, Belorussians. Soviet power is regarded by many as being no better than the German occupation, the Belorussians being caught between the two. This identification of the partisans—the representatives of Soviet power—with the Germans and their Polizai comes across when Rybak asks the *starosta* who fired the rifle shot: "People like you. They wanted some vodka."[36]

Rybak readily accepts the food provided by the old couple; Sotnikov conspicuously refuses to eat anything. Rybak appears to have compromised himself, whereas Sotnikov has not. Sotnikov, it would seem, continues to adhere to his code of duty, whereas Rybak shows himself to be an opportunist: Food is food, whoever provides it. We might also see Sotnikov's refusal to take food as prudence, since he recalls an incident in the war when an apparently friendly woman gave him food and then sent for the Germans. Unanswered is why people behave in this way. Why is there not complete resistance to the German occupation? Sotnikov's unyielding stance toward the Germans tends to impair his ability to understand the predicament of others who have not embarked on a course of armed resistance. He seems oblivious to the fact that there are alternative ways of resisting the Germans. That the old man, Petr, has been press-ganged into becoming the *starosta* leaves Sotnikov unmoved: "He could find no sympathy for a man who agreed to serve the Germans and who more or less carried out this service. That he had some kind of excuses for this didn't trouble Sotnikov, who already understood the price of such justification. In the cruel struggle against fascism, one must not take into account any, even the most deserving, reasons. Victory would come only in the face of any reasons."[37]

Bearing in mind that this story was published in 1970, when censorship of literature—particularly anything to do with the war—was severe, we must consider the possibility that this passage has more to do with appeasing the censorship apparatus than with revealing anything about the character of the protagonist. If, however, we take Sotnikov at face value, then his response to the dilemma of the old couple is not entirely satisfactory. He implies criticism of the preparations for war, and in the conversation with Rybak about their past service, he pointedly comments on the long eastward journey they have made, the retreat of the Red Army. His recollections of the 1941 summer retreat, for all the undoubted bravery and skill of his gun crews, show that something has gone wrong. Sotnikov's uncompromising response to the old couple's predicament, which is not of their making, is at odds with his nonjudgmental approach to the Soviet state and Stalin, who must share some of the blame. There is also something faintly preposterous about Sotnikov's refusal to accept food from the couple, given his physical state and the uncertainties of partisan warfare. Would he similarly refuse to take food or water provided by the Germans when he is held in captivity? And what of the slaughtered sheep that Rybak takes from the old man? Are his fellow partisans, starving and freezing, to be denied this beast, taken from the reluctant *starosta*, because Sotnikov deems it to be tainted flesh?

Bykov himself implies criticism of Sotnikov's doctrinaire attitudes toward Petr, who, when arrested and put in the same cell as Sotnikov and Rybak, shows himself to be made of sterner stuff than Sotnikov believed. Moreover, Petr raises the question of the dangers of moral and intellectual relativism. He notes that their interrogator once went around the villages agitating against God and religion; now he works for the Germans. And why had they ignored the plight of the Jews? "They began with the Jews," argues Petr, echoing Niemöller's admonition, "and look, they're finishing with us."[38] Then he turns to the painful question of why people become traitors: "The fascists—well, that's clear; they're alien people, nothing else to be expected. But what about our people who are with them? How are we to understand them? They've lived among us, eaten with us, they've looked people in the eye, and these days they have a rifle and they want to shoot people. And they do!"[39] In other words, those, like Rybak and the interrogator, who are driven by moral relativism will serve either Communism or National Socialism if necessary for survival.

For Sotnikov, duty is an absolute, and although it could conceivably be identified with service to the Red Army, it is in its ultimate form an abstract concept that stands above the Soviet state and politics. It is duty for its own sake and much closer to that calling enunciated by the German general von Seeckt (1866-1936). In his cell in between beatings, Sotnikov recollects in a dream his childhood fascination with his father's Mauser pistol. The pistol confers power on the holder, and the young Sotnikov is like any boy who would be Prometheus and steal the power of the gods. Naturally the temptation is too powerful; he succumbs and accidentally discharges the weapon. Sotnikov confesses to his father, giving him to understand that the moral impetus for owning up to the deed came from him, the sinner, not from his mother. The episode is a turning point in Sotnikov's moral education: "Generally speaking he got away with his disobedience quite lightly. He avoided a beating with the strap. But his fainthearted nod left a painful scar in his soul. This was a lesson for his whole life. And thereafter he never lied to his father or anybody else. He stuck to his answer while looking people in the eye."[40] It is the sense of duty to something higher—maybe to God, maybe to the ethos of soldierly duty inspired by his father—that sustains Sotnikov in his ordeal. Of crude Soviet clichés we find no trace at all, and it must have irritated Soviet critics to find Sotnikov awaiting his execution in quiet contemplation of duty and honor, not of the party and Lenin. Even the comment that he is an enemy of fascism is not compelling. Presumably even dyed-in-the-wool enemies of Communism can achieve some freedom from their executioners by coming to terms with their deaths. Rybak as Judas and Sotnikov defying his tormentors and preparing to meet his death invite speculation on whether we are reading an allegory of Christ's betrayal, death, and resurrection.[41] The dangerous quest undertaken by Rybak and Sotnikov often suggests a spiritual journey, a time of trial for both men that is only marginally connected with the war and could easily be accommodated in a completely different setting. The trial is one of faith, essentially a test of the belief that there is something greater than the flesh. Perhaps the greatest compliment that Rybak pays Sotnikov is the fact that despite all his justifications, Rybak knows that he has done wrong and that he is incapable of expiating his guilt.

Sotnikov's thoughts on his imminent death and its meaning are linked to his movement through the cemetery. He ponders the significance of crosses, humankind's desire to be remembered. His own memorial will be his bravery in the face of death. The fate of a Soviet colonel captured by the Germans who hurls abuse at his German tormentors inspires him: "It goes without saying that the colonel was later shot, but those few minutes before his execution were his triumph, his last feat of bravery, certainly no less difficult than anything on the battlefield."[42] The final line would have reminded Soviet readers of the state's scandalous treatment of Soviet prisoners. The colonel is unaware that his cursing is heard by some of his own people through the walls of the barracks. The colonel's end anticipates that of Sotnikov himself. The brave act is witnessed, as Sotnikov's act will be, and the memory lives on. Sotnikov's approach to his own death is essentially free of any political creed. The condemned man must try to make his own peace with the life he is about to depart, and to that extent he leaves the world in the same way that he entered it: alone. The dignity and the courage with which he faces the end can be their own reward, the ultimate freedom from tyranny and flesh. Sotnikov secures this last chance for himself by kicking away the log on which he stands, thus preempting the hangman and meeting his death as a free man.

Sotnikov's magnificent defiance in the face of appalling suffering should not, I suggest, prevent us from inquiring whether his sense of duty and the moral security it affords do in some way blind him to the motives of others. Naturally he is hurt and surprised by Rybak's behavior, and the problem of Rybak's treachery is compounded by the fact that Sotnikov does not believe him to be a traitor or a coward:

> Without a doubt, either from fear or from hatred people are capable of any treachery, but Rybak, it seems, was not a traitor, nor was he a coward. How many opportunities had he had to desert to the Polizai, and there were many opportunities when he could have behaved like a coward, yet he always behaved honorably, at the very least no worse than the rest. There must be something missing in him—strength of character or lack of principles. Or perhaps it was simply a matter of selfish calculation for the sake of saving his own skin, which always makes for treachery. But when all is said and done, there is something on earth immeasurably more important than one's own skin.[43]

Sotnikov's absolutism clashes, I suggest, with the state creed of Marxism-Leninism. In a society that denies the existence of God and aggressively promotes atheism and materialism, why should there be something "immeasurably more important than one's own skin"?

Sotnikov's sense of duty also clashes with the practical demands of the task in hand. A man severely weakened by a chest infection, with a loud cough, is unsuited for the exhausting task of foraging for food in the middle of winter. In his weakened state, he is manifestly a liability to Rybak, the fully fit partner, endangering both their lives. This situation shows a lapse of professional judgment on the part of Sotnikov, who as a regular soldier must have been well aware that a chronic cough should exclude an individual from taking part in any mission that depends on stealth and silence for success. Sotnikov's cough sets off an unfortunate sequence of events. His illness has so weakened him that he is unable to break contact with the Polizai, as a result of which he is wounded in the leg, a further impediment to his usefulness and another burden for Rybak. The time lost by his illness and wound and the onset of dawn compel the two men to find shelter in a house. The house is inhabited by a mother and two children, and in German-occupied Belorussia, the presence of the partisans exposes this family to great danger. It is, of course, Sotnikov's dreadful cough that betrays his and Rybak's presence in the attic when the Polizai call, with the expected consequences for mother and daughters.

Even before Sotnikov's cough gives them away, we see the first signs of Rybak's rejection of his fellow partisan: "Various feelings toward him [Sotnikov] started to mix themselves up in his consciousness: involuntary pity that so much could happen to one person (as if the illness was not enough, he was then wounded), but at the same time an indefinite feeling of irritation appeared, a presentiment that Sotnikov had brought all these troubles down on the two of them."[44] In fact, Rybak's presentiment that Sotnikov is somehow responsible for their plight is hinted at soon after the two men set out on their mission. They come across a house and property laid waste by the Germans in antipartisan operations: "Rybak realized that their luck was starting to go against them, and for the first time he started to think that their bad luck was ceasing to be a matter of chance."[45] Sotnikov's response to this act of German revenge is to posit that "somebody gave them away."[46] This early encounter prefigures not only the eventual fate of Sotnikov and Rybak but also Sotnikov's pivotal role: It is his cough that betrays him and Rybak to the Polizai. If Rybak stands condemned for his treacherous pursuit of self-interest, the defiant manner of Sotnikov's dying should not obscure the fact that a Seecktian dedication to some abstract notion of duty—the behavior of the British colonel in The Bridge on the River Kwai (1957) also comes to mind—that is uncoupled from an appreciation of practical, often sordid realities can be every bit as selfishly destructive.

The Obelisk (1972)

Bykov's stories are straightforward, yet they give rise to moral dilemmas and complicated problems. The main themes of The Obelisk are memory and memories of the war and the reluctance of those living in the present to face up to them. Many years after the war, the narrator learns that Miklashevich, a teacher who was a partisan during the war, has died. At the teacher's funeral, he meets another partisan, Tkachuk, who is bitter that Miklashevich's mentor, Moroz, has only just been recognized for his part in resisting the Germans. The eponymous obelisk has been erected largely due to the efforts of Miklashevich and is intended to commemorate a group of young partisans who were executed by the Germans in 1942. Miklashevich was the sole survivor. This apparently simple history hides a problem that until very recently the party did not want discussed or remembered, namely, the role of the village teacher, Moroz, the forgotten mentor of the young partisans, and Moroz's own behavior during the German occupation.

Miklashevich's funeral is hijacked by the local party official, who in a speech full of Soviet clichés conspicuously ignores the role of Moroz. Tkachuk argues that the party has deliberately deleted Moroz from the historical memory. Only very recently, since his ideological rehabilitation, has Moroz's name been added to the list of names on the obelisk. The clash at the funeral between the party official and Tkachuk reflects a view of truth that is ubiquitous in Bykov's work, and indeed in much of the best literature about the war. Truth, in keeping with the character and experiences of Tkachuk and the war itself, is sometimes rough and abrasive. Lies, like the party official, are all too often smooth, comforting, and polished.

As a teacher, Moroz does things his way. There is something unyielding, a strength of spirit and character, about Moroz, hinted at perhaps in his name, which in view of Bykov's obsession with cold seems not insignificant. Even before the war, Moroz is dogged by scandal. A schoolboy whom Moroz has befriended wants to live with him because his own father beats him, and the case ends up involving the local prosecutor. Moroz has the ability to get close to people, especially those who are wounded in some way.

What damns Moroz in the eyes of the party is that he continues to teach in the local school after the Germans arrive. This immediately gives rise to accusations of collaboration: "Well, what a change! I would've expected this from some, but not from Moroz. And at this juncture the prosecutor expressed himself along the lines that in his own time, one ought to have repressed that Moroz—he's not one of ours. I say nothing. I keep thinking, thinking, and I just can't get it into my head that Moroz is a teacher for the Germans."[47] Eventually the partisans pay Moroz a visit. He defends himself thus: "I teach nothing bad. But a school is necessary, and if we don't teach, then they'll make a bad job of it. I've not been trying to make something of these lads for the last two years only to let them become dehumanized now. I'll still fight on their behalf. Insofar as I can, to be sure."[48]

The narrator concedes that Moroz may be right and in making this concession highlights one of the crucial problems of living under German occupation: the conflict between resisting the Germans and the

banal, prosaic details of occupation itself; the obligation of every loyal Soviet citizen to resist the Germans and the rather obvious, though less
glamorous, requirement that life must go on. In the Soviet context,
Moroz runs the risk of being accused of collaborating with the enemy,
though the mere fact that he lives in the German-occupied territories condemns him and others to suspicion. The narrator acknowledges the demands of the present—to resist the Germans—but also recognizes that
Moroz is working for the future, for the time when the Germans will no
longer be there. To believe that there will not be a time when the Germans
will be absent is not to believe in the future.

Two important intellectual and moral influences on Moroz, both of
which explain the resolution of The Obelisk, are Tolstoy and Dostoyevsky.
Tolstoy inspires his final act of nonresistance to evil, and a patient who
was in hospital with him alludes to the other great Russian writer by one of
his best-known aphorisms: "He kept reading from some thick book,
mainly to himself, but sometimes aloud. I forget the name of the author
. . . I recall it went something like that if there was no God, then there was
no devil, and that means that there is no heaven, no hell. Everything is possible. Killing and pardoning."[49] That Miklashevich, one of Moroz's students, realizes the significance of Dostoyevsky tends to vindicate Moroz's
choice to continue teaching during the years of occupation. Moroz has en-
sured that the moral and intellectual links between the generations have
not been broken by the German invaders. We might see this result as his
heroic deed (podvig), or one of them at least, and one that deserves recognition. The emphasis on Tolstoy and especially Dostoyevsky as influences
on Moroz is also a swipe at the Soviet state. If, as the godless state maintains, there is no God, then anything, including collaboration, is permitted. Moroz's teachings provide the moral armory to resist the German occupation, whereas the relativism of the Soviet state does not. We have an
example of this in the story itself.

Two lads from the village of Sel'tso join the German-sponsored Polizai.
The first ends up being shot by the Germans; the second, called Cain
throughout the region, serves his German masters well. Cain's metamor-
phosis is important:

> Before the war he lived with his father on the farm. He was young,
> unmarried—a lad just like any other. Nobody had a bad word to say
> against him before the war. Then the Germans came, and he was

transformed. That's conditions for you. Probably in one set of conditions one part of a person's character is uncovered and in others, another. Therefore every time has its own heroes. . . . In the summer of '43 he disappeared somewhere. Maybe he got a bullet, but perhaps he's living a life of luxury in the West. People such as him don't get burned by fire or drown in water.[50]

The appeal to the biblical parable of Cain and Abel can be effective only within a moral framework of good and evil, of truth and falsehood. God punishes Cain because he has slain his brother: "When thou tillest the ground, it shall not henceforth yield unto thee her strength; a fugitive and a vagabond shalt thou be in the earth" (Genesis 4:12).[51] The biblical Cain does not deny God, but the Cain of *The Obelisk* lives in a state that preaches atheism, aspires to replace God in the hearts and minds of its citizens, and asserts and imposes the absolutism of class war. In the Soviet scheme of things, Bykov's Cain is not automatically the sinner, for it is the Soviet state that has slaughtered millions of Soviet peasants and cast them adrift from the land, making them fugitives and vagabonds and driving some of them, such as Cain, into the arms of the invader. If that premise is granted, then what is the reason the young partisans want to kill Cain, an attempt that sets off the sequence of events leading to Moroz's execution? Are the partisan defenders of Soviet power, Cain's would-be assassins, any better than its violators? Moroz's injunction to the schoolboys that Cain not be killed may well owe something to Tolstoy's concept of nonresistance against evil, and also perhaps to an understanding that the partisan movement does not possess all the moral arguments and solutions to the problem of the German occupation. Moroz's decision to continue teaching might be based on this realization.

The assassination attempt goes ahead, but it fails, and one of the boys is seen. The Germans arrest the boys and demand that Moroz surrender himself or the boys will be executed. The partisans think Moroz is crazy to believe the Germans and wrong to surrender. The assassination attempt having been made, rightly or wrongly, the conflict becomes that between the general cause of the partisans fighting the Germans, and trying to maintain cohesion and discipline, and Moroz's sense of duty and moral worth, which operates independently of the partisan collective and Soviet society. Moroz surrenders and is duly led to execution with the boys. The manner of his dying and his last words remind us of Sotnikov:

And he himself tried to be cheerful, as far as, of course, he was able. He said that a man's life was nothing when measured against eternity and that fifteen or sixteen years is nothing more than an instant before the face of eternity. He went on to say that thousands of people had been born in Sel'tso; they had lived and passed into oblivion and nobody knows them or remembers any trace of their existence. But they would be remembered, and that for them should serve as the highest award, the very highest of all possible awards on earth.[52]

Coming to a final judgment regarding Moroz's fate, as with so much in Bykov's works, is not easy. Tkachuk proposes to the narrator that it is a heroic story; the visitor is not so sure. By the time Tkachuk has told the story, the night is setting in: "The night had gotten a little darker, or so it seemed coming in from the light."[53] A convenient metaphor of the gray areas, this moment tends to blur or rather reinforce the views of the two men: Tkachuk is quite clear that Moroz's deed is an act of heroism; the visitor believes that it is not so clear-cut, that perhaps Moroz was stupid to throw away his life because his death meant the villagers lost his services as a teacher. The changes from light to darkness and darkness to light frequently facilitate the transitions from present to past and back. The transition from light to half light and darkness—as in the frequent use here and elsewhere in Bykov's work of the verb *stemnet'* (to grow dark)—serves as a metaphor of the transition from clarity to confusion, the moment between the past and the present, a reminder that things in war are not quite what they seem.

In the final scene, the two men are given a lift by the party official. He has, he says, nothing against Moroz now that his name has been rehabilitated, thus arrogating to the party the exclusive right to judge the past. The whole question of collective action and approval once again surfaces. "But," Tkachuk counters, "he was not repressed. He was simply forgotten."[54] The party official counters with the inevitable, telling question: "And what would have happened if every partisan had behaved like Moroz?"[55] We return to the start of the dispute, and the question of Moroz's bravery or otherwise is left unresolved.

The Wolf Pack (1974)

Some thirty years after the war, Levchuk, a former partisan, pays a visit to a young man, the son of partisans who were both killed in the war. Finding his host out, Levchuk recalls the past and the circumstances that have brought him there. *The Wolf Pack* is a multilayered story of treachery, love, and loyalty. The wolves appear in many guises: They are the indigenous wolves of Belorussia, the primeval presence and reminder of an ancient mutual enmity, who are always ready to attack and kill humans in the harsh winters; they are the partisan traitors who are wolves to their fellow humans; and they are the German *Partisanenjäger* who, in an exceptionally powerful climax to this story, hunt the narrator, Levchuk, through the marshes of Belorussia. With relentless and brutal honesty, Bykov dispels many of the official Soviet myths about partisan warfare.

Wounded in the shoulder, Levchuk, along with the partisans' radio operator, Klava, who is pregnant; a badly wounded soldier, Tikhonov; and Griboed, is to be evacuated. So begin two grim days of escape and evasion. Against the advice of the partisan scouts, who have declared a forest track to be safe, Levchuk decides to leave the track and cross the marshes. The others object, mainly out of a fear of the unknown. The trackless, uncharted marsh represents terra incognita, and they would rather stick to the track with its false sense of security. The atmosphere of menace that pervades nearly every Bykov story would be inconceivable without wilderness, marsh, snow, and forest. Yet for all the sense of menace, the wilderness can be trusted in a way in which humankind cannot. Levchuk's instincts tell him that the track is not safe, that the Germans are waiting in ambush (as they are). The question left unanswered at this stage is whether the Germans were merely lucky or whether the partisans harbor a traitor.

In a digression, we learn that one traitor has already been identified, which leads to the death of Platonov, the group's leader. In keeping with his skepticism, Levchuk suggests that Platonov was too trusting: "He betrayed [izmenil] himself only on one occasion, having acted hurriedly, without thinking, and that lack of thought cost him his life."[56] Two Red Army soldiers join their group, ostensibly having escaped from the Germans. One, Kudriavtsev, says that the other soldier, Shevtsov, was interrogated by the Germans, and expresses a suspicion that he is a German agent. A search yields a German cipher, and Shevtsov is executed. This episode dramatically enhances Kudriavtsev's credibility and accelerates his acceptance into the group. We suspect that the other soldier has been sacrificed precisely for this reason.

Kudriavtsev is a familiar character in Bykov's fiction (compare him to Rybak in *Sotnikov*, Blishchinskii in *A Page from the Front*, and Golubin in *To Set out and Not Return*). Socially successful and engaging, he is everybody's friend, and it is this social success that enables him to lure Platonov into a German ambush in which he is killed. What adds to Bykov's theme—the manner of Platonov's death being an occupational hazard of partisan warfare—is the uncertainty regarding the identity of the father of Klava's child. Of significance here, and for the story as a whole, it is hinted, is the obvious sexual attraction that Klava feels for Kudriavtsev. Bykov implies, though very lightly, that Klava has not been faithful to Platonov.

The ambiguity concerning the father helps to explain what at first appears to be Levchuk's ungracious behavior toward Klava: "He did not console her because he did not know how to, and, moreover, he considered her guilty for what had happened to her."[57] In the circumstances in which the partisans find themselves, and by the very nature of war itself, a pregnant woman is a liability. The finger of suspicion points at Kudriavtsev, the traitor, rather than at Platonov. This is the guilt to which Levchuk refers, and it makes Klava, who realizes with Platonov's death that she too has been duped, "inconsolable."

The child is born in what remains of a village laid waste by the Germans and the Polizai. Bykov paints a scene of devastation, one that was common throughout German-occupied Belorussia and was not unknown during the Sovietization and collectivization of Belorussia. The scene is a hint that not much separates Soviet power from that of the Germans:

> Levchuk had expected to see some buildings, or at the very least
> some thatched roofs with chimneys—the normal signs that there
> was a village nearby, but he saw none of this. Its past here could be
> guessed at merely by the several tall trees that were visible a little way
> beyond the rye field. Approaching closer, they saw from behind the
> weed-infested hedges the smoke-stained remains of the stoves and,
> in places, the charred, unburned corners of the sheds and wooden
> beams laid out in the yards covered in grass. Of the many buildings,
> only the foundation stones remained. Trees close to the fires stood
> dried out, with branches bereft of any leaves. The tall lime tree
> standing above the well was green only on one side. Scorched, the
> other side stretched out its twigs in a strange way to the sky. In the
> flattened and uncultivated gardens lay scattered and broken tubs,
> various domestic utensils, sticks, and gray dried-out rags. By the
> look of it, the village had been burned down in the spring, just before

the gardens were plowed up. The winter crops that were growing in the field no longer belonged to anyone, and spring crops were nowhere to be seen. The field next to the gardens lay neglected, densely covered with goosefoot and pastor's lettuce.[58]

That Klava should give birth to her son in this wasteland has a certain symbolism for the time frames, both war and postwar. If Kudriavtsev is indeed the father, then it seems somehow apposite that the mother at the time of birth should be reminded of what is at stake. Retrospectively, we can see the child's birth in that place, at that dark hour, as a symbol of hope for the future, hope that the Germans will not destroy Belorussia.

The child safely delivered by Griboed, Bykov returns to the issue of its paternity in a way that forces the reader to ponder the same question. For example, Levchuk reluctantly agrees with Griboed that the child is just like Platonov. At this moment, we ask whether the child's paternity is the subject of Levchuk's postwar visit. Has he come with the aim of telling the adult son the truth? Or will he keep his doubts to himself and maintain the fiction? on cue, as if to reinforce our skepticism, the barn is surrounded by a detachment of Polizai led by none other than Kudriavtsev. His turning up immediately after Klava has given birth appears to be no coincidence in the context of the ambiguity and uncertainty surrounding the identity of the father. We might see his appearance as a gruesome parody of the father's seeing his newborn child for the first time. Like Golubin in To Set out and Not Return, who, having shot Zosia, returns to the place where he shot her, Kudriavtsev returns, as it were, to the scene of the crime—or rather to his partner in crime, Klava. A further hint comes from Kudriavtsev himself. Levchuk and Griboed are free to go, he says, if they hand over the signaler. Kudriavtsev's conspicuous use of the diminutive Russian form for a radio operator, radistochka, a term of affection—perhaps the same epithet he first used in seducing her—gives the game away. Kudriavtsev's demand hardens Levchuk's suspicions regarding Klava and explains his harsh treatment of her when she volunteers to hand herself over and leave the child with Levchuk.

After the barn is set ablaze by the Polizai, Levchuk cannot find Klava or the child in the smoke and confusion. Given Kudriavtsev's specific demand that she be handed over and the fact that she volunteered to go, there is a possibility that she has gone to Kudriavtsev after all. On a number of occasions after Levchuk escapes from the fire, Bykov points us toward this conclusion. Levchuk repeatedly speculates on the fate of Griboed and Klava, especially the latter:

He was tormented by the question of what had happened to Klava. And what was Griboed's fate? In any case, Griboed is most likely there and still is; he would hardly have succeeded in leaping to the door. But where had Klava disappeared to? How had she crawled out of the threshing barn? It was as if she had been swallowed up by the ground. He did not catch sight of her anywhere.[59]

This is the fourth occasion in The Wolf Pack in which Levchuk implants doubt in the reader's mind regarding Klava's loyalties. Having escaped from the barn, Levchuk feels compelled to return. He finds Griboed's body. And how did Griboed die? At the hands of the Polizai? Or did Klava kill him to make good her escape? Klava has "disappeared without a trace."[60] It is at this precise moment that two quite different sounds link Klava's disappearance: The first is the sound of the Germans' dogs as the climactic manhunt is about to begin, and the second is the crying of Klava's child, abandoned in the rye field, with no trace of the mother. "It seemed to him that Klava could be lying somewhere as well. But Klava was not there, just her son, who inexplicably happened to be there."[61] The juxtaposition of Levchuk's thoughts on Klava's fate and the barking of the German tracker dogs invites us to ask questions that have no clear-cut answers. The last we see of Klava and her son is in the barn. How did her son end up in the field? Did she leave him there when she ran to Kudriavtsev?

Bykov had already grappled with this sort of problem in To Live until Dawn, published two years earlier. Two soldiers in a patrol inexplicably disappear. The eventual explanation of what happened casts light on what happened to Klava. In To Live until Dawn, the possibility that the two soldiers deserted is explicit, whereas in The Wolf Pack, with regard to Klava, it is hinted at. In both novels, Bykov uses an almost identical sentence to suggest that treachery cannot be ruled out. The key difference is that the soldiers' absence is eventually explained in To Live until Dawn, whereas the question of Klava's disappearance is left unanswered. Together with the other hints, this uncertainty strengthens the suspicions against her.

The possibility—and we must admit that it is just that, all the evidence being circumstantial, allusive, elusive, fragmentary, and psychological—that Kudriavtsev is the child's father adds a rather nasty twist to the theme of treachery. Platonov has been betrayed twice: once by Kudriavtsev, who led him into the ambush, and again by Klava, the woman he loved. If indeed Kudriavtsev is the father of Klava's son, then we might see the Klava-Kudriavtsev-Platonov triangle as an allegory of the incestuous nature of partisan warfare itself: Today's friends are tomorrow's traitors. Political loyalty and allegiances are like sexual partners, to be changed when convenient. If the man identified at the story's end is Kudriavtsev's son, then he is the son of a traitor, which was not a pleasant situation in the Soviet Union. Levchuk, it seems, will follow the example of Vasilevich in *The Dead Feel No Pain*. Even if he does suspect something, he will maintain the fiction, the holy lie, that the child is Platonov's so that the sins of the fathers shall not be visited on the sons.

The Sign of Misfortune (1983)

One of Bykov's remarkable qualities as a writer is his ability to find and to exploit an apparently inexhaustible seam of observations and insights into human behavior in war. In *The Sign of Misfortune*, Bykov returns to his familiar—and from the point of view of Soviet censorship dangerous—themes: life under German occupation and the moral choices that must be made in order to survive. What makes *The Sign of Misfortune* subversive of Soviet order and its enforced historiographical line is not merely Bykov's point that Soviet citizens were willing to serve in the German-controlled Polizai or to assist in the rounding up of Jews but that he also invites the alert reader to consider the possibility that Soviet behavior in the 1930s was not far removed from Nazi behavior during the years of occupation. In some ways, it was worse.

Every work in Bykov's partisan warfare cycle makes the point that collectivization acted as a recruiting agent for the Nazis. In *The Sign of Misfortune*, Bykov moves beyond the consequences of collectivization in terms of attitudes toward the Germans; now the focus is on the Soviet attitude toward property and, to take it one stage further, possession (and dispossession). The "sign of misfortune" hangs, vulturine, over every plot line: the impending arrival of the Germans; the relentless harassment of the work's two heroes, husband and wife Petrok and Stepanida, by the Germans and the Polizai; and the wave of arrests in the 1930s. Arguably its most devastating manifestation is the assault on the institution of property. A society that tolerates and encourages the seizure of land under the Marxist slogan of "the expropriation of the expropriators" is one that is truly cursed and, as events showed, bitterly disunited in the face of the German occupation.

Bykov repeatedly stresses the powerful innate drive to own land and property, and indeed the drive to acquire both is a powerful factor in both

Petrok's and Stepanida's calculations. Her feelings for a particular field, known locally as Golgotha, the full significance of which name is revealed later, are deep and maternal:

> The Germans would hardly give the land to the peasants. They knew that once you let it out of your hands, you never get it back. No matter what it was, this piece of land, this godforsaken hillock with the name of Golgotha, she felt sorry for it, as a mother might feel sorry for an only child that was ill. How many times had she gone out there on her old legs; how much work had she done with her exhausted hands! How many years had she and Petrok plowed, sown, harvested, covered the field with manure, and broken up the heavy lumps of clay.[62]

At this stage in the story, the picture we have of Stepanida and Petrok is of a hardworking couple who live by their own labor. In various asides we are given to understand that what they have is theirs by right and that it has been lawfully acquired. Stepanida's comments on her diploma are intended to make the point that she respects private property; that it must be earned: "I did not get it for stealing property. It's for my own hard work."[63] This picture of a decent couple makes the arrival of the Germans and their vandalism all the more shocking. The Germans expel the couple from their house. They plunder their scarce reserves of food and in a fit of temper kill their cow. Not surprisingly, the couple themselves seem to think that they have been singled out in some way. Petrok muses that "God has visited punishment on two old people. But why, though?"[64] Later he agonizes over why the Germans destroyed the vegetable garden: "Well, there's God's punishment—thought Petrok with a heavy heart.—But what are the sins? And precisely why has all this fallen on me?"[65] Even Stepanida, by far the tougher of the two, seems overwhelmed by their cruel and sudden misfortune: "What had she done wrong against God and conscience; why had such punishment fallen upon her and other people? Why had these strangers invaded her life, which was difficult enough already, and turned everything upside down and deprived a person of even the slightest hope for the future?"[66]

Initially our reaction to the way the couple are treated by the Germans is to regard it as the outcome of war. The Germans are rapacious invaders who respect nothing and plunder at will. The question is whether anything other than the Germans and the war might explain the couple's plight. They themselves seem to harbor a suspicion that they are being punished in some way and for something that may not be directly related to the war. Human memory, "endowed with that ability to change the past into the present and to link the present with the future,"[67] in the concluding lines of Bykov's powerful prologue, points the way back to the first two decades of Soviet power.

Stepanida and Petrok's agonizing questions about the source of the calamity that has befallen them and others is not properly addressed until chapter 12, one of a number of flashback chapters. The key events are the reallocation of land after the Civil War and collectivization. As a member of the poverty committee, a party-created device for forcing collectivization upon the village, Stepanida is revealed as an activist. Unlike her husband, she is no passive bystander but a willing instrument of the party.

Kosmachev, the party official, attempts to browbeat the villagers into giving up their property rights and joining the collective. His assertion that "the whole country was amicably moving toward collectivization"[68] is a lie designed to apply further pressure to the villagers. Coercion, not persuasion, is the preferred method. One person volunteers to join the collective, then calls on another to follow his lead, and so on. Stepanida is uncomfortable with this procedure and, significantly, does not show the same strength of character that she shows in dealing with the Germans. Any opposition she might muster is already compromised because, as we learn here, she and Petrok have already been allocated five acres of the IAkhimovskii estate. Here too we see the seeds of the bitter enmity between Stepanida and a neighbor, Guzh, that becomes clear during the German occupation. Guzh senior refuses to join the collective: "Guzh sat there as if awaiting death, stubborn and silent, his lips tightly shut, looking into the corner where at one time icons used to hang but where now, barely visible through the tobacco smoke, could be seen a portrait of Karl Marx nailed to the wall."[69] The displacement of the icons by a portrait of Marx reflects the basic clash between the tenth commandment and the Marxist idea of the expropriation of the expropriators.

Defending what she takes to be her own property against the Germans, Stepanida is implacable. She wastes the cow's milk so as to deny it to the Germans. For this she is beaten. In some ways, her punishment is not linked solely to the cow. The clue is in her reaction; she complains that she has been whipped "in her own yard."[70] The begged question that is not immediately obvious in this disgraceful beating of an old woman is whether the yard is indeed her own. At this stage, two questions lie dormant: Are she and Petrok the rightful owners? Are they not in their own way expropriators, like the Germans? Her deliberate wasting of the milk demonstrates something fundamental about ownership, an attitude that we all recognize and that was a clear characteristic of the peasant response to collectivization in the 1930s: This is mine; if I can't have it, then neither shall anyone else. The distinction is made even between husband and wife. Taking the milked cow back to the Germans, Petrok acknowledges that "the cow was not his property; it belonged more to his wife."[71] Stepanida's instinct for private property or personal ownership—as we have already seen in her deep love for the Golgotha field—is demonstrably at odds with her taking part in the dispossession of so-called kulaks. Her strong sense that the Germans are violating her property rights is implicit condemnation of the Soviet state's seizure of land and farm equipment and thus of her own role as a party activist.

Bykov continues to explore the theme of expropriation in chapters 13 and 14. Stepanida worked for the IAkhimovskii estate as hired labor. The fundamental desire to own land, a drive that the Soviet state seeks to eradicate, is evident when she and Petrok acquire some property. Petrok is overjoyed, though somewhat ambiguously pointing out to Stepanida that if one particular local can be dispossessed as a kulak, then none of them is safe: "Who else will be dispossessed as a kulak in a couple of years?"[72] For what comes later under the German occupation, this question is of the greatest relevance. In the manner of receiving the land—taken from Pan IAkhimovskii—and allocating it to the new owners, Stepanida and Petrok, "by right of expropriation,"[73] we see the source of much misery and the beginnings of the curse. However much she tries to persuade herself that the land has been lawfully acquired, Stepanida is aware of a nagging sense of guilt:

> Even if just confined to her thoughts and hopes, she nevertheless coveted another's property, something she had not permitted herself in all these years of service at IAkhimovshchina, where with all her might, through need and poverty, she had guarded her honor and endeavoured to make sure that nobody could ever reproach her for anything. . . . Now these changes had stirred up her conscience. How should she be? How should she live were she not to take the land, were she to renounce it? But were she to take it, how could she look the owner in the eye?[74]

Despite these feelings, Stepanida persuades herself that acquiring the land is a good thing: "Ahead of them lay a life of freedom with many worries, hard work, but one without compulsion, a life where everything bad and good would depend on the two of them alone and on nobody else. This was happiness that raised them to heaven, a stroke of good fortune of which one could really dream."[75]

Here we see the heart of the whole problem surrounding the attempt to build a better life based on Marxist expropriation of the expropriators. Stepanida knows, despite her dissembling to herself and all her arguments, that she is the recipient of stolen property. She recognizes as much when she admits that she covets another's property. Accepting the stolen land allocated by the party makes her and others accessories to the theft. One can accept her apologies to IAkhimovskii for what has happened, but, as he points out, she did not refuse to take the land. When he tells her that "it is a sin to covet another's property,"[76] he echoes the warnings of her own conscience. By this stage, however, with the expropriation completed and IAkhimovskii dispossessed, Stepanida no longer seems willing to heed the voice of conscience. Her unspoken response to IAkhimovskii—"How can this property be alien to me?"[77]—suggests that she sees the whole process as normal, the natural order of things, somehow a just reward for her long years of loyal service to the estate. The property and title to the land have, however, not been transferred in accordance with the customary norms of alienation, and so her question invites the answer that the property is indeed "alien"—not hers, that is, in any strict legal or even moral sense because it has not been alienated, merely expropriated.

Nor are the omens good. Some time later Petrok finds a dead lark, which Stepanida takes to be "a clear harbinger of misfortune."[78] Pan IAkhimovskii never recovers from the loss of his land and house and commits suicide. As if to reinforce the point, the horse dies of exhaustion while plowing Golgotha. The good life gives way to a wretched and bitter struggle. The land refuses to give up its riches. As Petrok realizes, "It's cursed, this hill. We had no land, but this is not land either."[79] The arrival of the Germans and, even worse, the predations of their Polizai auxiliaries is the final misfortune to fall upon Petrok and Stepanida. The Germans are the new agents of expropriation. Petrok's oft-used words when justifying his backbreaking labor on Golgotha—"As you earn, so you will receive"—now take on a far more sinister meaning. It also helps to end the uncertainty surrounding the cause of the couple's punishment. True, Stepanida and Petrok did not initiate the dispossession of IAkhimovskii, but they were the prime beneficiaries, and Stepanida colluded in the dispossession of Guzh senior.

Collaborator and member of the hated Polizai though he is, Guzh junior is nevertheless substantially correct in his assessment of Stepanida's role in the village before the war: "You're an ignorant woman, are you? And who organized the collective farms? Who forced the women into the reading rooms? Ignorant woman, are you? And the dispossession?"[80] Her claim that she is just an ignorant woman is not true. Bykov's use of the adverb "pensively" (zadumchivo) to qualify her response to Guzh suggests that her attitude toward collectivization may have shifted; that she realizes that she was instrumental, at least in part, in creating the bitterness that has devoured Guzh.

Another incident, again involving Guzh junior and Stepanida, this time before the war, illustrates the morally and societally destructive consequences of state-sponsored expropriation. Guzh junior opportunistically robs Stepanida in the forest. She feels a sense of violation and humiliation; she believes that Soviet power will deal with these bandits. The trouble is, of course, that Soviet power appears to be no better than the bandits in the woods, and she, by taking part in the dispossession of others, is arguably a bandit herself, working on behalf of Soviet power. If banditry is acceptable, then Guzh is behaving according to the norms of the Soviet state. In another bout of theft, Petrok loses his horse. He says of the thieves, "They have nothing to lose. They are like wolves in the forest."[81] Again, if the new law is expropriation, an assault on private property rights, then stealing horses and robbing people is the way to live. The common ownership of the means of production negates the concept of theft because if all are owners in common, how can one rob one's own property?

One expropriation leads to another. The Germans in a sense are agents of retribution. In demonstrating the moral and ethical weakness of Stepanida's and Petrok's claim to the land, Bykov is really exposing the whole program of Soviet collectivization to scrutiny. Here was an absolute disaster that claimed millions of lives and forcibly transferred millions of acres of land from private ownership to the state. Stepanida's willingness to waste the cow's milk rather than let the Germans drink it is one small example of the same kind of resistance that occurred during collectivization, when peasants slaughtered their livestock in the millions rather than let their stock be carried away by party activists. And why should we stop at collectivization? Based on expropriation of property, the Bolshevik revolution, when Russia, in Solzhenitsyn's words, succumbed "to the cheap calls to theft and desertion," was the sign of misfortune that hung over the Soviet Union from its inception until 1991.[82]

The two scenes of destruction with which *The Sign of Misfortune* begins and ends are linked and reinforce this message. In the concluding scene, Stepanida sets the farmstead alight, a final act of rebellion, as the Polizai try to break down the doors to recover a bomb. This scene returns us to the prologue:

> People and time had not left much behind here of what was once a sprawling and expansive farm estate. Here and there a few remains could be seen on the surface; a foundation stone, a sunken mound of bricks and two stone steps near the former entrance. These entrance blocks rested on the same place as they had for many years past, and the small reddish ants somewhere close by who had selected themselves a dwelling scurried about their affairs on the lower step, which went into the ground. . . . Nothing remained of the well; the framework had rotted away, or perhaps people had destroyed it. The water that was never extracted dried up, retreating to the depths of the earth. In place of the hut that used to stand here, a thorny wild pear tree stretched toward the light from the weeds; perhaps it was the offshoot of the pears that once grew here, or maybe a self-sprouting one brought in by the birds from the forest.
>
> From the main road very little indicated that there had ever been a farm estate here, merely one of the two lime trees that had stood in all their splendor besides the gates of the estate. Of the other there was no trace, and indeed the one that remained was a pitiful sight. . . . For some reason the birds that flew out of the forest never settled on its branches, preferring the tall alder nearby. Possibly the crows remembered something, and perhaps with their ancient instinct they could sense the spirit of unhappiness in the mutilated tree, the sign of ancient misfortune. This fateful sign lay over everything here.[83]

The sign of disaster, the curse that has fallen on Petrok and Stepanida, and by implication on Belorussia and on the Soviet Union, is the violation of another's property, not in any narrow juridical sense but in the sense of the biblical injunction that, among other things, "thou shalt not covet thy neighbour's house" (Exodus 20:17). Class war, the call "to expropriate the expropriators," is a violation of God's law. The outcome of expropriation in *The Sign of Misfortune* implies that the institution of private property must be upheld as a fundamental principle of a just and stable society.

As the story moves to its incendiary conclusion, Stepanida comes as close as she psychologically can to an admission that collectivization was wrong and that she helped to create the situation that has made her life so miserable:

> In all probability a person was made in such a way that he would respond to good with good and was hardly able to respond to evil with good. Evil could give rise to nothing other than evil. Nothing else was possible. The trouble is that human goodness is defenseless before evil. Evil can only be dealt with by strength and only deterred by punishment. Only the thought of the inevitability of punishment could restrain its predatory instinct and force it to think. Were there no punishment, then chaos, of which it was spoken in the Bible, would reign on earth.[84]

When she notes that "evil could give rise to nothing other than evil" she recognizes, albeit reluctantly, that no notion of the good and just society can be based on a foundation of evil. It may well be that this supplies a clue as to how we should interpret the final, somewhat enigmatic sentence of this work: "But the bomb was awaiting its time."[85] Are we to see the bomb as a metaphor of the Soviet state's disastrous war against private property and the individual freedoms that go with it, which will eventually be its undoing?[86]

The Quarry (1986)

Four decades after the war, Ageev, former soldier and partisan and the sole survivor of a German firing squad, returns to a quarry, the site of the execution, in the hope that he will find the remains of a woman who was arrested through his carelessness and lack of foresight. In his quest, Ageev resembles an archaeologist who painstakingly tries to rebuild a picture of the past, yet his excavation of the quarry is driven as much by the moral problems of life under German occupation and his own behavior as by the search for physical remains. Published on the threshold of glasnost and perestroika, The Quarry reflects the author's tenacious and relentless obsession with the past, with a war that is so reluctant to release its grip on the survivors.

Ageev's unit is overwhelmed by the German assault in 1941. Managing to break out of German encirclement, he and another soldier, Molokovich, who will later die in the quarry, end up in a village far behind the German lines. Their chances of making it back to the Soviet lines now virtually nil, the two men lie low in the Belorussian village. Wounded, Ageev finds shelter in the house of Baranovskaia, the widow of a priest. Both men are recruited by the local partisans to work in the underground. Ageev's situation is complicated by Drozdenko, the head of the Polizai, who immediately sees through his unconvincing story that he is Baranovskaia's son and tries to recruit him. Ageev allows himself to be persuaded to work for the partisans while still wounded, when more prudent counsels should have prevailed. Under pressure from Drozdenko, he also signs a document in which he consents to cooperate with the Polizai. Realizing that he has made a terrible mistake, he informs his partisan contact, but his honesty does him no good. The partisans suspect that Ageev is playing a double game, and his refusal to become an active agent for the Polizai, as opposed to a mere signatory of an agreement, inspires suspicion from the Polizai that he is working for the partisans. Ageev, whom Bykov shows to be an honest and loyal soldier, is completely out of his depth in this underground war, this snake pit of treachery, lying, and betrayal. Former loyalties count for nothing. Ageev shares the fate of so many of Bykov's characters, and, in one of the author's favorite similes (see, for example, The Kruglianskii Bridge and Sotnikov), "he felt himself to be on the blade of a knife, on a powder barrel in a fire."[87]

Ageev's quest represents only one of a number of "pasts" that are uncovered in The Quarry. During his period of recuperation in Baranovskaia's house, Ageev, the Red Army officer, receives a firsthand account of what happened in the rural districts after 1917: the Civil War; the destruction and vandalism inflicted on the churches; the persecution of Baranovskaia's husband, Father Kirill; and the prosecution of class war and collectivization. Like Pan IAkhimovskii in The Sign of Misfortune, Baranovskaia is critical of the seizure and destruction of private property. In another echo of The Sign of Misfortune—Stepanida's belated realization that good cannot be created on the basis of evil—Baranovskaia rejects the Soviet experiment because, as she tells Ageev: "goodness is impossible without God."[88] In another blow to Ageev's Soviet education, she tells him, "Well, were you to read Dostoyevsky, you would know that if you don't let God into your soul, then the devil will invariably settle there."[89] Ageev's succumbing to Drozdenko's pressure tends to support Baranovskaia's belief that without faith in God, or something other than the party to turn to, human beings will do anything because they have no inner moral resources on which to fall back.

Baranovskaia's obvious approval of Dostoyevsky and the discovery of Father Kirill's copy of *The Devils* (1871–1872) imply some connection between *The Quarry* and Dostoyevsky's themes. Indeed, the various comings and goings to the house are reminiscent of a Dostoyevsky novel, as if all the visitors are in one way or another involved in the temptation of Ageev. Koveshko, the Belorussian patriot who has thrown in his lot with the Germans, is particularly sinister. He refers to Ageev as Neponiatlivyi— the Russian means "stupid" or "dull"—presumably because Ageev fails to see that the game is up for the Soviet Union. We see an explicit reference to Smerdiakov in Dostoyevsky's *The Brothers Karamazov* (1879–1880) when Koveshko says to Ageev, "Well, it is pleasant, don't you know, to talk with an intelligent man."[90] Smerdiakov is infatuated with the French and Napoleon, despising the Russians, whereas Koveshko admires the Germans and Hitler.

The chance discovery of Father Kirill's trunk containing long-forgotten books and journals confronts Ageev with yet another past to which he has been denied access in the Soviet period. Browsing through one of the old pre-1917 journals, which deals with World War I, he is interested in the Russian soldiers:

> He was looking for something different—he sought something about the traitors and betrayers of that time, of the type of today's Polizai, deserters, those like Drozdenko. You see, at that time there were battles in these very same places, and half of Belorussia was under the Germans and in all probability at that time there would have been German stooges about whom the journal *Niva* would have written or at the very least mentioned. But *Niva* was silent on this question, as if there were none at all.
>
> And perhaps there were none at all?[91]

Here Bykov returns to the destructive consequences of Communism on national loyalty and identity, a theme that runs throughout his entire work. Under communist rule, loyalty to the national culture, language, and folkways of Belorussia was a form of counterrevolution that was ruthlessly punished. Some may be attracted by the arid demands of ideological loyalty, but such notions have never been the enduring basis of any nation. Nations are made and sustained by the sacrifice of blood. They are held together by common culture, language, and history. Marxism-Leninism and Internationalism proved to be anemic substitutes. Of Belorussian, during one of his visits to Ageev, Koveshko says, "An ancient language, you know, going back to pagan times, from the times of the Great Principality. Not so easy to eradicate it, if over the centuries the Russians have not managed to do so.'"[92] The painful, shocking discovery for the Soviet regime between 1941 and 1945 was that, by declaring the nation to be illegitimate and counterrevolutionary, a bourgeois construct, the regime made collaboration with the Germans all the more likely. However outraged Soviet readers may have been by types such as Drozdenko and Koveshko in The Quarry—Lazar' Lazarev, a leading Bykov scholar, passes over this question entirely—the Soviet system, by trying to destroy and undermine national loyalty, helped to destroy the very quality of loyalty itself. Loyalty now meant the ruthless pursuit of self-interest and survival at all costs. Who then is the stooge, Drozdenko, who collaborates with the Germans, albeit out of purely selfish considerations, or Ageev, who despite a crash course in Belorussia's proud past courtesy of Maria (the young woman whom he meets in the village and the reason for his post-war quest), Baranovskaia, and Father Kirill's journals, regards Sovietized Belorussia as superior to what existed before? Is there indeed any difference in approach between Koveshko and Ageev? Koveshko has convinced himself that the communists are "evil number one" and that the future lies with Germany. Ageev, the Belorussian, has also turned to an outside power, the Soviet Union, for salvation. Ageev is also mute on the question of "the laws of history,"[93] which Koveshko uses to justify the actions of the Germans. An appeal to "the laws of history" is precisely the formula that a communist would use to justify mass murder and class war. What then is the difference between the Nazis and the communists? Ageev offers no answer.

A sense of loyalty and a fear of treachery are the twin forces that drive Ageev's obsessive excavations of the quarry and create the psychological tension in The Quarry. After the village was liberated, the remains of only three bodies were uncovered: Molokovich; Zyl, a saboteur; and Kisliakov, a partisan. There is no trace of Maria, and her name is not included on the memorial obelisk. One thing that must be considered is the possibility that the girl was an agent of the Polizai. Ageev is tormented by the fact that her name is not on the memorial and that there is no trace of her, no local memory:

> But why was she not there? Had she really survived? Or had she perished in some other place, perhaps in a German concentration camp or after having been taken away from the area? Of course,

during that time anything could have happened. But Ageev had lived through the last four decades in the certainty that she had not avoided their common fate. At the very least the terrible events of that autumn had not left any hope for anybody. All of them were doomed, and only he by a quirk of chance had returned from the dead. But two lucky chances in their situation—that would be too much, and he was unable to believe in the second one.[94]

Realistically there are only two serious outcomes: Either she was shot somewhere else, or she betrayed Ageev and survived the war. The absence of any documentary evidence that might clarify her fate has alarming implications that, in the way Bykov lays them before the reader, are somewhat ambiguous: "Ageev understood that he was not so much hungry for news of her fate but rather was trying to deceive himself so as to avoid that final, for him impossible, answer. This answer could carry in itself the most terrible result."[95] At this stage it is not clear what is meant by "the most terrible result." Is it that she is dead or, worse still, that she was a German agent?

Arrested by the Polizai, Ageev is tormented by the possibility that Maria gave him away, a realistic one given that she may well have been tortured:

> The main and most terrible thing for him was, nevertheless, clear: Maria had been caught. Apparently she had been captured with her damning load. But how did they know about her? Had Maria betrayed him, said something, named him? Of course, the possibilities open to them of getting a confession were numerous, even more so from an inexperienced, green girl, to which end they would certainly not spare any efforts. But nevertheless . . . Nevertheless he did not want to believe that she would betray him so quickly. She could not betray him because she loved him, and for him such a blow from her would be more terrible than any failure, worse than death.
>
> Nevertheless, he could come up with nothing else at all. Not a single soul knew of their relationship in the village, neither the neighbors, the Polizai, nor their people. How were the Polizai able to link her with him? And within a matter of hours after her being detained?[96]

Under German occupation, and especially in Vasil' Bykov's stories, things are never straightforward. At this stage in *The Quarry*, Ageev must consider the possibility that Maria has betrayed him. Indeed, just after they first met,

Ageev considered that she may have been planted by the Germans or the Polizai: "Has she perhaps been sent on some secret task? Has she been recruited and indoctrinated? No, that's not possible. In such a case everything would certainly be done with greater cunning and more logic. But it has happened naively, brazenly, foolishly."[97] Is that perhaps where the cunning lies?

There are two scenarios for any betrayal. In the worst case, she has been sent to spy on Ageev, possibly by Drozdenko. Her interest in Belorussian culture, history, and language, all of which would align her more closely with the anti-Soviet sentiments of Koveshko than with the pro-Soviet ones of Ageev, represent a challenge to the Soviet identity that the Bolsheviks wanted to impose on Belorussia. Study of such topics would also have been a dangerous pursuit immediately before the war and likely initially to have made her sympathetic toward the Germans. Her father's death four years earlier, in 1937, points to his being a victim of the purges. Explicit clarification is not forthcoming from Maria, possibly because it might make Ageev suspect her of harboring anti-Soviet sentiments and make him wary of her. It's worth noting that he maintains the fiction with her that he is Oleg, Baranovskaia's son; even after they have become sexually intimate, he does not tell her his proper name. If her aim is to deceive Ageev, then what better way than to tell him that she is pregnant, so inspiring in him a deeper love and trust, all the better to trick him into revealing information? Ageev has no way of knowing for certain whether she is pregnant.

Was she arrested with the explosives at the station, or did she go straight to the Polizai? The other disturbing piece of evidence, or rather lack of evidence, is the absence of any human remains in the quarry. Only three bodies were exhumed. The lack of a body, unfortunately for Ageev's state of mind, suggests something too horrible to contemplate: that the confrontation in front of Drozdenko was a carefully orchestrated sham. Psychologically the love story may well be Bykov's masterstroke, for by compelling the reader to consider with Ageev that Maria may well be a German agent, Bykov weakens or destroys for good the vicarious pleasure that we have derived from seeing their love unfold. We are no longer bystanders: The love story amid the gruesome war and all its suffering has embroiled us as well. Like Ageev, we desperately want to believe that this was real love, untainted by the Germans or the loathsome Polizai.

Fortunately, a less dreadful outcome—for both reader and Ageev—was that Maria, like Kisliakov, was broken during interrogation; that she was offered life for herself and her unborn child if she betrayed Ageev. If so, can we blame a young woman for behaving in such a way, for making a Sophie's choice? There may even be some kind of rough justice in her decision. What right did Ageev have to send her to the station? Drozdenko's taunting of Ageev in front of Maria is cruel but true: "You loaded her up with the explosives! Carry this to the station! Did you think where you were sending her to? You sent her to her death!"[98] Ageev and Maria's love is reminiscent of the illicit, brief love between Julia and Winston in George Orwell's 1984. Under the pressure and torture of the Thought Police, they betray one another. By the time his excavations are over, Ageev has accepted that he destroyed Maria. He has not found the past; it has come to him.

The Great Freeze (1993)

The Great Freeze concentrates on the life and fate of a communist partisan, Azevich, the lone survivor of his group who is trying to evade capture. Pursued by the Germans; weakened by an acute bout of pneumonia, which has just killed the group's commissar; and unable to trust the local population, his own people, Azevich wanders across the winter countryside, trying to find what shelter and succor he can. Terrain and weather both conspire against him. Bykov's story inspires the same atmosphere of menace as Angelo Jank's sinister winter painting, Der Tod im Baum (1897). In a number of flashbacks, which occur in dreams induced by bouts of fever, Azevich recalls collectivization and the attempt by the party activists, including himself, to destroy the old rural way of life in the 1930s. Published after the Soviet collapse, The Great Freeze is an explicit condemnation of collectivization and its corrupting effects.

The Azevich of the 1930s is a simple farm lad who is seduced by the promises of Communism. Appointed as the coach driver of a local communist official, Zaruba, he witnesses the attempts by the party to cajole and eventually to terrorize the peasants into accepting the collective farm. The arrests begin, and various "enemies of the people" start to disappear. The web of personal relationships, always important in rural areas, disintegrates or is poisoned by the demands of class war. Religious affiliation of any kind is regarded as backward, and those who speak out on behalf of Belorussia are seen as dangerous "nationalist elements," at odds with "the progressive morals of a new age."[99]

Among the party hopefuls, things are even worse. Joining a discussion group on Lenin, Azevich falls under the influence of Polina, a party activist who uses him for her own ends, specifically to acquire evidence that will undermine Zaruba's position (there is a strong suspicion that she is work-ing for the NKVD). She persuades him that Zaruba is a secret White Guard and counterrevolutionary. Azevich signs the *donos* that destroys Zaruba, thus beginning the process of his own moral compromise and making his own material contribution to the atmosphere of terror that appears to be running out of control: "Meanwhile the organs regularly wielded their knife among the regional leadership. People were taken in spring and sum-mer. Azevich had long since stopped racking his head as to why some per-son or other had been arrested. Like everyone around him, he already knew that anyone could be arrested, as long as some excuse could be found. No matter, people were arrested without any cause as well. This was like fate, like some sudden, foul illness."[100]

As his moral and intellectual corruption progresses, Azevich's mother and father sense that their son has joined the ranks of the enemy. He incurs bitter reproaches from his mother:

> The peasants are being driven into the collective farms and
> everything is being taken from the collective farm workers: bread,
> potatoes, seeds, equipment and horses. Oh, there will be famine, oh
> we'll be eating grass and chaff; what is going on! What are these
> bosses of yours; have they gone out of their minds or what? Is it
> really possible to treat their own people like this? What are we guilty
> of? Or are they monsters or what?[101]

Once in the party, Azevich fully participates in the systematic destruction of rural life, the symbol and substance of which is the village millstone. De-stroying millstones is far more than the state's preventing the independent milling and baking of bread, thus forcing dependence on the collective farm, it is above all an attack on the old customs of the village, the arrival of a brutal and ruthless modernity. That Azevich actively cooperates in this sa-tanic vandalism compromises him—he destroys the millstones in his own village—and chains him to the party, the real "enemy of the people."

The party and its enforcers, the partisans, as "enemies of Belorussia," are a major theme in Azevich's ordeal by cold. One chance encounter un-derlines the party's ruthlessness toward its own. Azevich meets an old woman and two orphaned children, their father shot by the partisans be-cause he interceded on behalf of a German. As the old woman recounts the death of the children's father, Azevich ponders how such things could happen:

Azevich sat in silence and thought. But what could he do; how could he console the children? Maybe what happened was necessary, but maybe not. How are we to understand who is guilty? Of course, it's the war that is to blame, the universal cruelty, hatred, and intransigence, which had torn people's souls. People shot, destroyed, and plundered; if only there was more blood, the enemy's and ours. But did this really all start only with the war; was the same thing not going on before the war? . . . We were waging war against one another long ago, with no little success. Not for nothing was it said: Strike your own so that the enemy was afraid. The enemy was in fact not that frightened, but our own people were smashed. . . . So as not to go out of one's mind, one should leave this matter alone. We can sort things out after the war.[102]

Repeatedly he is confronted with the hostility of the local population to himself and what he represents. An old man feeds him and then sets off to fetch the Polizai. In one scene set in a poorly lighted room—one of Bykov's favorite metaphors of uncertain loyalties and potential treachery—Voiteshonok, a former friend, compels a reluctant Azevich to face up to what he has done. Implied is the idea that those who join the Polizai, or in Voiteshonok's case are somewhat lukewarm to the partisans, are not necessarily the traitors; those such as Azevich, who turned against their own in the 1930s, have questions to answer as well. Azevich starts to realize this. His isolation from his own people is highlighted by the fact that he cannot return to any of the familiar haunts, even his own native village: "Well, what a wretched life, or the war, or cursed fate, when he could not go to where he wanted, where there was refuge and safety."[103] Azevich begins to understand that collectivization and the arrests are not some freak event but a human-made catastrophe, the deliberate work of people like himself who did the party's bidding, becoming the party's willing servant and agent.

Weather in this story is overwhelming. Nearly all recollections of past deeds are accompanied by comments on the severe cold (the *stuzha* of the title). Cold is associated with the secret police and the party, a coldness of heart that makes it possible to inflict starvation on one's fellows in the name of the new world. Under German occupation, cold is more than a metaphor of ideological pitilessness. It is a relentless physical presence that torments Azevich and punishes him for the past. After he leaves the woman and children, Azevich finds himself in the center of a snowstorm.

The elements seem to be attacking him. Rural life and submission to nature, on which he, as a party activist, declared war, seem to be seeking revenge or punishment for past sins:

> The freezing cold tore him to pieces; his body was racked by shivering. Apart from walking, there was no way to keep warm. . . . And barely had he thought that it would probably start to snow than it actually started to fall thick and heavy, as if it was scattered from a sack. The wind drove and drove the snow and sleet about, piling it up on the grass, crossing his back and across his shoulders. . . . Perhaps the best thing would be to find some shelter somewhere from this snowy maelstrom and sit it out and wait. If only he would come across some kind of shelter or pine thicket or tree. But nowhere in the area was there even a single tree. The wind and snow raged across the whole space. After the sleet, big lumps of snow fell from the sky, stuck to his shoulders, and settled on his head and in the folds of his greatcoat, quickly covering the ground. . . . Azevich realized that there was a precipice ahead. Overgrown with bushes, it lay across his path like a wide gap. What could he do? Which way should he go to get around it? And would it be possible to bypass it? Through the thick foam of snow, Azevich could just about make things out, and going slowly he climbed down into the gray mass of the precipice. Holding on to the slippery, cold branches, he had covered about ten or so paces when he fell, falling down the grassy slope almost to the very bottom on his buttocks. Here at the bottom it was somewhat quieter, although above him floods of snow were being carried about the whole area of the precipice. Azevich sat for a while, struggling for breath. He was no longer cold; it was stuffy, and he was drenched from sweat. The edges of his greatcoat and trousers were soaked. His heart beat furiously. He could not bear to stand; he wanted to close his eyes and sit in this gully, which was overgrown with hazel bushes, but the danger of falling asleep and freezing to death forced him to pull himself together and stand up. He had to get himself out of this snow trap.[104]

Embedded in *ovrag* (gully), *vrag*—"enemy" in Russian—alludes to past and present. The gully episode is an effective metaphor of his moral fall, ascent, and return to his people, his moral rehabilitation from Communism. Delirious, "hellishly cold,"[105] and aware that he might be dying, he realizes that he has wasted his life:

He was prepared to turn himself inside out in order to carry out any task such as would be demanded from a Bolshevik. And what was the result? Whose hand guided his diligence? Not his, that's for sure. . . . He lived according to another's conscience, according to alien laws; he used the resources of others. Life and people used him as they thought fit. He was a convenient instrument in the hands of others, weak-willed, always available for their use.[106]

Azevich is saved by a chance meeting with a woman who gives him bread and water. His receiving the bread in this way serves as a reminder of his past sins and in another way suggests forgiveness on the part of those against whom he has sinned. The woman's son, like Azevich, joined the party and did everything that was required of him, yet he was still arrested. The woman's forgiveness of Azevich—whom she recognizes from before the war—has a message for contemporary Belorussia (now Belarus), trying to rebuild itself after the Soviet era: that resurrection of the nation demands forgiveness, or at least not mindless vengeance.

Azevich's eventual survival and the death of the commissar at the start of *The Great Freeze* are symbolically linked as Bykov explores the impact of collectivization on Belorussia during the 1930s and the way in which it made collaboration with the German invader all the easier for those who hated the Bolsheviks. Those same Bolsheviks who pushed through the party's policies in the 1930s now find themselves outcasts under German occupation. In a sense they are the victims of policies they inflicted on their own people in the 1930s. The commissar's death from pneumonia and Azevich's descent into exhaustion and the threat of death can be seen as punishment for their moral and cultural betrayal of their native Belorussia. Azevich's path from physical prostration and near death to improved health is perhaps complete when at the end of the story he crosses himself. Having abandoned God as a communist, Azevich, the reborn Belorussian, as it were, rediscovers Him. He has cast off the incubus of godless Communism and returned to his people.

Conclusion

The fact that some of Bykov's work—*The Dead Feel No Pain, Sotnikov, The Sign of Misfortune,* and *The Quarry*—was published during the Soviet period would appear to be one of the more astonishing inconsistencies or failings of the censorship apparatus. The answer to this riddle may lie in the fact that, whereas *Life and Fate*, with its epic format and direct questioning of the Soviet state's legitimacy, terrified the censors and the KGB, Bykov's stories are particularist: They deal with individual renegades or heroes and apparently eschew the bigger picture found in *Life and Fate*. I say "apparently" because the cumulative effect of Bykov's work was just as threatening to Soviet orthodoxy. *Life and Fate* represented a full-scale frontal assault—clear and present ideological danger to the Soviet state—whereas Bykov's work could be likened to a campaign of partisan warfare, of indefatigable, relentless attrition. This effect reflects not just a determination on Bykov's part to get at the truth of what happened but also an insatiable curiosity about the reasons people behave as they do when "cruel are the times." In reading Bykov, we are in the realm of critical thresholds. In many of Bykov's stories, his characters are on a knife edge, to use the author's metaphor. What is the apparently infinitesimal measure of change that causes one man to become a traitor while the other remains loyal? And would these treacherous tendencies ever have been revealed had it not been for the war? The really bleak message that emerges from Bykov's fiction is that when it gets down to this sort of highly individual war, others cannot be trusted—you are on your own. The qualities needed to wage this kind of war—partisan warfare especially—are a complete reversal of the collectivist ethos of Soviet society.

The basic plot varies, but Bykov returns to the same questions—loyalty, honor, self-sacrifice, ostracism, collaboration, and fear—and examines them from many different standpoints. The themes never change, but the settings, the slight variations, always produce the unexpected, an often startling and unsettling insight into human behavior, as for example in *Sotnikov*, *The Obelisk*, and *The Wolf Pack*. The corpus of Bykov's writing from *The Third Flare* through *The Quarry* to *The Swamp* is a study of man as traitor, coward, martyr, patriot, and soldier in war and in peace. Flashbacks—a standard device of Bykov's stories—are intended to alert the reader to the fact that not all the moral dilemmas associated with war disappear when the guns fall silent, one of the things that made *The Dead Feel No Pain* so controversial and its author particularly uncongenial to the party in Belorussia. Comparing Bykov's work that was published during the Soviet era with that published after 1991, we are left with an unmistakable impression of honesty and steadfast commitment to the truth. *The Great Freeze* comes as no great surprise because we have read it all before. It is what we have come to expect. Bykov has remained true to his calling, remaining at his post to the end. His work represented an intolerable challenge to more conventional views about the war.

In the next chapter, I examine two attempts to counter the ideological insurgency initiated by Bykov and others.

4 The Imperium Ripostes: The Return of the Vozhd'

Who was the first person on earth who told a falsehood? . . . And wouldn't it be
interesting to know why he lied for the first time?
—Question asked by Stalin in Ivan Stadniuk, *War*

*Pioneered by Viktor Astaf'ev, Grigorii Baklanov, Vasil' Bykov, IUrii Bondarev, Anatolii
Kuznetsov, Viktor Nekrasov, Konstantin Simonov, and others, a clear split between dissenting
and party-sanctioned interpretations of the war had emerged by the end of the 1960s. Across a
whole range of themes, including Stalin's competence, Soviet readiness for war, the role of the
Special Sections, and collaboration, party orthodoxy faced cogent challenges. It would,
however, be a serious error to dismiss the official view of the war as one that commanded no
support or to say that where such support could be mustered, it was induced only by coercion or
self-interest. Two major novels, Ivan Stadniuk's War and Vladimir Bogomolov's In August
1944, which were published in the Brezhnev era, show that not all writers subscribed to the
post-Stalin revisionism of the war theme in literature. Stadniuk sets out to persuade us that
Stalin was after all a military genius, and Bogomolov would have us believe that the
counterintelligence and internal security operatives of SMERSH and the NKVD were the war's
unsung heroes.*

Stalin the Redeemer

Having convinced themselves that objective truth was a bourgeois fiction
designed to perpetuate the hegemony of the ruling class, Soviet Marxists
could reasonably argue that Soviet historians and writers who deviated from
the ideological norms of Soviet historiography and literary criticism, for example, by asserting that Stalin was responsible for the catastrophic defeats of
1941, were motivated not by any objective factors but by more sinister ambitions. They had succumbed to heresy and were guilty of ideological deviation-
ism and revisionism. In effect, they were assisting the enemies of the Soviet
Union in the propaganda war with the West, one of the main accusations that
was leveled at Nekrich. From the point of view of antirevisionism, Ivan
Stadniuk's long novel *Voina* (War, 1970–1980) and Vladimir Bogomolov's *V
avguste 1944 goda* (In August 1944, 1974) were landmarks in the battle against
widely read and popular dissenters such as Baklanov and Bykov.

War is in part a reaction to what Stadniuk believes to be the self-doubt
and gloomy introspection that have established an unhealthy niche in

Soviet-Russian war literature since 1953. Only a Marxist-Leninist analysis, he argues, can do justice to the theme: "The writer who combines his art with the universal, historic feat of arms of the Soviet people in the Great Patriotic War will be unable to attain those profound truths and to make serious general conclusions if he does not proceed from Marxist-Leninist historicism."[1]

Stadniuk's target is not just revisionist writers and historians, with what he perceives as their failure to get things right, but also the opportunists who now hope to make a name for themselves:

> This was a serious time. . . . Chroniclers, philosophers, and eloquent orators of all continents will focus their gaze on it. And among them will be those who will permit themselves to judge the events of those days without due understanding of their complex, tragic nature, who will view them from positions of a certain philosophical-historical Daltonism. And others, having shamefully forgotten about their former beliefs and public assertions, will start to seek out the pendulum of the "new" time. They will take the recurrent squeaking of a weather vane on someone else's rooftop for the voice of truth. . . . Looking at the past through the prism of their inflamed imagination, they will start to replace the truth by lies and their own ignorance, presenting the fruits of their labors as the insights of genius reconstructing an original and universal history.
>
> However, for the great good fortune of history, those forces that protect the truth are insurmountable.[2]

According to Stadniuk, Soviet strategy and the conduct of the war were fundamentally sound. Chaos, fear, and uncertainty there were; yet if we analyze the deep structure of the war, its causes and politics, insists Stadniuk, we cannot fail to see Stalin's farsighted policies at work, especially with regard to the sequence of events leading up to and extending immediately beyond 22 June 1941. Stadniuk portrays Stalin as a wise war leader, a master strategist, and a profound thinker. With Stalin at the helm, Stadniuk asserts, defeat is impossible and victory is inevitable. These assertions would not be out of place in Shpanov's military fantasy.

Now, to argue that War is merely the crude propaganda of a disgruntled neo-Stalinist would not do the author justice. The book certainly contains organized lying and propagandistic purpose against the backdrop of the Cold War and the attempts, encouraged by Brezhnev, to try to arrest and even to reverse certain historiographical trends. The primary purpose in reading and studying *War* lies not in any promise of encountering an epic war novel but rather in examining the mechanics of hagiography and myth-making and the often breathtakingly cynical distortions and omissions employed by Stadniuk to achieve these ends. Moreover, Stadniuk's obsessive reconstruction of the Soviet Union's war reveals something of the deep craving that all nations experience when confronted with catastrophe on the scale of the German invasion. *War*, contrary to the author's intent, underlines just how close the Soviet Union came to being defeated, a possibility that at the time of the novel's publication, some forty years after the German invasion, still exercised the minds of the Soviet leadership.

Stadniuk's own brand of orthodoxy is reflected in his pursuit of several clearly defined goals. The first, and perhaps the most important, as the title of this chapter suggests, is to overcome the attacks on Stalin and to claim a place for him in the pantheon of great military thinkers. In view of what happened on 22 June 1941 and the inexorable and observed buildup of German military power on the Soviet Union's borders prior to that fateful Sunday, this project involves a lot of omissions and amputations. Stadniuk, like his hero, is no reluctant surgeon, and the history of the mid–twentieth century endures some traumatic and invasive surgery from the author's saws, scalpels, and drills.

In attempting to salvage Stalin's reputation as a military leader, Stadniuk is obviously aware that some explanation must be found for what went so horrendously wrong. To exonerate Stalin, Stadniuk seeks the necessary scapegoats in the military, focusing especially on General Pavlov and his staff. Things would not have been as easy for the invading Germans, we are to believe, had Pavlov been up to his job. In blaming selected Soviet generals for the Red Army's failure to stand up to the Wehrmacht, Stadniuk almost completely ignores the purges of the army and their disastrous effects on doctrine, training, equipment, and morale. Stadniuk's short course in Soviet history also omits the role of the NKVD and the Special Sections in the army. His depiction of these organs, apart from their readiness to see traitors under every stone, bears little resemblance to what we find in the work of Astaf'ev, Baklanov, Grossman, and Bykov, and this startling difference is itself of great interest.

In resurrecting Stalin's reputation, Stadniuk has to explain away a formidable catalog of errors that would deter all but the most determined of hagiographers. First, he must show that Stalin was aware of the concentration of German military forces on the Soviet Union's borders and that he understood its full significance. Second, as a consequence of Stalin's understanding of what was at stake, he must account for the dazzling success of the German Blitzkrieg. Third, he must convince the reader that the failures of the Red Army in both the Russo-Finnish winter war of 1939–1940 and after 22 June 1941 could not be laid at Stalin's feet. Fourth, he must demonstrate that Stalin's fears about British intentions—the idea that the British were trying to play Germany off against the Soviet Union—were not the paranoid ravings of an isolated tyrant but had some substance. Fifth, we are to believe that by the time of the German invasion, all the "social and class contradictions" arising from the tsarist past and the transition to the Soviet state had been resolved to the point that the Germans were greeted by implacable resistance from the local population. If he were able to make a convincing case on all these points, and some related ones as well, Stadniuk would be in a strong position to claim that Bykov, Baklanov, and many others were at best defeatist and at worst the witting or unwitting tools of the West.

Two immediate problem areas for Stadniuk in the period leading up to the German invasion are the TASS communiqué of 13 June 1941, which was published in *Pravda* on 14 June 1941, and the Non-aggression Pact with Germany that was signed in 1939. Chumakov, a leading player in the novel, whom Stadniuk portrays as an exemplar of the very best in Soviet generalship, is given to understand the full significance of the TASS announcement by a fellow officer:

> The TASS announcement is an action of the state's line in foreign policy. You know the famous formula that war is a continuation of policy by other means. While there is no war, one thing is demanded of us military men: to strengthen our military might and to be ready, but . . . neither to give any sign of our misgivings, nor anything of our preparations. To avoid any conflicts whatever. Even an accidental shot on the border from our side could be viewed as provocation.[3]

Here Stadniuk starts to lay one of the foundations of his revisionist novel, namely, that the TASS communiqué promulgated a week before the German invasion was a carefully conceived response on the part of the Soviet Union to the German preparations for invasion. The enlistment of Clausewitz's formula is intended to show that everything is under control, that the Soviet Union talks and acts peacefully but prepares for any eventuality, that it talks softly but carries a big stick.

Added authority is imparted to this interpretation by the Soviet Union's own Clausewitz, the intellectual mentor to Chumakov and other senior Soviet military leaders, the professor of military history Nil Ignatovich Romanov, who, somewhat incongruously from a metaphorical standpoint, is dying. Romanov dismisses Hitler with the comforting remark that he is "the most remarkable charlatan of the twentieth century,"[4] an assessment that does not sit easily with the fact that huge areas of Western Europe were by then under German control. Romanov refers to the pact, arguing that since Germany is observing its terms, so must the Soviet Union. In fact, at this stage, the real villains of the piece, according to Romanov, are the British, who are trying to turn Germany against the Soviet Union. For the Soviet reader, denied any knowledge about the scale of German border violations, this claim is grossly misleading. It is an interesting question whether, in the context of the 1970s, the discussion of the pact with Germany is intended to justify détente with the West while also highlighting the dangers: The Soviet Union is committed to peace and détente, but naturally we do not trust the West, and vigilance—that pervasive standard of Soviet propaganda—is required.

In *War*, Romanov reinforces the dominant view of the pact as a measure of pure expediency intended to win time. At no stage was Stalin fooled by Hitler's real intentions. In a grossly propagandistic soliloquy, conveniently using the evasive and exculpatory first-person plural, Stalin, the straight talker who always lays his cards on the table, explains what went wrong:

> Yes, there was not enough time; we miscalculated with regard to the time scale—he said in such a tone, as if only now he had become convinced of this truth.—But, well, we weighed up literally everything, apparently, and demonstrated our sincerity in striving for peace. We had no intention of attacking anyone and pursued the well-known rule according to which sincerity in politics and diplomacy is the mother of truth and the sign of honest people . . . Nevertheless, we forgot for a while that they and we have a different set of scales, a different truth and different concept of honesty. That is where we miscalculated. But Hitler, having perfidiously violated the treaty, has decisively miscalculated in everything! . . . He will be destroyed! . . . Even if Hess did in actual fact secure some guarantees from Churchill, the fascist Führer had better not bank on that! . . . Not on that! Although it will be very difficult for us.[5]

We encounter the same kind of cynicism, located somewhere between breathtaking and Pythonesque, in Stalin's dealings with Ribbentrop. Stalin, while presumably looking Ribbentrop in the eye and barely able to suppress a desire to collapse into hysterical laughter, responds to the proposal from the German foreign minister that the preamble to the pact should include a statement about the new era of German-Soviet friendship: "The Soviet government would not honestly be able to assure the Soviet people of the fact that friendly relations existed with Germany if for the last six years the Nazi government had been emptying rubbish all over the Soviet government."[6]

Stadniuk also strives to present the most rapacious elements in the Molotov-Ribbentrop Pact, the annexations that extended the Soviet Union's western borders, as something quite just and even in accordance with the wishes of the people of those regions. Romanov talks, in passing, of the "reunification of the western regions of Ukraine and Belorussia with us" and "the reestablishment of Soviet power in the Baltic Republics."[7] Of Katyn there is no mention at all.

Returning to Stalin's plans, Romanov seeks once again to justify the Soviet Union's behavior toward Germany in the light of imminent aggression:

> But I suppose that Stalin and indeed the general staff are still hoping to restrain Hitler. They have adopted a position which is by no means new in the history of relations between hostile states: not to provide any *casus belli*. Obligations in accordance with the trade agreement are probably being carried out by us to the letter. We have even closed down our missions and embassies in those countries which Germany has seized. . . . We are taking all measures to ensure that everything stays calm on the borders, despite the provocations and despite the fact that on the other side of the border troops are being concentrated. The TASS communiqué . . . is the final attempt, it seems to me, to bring Hitler to his senses.[8]

Stalin, insists Romanov, is well aware of all this but realizes that were he to order a full-scale mobilization, war would follow. He refers to the work of the Prussian officer Heinrich von Bülow (1757–1807), who argued that the task of strategy was to achieve the goals of war without battle.

The various references to Clausewitz's *On War* that occur throughout *War* along with references to some of the military thinkers cited by Clausewitz, such as Bülow and Henry Lloyd (1720–1783), create an impression of depth in strategic thinking. They are, however, little more than name-dropping. Stadniuk's own title would seem to be deliberately chosen with Clausewitz in mind, the discussion and Soviet practice of war under the control of Stalin serving as a riposte to the "bourgeois scholar of war." Stadniuk's book is war, whereas Clausewitz, Stadniuk hints, just wrote about it. With regard to Clausewitz, Stadniuk is selective. He can cite the German author's underlining of the relationship between diplomacy and war, which Stadniuk uses to justify Stalin's incompetence and failure to take the necessary timely steps, but he ignores Clausewitz's thoughts on defense and attack in books 6 and 7, respectively, of *On War*, which were of the greatest relevance for the Soviet state in 1941.

Romanov's analysis of the Russo-Finnish winter war is also intended to demonstrate the hostile intent of the Western powers toward the Soviet Union. Romanov instructs us that the Finnish war was planned by the imperialists and aimed at the Soviet Union. The idea was to start a war with the Soviet Union and then get Germany to join in. According to Romanov, France and Britain made the decision to go to war against the Soviet Union on 19 December 1939. The plan was to attack the Soviet Union from the north and the south: in the north through Finland; in the south with divisions from Yugoslavia, Turkey, Romania, and Greece and air attacks carried out by the British from bases in the Middle East. Faced with this vast coalition of enemy forces, the Soviet high command, after the obligatory "profound analysis of the situation,"[9] concluded that a peace treaty had to be imposed on Finland as soon as possible by force of arms. The Soviet Union did achieve its aims, though at a very high cost and after an embarrassingly weak performance against the Finns. Romanov notes the poor performance of the Red Army but bypasses the demoralizing impact of the purges. He suggests that Trotsky's machinations, the purges, and the Allies' attempt to invade through Finland must all be seen as part of the grand anti-Soviet coalition. Regarding the purges, which had a marked impact on the Red Army's conduct of the war, the best that Shaposhnikov, one of Stalin's cronies with whom Romanov discusses the war, can do is refer to "the tragic mistakes."[10] Having reaffirmed his belief in Bukharin's and Trotsky's crimes against the Soviet state, Romanov, in a tortuous circumlocution, solemnly insists, "And the tragedy of the innocent begins with the guilt of the guilty. . . . However, the guilt of the guilty never justifies the tragedy of the innocent."[11] In other words, it is regrettable but unavoidable that innocent people were arrested and shot. The main thing is that the "guilty" were uncovered. No good is served by dwelling on the "errors" of the past. In the same vein, at the end of book 2, and with the military situation now desperate, Shaposhnikov magnanimously shows himself able to forget the past: "Should we not return several talented people to the army . . . those who were repressed or removed as a result of a misunderstanding?"[12]

Soviet propagandists, writers, and historians have made a great deal of Churchill's declared and well-known hostility to the Soviet state in order to argue that all the offers of help made by the British prime minister were intended to embroil the Soviet Union in a war with Germany. A great many ex-Soviet citizens—certainly not all of whom are admirers of Stalin—stubbornly persist in the belief that Churchill was conspiring with Hitler against the Soviet Union. Churchill's letter warning of hostile German intent is viewed with intense suspicion as an attempt on his part to provoke a war between Germany and the Soviet Union. Rudolf Hess's sudden dramatic flight to Britain on 10 May 1941 sent the conspiracy theorists into overdrive. Picking at this particular sore is irresistible for Stadniuk, both before and after the German invasion. As far as Stadniuk is concerned, Churchill is to blame for the Soviet Union's diplomatic ills. Churchill is perfidious Albion incarnate: "You see, it was precisely British duplicity, the inherited perfidy of that scion of the house of Marlborough—Winston Leonard Spencer Churchill—with its policy of setting Germany against the Soviet Union that created the murky atmosphere in Europe in which it was difficult to distinguish between imaginary and true dangers."[13]

In the politburo's discussion of Churchill's speech on the occasion of the German invasion, Stalin, looking suitably serious, one assumes, asks two questions, which apart from philosophical interest and his qualifications to provide the answers show that Stalin can enjoy a joke at his own expense: "Who was the first person on earth who told a falsehood? . . . And wouldn't it be interesting to know why he lied for the first time?"[14]

Stadniuk's attempt to stick much of the blame for the abysmal performance of the Red Army on General Pavlov is an especially scandalous and ugly example of his antirevisionism. The process of undermining Pavlov begins very early in *War*. It centers on Pavlov's grasp of doctrine and his alleged failures of leadership. Toward the end of book 2, two similar, ominous noises are made about General Kirponos, the commander of the South-West Front.

In an article that he sends to Shaposhnikov, Chumakov analyzes the success of the German armored units in France in 1940. The article is well received and leads to his being appointed to command a newly created mechanized corps. The comments on the creation of these units are relevant to what comes later in the attacks on Pavlov because they are part of the process by which Stadniuk incrementally builds the case for Pavlov's being dismissed and eventually shot. In an oblique reference to Pavlov, who served in Spain and was made a Hero of the Soviet Union, Chumakov notes that the Soviet mechanized formations predated the German success: "As early as 1932, such formations were created in the Red Army. But in 1939, whether from not looking hard enough at the peculiarities and the difficulties of the war in Spain, or whether for other reasons, it was decided that smaller, mobile armored formations would be easier to maneuver in battle."[15]

Chumakov's thoughts on the new formations and their earlier use are directly related to Pavlov. The two men knew each other in the Spanish Civil War, and Chumakov wonders whether Pavlov is worthy of his promotion and new appointment: "Has Pavlov, the military leader, emerged from Pavlov the bold commander? . . . And does the new general of the army understand that he is responsible for the combat-readiness of one of the most powerful advance guards of the Red Army, which functioned as a screen in front of the main entrances into the Soviet Union?"[16]

Later in the novel, as Pavlov's professional situation is in catastrophic decline, we learn in a flashback that Romanov has also expressed fears that Pavlov may have been promoted beyond his abilities. Returning to the concerns enunciated by Chumakov, Romanov holds Pavlov responsible for impeding the development of mobile armored formations: "But Pavlov, without conducting a comprehensive analysis of the experience of the battles in Spain in which he had taken part, started from nowhere to prove that the corps organization of tank troops was too awkward and, supported by the chairman of the commission, Marshal Kulikov, proposed that the tank corps be disbanded."[17]

That one of the Soviet Union's leading military theorists and a senior Soviet general both expressed doubts about Pavlov naturally serves Stadniuk's purposes nicely. Things, it is hinted, could be even worse. In a discussion of Pavlov's failings, we are told that he was captured by the Germans in World War I. In a world dominated by Stalinist paranoia, this could easily be interpreted to mean that Pavlov was a German agent and that his recommendation to disband the large tank formations on the eve of war was made at the behest of his German spymasters. Stadniuk at this stage in the novel, one suspects, is leading his Soviet readers in precisely that direction.

Aware that he has been tricked by the Germans, Stalin starts to seek scapegoats. His ire falls on Pavlov:

> Nobody knows anything definite about what is happening on the border! . . . Pavlov has no contact even with the headquarters of his armies! . . . The directive to the troops, he says, was late. . . . Why was it late? Why is the matter put in such a way that the directive was late? And what if we had not managed to issue a directive? Surely an army can be in a state of combat-readiness without a directive! . . . Surely I don't have to order my watch to tick! Surely I don't have to remind my heart that it mustn't stop! . . . We had to send the nannies—Marshals Shaposhnikov and Kulik—to Pavlov. . . . And you proposed that I made a radio broadcast! . . . I will have occasion to speak all right![18]

If, as Stalin suggests, a directive is not necessary for an army to be in a state of combat-readiness, then one must wonder why it was sent in the first place. Stalin's attack on what he perceives to be a lack of initiative on Pavlov's part is an attempt to hide the institutional and operational failings of the Red Army caused in large part by the decapitation of the army and the fear of showing initiative (contradictory warnings, for example, about not reacting to German provocation). It could be argued that failure to react to German violation of Soviet air space and border incidents actually encouraged the Germans. A robust and widely publicized diplomatic response probably would not have stopped the Germans from invading, but it would have steeled the Red Army and Soviet population to expect an invasion, thus ending the demoralizing uncertainty caused by orders not to incite the Germans and reducing the shock factor of the invasion. This uncertainty and lack of initiative cost the Red Army dear.[19] Stalin, as head of state, was to blame, not Pavlov. As the situation becomes worse, other Soviet generals chime in against Pavlov. Vatutin helpfully notes that "Pavlov and his headquarters have made a number of miscalculations."[20] But what counts for Stalin's reputation as war leader is what was happening in the crucial days before the Germans invaded. Stalin's response to Vatutin suggests that Pavlov is already doomed: "Your Pavlov will have to answer for this!—Stalin raised his voice for the first time. During the week before the war he assured me over the phone that he had personally gone to the border; that he had not come across any masses of German troops at all, and he called rumors of war provocations! And he cited his own reconnaissance, which he asserted was working very well!"[21]

Stalin's mention of "the radio broadcast" is also intended to be exculpatory because it was Molotov, not Stalin, who made the first announcement of the German invasion. Stadniuk disingenuously informs us that Molotov was authorized to make this address on behalf of the Soviet government, thus bypassing the obvious question of Stalin's failure to deliver the address as the Soviet leader. The evidence points to Stalin's complete shock and nervous prostration when informed of the German invasion. Perhaps despite his best intentions, or possibly because Stalin's cowardice when confronted with the news of the German invasion cannot be struck off the historical record, Stadniuk gives some idea of Stalin's state of mind and strives to create a grotesque justification for his hero: "From everything it was evident that Stalin was uneasy. He, it seemed, right up to the very last moment had not believed in what had happened. As if he was hoping for a miracle and was expecting a phone call from the general staff reporting that there was no war, that the Germans had initiated an unprecedented provocation and now it was necessary to settle a complicated, bloody conflict with its far-reaching consequences."[22]

Stalin was in no position to order the recall and execution of Pavlov and others. His failure to deliver this initial, crucial address must be seen as an act of cowardice. There are no obvious mitigating circumstances, and even if there were, Soviet soldiers were soon going to be executed for a lot less with absolutely no mercy being shown. In *War*, Pavlov is made to assume all the failings and myopia that should more properly be attributed to Stalin: It is Pavlov's fault that nobody took the threat of war seriously; it is Pavlov's fault that the necessary preparations were not made in time; and it is Pavlov's fault that so many aircraft were destroyed.[23] Stalin's insistence that diplomacy is based on facts, that facts are the sole basis for making decisions,[24] appears ludicrous when measured against his failure to face up to the *facts* of German border violations and troop concentrations.[25] The description of Pavlov's state of mind put forward by Stadniuk to explain these failings could easily be a description of Stalin:

> It was necessary to understand the harsh temper of this forty-four-year-old general of the army. In the indignation of his irascible and fragmentary judgments, he spared nobody: neither the leaders in the People's Commissariat for Defence, who so insistently warned of possible provocations, nor himself, who blindly believed that in the first place it was not generals who should anticipate war but

diplomats and politicians and who therefore in anticipation of war adopted a relaxed approach and did not do a great deal that he could have done; he did not forgive those commanders of the armies who never decisively sounded the alarm; or his staff officers who were sensitive to their superiors' opinions and who looked with disbelief at the army intelligence reports fraught with menace.[26]

Stalin's speech of 3 July 1941 provides Stadniuk with another opportunity to engage in some inventive editing. Extracts of the speech with Stadniuk's interpolations are designed to remove any stain of incompetence, above all that of trusting the Germans. The subsequent discussion of military theory is intended to promote not merely Stalin as a great military thinker but also as the legitimate heir of Lenin. "For a politician," notes Stadniuk, "the most important problems of the class struggle are precisely questions of war and peace."[27] Stadniuk says that Stalin has devoted his energies to studying the latest military doctrines and theories, the new equipment, and the cooperation of different arms and units. This leads to another swipe at the hapless Pavlov:

> Unfortunately, not all the transfers of military district commanders turned out to be successful. The thought of this gnawed away painfully at one's heart. How many times in these days had Stalin recalled Pavlov, struggling to understand all the more deeply the level of his own error when six months ago he had agreed to his appointment to the Minsk district command and tried to clarify the objective measure of Pavlov's own guilt for what had happened on the Western front. Even if one took into account that Pavlov was not to blame for the deficiencies in equipping and supplying the military district, now the measure of his guilt seemed to Stalin to be large.[28]

When Pavlov is eventually relieved of his command, Voroshilov informs him of the reasons for his dismissal: "You didn't do what you as the commander of the border district were obliged to do and what was not the government's responsibility! You ought to have assembled the troops and placed them in a state of battle-readiness on the basis of planned training. Why was the artillery on the training areas at such a time, and why did it have an issue of ammunition sufficient only for training purposes? And how could you allow your aircraft to be attacked?"[29]

Given Stalin's fears about upsetting the Germans, Soviet generals had very little room to maneuver. The idea that there were clearly demarcated areas of government (party) and army responsibility carries little weight in this context. Placing troops at heightened levels of battle-readiness was also very much at odds with not wanting to provoke the Germans. Blaming Pavlov for allowing his aircraft to be attacked is another attempt to exculpate Stalin. If war were imminent, then the sensible precaution would be to disperse aircraft and to deploy them further to the rear—operations that would have been noted by German air reconnaissance and thus hinted that the Soviet High Command suspected something was afoot. The failure to allow for such dispersal is another direct consequence arising from Stalin's fears of provoking the Germans. And to compound Pavlov's criminal negligence, Stalin, Stadniuk tells us, was intimately acquainted with the developments taking place in the Luftwaffe and was ensuring that the necessary countermeasures were taken by the Soviet Air Force. We are to understand that there was no shortage of good aircraft in place to meet the German threat. The problem was incompetent generals, such as Pavlov, who "wrecked" all the hard work.

Pavlov's fate is sealed with the arrival of Timoshenko's deputy, Lev Mekhlis, the cause of so much misery in the Red Army. In a speech to the assembled generals, he alludes to Pavlov: "However, comrades . . . I must in confidence say that at some time another bitter and harsh truth will also become known. The names of those people who are to blame will become known, and it is entirely possible that their base treachery is responsible for the fact that the Red Army has withdrawn so far from our borders. . . . These people, regardless of their former military ranks and services, will be condemned and severely punished!"[30]

As far as Stadniuk is concerned, Mekhlis's main flaws are a "suspicious nature and abrasiveness in dealing with people,"[31] an assessment that ignores the fact that Mekhlis represents the very essence of dual command and the crippling legacy of the purges. An example of Mekhlis's damaging supervigilance is his assertion that Pavlov is suspected of having made some kind of deal with the Germans. Timoshenko is so angered by this accusation that he telephones Stalin with this unconvincing defense of Pavlov: "Mekhlis suspects Pavlov and his former staff officers of being traitors, of having made some kind of a deal with the Germans. . . . I consider this to be rubbish, and Mekhlis demands that the investigator gets confessions from the arrested."[32] The whole exchange is a grossly cynical and artificial construction.

Presumably, Stadniuk would have his Soviet audience believe that people such as Mekhlis were actively prevented from interfering with due process—even in fact that there was such a thing, and that beatings and torture were not used to extract confessions from those arrested. Again, Mekhlis's interference in military decision-making and the way in which Stadniuk shows the response of soldiers to Mekhlis's efforts are designed to mislead. Initiative is essential, but it is initiative that party ideologues such as Mekhlis find suspicious, treating it almost as if it were one step removed from going over to the Germans. The obvious case in point is Colonel Malyshev's decision to blow up the two bridges over the Dnieper so as to deny their use to the advancing Germans (book 3, chapter 19). German saboteurs dressed as Soviet troops present forged orders transferring responsibility for bridge security to them. Malyshev sees through their trick, and the bridges are blown. The obvious inference to be drawn in the atmosphere of panic, confusion, and paranoia is that Malyshev is himself a German agent acting on orders: Summary execution rather than a time-consuming investigation to establish what actually happened would have been highly likely. Yet "common sense triumphs,"[33] somehow, and Malyshev is not punished.

There are several other incidents in *War* involving the Special Section and the NKVD that have little in common with the assessments of other Soviet writers and leave a reader with the impression that Stadniuk is simply passing over the darker sides of these agencies. Chumakov has a number of serious encounters with the Special Section, any one of which could be fatal, yet he breezes through unscathed. The first concerns the way he is treated after his unit is encircled by the Germans and manages to break out and get back to the Soviet lines, a familiar theme in Soviet war literature. He is welcomed back to the fold without any bother or taint of suspicion. In 1937, while he is in Spain, Chumakov is denounced by a Colonel Rukatov, who accuses him of engaging in counterrevolutionary activity. Chumakov learns of this from a *chekist*, and, remarkably, nothing happens to him. Stadniuk repeatedly fails to confront the real nature of 1937, implying that the purges were a minor event in the life of the army and that isolated incidents of officers' being denounced were the work of envious failures such as Rukatov rather than reflecting any fundamental problem in Stalin's Soviet Union or being orchestrated from above. Having himself been wrongly accused and survived, Chumakov is strangely unruffled by the assertions of a colleague regarding the purges: "But the main thing is that we succeeded in disarming a huge conspiracy. . . . You understand what threatened us? The

Red Army from top to bottom was in the hands of enemies of the people!"[34] Chumakov makes no real attempt to challenge Mikofin's conspiracy theories, yet he acknowledges that he could have vouched for one or two of the accused.[35] Chumakov, we learn, knew IAkir, who perished in the purges, a dangerous connection. He recalls a discussion he had with IAkir after he was appointed to the headquarters of the Ukrainian military district. IAkir asked him for his thoughts on the future war: whether operations would be fought not only on the territory of the enemy but also on Soviet territory. This seemingly innocuous question had major consequences in the lead-up to the 1937 purges of the military. An offensive strategy would support Trotsky's call for worldwide revolution, whereas a defensive strategy would be in line with Stalin's concept of socialism in one country. During the purges, an officer's stance on this question was a matter of life and death. Note, however, Stalin's pitiful excuse after the Germans have invaded that "Soviet military theory had not seriously concerned itself with the problems of major defensive battles,"[36] implying that the Red Army was designed only for offensive operations—an idea that is clearly at odds with the requirement not to "provoke" the Germans and, as already noted, is a serious failure. What kind of professional army, particularly one charged with the duty of defending a large land mass, fails to devote sufficient attention to large-scale defensive operations? The failure is surely Stalin's. Do these exchanges lend any support to the central thesis of The Icebreaker?

Links with any foreigners were especially dangerous, and in the course of the German advance, the chance capture of a German colonel places Chumakov in danger. In 1935, this colonel, a Sudeten German, was a member of the Czechoslovak military delegation that watched the Soviet summer exercises. After the colonel is badly injured in an accident, only a blood transfusion—the blood donated by Chumakov—saves his life. Here is sufficient material to build a case against Chumakov for being a German or Czechoslovak spy, which together with the later accusation of counterrevolutionary activity could have proved fatal. Reacting to the German's taunts that the Soviet Union is finished, Chumakov refers to Themistocles's speech in 489 B.C., just before the Battle of Salamis, an extract from which provides the epigraph for book 3. In an apparently hopeless situation, the Greeks prevailed. Given that Stadniuk argues repeatedly that war is a test of social-moral structures, the analogy with Greece's victory is somewhat embarrassing, for Greece was the preeminent free-trading, private property-owning state of the ancient world.[37]

Large-scale collaboration and mass desertion from Red Army units are conspicuously absent from *War*, though Stadniuk perhaps has them both in mind when he mentions Stalin's thoughts on fifth columns. Of all the countries attacked by Germany, only the Soviet Union, according to Stalin, has not produced a fifth column. Stalin's attempt to account for the absence of such a fifth column is pure wishful thinking and, as events were already showing, is disastrously wrong in view of what is happening in Belorussia, Ukraine, and the Baltic states: "By the start of the war, regardless of our quite recent bourgeois past, we had neither the social basis nor the forces capable of giving rise to a 'fifth column,' and this, taking into account the fact that the October Revolution took away the property of thousands and thousands of people, leaving them only the right to labor and live like everybody else."[38]

Turning on Mekhlis—as Stadniuk would have us believe—for putting forward the idea that Pavlov or any other Soviet officer could possibly work for the Germans, Stalin in another bout of cynicism ridicules the mere possibility of Pavlov's being a traitor to support his view that the Soviet Union is "traitor-free": "To suppose that Pavlov, a former peasant, who had become a general of the army and Hero of the Soviet Union, could do some kind of a deal with the fascists against the workers-peasants state!—Having stopped, Stalin only turned his head toward Mekhlis. His sidelong glance expressed indignation.—But you see, it was precisely you who dispatched the generals to Moscow from Smolensk to be put before a court with this accusation!"[39] Even as he is about to be executed, Pavlov is still useful to his master in the propaganda war. Moreover, Stalin's defense of Pavlov is something of a hostage to fortune, since Pavlov's background and rise in the military come very close to those of General Vlasov.

What Stadniuk attempts to do here, as elsewhere in *War*, is to justify the purges and the Great Terror ex post facto. The reason, according to Stalin, that there was no German-inspired fifth column in the Soviet Union, just monolithic unity, was that Stalin, as early as the mid-1930s, anticipating the German attack, prophylactically eliminated all the Trotskyist and counter-revolutionary groups, especially those in the armed forces.

Stalin's complacent attitude toward a fifth column notwithstanding, the German Abwehr under the command of Admiral Canaris successfully deployed a large Russian-speaking fifth column inside the Soviet Union. Stadniuk does not ignore these spies, but for the sake of consistency with Stalin's assertions about the absence of any homegrown fifth column in the

Soviet Union, he shows the German-trained saboteurs to be exiles, disaffected and bitter at having lost everything after 1917. The two main culprits are the Glinskii brothers, Nikolai and Vladimir, minor aristocrats who declared war on the Bolshevik state from its beginning. Nikolai may be said to represent capitalism. Surviving the Civil War, he does very well out of the New Economic Policy (NEP), managing to remain one step ahead of the secret police while acting as the banker of an underground counterrevolutionary group. By the time of the German invasion, we find him in Moscow, living under the name of Prokhorovich and, significantly, employed as the *dvornik* in the same apartment complex that houses Chumakov's wife and Romanov. Vladimir, who lives a life of grinding poverty in exile in France, is a far more interesting character. In desperation, he joins the French Foreign Legion. A chance meeting with a German journalist on his discharge from the legion in 1935 leads to his being recruited by the German Abwehr. The pages devoted by Stadniuk to Glinskii's life in exile—the poverty, the loss of status and property, the susceptibility to the ideas of Nietzsche and Hitler—are perhaps designed to offer a social, psychological profile, by no means outrageous, of the type of individual who was attracted to the Nazis. Vladimir's German benefactors now provide a focus for his anti-Sovietism and a sense of purpose in an otherwise aimless existence. They have effectively harnessed his deep resentments for their own ends.

Even allowing for the dire affects of Soviet censorship, I suspect that there must have been many Soviet readers, with firsthand experiences of the war, who reacted with disgust upon reading *War*. The problem is not just Stadniuk's combination of cynicism and apparent sincerity but also the impossibility of mounting any kind of critical challenge when the novel was published. Writers who for whatever reasons omit, distort, or lie about the experiences of such a terrible war do not serve the interests of the present or the memory of the fallen. With this in mind, the most damning judgment on *War* can be found in the novel itself, in two extracts from Romanov's notebooks: "Who does not know the truth of his past is not worthy of the future"[40] and "Falsehood about a nation's heroic past gives rise to a lack of faith in the present. . . . Such falsehood takes the shine off the most glorious feats of the present and insults the feelings of the people."[41]

The *Osobist* as Hero

Among students of Russian literature in the West, Vladimir Bogomolov is best known as the author of two *povesti, Ivan* (1957) and *Zosia* (1965).[42]

Less well known—in fact, almost entirely ignored in the West—is his much longer and far more orthodox In August 1944,[43] a fast-moving tale of a SMERSH counterintelligence team in pursuit of German agents operating behind Soviet lines. Two English-language surveys of Soviet Russian war literature published in the 1980s completely ignore the novel,[44] and two major reference works of Russian literature do not include any essays on Bogomolov, even on the better-known shorter works, Zosia and Ivan.[45]

Two factors might explain this neglect or indifference. The first is a general lack of interest in the Soviet Russian war novel per se and the assumption that the orthodox, even neo-Stalinist, position adopted by Bogomolov in his novel renders In August 1944 ipso facto unreadable or unworthy of serious study. A second consideration probably has more to do with the date of publication: 1974 was the year when Solzhenitsyn's position in the Soviet Union, as both a writer and an anticommunist prophet, was rapidly becoming untenable, and his expulsion that same year tended to dominate Western interest in the Soviet literary world. As the activities of dissidents gained greater importance, particularly after the signing of the Final Act of the Helsinki Accords on Security and Cooperation in Europe in 1975, there was little interest in more orthodox writers who, rightly or wrongly, were perceived as apologists for the Communist Party. One interesting point noted by Hedrick Smith is that in the Soviet Union of the 1970s, the spy enjoyed cult status in the state media and was regarded as a national hero, whereas in the West, especially in the United States, considerable ill feeling was directed against the Central Intelligence Agency (CIA).[46]

Unusually for a Soviet writer adopting an ideologically orthodox position, Bogomolov's fictional account of the counterintelligence war is both entertaining and convincing. Consequently it is an effective challenge to much of the very best in Soviet Russian war literature. Bogomolov achieves this effect by virtue of his mastery of counterintelligence jargon and detail, by selective omissions, and by narrative technique. In August 1944 is certainly worth reading and studying. It is a fast-moving and exciting spy and war novel in its own right. What starts out as a routine search for German agents rapidly escalates into a massive manhunt for an especially dangerous and daring German spy team, code name Neman, that, if successful, will compromise the planning for and success of a major Soviet offensive and Stalin's plans for the final attack on Germany. Stalin takes control, and all the counterintelligence resources of the state are deployed against the German agents. The manner in which Bogomolov blends a mixture of fact, fiction, and omission results in a powerful challenge to a large body of Soviet-Russian war literature written before and after *In August 1944*, according to which the *osobist*, SMERSH, and NKVD operatives, as well as the commissars, were enemies of ordinary soldiers because of their preoccupation with pursuing cruel ideological vendettas rather than fighting the Germans. Worse still, their military expertise and authority were inflated to the detriment of the professional military in order to enhance the status of the party.

Commissars and other representatives of these organs are portrayed with varying degrees of criticism in, for example, Vasilii Grossman's *Narod bessmerten* (The People Are Immortal, 1942), *For a Just Cause*, and *Life and Fate*; Emmanuil Kazakevich's *Star*; Grigorii Baklanov's *July 1941*; and Vasil' Bykov's *The Dead Feel No Pain*. In addition to Georgii Vladimov's *The General and His Army*, the other major war novels of the 1990s—Viktor Astaf'ev's *The Damned and the Dead*, Vasil' Bykov's *The Great Freeze*, and Vladimir But's *Heads—Tails*—all contain highly critical portrayals of *smershovtsy* and NKVD men. *The General and His Army* is of particular relevance because Vladimov's sympathetic portrayal of Andrei Vlasov and a particularly savage portrayal of a SMERSH operative, as well as many other related themes, seem to be a calculated response to Bogomolov's *In August 1944* (I examine Vladimov's novel in chapter 7).

In what appears to be a deliberate echo of Churchill's words uttered on 20 August 1940 at the height of the Battle of Britain—"Never in the field of human conflict was so much owed by so many to so few"—Bogomolov dedicates his novel "to the few to whom the many are indebted." The men from SMERSH, the Soviet few, were all that stood between Soviet Russia and defeat, or so Bogomolov would have us believe. His SMERSH officers, Alekhin, Tamantsev, and Blinov, are part of an "operational-investigative group." Alekhin, the group's leader, is the specialist in interrogation, the one who through relentless questioning can break down even the best cover story. Tamantsev is the exemplary SMERSH agent, the 007 of the trio: He is the specialist in shooting on the move and unarmed combat, the agent who can capture an armed enemy without killing him. Blinov is the novice officer under instruction. Radio signals emanating from a clandestine transmitter have been intercepted, and the team is trying to track down the location of the transmission. The search is played out in the dense forests and ravines of Belorussia and Western Ukraine in August 1944.

Although the main enemy is still, at this stage of the war, the German army, conducting a fighting retreat westward, various groups of anticommunist nationalists and others hostile to Communism are emerging as the new threat to Soviet power. In the early stages of the investigation, one Kazimir Pavlovskii, the son of a German, emerges as a prime suspect. His father was arrested as a *Volksdeutsche*, for betrayal of the motherland and for signing the *Volksliste*.[47] Given the way in which the non-Russian ethnic groups were treated by Stalin, Alekhin's statement that he cannot see what exactly is criminal in the father's behavior is disingenuous, to say the least. The record of the interrogation includes questions about those who participated in the mass shootings of Soviet prisoners of war, yet there is no mention by Bogomolov of the way in which Soviet prisoners of war were treated by their own side. For Soviet soldiers, the mere fact of having experienced *okruzhenie* or having been a prisoner of war was regarded as proof of treachery. In the same report, it is revealed that Pavlovskii's mother was convicted of anti-Soviet activity. Revealing this background information through the medium of an official report relieves Bogomolov of the dangerous ideological task—in 1974—of examining Pavlovskii's motives for becoming a German agent in the first place, and thus of discussing the way that the Soviet state treated national minorities.

The motives of the *Volksdeutsche* could plausibly be explained by their commitment to a pan-German empire in the East in which they could expect to be prime beneficiaries. Less easy to explain—certainly in 1974— would be why Soviet citizens fought for the Germans. In one of his searches, Tamantsev comes across the body of woman in a uniform bearing the letters ROA, the acronym of the Russian Liberation Army (Russkaia Osvoboditel'naia Armiia). In the text, the meaning of the acronym is not explained, which might be due to squeamishness about the ideological implications of a Russian army of liberation, specifically the notion of "liberation"—from whom or what?—or to a tacit recognition that many Soviet readers would know the significance of the ROA despite the official blackout. In a skillful propagandistic touch that identifies the German SS with the ROA—and thus with Vlasov—we are told that the woman is wearing SS-issue trousers and that two other bodies are those of SS men.

Detail on the nationalist threat comes from two sources: Alekhin and his men, as they pursue their quarry, and the insertion into the narrative of situation reports (sitreps), in effect twenty-one separate chapters out of a total of ninety-nine. Bogomolov uses sitreps, summaries, and intelligence briefings, which we are given to understand are based on authentic but bowdlerized originals, to fill in background detail and to retard or to accelerate the narrative as well as to create excitement and to arouse interest. The first sitrep is written in the aftermath of the immediate return of the Red Army to Belorussia after more than three years of German occupation. The sitrep draws attention to the presence of large numbers of traitors and the underground nationalist movements, all of which are hostile to the Soviet Union. Isolated groups of German stragglers are also seen as a threat because they have been instructed by their leaders to stay behind the lines and report Soviet troop movements back to the German high command. Of great interest for the theme of the novel is the detail given by Bogomolov on what are undoubtedly regarded as the main enemy, the internal ideological opponents of the regime. These are the Ukrainian Insurgent Army (Ukrainska Povstanska Armia, or UPA), Lithuanian nationalists, and Polish resistance groups supplied by London, especially the Armia Kraiova (AK). The sitrep notes regarding the latter:

> As has been established, the Polish underground has been given a directive by the London center to conduct subversive activities in the rear echelons of the Red Army. For these purposes, orders have been given to maintain a large part of the detachments, weapons, and radio transmitters and receivers illegally. In June of this year, Colonel Fieldorf, who visited the Vilenskii and Novogrudskii districts, issued specific instructions while there. With the arrival of the Red Army, the following orders were to be carried out: (a) to undermine all the measures taken by the military and civilian authorities; (b) to sabotage lines of communications at the front and to implement terrorist attacks on Soviet military personnel, local officials and activists; (c) to collect and pass on by code to General Bor-Komorowski and directly to London intelligence information about the Red Army and the situation in the rear.[48]

In a footnote, another suggestion that we are dealing with official documents, Bogomolov describes the AK as follows:

> Armia Kraiova (AK) is an armed, underground organization of the Polish émigré government in London, operating on the territories of Poland, southern Lithuania, and the western districts of Ukraine and Belorussia. In 1944–1945, acting on orders of the London center, the AK conducted underground work in the Soviet rear areas. They killed officers and soldiers of the Red Army and Soviet officials, carried out espionage and sabotage, and robbed the civilian population. Members of the AK frequently wore the uniforms of the Red Army.[49]

The sitrep provides details of incidents in which Soviet troops and officers have been killed by members of these nationalist groups in ambushes and explosions. Nor are the attacks confined to the soldiers of the Red Army. The infrastructure of the communist administration is also under attack, with civilian communist officials the target of assassination and intimidation. The author's intention is no doubt to arouse anger in the Soviet reader toward the nationalists and separatists who are murdering their liberators. It is implied that the nationalists and separatists are Nazi sympathizers, and no account is given of the bitter struggle waged by, for example, the Ukrainian Insurgent Army against the German occupiers.[50] Conspicuously absent from this account—one of many omissions—is an explanation of why there is such opposition to the Red Army in the first place. In conclusions that closely match Grossman's in *Life and Fate*, Yuriy Tys-Krokhhmaliuk provides the answer: "The Nazis and the Russians were equally guilty in pillaging and razing the Ukrainian villages. They competed in terror; each diligently studied the methods of the other in endeavoring to perfect genocide."[51]

Bogomolov's interposition of operational reports and sitreps in the narrative is in fact a staple of the genre that has been used by Western thriller writers such as Frederick Forsyth, Tom Clancy, and Ian Fleming with great effect. Also like Forsyth and other spy novelists, Bogomolov goes into painstaking technical detail regarding the tools, jargon, and tradecraft of espionage and counterespionage, all of which serve to enhance the story's verisimilitude, suggesting that it is a biographical rather than a fictional account—even, perhaps, that it was written with the express approval and encouragement of the KGB. For example, on searching the probable site used by enemy agents to send a radio message back to base, Tamantsev finds the remnants of a cucumber. Alekhin, it turns out, was an agronomist before joining SMERSH and concludes that this type of cucumber is not native to the area. Although this conclusion reflects well on the extreme professionalism of the SMERSH trio, it may also be seen as a diversionary ploy by Bogomolov, a compensatory mechanism whereby he, overwhelming the reader with forensic detail, manages to plug lacunae in the historical and political background and thus obviate any discussion of Soviet strategic motives. Manipulated in this way, the reader becomes a participant (or perhaps victim) in the game of deception and counterdeception, a fellow sojourner in a treacherous landscape. Counterintelligence jargon, which Bogomolov uses liberally throughout *In August 1944*, serves the same purpose as the plethora of forensic detail. The following examples can be noted: chistil'shchik (special agent of a counterintelligence unit), volkodav (a special agent, or spycatcher, who is able to take alive a well-trained and armed enemy agent who is resisting arrest), parsh (enemy parachutist-agent, or an enemy able to put up strong resistance), zelenaia tropa (an attempt to cross the lines at an interunit boundary), streliat' po-makedonski (shooting on the move with two pistols at a moving target, one of Tamantsev's specialties), kachat' na kosvennykh (indirect questions designed to reveal inconsistencies), predel'nyi rezhim (a system of heightened security checks in an emergency situation), flanery (enemy agents in the uniform of the Red Army who move from place to place reporting troop movements), marshrutniki (agents who move about on trains), and moment istiny (the moment of truth, defined by Bogomolov as "the moment when information received from a captured agent furthers the rounding up of the group and the completion of the case").[52] These specialist terms, real or concocted by the author, invite the reader to enter the exclusive world of counterintelligence and to identify with Bogomolov's SMERSH heroes.[53]

In the fiction of Astaf'ev, Baklanov, Grossman, and Vladimov, the 1941 retreat is shown as being exacerbated by the interference of political commissars in military decision-making. Hysteria about German agents leads to innocent soldiers' being arbitrarily executed as spies and suspected deserters. Through the eyes of Alekhin and Tamantsev, Bogomolov uses flashbacks in an attempt to show that fears about the penetration of German agents were real, that harsh measures were justified, and by implication that summary executions were necessary to restore order.

Tamantsev recalls in the first days of the war being part of a team that intercepted German agents whose documents appeared to be in perfect order. In another incident, a grief-stricken old woman wandering around in the area of Smolensk station is not quite what she seems: She turns out to be a German spy reporting troop movements. After she is captured, Alekhin reports, "I saw her a week later in the course of the investigation: in complete control of herself, a cold glance, lips tightly shut, a proud bearing. Her entire appearance exuded an air of contempt and hatred. She categorically refused to answer any questions, remaining silent to the end. Nevertheless, her guilt was established by the evidence of the radio operator and personal belongings. She was condemned and executed."[54]

These incidents are designed to elicit sympathy, to show the border guards as heroes, as vigilant defenders of the motherland. Significantly,

Alekhin describes the spy as a "Russified German woman,"[55] implying that Russians of German origin are especially suspect. Stalin certainly thought so. Volga Germans, along with other nationalities—Ingush, Crimean Tatars, Balkars, Karachai, and Kalmyks—were deported with huge loss of life between November 1943 and June 1944. In another blind spot, Alekhin, trying to isolate potential German agents in Grodno and Belostok, notes that one inhabitant managed to escape from Treblinka (one of the worst of the Nazi death camps). Bogomolov conspicuously refrains from mentioning anything about the extermination of Jews or that having been captured by the Germans was, should one manage to escape, the cause of a soldier's being regarded with profound suspicion.

In attempting to restore the reputation of SMERSH operatives, Bogomolov tries to show that much of the soldiers' hostility toward SMERSH is based on ignorance. SMERSH operatives work in the land of mirrors: Things are never what they seem, and only the agents' training and dedication allow them to see through the enemy's deceptions. Captain Anikushin, the SMERSH team's army liaison officer, betrays, Bogomolov suggests, all the standard prejudices of the soldier: "The captain did not like being instructed, in the same way that he did not like the word 'vigilance.' Moreover, he was completely convinced, like the majority of people, that were he ever in his life to meet a saboteur or spy, he would recognize one immediately."[56] "The captain did not like these *osobisty*. He considered them privileged idlers, with an inflated opinion of themselves. 'They wander about behind our lines'—he was certain—'they fancied themselves heroes.'"[57]

Anikushin's inexperience is exposed by Bogomolov as the three German agents, all possessing impeccable documentation, are apprehended and interrogated by Alekhin. Anikushin identifies with the officers, believing that they are who they say they are and that their treatment is yet another example of the heavy-handed SMERSH at work. At this very moment, a recollection from the summer of 1942 intrudes. His unit received a signal to abandon its position and heavy equipment and retreat to the Volga. Anikushin refused to obey the order and stayed put. His fellow officer retreated. Later it turned out that the order had been given by a Soviet officer who had been captured and persuaded to work for the Germans. Those Soviet officers who obeyed the false order were shot under the provisions of Stalin's "not a step backward" order (Order № 227). Anikushin realizes that "this episode particularly confirmed to him the necessity of never being just quiet, of being an unthinking participant, but of acting in such complicated situations as

dictated by his conscience and conviction."[58] On the face of things, his behavior and sentiments appear laudable. The trouble is that such a display of
initiative was precisely the fault line between the class of ideological functionaries—SMERSH, the NKVD, and commissars—and the professional
soldier that caused so many lives to be thrown away. In the situation just described, the decision to stay or to retreat (as ordered over the radio) was a
gamble either way. There can hardly be any justification for shooting soldiers merely because their officers fell for a *ruse de guerre*. And the decision
whether to retreat—as frequently dictated by the speed of the German advance—or to stay put was one to be made by soldiers, not political commissars. On this occasion, Anikushin won the draw.

Anikushin recalls another incident involving the *osobisty*. In the middle
of a desperate battle, three soldiers were discovered to be missing. As a
result, he was subjected to prolonged interrogation, under suspicion that
he had in some unspecified way colluded with the absent soldiers. Again,
as with the false radio signal, the reader's sympathies are with Anikushin,
but not, I suggest, with Bogomolov's disingenuous attempt to show that
this sort of pointless, harassing interrogation is somehow justified. The
basis for suspecting these soldiers was the fact that they had, in the Soviet
euphemism, "lived on territory temporarily occupied by the enemy."[59] In
other words, there was no evidence at all that they had collaborated with
the Germans. They, like millions of Soviet citizens abandoned to their
fate by the Red Army, were victims of circumstances completely beyond
their control. In attempting to persuade the reader that Anikushin is a
loyal Soviet officer and that the attentions of the *osobisty* are unjustified,
Bogomolov merely draws attention to the hysterical paranoia of the *osobisty* and the paranoia of Soviet society in general, whether in war or
peace: "But he, Anikushin, had never lived in German-occupied territory.
And he had not spent a single hour in captivity or encirclement. And he
had no repressed relatives either here or abroad, even distant ones. . . .
Regarding all the paragraphs of all the forms, his life was beyond reproach, as clean as glass."[60] The obvious fear that is associated with having been in German captivity or encirclement makes a mockery of one of
the official documents, cited by Bogomolov, according to which the organs are prepared to forgive traitors or informers if they assist in the capture of the German spy team.

As the interrogation of the suspects progresses, Anikushin becomes
ever more indignant at the way they are handled:

And just look at these insolent, unpunishable people, so sure of the fact that they are above the law, who on some arbitrary whim have searched his brothers in arms, frontline soldiers who in a week or two will have to shed their blood in defence of the motherland.

Indeed, just who is this Alekhin?! Some careerist opportunist or other. Probably from the sticks, maybe with five, maximum seven, classes behind him. He ended up with the *osobisty* on the basis of clean paperwork. Picked up a few words of the bosses, city expressions and military terms, and thinks he can do anything he likes.[61]

Soviet readers, especially former soldiers, perhaps despite Bogomolov's best intentions, would, one suspects, have readily agreed with Anikushin. Certainly the weight of evidence recorded in Soviet-Russian war literature (and the history of the prewar and postwar periods) leads to the view that the *osobisty* behaved precisely in the way described by the indignant Anikushin and that many of the *osobisty* were, as Anikushin characterizes them, ruthless individuals looking for the main chance. Anikushin's intention to write to Stalin to protest the behavior of the *osobisty* is another of Bogomolov's jokes at the expense of the army officer, and indeed of the many naive Soviet citizens who during the Terror wrote to Stalin in the belief that he knew nothing, that his unscrupulous subordinates were acting without his knowledge. Moreover, in his attempt to set Anikushin up for a fall (those stopped are, of course, enemy agents, as only the professional vigilance of the *osobisty* could detect), Bogomolov ends up parodying and thus demythologizing—unwittingly, perhaps—the standard liturgy of Soviet wartime propaganda: "brothers in arms," "shedding their blood," and "defense of the motherland." These three suspects, as we eventually find out, are not Anikushin's brothers in arms, but then neither were the NKVD detachments who on the slightest suspicion—and suspicion was enough—arbitrarily shot down retreating Soviet soldiers in 1941 and 1942. In the subsequent shootout with the German agents, Anikushin is killed—Bogomolov, we feel, relishes killing him off—and the expertise of Alekhin's team is vindicated.

The SMERSH trio's relationship to the army officer, Anikushin, parallels the grander relationship between Stalin and the Soviet high command. In chapter 56, titled "At the HQ of the Supreme Commander," Bogomolov examines Stalin's military thinking and the importance of counterintelligence for the survival of the Soviet state. Though by no means a slavish encomium of Stalin, it occasionally borders on hagiography. Bogomolov attempts to restore Stalin's reputation, and it is here that some of the most serious historical omissions can be noted. This chapter explains the essence of the operations to round up and liquidate the various operational units of German spies behind the Soviet lines.

The alarm caused by the presence of German agents must be understood in the light of Hitler's surprise attack on the Soviet Union. Stalin, argues Bogomolov, was "monstrously deceived" by his intuition[62] in June 1941, and since that time Stalin has paid special attention to the need to deceive the Germans about the time and place of major operations. Bogomolov carefully avoids the word used by Stalin in his address of 3 July 1941 to describe Hitler's breaking faith, *verolomnyi*, for this act of "faith-breaking" merely underlines Stalin's failure to see through Hitler's false promises. Bogomolov's attempt to persuade us that Stalin was the supreme exponent of counterintelligence does not succeed, mainly because it rather clumsily bypasses the fact that there was plenty of intelligence regarding Hitler's intentions, which Stalin ignored. If the hapless Anikushin discovers only too late that "things are not what they seem," the same is true of Stalin. For Stalin, the moment of truth is 22 June 1941, when the real nature of Hitler's intentions is finally revealed.[63] And at the tactical level of operations, even down to the changing, shifting loyalties of Soviet citizens living under German occupation, the same is true. Truth—that is, where their real loyalties lie—is a matter of life and death. The deceivers are those who survive. The expert liar, the dissembler and deceiver, is he who recognizes the truth. The apparent truth-teller is potentially the expert liar. Bogomolov notes with approval Churchill's remark to Stalin made during the Teheran conference that "truth has to be protected by lies."[64]

Deceived by Hitler, Stalin accordingly formulates three essential principles associated with the element of surprise: (1) Surprise catches the enemy unprepared so that his troops are unfavorably disposed to deal with the blow; (2) surprise compels the enemy to react to the attacker's plan, thus losing the initiative; and (3) surprise weakens the faith and confidence of the defending troops in their high command. However, this very reaction of Stalin's raises questions that Bogomolov is reluctant to address. What was the nature of Hitler's "monstrous deception"? Why did Stalin trust Hitler? The answer is the Molotov-Ribbentrop Non-aggression Pact, which prepared the way for Poland to be invaded and the Baltic states to be incorporated into the Soviet Union.

All three consequences of the element of surprise cited by Stalin were, of course, achieved by the German high command. Stalin refused to act on sound intelligence that a German attack was impending. The Germans achieved complete tactical surprise along the entire front, and the Soviet army was infected by an almost catastrophic loss of faith in itself as it was forced to retreat. Another key omission on Bogomolov's part, as in Stadniuk's novel, is his failure to discuss the consequences of the purges on the Red Army's ability to wage modern war. Again, Bogomolov says nothing of Stalin's responsibility for this state of affairs, his nervous collapse when told of the German attack, or his failure to address the Soviet people as soon as the invasion started. Soviet officers were shot for a lot less.

As a result of the brutal lessons inflicted by the Germans, Stalin comes to the following conclusion:

> From this it follows that the successful outcome of any operation depends to a considerable degree on secrecy and deception measures. From this it follows that a victory which is achieved without surprise, at the expense of numerical superiority, does not bear the stamp of a commander's talent and is achieved at much greater cost. From this it follows that it is necessary at all costs to hide one's intentions, to create a threat simultaneously at several places, thereby compelling the enemy to disperse his forces. From this it follows that it is necessary to make a show of preparing for an offensive in one place and making secret preparations for one in another place, while trying in all situations to catch the enemy unawares.[65]

The plodding and repetitive use of logical transitions ("from this it follows"), intended no doubt to show Stalin's superior strategic reasoning, draws attention to the state of the military art in the Soviet Union. Did it really take three million German soldiers, thousands of tanks, and the total destruction of the Soviet Air Force to bring home to Stalin the potency of the factor of surprise on 22 June 1941? Far from rescuing Stalin's military reputation, Bogomolov merely underlines his slowness to learn, the clumsy nature of Soviet ideological control of the army, and the dreadful cost in Soviet lives. We get an altogether more brutal—and accurate—assessment of Stalin's failure to apprehend the nature and scale of the Nazi threat from Churchill, whose comments also serve as an apposite response to Stadniuk's machinations:

War is mainly a catalogue of blunders, but it may be doubted whether any mistake in history has equalled that of which Stalin and the Communist chiefs were guilty when they cast away all possibilities in the Balkans and supinely waited, or were incapable of realising, the fearful onslaught which impended upon Russia. We have hitherto rated them as selfish calculators. In this period they were proved simpletons as well. The force, the mass, the bravery and endurance of Mother Russia had still to be thrown into the scales. But so far as strategy, policy, foresight, competence are arbiters, Stalin and his commissars showed themselves at this moment the most completely outwitted bunglers of the Second World War.[66]

Looming large in all Stalin's strategic planning at this stage of the war—August 1944—is the Polish question. As becomes clear from operational reports, the search for the German spy team, the Polish question, and especially the Warsaw uprising are intimately linked. In fact, the Polish question emerges in the early stages of Alekhin's investigation. The trail leads to a Polish woman in whose house two prime suspects have stayed. Alekhin, in order to secure her full cooperation, has to tell her something of his suspicions. Having ascertained that her husband died fighting against the Germans in 1939, Alekhin tries to win her over by suggesting that Poland and the Soviet Union have a common cause against the Germans. Up to a point, this statement is true, though it conveniently ignores the Soviet-German partition of Poland made possible by the Molotov-Ribbentrop Pact. With the Germans retreating, the Poles now aspire to regain their independence from both Germany and the Soviet Union. For a majority of Poles, the new enemy is now the Soviet Union. The fact that a photograph of Marshal Pilsudski, the great Polish patriot, adorns the wall points to the woman's loyalties.[67] Having surreptitiously noted the photograph, Alekhin nevertheless adopts a sympathetic pose that is purely tactical: "What could I say to her? . . . I knew that there was an uprising in Warsaw, that it had been started by the AK, but that thousands of Poles were fighting. Already in its third week there were ferocious battles in the city. People who were more or less unarmed were resisting German tanks, planes, and artillery. Thousands were dying every day."[68]

Unsaid is the fact that a large Soviet army located outside Warsaw under the command of Marshal Rokossovskii refused to come to the aid of the Polish uprising. Operational documents—dated 15 August 1944—cited by

Bogomolov provide details of an AK radio team surrounded by Soviet counterintelligence. Bogomolov implies that the Warsaw uprising against the Germans is really part of a much wider uprising against the Soviet Union in Belorussia and Ukraine.

The Warsaw uprising is an attempt to liberate Warsaw from the Germans before the Red Army can get there, and ultimately to prevent the Red Army from coming to Warsaw and Poland. From the Soviet point of view, this would create serious problems for the projected plan for taking Germany. Of interest is the fact that in the incident referred to in the operational documents, the radio used by the Polish group is of British origin; the implication is that the whole uprising is being organized by the British and is part of an attempt to destabilize the Soviet occupation of Poland in order to keep the Red Army out of Poland and the Baltics. Vying with the Polish Home Army for control of the country are the communist-controlled People's Army (Armia Ludowa) and the National Armed Forces (Narodowe Sily Zbrojne). Of the three groups, the nationalist Polish Home Army was the main threat to Soviet ambitions in Poland. Many Polish survivors of the uprising believed that Stalin ordered Rokossovskii's army to halt outside Warsaw to enable the Germans to eradicate the Polish Home Army.[69]

Despite Bogomolov's best attempts to show the return of the Soviet security forces and army as an act of liberation—a somewhat thankless task—the attitude of Alekhin and Tamantsev toward the locals betrays a certain contempt that is far more consistent with the mind-set of occupiers, or rather reoccupiers, than liberators. In the administrative chaos created by the German retreat, private trading has once again asserted itself, and Alekhin's reaction is one of mild disgust: "Private trading in the liberated towns amazed Andrey. He could not understand business activity. A bourgeois, as it seemed to him from books and the cinema, would probably look just like these satisfied people behind the stalls."[70] Convinced that this is the return of NEP, Tamantsev reacts even more strongly: "A certain resurgence of private capital and speculators. Time will come when they will be clamped down upon and have the fear of God put into them!"[71]

In a letter home, Alekhin expresses a very low opinion of the local inhabitants: "The population here consists of Poles and Belorussians, but they are so-called 'Westerners.' They are cowed and backward people, and unsympathetic to us. In the month since I have been here I have not met a person in a single village who has had more than three or four grades of education. Our Russian people are far more cultured."[72] According to Alekhin's orthodox Soviet-Marxist stance, the reason these people are allegedly poor, stupid, and lacking culture comparable to that enjoyed in the Soviet Union is because the institutions of private property and religion are so strong.[73] Alekhin's contemptuous dismissal of the local population—no fraternal socialist feelings here—parallels the contempt expressed by German soldiers who, imbued with the cult of the *Untermensch*, regarded the Soviet population, and especially Soviet prisoners of war, as subhuman.

The tone of Alekhin's letter and the threat from Tamantsev that this resurgence of NEP-like capitalism will be crushed come with a sinister warning, namely, that full Sovietization will be reimposed as soon as possible. "Reimposition" is the precise word here, for in the period between the German invasion of Poland (1939) and the German invasion of the Soviet Union (1941), the Soviet zones in Poland and the Baltic states were brutally and bloodily Sovietized. It was during this period that Stalin sanctioned the mass murder of 21,857 Polish officers, officials, and intellectuals at Katyn and other sites in what is now widely known as the Katyn massacre.[74] Before retreating eastward in the summer of 1941, NKVD units in Ukraine shot prisoners who could not be evacuated because of the speed of the German advance.[75] When the NKVD returned in 1944, many Belorussians clearly preferred to take their chances with the retreating Germans rather than suffer the reimposition of Soviet rule.[76] Nor did the war between the NKVD and various nationalist groups in parts of Poland, the Baltic states, and Ukraine peter out in 1945 with the official end of World War II. For example, the UPA fought the NKVD and its agents provocateurs until 1952.[77]

As a spy or detective novel, the strength of In August 1944 lies in the author's command of the minutiae of counterintelligence and the obligatory false trails. The weaknesses are to be found in the bigger picture and to a lesser extent in the characterization of the three SMERSH men and their interaction with the Red Army represented by Anikushin. The exciting account of the pursuit and eventual destruction of the German agents, legitimate targets in the war with the German enemy, largely ignores the sadistic, ideological vendettas waged by the NKVD and SMERSH as the Red Army recaptured territory as well as the whole question of collaboration and the daily struggle under German occupation.

Conclusion

The reader who comes to *War* and *In August 1944* after Bykov's *The Dead Feel No Pain* or Grossman's *Life and Fate* is confronted with something of a problem, which appears straightforward but is not really so. Is the view of war offered by Bykov and Grossman a more honest, more reliable, more truthful one than those found in *War* and in *In August 1944*? If so, does that mean that *War* and *In August 1944* are to be regarded not as honestly flawed, fictional accounts of the war but as deliberate distortions intended to sustain an essentially ideological interpretation of the war on the eastern front?

Truth, lying, and Stalin's belated obsession with the aesthetics of deception are major themes in Stadniuk's and Bogomolov's novels. In trying to persuade us that their vision of the war is the one that counts, both authors appear fully to grasp the essence of Sun Tzu's maxim that "all warfare is based on deception."[78] Warfare on the ideological front is no different. Stadniuk wants us to see *War* as an attempt to uncover and to assert the historical truth; to this end, he concentrates on well-documented historical events: the TASS communiqué of 13 June 1941, the events of 22 June 1941, Stalin's role, and the fate of Pavlov. To the extent that there is some consensus regarding what happened before and after the German invasion, some objective measure for assessing Stadniuk's novel, which purports to be a historically truthful epic, can also be said to exist. Even Stadniuk does not subscribe to fashionable shibboleths that truth is only perspective or that we can never know the truth. On this basis, the picture of Stalin and his machinations offered in *War* is simply inconsistent, to put it mildly, with what we know, and with what was known when the novel was first published. *War* is indeed ideological whitewash. There are simply too many omissions and distortions for it to be a credible account. Any credibility that accrues to it is secured only by the censor's denying the opposition a voice. Once glasnost denied *War* its bodyguard, Stadniuk felt the suppressed and delayed wrath of critical opinion. In any case, the huge amount of declassified material on this question that was published throughout the 1990s, and continues to be supplemented, puts the matter beyond any doubt. For example, the two volumes of *1941 god* (1998), which deal with the period before and immediately after the German invasion, reveal just how detailed was the information that Stalin received concerning the concentration of German military forces on the Soviet Union's borders. The failure to act was Stalin's. Likewise, the interrogation protocols of General Pavlov, who was arrested on 4 July 1941, show that the charge of treason, a despicable accusation, was indeed the line of attack used against him.[79]

Bogomolov's main theme, the moment of truth, does, I believe, have some wider relevance for war literature as a whole. War literature is not one all-encompassing moment of truth but is made up of a number of discrete moments of truth—to borrow Solzhenitsyn's calculus metaphor—which, taken together, give us the big or bigger picture. No single writer gives us everything. The big (or bigger) picture comprises the efforts of all writers in the field. Among writers, Bogomolov's view of the war and especially of SMERSH is a minority one, yet it cannot simply be dismissed. Counterespionage is necessary and dangerous work; the Germans were trying to sabotage the Soviet war effort: all true. The trouble is that Bogomolov avoids too many of the deeper questions related to his theme. This is the main difference between Stadniuk and Bogomolov and dissenting writers such as Bykov and Grossman. Individually, Bykov and Grossman do not represent the last word on the subject of the war. For example, Grossman may be wrong about the source of Russian resistance at Stalingrad. Yet Bykov's and Grossman's depictions of the war are far closer to the historical record and, importantly, lack that conscious attempt to deceive, which is the hallmark of Stadniuk, and to mislead, in the case of Bogomolov.

In a curious way, both Stadniuk and Bogomolov confirm Churchill's belief that the truth—in this case the real nature of the Soviet state in war and in peace—must be protected by an escort of lies. Once the escort of lies was removed, as it was in the late 1980s, the Soviet state, unable to withstand open and critical scrutiny, collapsed. However, the collapse of the Soviet state in no way diminishes the bloody sacrifices of the Red Army and its final victory on the Volga, the theme of the next two chapters.

5 The Hinge of Fate: The Battle of Stalingrad in Soviet-Russian War Literature

"For a Just Cause"! That was the title of the remarkable book by that great, Russian writer Vasilii Grossman. It is dedicated to Stalingrad, one of the greatest battles in the history of war. Were he to wake up now, Vasilii Semenovich would shudder at the title. Clever, even wise, someone who knew much that we did not know, totally truthful, even he considered that at that time we were fighting for a just cause.

The enemy will be destroyed! Victory will be ours! But our cause proved to be unjust. And in that was the tragedy of my generation. And mine as well . . .
—Viktor Nekrasov, "Forty Years Later"

The battle of Stalingrad maintains a huge presence in Soviet-Russian war literature and historiography, reinforcing some of the deepest-held beliefs about the nature of the Soviet state. Likewise, Stalingrad occupies a major place in German war literature and historiography. Nor is fascination with the battle confined to the two former enemies. The recent commercial success of Antony Beevor's Stalingrad (1998), which uses a format similar to William Craig's earlier book, Enemy at the Gates: The Battle for Stalingrad (1973), as well as films such as Joseph Vilsmaier's Stalingrad (1992) and Jean-Jacques Annaud's Enemy at the Gates (2001), suggests that English-speaking audiences are just as obsessed with the battle. In this chapter, I examine the portrayal of the battle in Soviet journalism and literature (the works of Viktor Nekrasov, Konstantin Simonov, IUrii Bondarev, and Vasilii Grossman), where it is transformed from a looming catastrophe into an exemplar of Soviet resilience and vindication of Stalin and his policies (or otherwise in one important case) and from there into an iconic victory over Nazi Germany.

Introduction

The defeat of the German 6th Army at Stalingrad in 1943 and indeed the whole story of Hitler's duel with Stalin are irresistibly fascinating for writers and historians. It was, after all, on the Eastern front that the two totalitarian states of National Socialist Germany and the Soviet Union contested the dominion of Europe in a protracted ordeal of fire, blood, and ideology. Nearly seven decades after the end of World War II, there seems to be no sign that the viewing and reading public is suffering from combat fatigue. Quite the reverse, in fact; the appetite for books, films, and documentaries, serious or otherwise, seems insatiable, especially with regard to Nazi Germany and the Eastern front.

There are several explanations for this continuing obsession. First, there is the sheer scale and duration of World War II, the savagery and all the horrors and wonders of modern technology that emerged from it. Second, we are drawn to war by human folly, bravery, endurance, heroism, misery, and wickedness. Thermopylae, Marathon, Cannae, Verdun, the Somme, and the battles on the Eastern front in World War II will continue to hold our attention even if future histories of postheroic war will dazzle us with accounts of remote-controlled, "intelligent" munitions and other, yet-to-be-invented, biotechnological horrors. Third, certain battles—those at "the hinge of fate," to use Churchill's expression[1]—provide a crucial frame of reference for justifying and explaining the course of history. Nations and states crave the comfort of half truths, glorious falsification, omission, and myths. The iconic battle satisfies this deep need, inspiring and nurturing national pride and legitimizing leaders. The outcome at Stalingrad, Marxist-Leninist interpreters claimed, was an emphatic demonstration of the Soviet system's superiority in war and peace. Churchill, while paying generous tribute to the Soviet contribution to the Allied cause—"a wonderful achievement"[2] is how he described the defeat of the 6th Army—was nevertheless well aware of the deeper significance of the Soviet victory and what it meant for postwar Europe: "This crushing disaster to the German arms ended Hitler's prodigious effort to conquer Russia by force of arms, and destroy Communism by an equally odious form of totalitarian tyranny."[3] Fourth, we must consider the spectacular collapse of the Soviet empire in 1991, which made it possible for historians to reevaluate the history of the war in a way that was impossible while the prerogatives of Soviet censorship and Marxist-Leninist ideology impinged upon academic freedom. Under conditions of Soviet-style censorship, truth is indeed the first casualty, but thankfully it has proved to be a magnificent survivor. Over the past fifteen years a great deal has been achieved, and we can expect more to come over the next decade or two. At that stage, historians and students of the battle might be able to sign their own cease-fire.

Stalingrad fascinates writers and historians because it magnifies and intensifies the horrors of war on the Eastern front, giving a truly demonic hue to the main players as they wage total war.[4] Confident that the capture of Stalingrad will be the knockout blow that will secure victory, Hitler urges his army on; Stalin struggles to stem the tide so as to save himself and his dangerously weakened regime. The relentless infantry attacks and counterattacks are redolent of the attrition battles in World War I. The killing and dying are on the same pitiless, industrial scale. Nor can modern weapons obscure the fact that both combatants deliberately evoked and nurtured deep hatred of one another. Our remote ancestors' propensity for violence was spontaneous and local; in the twentieth century it was global, systematic, and planned. It is therefore not entirely accurate to characterize Stalingrad and the other battles on the Eastern front as a regression to barbarism. Rather they represent a progression to a new type of barbarism, one dominated by technology and influenced by the mass media. The nightmare of two huge armies reduced to fighting over the ruins of a city does not lead, as Nazi ideology believed, to the birth of the Nietzschean *Übermensch* or to the figure of the *Urmensch*, both exalted in Jünger's work, but to a brutal parody of both, a degraded, modern savage who, armed with his hand grenades and machine guns and with his ideological indoctrination, can claim no innocence or nobility.

Maybe inspiration is to be found in the way in which the two adversaries responded to their various misfortunes. In September and October 1942, there seems to have been a realization among the Russian defenders that the moment of truth had arrived. In "Volga—Stalingrad," written at the beginning of September, Grossman records the change in mood: "However, the idea of the Volga and Stalingrad, about the main and decisive battle, dominates everyone's thoughts: old men; women; the fighters in the workers' battalions; the tank soldiers, airmen, and artillerymen."[5] This hardening in attitude among the defenders and civilians—whether inspired by brutal expediency and harsh military discipline or by a retreat to what Samuel Johnson rather uncharitably called the "last refuge of a scoundrel"—may be regarded as one of the battle's turning points.

An obvious consequence of Soviet tenacity, and one that was fully appreciated in the West at the time, was the persistent inability of the Germans to administer the coup de grâce. Just when news of Stalingrad's fall seemed imminent, the German attack was stopped in its tracks. Sheer delay conveyed a hint of the tenacious resistance being offered. The Germans fighting in Stalingrad were under no illusion about the hardening of Soviet resistance, whatever Goebbels was telling the world. German reports repeatedly stressed the severity of the fighting: "The enemy fights bitterly for every house."[6] One officer complained that the Russians were waging a "war of attrition" (*Zermürbungskampf*).[7] In a report to General Friedrich Paulus, Lieutenant General Strecker, commander of XI Corps, noted that the effectiveness of his soldiers was being degraded by the cumulative effects of severe

fighting, continual guard duty, insufficient food, and unhygienic conditions. Worse still: "The NCOs have been decimated,"[8] and, providing some
vindication for Air Chief Marshal Sir Arthur Harris, Strecker writes that
news of RAF bombing raids over Germany was affecting the soldier's morale: "He is burdened by worry of what is happening in the air attacks at
home."[9]

Likewise, the agony and endurance of the encircled 6th Army are both
dreadful and inspiring. Indeed, there is even something miraculous, a hint
of divine punishment and reward, in the dramatic reversal of fortunes of the
two armies. The Red Army endures and wins—albeit at dreadful cost—
whereas the once triumphant 6th Army is reduced to a starving, freezing
mass, the psychological and military shock of defeat all the more devastating for being so unexpected, so unbelievable, after the spectacular successes of the summer of 1942.[10] Charles de Gaulle, who startled Alexander
Werth in Moscow in 1944 with his praise of German arms, grasped something of the dark grandeur and magnitude of German military ambitions
and how close they came to being realized. Interrupting Werth, who had
believed him to be praising the Russians, De Gaulle said, "Mais non, je ne
parle pas des Russes, je parle des Allemands. Tout de même, avoir poussé jusque là."[11]

De Gaulle's rational appraisal of German military achievement is a necessary corrective to the enormous power that the Soviet victory exercises
over Western and Russian imaginations.[12] Stalingrad is always cited as the
paradigm of operational encirclement, as if the Red Army were the leading
exponent of this strategy. Soviet-Russian war literature and historiography
have no hesitation in asserting this view. This perspective fails to do justice
to the military brilliance of the German generals, who relentlessly and skill-
fully repeated the pattern of encirclement and destruction of whole Soviet
armies in the summers of 1941 and 1942. The question to answer, or at least
attempt to answer, is where the Soviet success at Stalingrad stands in relation to the line of German successes stretching from the Briansk and Central fronts of 1941 to the virtual rout of the Red Army in the summer of 1942.
German retreats were invariably well planned and well executed and, as the
Soviet and Anglo-American armies were to discover to their cost, could still
pack a considerable punch (in Kharkov, 1943; the Battle of the Bulge, 1944;
Budapest, 1945; and the Battle of Berlin, 1945). Time and time again, the
German generals were able to extricate themselves from disastrous situations, often not of their own making. We should be grateful that Hitler's re-
lationship with the German general staff disintegrated.

When surrounded and beyond help, the 6th Army held out for nearly two and a half months in appalling conditions. (Compare its fighting spirit with that of the British garrison under the command of General Percival at Singapore in 1942.) In similar circumstances, the Soviet precedent was the collapse of command and control structures, resulting in stampede and desertion. Much bravery and endurance there was, but all too often these qualities were squandered by incompetence and by officers who were psychologically damaged by the purges and fearful of the party's wrath. In discussing German military success, there is a marked tendency to play down achievements. So accustomed are we to German victories that we take them for granted. When the Germans are eventually shown to be fallible, we are amazed. Conversely, we are so accustomed to Soviet military disasters that we are impressed by a success—even more so when, as in the case of Stalingrad, it involved much courage and sacrifice and held our attention for so long. Thus, we tend to magnify the battle's significance, which by the law of contrast should serve only to underline the preceding failures.

Review of the Literature

A review of Russian and Western sources indicates a large number of works on the battle of Stalingrad, ranging from novels and memoirs to historical and military studies.[13] Important are the memoirs of senior Soviet officers, especially Vasilii Chuikov's *Nachalo puti* (The Beginning of the Road, 1967),[14] A. M. Samsonov's *Stalingradskaia bitva* (The Battle of Stalingrad), a fourth edition of which appeared in 1989,[15] and Vasilii Zaitsev's sniper biography, *Za Volgoi zemli dlia nas ne bylo: Zapiski snaipera* (Beyond the Volga There Was No Land for Us: Notes of a Sniper, 1971).[16]

Some of the best-known Soviet novels are those by Konstantin Simonov, *Dni i nochi* (Days and Nights, 1943–1944); Viktor Nekrasov, *V okopakh Stalingrada* (In the Trenches of Stalingrad, 1946); and IUrii Bondarev, *Goriachii sneg* (Hot Snow, 1969).[17] All three writers were at Stalingrad—Simonov as a war correspondent, Bondarev as an artillery officer, and Nekrasov as a sapper officer—and offer interesting and important perspectives on the battle. *Days and Nights* is a straightforward, robust account of the street fighting. On the other hand, *In the Trenches of Stalingrad*, published just as the *Zhdanovshchina* was launched, is full of critical hints about the conduct of the war. It is remarkable that it was published at all in 1946. In terms of the author's often thinly veiled criticisms, it is ten to fifteen years ahead of its time. Certainly it comes as no surprise that Nekrasov fell foul of Soviet officialdom and went into exile. *Hot Snow* attempts a majestic sweep concentrating on the German attempts to break through the Soviet encirclement and relieve the 6th Army. Even though Bondarev, Simonov, and Nekrasov diverge in the emphasis they attach to certain themes, they represent a spectrum of writing that can be accommodated within Soviet war literature.

The same cannot be said of Vasilii Grossman's Stalingrad epic, *Zhizn' i sud'ba* (Life and Fate), which stands in splendid and heretical isolation and must be regarded as a special case, on a par with Solzhenitsyn's major works. Beginning his writing career in the 1930s, Grossman was a literary outcast by the time of his death in 1964. In *Life and Fate*, he attacks Stalin and Stalinism, concluding, like Churchill before him, that Communism and National Socialism were equally odious forms of totalitarian tyranny and that the outcome at Stalingrad served only to perpetuate Stalin's reign of terror. Best known for *Life and Fate*, which, together with the publication of *Vse techet* (Forever Flowing, 1989), marks the highlights of the glasnost years, Grossman wrote two other works that deal with Stalingrad but that tend to be overshadowed, understandably, by *Life and Fate*. Published in 1943, immediately after the German surrender, *Stalingradskie ocherki* (The Stalingrad Sketches) is a collection of Grossman's articles written for the Red Army newspaper, *Krasnaia zvezda*. For the most part, they read well and provide useful insights into Grossman's intellectual defection from the Soviet state. The same is true of *Za pravoe delo* (For a Just Cause, 1952), the precursor volume to *Life and Fate*, which, despite having been published just before Stalin's death, can hardly be regarded as an orthodox Soviet war novel.

Soviet Journalism at Stalingrad

Before I turn to a discussion of Bondarev, Simonov, Nekrasov, and Grossman, some remarks on the role of Soviet wartime journalism are merited because Soviet journalists and frontline correspondents help to determine many of the themes in postwar novels and *povesti*. Moreover, journalists responding to the unfolding crisis give a feeling for the time that is absent in the novels written well after the danger passed.

As memories of the Cold War start to fade, and journalism in the Russian Federation now operates in ways if not identical to yet recognizably compatible with its Western counterparts, it is easy to forget that Soviet and Western journalists operated in two different universes. Soviet journalists were compelled to interpret the world within a strict ideological framework. Western journalism encouraged skepticism, impartiality, and objectivity, all of which

were rejected by Lenin and his followers as bourgeois ruses to secure and retain power. Ideologically slanted reporting is not uninteresting per se, but it
requires certain skills to decode. Lacking these skills, Western readers
found Soviet English-language publicity material dull.

During the war, however, there was a certain loosening of party control.
In fact, such a loosening was probably unavoidable. In the aftermath of the
fall of Rostov in 1942, for example, a definite sense of impending doom is
detectable in the Soviet press. Chuikov, the commander of the 62nd Army;
Vasilii Zaitsev; Konstantin Simonov; Vasilii Grossman; and Viktor Nekrasov repeatedly stress this backs-to-the-wall factor, which is explicit in the
title of Zaitsev's *Notes of a Sniper*. The critical nature of the crisis could not be
glossed over: millions of dead and prisoners, military incompetence, constant retreat, and humiliating setbacks. Explanations had to be proffered
for the failure of the Red Army to stop Hitler's armies. Of the general Soviet
mood in the late summer of 1942, Earl Ziemke writes, "Morale of the troops
and the people showed signs of breaking. The burden of suffering, of defeats, and of mistakes weighed more heavily than at any time in the war.
The confidence and hope the winter's successes had raised were dissipated.
The Soviet command, it appeared, might have taken its people close to the
edge of disaster too many times."[18]

As German successes continued, room had to be made for a note of realism among the strident claims that the Soviet army was stopping the Germans. As Matthew Gallagher has pointed out, "However well motivated a
writer might be, he could not but run afoul of the inherent contradiction
between reality as politically idealized and reality as observed."[19]

Despite the common foe—but not necessarily the common cause—
Western correspondents based in the Soviet Union, even when their pro-
Soviet sympathies were well known, were regarded with intense suspicion
by the Soviet authorities. The American Walter Kerr and Wallace Carroll
and the British Philip Jordan, Alexander Werth, Charlotte Haldane, and
Ralph Parker, some of the most famous Western correspondents of the
day, were dispatched to the Soviet Union only to encounter implacable bureaucrats and censors. Western correspondents were not allowed anywhere
near Stalingrad while the battle was in progress. One important consequence of this control was that there were no checks and balances to counter Soviet reporting and no opportunities to verify its claims. Western correspondents were totally dependent on their Soviet hosts. Add to this
situation a natural desire to support an ally, to avoid embarrassing reports

that could be of use to the Germans, and it is clear that much Western reporting is unreliable and, depending on the correspondent's political sympathies, suspect. Western reporting was either secondhand or served as a
Soviet loudspeaker whose function, as far as the Soviet Union was concerned, was to present Soviet interests in as favorable light as possible in
order to influence domestic policy in the United States and Britain to the advantage of the Soviet Union.

Soviet press coverage of the Stalingrad battle embraced a number of
themes that, broadly speaking, can be contained within two categories. The
first category is the historical and political-ideological issues of the battle: its
historical significance; the development of Soviet military thought; selling
the idea of eventual victory to the Western Allies; the alleged depravity of
German culture and civilization; the need for a Second front to relieve the
pressure on the Eastern front and the implication that the absence of a Second front implied some dark Anglo-American motive; and, as the battle
moved toward its denouement, the skillful exploitation of the Soviet Union's
enhanced military prestige to influence the shape of postwar Europe.

The second category is on-the-spot reporting, which looks at the battle
from the sharp end. To this category can be added articles on such themes as
the peculiarities of street fighting; the promotion of General Rodimtsev's division in September 1942; the endurance of the Russian soldier; and the exploits of various snipers and scouts, or *razvedchiki*. By the end of the battle,
Soviet snipers such as Vasilii Zaitsev, Viktor Medvedev, and Anatolii Chek-
hov were household names. So successful are the Soviet accounts of the exploits of their own snipers, amplified by Western reporting, that we tend to
lose sight of the fact that the Germans employed snipers with the same
deadly zeal. All accounts of sniping at Stalingrad, be they Western or Soviet,
are devoted to Soviet exploits. The impression persists that German snipers
were repeatedly outmatched by their opponents, that German soldiers were
easy trophies. As the battle progresses, the Volga is promoted as uniquely
Russian, even becomes the symbol of Mother Russia, so that its protection
demands the ultimate sacrifice. Grossman, for example, refers to it as "the
river of Russian freedom."[20] Some article titles even create the sense that the
river represents a kind of moral threshold so that allowing the Germans to
cross it would be the final desecration, the rape of Russia.[21]

In the immediate aftermath of the summer disasters, a concerted press
campaign was launched against cowardice and deserters. Though not published during the war, Stalin's Order № 227 set the tone, demanding utter

ruthlessness. Articles with headlines such as "Slava geroiu, prezrenie—trusu!" (Glory to the Hero, Contempt for the Coward)[22] and "Zheleznaia distsiplina—osnova pobedy" (Iron Discipline Is the Basis of Victory)[23] were typical and indicate just how demoralized the army was. They left no doubt about the treatment that shirkers and deserters could expect to receive.

Some of the most striking changes in the Soviet wartime press—especially as the Germans advanced on Stalingrad—are evident in the many articles dealing with the professional shortcomings of the Red Army. The message was being driven home that competence and bravery were required. Serialized in *Pravda* between 24 and 27 August 1942, *Front* (The Front), a play by Alexander Korneichuk, addressed the failure to master the lessons of modern war.[24] The character General Gorlov is a senior officer whose reputation rests on his Civil War exploits. He is, as he admits, unimpressed by the technical gadgetry of modern war and convinced that wars are won by bravery alone. His intelligence officer has the unlikely name Udivitel'nyi (surprising) and, as implied by the name, is always being caught off balance by the Germans (appropriately, given Stalin's failures the previous summer). Korneichuk's aim is to obfuscate the reasons for the dire military situation. Lecturing the Red Army about the nature of modern war is all well and good, but who is to blame for the fact that the Germans are on the Volga?

In chapter 21 of *Life and Fate*, appropriately the reader's first encounter with the odious party bureaucrat Getmanov and his colleagues, Grossman is clear about the real significance of *The Front*: It is nothing less than an attempt to absolve the Greatest Strategist of All Time from any responsibility and to convince the Soviet public that "the failures of the war are linked to stupid generals unable to carry out the instructions of an infallible Supreme Command."[25] In fact, *The Front* is a typical piece of low Marxist agitprop. It is difficult to believe that it had any effect except to damage officer morale and antagonize an already hard-pressed military, which had no forum in which to reply to such vicious baiting. As a propaganda piece, the real aim of *The Front* was to obscure the deeper, systemic causes of failure—dual command being one—and to shift the blame away from Stalin and the party machine.

As the situation became critical, baiting the army gave way to what appeared to be major concessions. A more important indication of the army's enhanced status was the abolition of the institution of commissars and the return of unity of command, *edinonachalie*, which was promulgated on 9 October 1942 as German attempts to break Russian resistance were reaching their climax. The timing was crucial. It was a clear signal to the army, and belated recognition by the party, that dual command was chaotic and counterproductive, at least for the time being.

All nations look to their past for inspiration at moments of great national peril. The Soviet present was no barrier to exploiting the Russian past, and every historical angle that could be brought to bear on the significance of the battle was used. At the end of July 1942, amid a ruthless tightening of discipline, the creation of three new military orders for senior officers was announced, conspicuously borrowed from the great soldier-patriots of the past: Suvorov; Nevskii, and Kutuzov. Anniversaries were also exploited. Thus, on 7 September 1942, the 130th anniversary of the Battle of Borodino was commemorated.[26] The intended message was that as Napoleon's armies were lured ever deeper into the Russian interior, so the Germans will be, so that decisive victory will elude Hitler's generals. A similar message can be found a month later in a piece titled "Faktor vremeni na voine" (The Time Factor in War).[27] War, it is argued, is a question of industrial capacity, of engines, which requires time. Mindful perhaps of another ally who had turned out to be less than friendly in June 1941, the party felt the need to justify the wartime alliance with the capitalist states of America and Britain. The concept of "coalition wars" appeared in the press. Once again historical precedents were press-ganged into service. Napoleon, it was pointed out, had been defeated by a coalition of allies; so would Hitler be.[28]

Stalingrad, formerly Tsaritsyn, and after Stalin's death Volgograd, was where the White Guards had been checked in the Civil War. Party history arrogates a special place to Stalin in the saving of Tsaritsyn. But the main message—that victory had been seized in the face of impending defeat—formed the basis of an article by Vasilii Grossman, "Tsaritsyn-Stalingrad" (1942), in *Krasnaia zvezda*. Grossman avoids hyperbolical praise of Stalin. The tone is sober, but calmly optimistic:

> One cannot even begin to compare the force applied by Krasnov's men in 1918 with that applied by the Germans in August 1942. The attacks of tank divisions, the terrible fire of thousands of artillery pieces and mortars, the ferocious assaults from the air—there was hardly anything of comparable force in the history of war. Everything in the conduct of war had changed over these decades. . . . And only one thing remained unchanged, remained as it was, as if it was not

the people of a new generation who set out to defend Stalingrad: the courageous heart of a great people.[29]

News of the encircling operation was, considering the aims, modestly reported at first, a reflection perhaps of the very real respect in which the German high command was held. An immediate German breakout was expected, and the press was hedging its bets in the event of German success. Toward the end of November, the tone of reporting becomes increasingly optimistic. One of the most famous headlines of this period was carried by *Pravda* on 23 November 1942: "Budet i na nashei ulitse prazdnik" (There Will be a Celebration in Our Street as Well).[30] After months of frustration, there was a smell of success, a hint of a big victory, which because of the earlier caution seemed to carry much greater conviction than the normal bellicose headlines. News from the front was encouraging. It was the end of November, and the Germans had still not taken Stalingrad. Words such as *nastuplenie* (offensive), for so long used to describe German military activity, were now being used—convincingly—about the Red Army; and there were prisoners of war.

December's press is avowedly confident of final victory. We can see the first of a series of articles dedicated to mobile warfare, the coordinated use of tanks and infantry, published at a time when the German perimeter was being systematically reduced. Once it was clear that the battle had unmistakably turned in favor of the Red Army, further efforts were made to enhance the prestige of the Soviet officer. Gold braid was ordered from Britain, and on 7 January 1943 it was announced in *Pravda* that *pogony* (shoulder boards) were to be reintroduced for officers.[31] Considerable space was given to drawings of the new uniforms. These articles, and announcements in January of major changes in the uniform and status of officers, indicate that the Red Army and the officer corps had found their confidence after so many disasters. The reasons for such public satisfaction were twofold. Not only had Stalingrad been defended but the Germans, the masters of encirclement operations, had been given a taste of their own medicine. The Soviet military could now claim—who in the Allied camp was brave enough to dispute it openly?—to have taken the crown of military excellence from its defeated opponents.

Articles from mid-January detail the substance of these claims. In his article "Klassicheskii sluchai" (A Classic Episode) Nikolai Tikhonov misses no opportunity to bait the German general staff:

The Germans are gluttons for meticulous investigation, particularly in the sphere of military history. The late Count Schlieffen, whose memory is worshipped by the German general staff, once propounded the principle of a modern Cannae. In the Battle of Cannae, Hannibal surrounded the Roman troops under Terentius Varro, annihilated some of them and took the rest prisoner. . . . Since Schlieffen's day, all the outstanding German military experts have dreamed of bringing about a Cannae for Germany's enemies. . . . The present war, however, has already provided the German command with a classic example of Cannae, of which Colonel General Paulus will be able to give all the details, for he was one of the principal actors in it.[32]

Centralized control and censorship of the Soviet press were well suited to the needs of a state waging total physical and ideological war. Soviet correspondents made a distinct contribution to victory and to the way in which the victory was perceived. We know from the accounts of those who participated in the battle that the reports of certain correspondents—Vasilii Grossman, Il'ia Ehrenburg, and Konstantin Simonov—exercised a great effect on military morale. Grossman's contributions at the time and later are especially powerful and enduring. Apart from the immediate and dramatic military changes, the Soviet victory had long-term repercussions for the perception of the war on the Eastern front and the prestige of the Soviet Union. Soviet coverage of Stalingrad promoted four distinct themes: The Soviet Union has turned the corner; the Germans cannot win the battle or the war on the Eastern front; the battle marks a unique contribution to the art of war and military thought; and a new perception of Russia has been born and tested in the crucible of Stalingrad.[33]

The Stalingrad Novels
Days and Nights (1943–1944)

In Days and Nights, Simonov, in keeping with other writers, manages to convey something of the exceptional ferocity of the fighting in September and October and the desperate nature of the struggle. Stalingrad marks the beginning of the central Asian steppes, "the edge of the world";[34] there is nowhere else to go. Saburov, whose battalion is about to join the battle, realizes just how bad things are:

He was drinking water from the Volga, but at the same time he was at war. These two ideas—war and the Volga—for all their obviousness just did not seem to belong together. From his childhood, from his school days, his whole life, the Volga was for him something so profound, something so eternally Russian that the fact that he was now standing on the bank of the Volga and drinking water from it, and that the Germans were on the other side, seemed to him to be unbelievable and preposterous.[35]

In many ways, *Days and Nights* is curiously restrained, even neutral, as if the long, hard-fought battle has exhausted the author. Indeed, one of the main themes is tiredness, the remorseless draining of physical and mental energy in a war of attrition. (We find the same emphasis on tiredness in all its insidious forms in two British naval classics, *HMS Ulysses* and *Destroyer Captain*.) Simonov's title is well chosen; it captures some of the universals of war wherever it is waged. Days and nights pass in a blur of fighting, lack of sleep, and cold. Simonov's soldiers, as is especially evident in the friendship between the two main officer characters, Saburov and Maslennikov, are sustained by patriotism and above all by comradeship.

Simonov touches on some sensitive themes. In the course of the battle, Saburov and his battalion are cut off by the Germans and surrounded. In such circumstances there is always the suspicion that the Soviet troops did not fight hard enough, that the mere fact of being surrounded is a stain, regardless of how it came about. Of Saburov's misfortune Simonov notes, "Saburov together with his battalion had ended up in a situation which in its endlessly diverse forms in war is known under the general term 'encirclement.'"[36] Encirclement, Simonov suggests, is an occupational hazard, not automatic evidence of low morale and poor leadership or, worse, desertion.

Altogether less satisfactory is Simonov's treatment of desertion. One of Saburov's soldiers, having seen his comrade crushed by a German tank, panics and crawls away in the direction of the Volga. Detained, he is accused of desertion. In the middle of the investigation, the Germans attack and Stepanov, the accused soldier, fights well. The charge is dropped. This outcome is not entirely credible. Under the circumstances of Stalingrad and Stalin's Order № 227, the punishment would have been immediate execution, not a prolonged investigation in the middle of a desperate battle. Nor is there any hint that the officer sent to conduct the investigation is in any way connected with the NKVD's Special Section.

Far more convincing and symptomatic of the clash between military discipline and efficiency inspired by Order № 227 are the hastily organized attacks. Saburov is ordered to recapture a supply dump and intends to wait until nightfall. A senior officer, Babchenko, reminds him of the "not a step backward" policy and demands that the attack be carried out immediately. Saburov's response makes sense: "I've read the order. But I don't want to put people where there's no need to put them, where it's possible to get everything back without hardly any losses."[37] The attack ends in failure, inviting criticism of Babchenko and even the order itself: "He [Babchenko] understood the words 'not a step backward' literally, without wanting to reckon with what today's losses would cost tomorrow, when the Germans would once again attack and there would be nothing with which to hold them back."[38] As if to exemplify the spirit of defiance that he believes is called for by Order № 227, Babchenko refuses to take cover during a German artillery attack. He is killed, and Saburov can now pursue his own plan for recapturing the lost dump: "Of course he regretted the fact that Babchenko had been killed, but at the same time he had a conscious, totally clear feeling of relief from the fact that now he could do things in the way he considered necessary and that the ridiculous attack thought up by Babchenko for the sake of his own prestige would not be repeated."[39]

For a work that was written while the war was still being fought, *Days and Nights* is remarkably free from many of the standard Soviet ideological themes. Stalin is in the background; the obligatory term "fascists" is used only sparingly when talking about the Germans; and the credit for stopping the Germans goes to the Red Army, not to the party and its commissars. The work concludes with the news of the Soviet counterattack in November, yet the object of salvation is conspicuously Russia, not the Soviet Union. Victory at Stalingrad, and finally in 1945, hints Simonov, is preeminently a Russian victory.

In the Trenches of Stalingrad (1946)

There are no obvious explanations, apart from authorization at the very top or conspicuous failure on the part of the Soviet censors, to account for the publication of In the Trenches of Stalingrad in 1946. That the novel was awarded a Stalin Prize in 1947 suggests a conscious decision to allow publication—one that may have been subsequently regretted. Along with Kazakevich's *Star* and Grossman's *For a Just Cause*, In the Trenches of Stalingrad is one of three works published while Stalin was alive that presented a far from flattering account of the war in general and the battle of Stalingrad in particular.

We find little evidence of a planned withdrawal; instead, the climate is one of panic in the face of the German advance. The summer retreat that finally ends in Stalingrad shows the Red Army in total disarray. The Germans seem unstoppable. The Red Army retreats to new, hastily constructed defensive lines only to abandon them as soon as the Germans appear. The atmosphere is one of chaos and senseless sacrifice. Kerzhentsev, the engineer officer, describes his unit's first action, near Kharkov: "Never been fired at before, at the front for the first time, we were switched from place to place, put in defense, withdrawn, redeployed, put in defense again. This was during the period of the Kharkov spring offensive. We used to get lost, get muddled up, confuse others, and we could not get used to being bombarded."[40]

In the retreat, Kerzhentsev is aware that he and his men are abandoning the civilian population to the Germans, and he has no answers: "I can't look at these faces, at these questioning, uncomprehending eyes. What can I say to them?"[41]

Nor does Nekrasov shirk the question of cowardice, real and imagined. In the retreat, two men desert their unit in the night, and a supply officer, Kaluzhskii, is clearly planning for the worst. Anticipating the possibility that he might be captured or encircled, he has removed his badges of rank and the red star from his belt. In accordance with Stavka Order № 270, 16 August 1941, commanders and commissars who removed badges of rank were regarded as deserters who were to be shot on the spot and whose families were to be arrested. Kaluzhskii reveals that he can get hold of civilian clothing, and as the situation in Stalingrad starts to become serious, he intimates that he can arrange a transfer out of Stalingrad for his fellow officers.

In another incident that takes place in Stalingrad, Nekrasov deals with something that was all too common in the aftermath of Stalin's disciplinary orders. Two understrength battalions are ordered to attack some fuel tanks, but the attack falters because of heavy German fire. Captain Abrosimov, regardless of the losses, wants to continue the attack. Shiriaev questions the wisdom of such a move, and Abrosimov threatens to shoot him on the spot for cowardice and disobeying orders. Although the incident is all too believable—similar ones being found in works by other writers—the outcome of this confrontation is not entirely convincing because it is Abrosimov who faces a tribunal, not Shiriaev. Abrosimov is depicted as the unthinking robot, whereas the regimental commander, Borodin, and Shiriaev are shown as being tactically flexible. The major's challenge to Abrosimov is based on a rational appraisal, a professional response, which in the atmosphere engendered by Stalin's orders was viewed with suspicion:

> The men went into the attack. But not how you wanted them to do it. The men went into the attack, having thought about what they were doing. And what did you do? Did you see what the first attack led to? It couldn't happen any other way. We had banked on artillery support. We had to strike the enemy immediately before he could get his act together. But it didn't work out. The enemy turned out to be stronger, more cunning than we thought. We couldn't suppress his fire positions. I sent the engineer to the second battalion. Shiriaev was there, a lad with a brain. He had everything ready to seize the German trenches since nighttime. And he'd got things done well. And you, Abrosimov, did what?[42]

Abrosimov is ultimately demoted and sent to a penal unit. Although such an outcome was common, it leaves the impression that rational, tactically sound counsels prevailed over the demands for mere obedience. Unfortunately, Abrosimov's orders, countermanding those of Borodin, are more consistent with the harsh discipline and ruthlessness that were demanded and expected of commanders at the time, especially in the aftermath of Order № 227, of which Nekrasov makes no mention. In the Soviet scheme of things it is actually Abrosimov who has behaved correctly.

Another reversal of what we have come to expect can be seen in the way army officers and the political section behave in the prelude to an attack. An army officer from divisional headquarters clearly annoys Kerzhentsev with his questions, whereas the officers from the political section, in complete contrast with what we find in many other war novels, mind their own business: "They're good lads; they understand that questions at this moment are irrelevant and get on with their own affairs in silence."[43]

If the tribunal involving Abrosimov appears to understate a particular problem, there are plenty of swipes at the Soviet leadership. Georgii Akimovich, who runs a power station in Stalingrad, asks a question that must have exercised the minds of a great many: "How are we going to fight the Germans? . . . The Germans have come from Berlin itself to Stalingrad in motorized transport, and we sit in trenches wearing jackets and overalls and armed with a model 1891 .375 rifle."[44] He also offers a not exactly flattering assessment of Red Army performance: "To get from the border to the Volga also takes some doing."[45] An apparently impressed Shiriaev also appears to damn Stalin with faint praise: "Nevertheless he's got willpower.—Who has?—Stalin has, of course. To hold the enemy in check with two retreats. Just think of it! In '41 and now here."[46]

The following exchange between Farber and Kerzhentsev is also highly charged. Despite the attempt to lay blame or indifference on themselves, this apparently innocent exchange points to the highest level in the Soviet Union: "'In short: did you know that there would be a war?'—'I sort of knew.'—'None of this "sort of"; you knew. And you knew that you would be taking part in it.'"[47]

For all the suffering and loss of life, Nekrasov manages to finish the novel on a note of celebration, albeit an exhausted one. Nearly three months after Hitler's speech of 9 November 1942, and with isolated pockets of Germans still surrendering, it is Chumak, the fiercely independent scout, who articulates the grandeur of what has been achieved. Chumak mocks Hitler's speech, in which the Führer claims that Stalingrad belongs to the Germans, apart from some Russians sitting in a few buildings:

> Well, there they are, those few buildings. There's Mamaev, flat and ugly. And there are the fuel tanks just like two boils on the top. Oh, and did they torment us. Even now it's disgusting to look at them. And behind those red ruins there—only the walls still stand like a sieve—Rodimtsev's positions began. A strip about two hundred yards wide. Just think, some two hundred wretched yards! To cross all of Belorussia, Ukraine, Donbass, the Kalmyk steppe and not manage to cross two hundred yards . . . ho, ho![48]

For a Just Cause (1952)

For a Just Cause is an account of the Soviet retreat that leads to Stalingrad in the late summer of 1942. Published at the height of the post-1945 purges—when Stalin is about to uncover an alleged plot by Jewish doctors to assassinate the Soviet leadership—For a Just Cause is, by the standards of the late Stalin period, a highly unusual novel. Hewn from the same Russian oak as War and Peace, For a Just Cause, like the later Life and Fate, is constructed on a series of contrasts between chapters based on a recurring pattern of three main types: personal-biographical narrative, historical-strategic/explicatory digression, and battle scenes. The overall effect is of a great interconnected web of personal relations, ideas, and events, a solar system that has Stalingrad at its center. Though Grossman is better known in and outside Russia for *Life and Fate*, it is tempting to reverse what might be regarded as a tendency to highlight the importance of *Life and Fate* at the expense of *For a Just Cause*. True enough, the path to *Life and Fate* leads through *For a Just Cause*, but it is also the case that *Life and Fate* is a worthy sequel to *For a Just Cause*.

Grossman's personal-biographical chapters are dominated by mother-son, wife-husband relationships. Spanning both *For a Just Cause* and *Life and Fate* are the family tragedies of the Shtrums and the sexual jealousy arising from the Krymov-Zhenia-Novikov triangle. In *For a Just Cause*, the focus is on the families of two soldiers: Vavilov and Berezkin. Vavilov is leaving his family, and Major Berezkin chances to meet his family on a Stalingrad street as the Germans are closing in.

Liudmila Shtrum is tormented by the fact that her son, Tolia, must go to war. Wounded, he dies in the hospital, and his mother, who visits his grave—the scene appearing in *Life and Fate*—is broken by her son's death. Viktor, Liudmila's husband, learns the fate of his own mother, who was murdered in the Berdichev ghetto, from her last letter, which is smuggled across the front line by Ikonnikov-Morzh (who will be the main source of moral challenge to Soviet and Nazi totalitarianism in *Life and Fate*). The text of the letter is finally revealed in *Life and Fate* and lays bare the administrative cruelty inflicted on Jews as they are deceived and rounded up for extermination. Liudmila's visit to her son's grave and Viktor's tormented rereading of his mother's last letter confront us with the full and dreadful agony of a mother's love for her son. We are in the presence of something sacred, the inner sanctum of maternal grief, and the pages must be handled with due reverence.

Abandoned by his wife, Krymov finds some solace in the comradeship afforded by the war. But no matter how hard he works to serve the cause, the memory of his wife, his longing for her, and the pain of his separation are always ready to ambush him when the exigencies of war momentarily recede. Krymov, we suspect, is not entirely honest with himself. The ideological justification for waging the war against the Germans that, as a commissar, he is obliged to lay before the soldiers in his unit is straightforward enough, but for all the talk of internationalism and the working class, the veteran Bolshevik is driven by something more primeval. He fights not for any ideological construct of Soviet Russia but for Mother Russia herself: Zhenia, his woman, is Russia. He would, we believe, happily die with terrible wounds if his last moments were to be spent in her arms. His arrest in *Life and Fate* precipitates a moment of decision for Zhenia: Is it to be Novikov or Krymov? Novikov's star appears to be in the ascendant. Aware that Krymov has been arrested and sent to Moscow, she sends him, now declared an "enemy of the people," a food parcel in the Lubianka, a brave thing to do in Stalin's time. Emotionally, at least, she seems to have returned to him.

The scenes involving Vavilov and Berezkin honestly reflect a painful experience of war familiar to any soldier—the separation of husband and wife. As Vavilov sets off to war, we sense that he will not return, and a miracle will be necessary for Berezkin's wife and child to survive. Grossman expertly exploits such scenes in order to secure an emotional response from the reader and also to prepare the ground for his later thesis that it was love of Russia, the defense of home and hearth, that held the Germans on the Volga, emphatically not the sterility of internationalism.

The historical-strategic chapters offer Grossman enormous scope to indulge his insightful speculations on the course of the war. For example, he obsessively returns to the summer of 1941, arguing that this experience hardened the survivors who will now stop the Germans at Stalingrad. The experiences of that summer are emphasized in the biographies of Novikov, Darenskii, Berezkin, and Krymov. Darenskii in his diaries reveals the fear and chaos of the early months yet manages to strike an optimistic note: "I'm convinced that the old Russian army would have collapsed from such blows, together with the tsarist regime. And we are holding out, which means we will hold out, which means we will be victorious."[49] That Darenskii was arrested in 1937, sent to a camp, and then released in 1940 renders this optimism somewhat forced. Darenskii, like Rokossovskii, survived the purge. Many did not, which surely must have had an impact on the Soviet response to the German invasion. Novikov recalls the first battles and the contradictory orders and confusion, the demand that Soviet commanders not respond to any provocation, even as the Germans were surging through the border regions. Novikov concludes that the main problem of the first few hours of the war was the breakdown in communications: "If communications had been intact, he believed, everything would have gone a lot differently."[50] Of Berezkin and the summer of 1941, Grossman notes, "The major had fought in the summer of 1941 in the forests of Western Belorussia and Ukraine. He had passed through the trials of the first days of the war and knew and had seen it all. A taciturn and shy person, the major listened to all the stories about the war with a quiet, restrained smile, amusing himself with the thought: 'Eh, lads, one can't talk or write about what I know.'"[51]

In his own retreat, Krymov sees the full range of human behavior in war: "Day and night Krymov headed eastward. On the way, he heard of General Colonel Kirponos's death; he read German leaflets about the fall of Moscow and Leningrad; he saw iron loyalty, treachery, despair, and unshakable belief."[52] Yet the summer of 1941 for Krymov, the commissar, means something fundamentally different from what it means to the professional officers. The German invasion awakens memories of the Civil War, Krymov's finest hour. He is reliving his past. For example, he feels a special sense of pride when he is addressed as "commissar" because the men know of Hitler's Kommissarbefehl (June 1941), the order to shoot all political officers and commissars on the spot. The irony, which is revealed only in *Life and Fate*, is that he will be arrested—and almost certainly shot—by his own side.

The frequency with which Grossman uses the summer of 1941 in the biographies of soldiers—Berezkin, Darenskii, Novikov in *For a Just Cause*, and Ershov in *Life and Fate*—suggests that by the time the Red Army reached Stalingrad, all the chaff had been removed, all the weaklings had been culled or otherwise eliminated; that what confronted the Germans at Stalingrad was the hard core of Russian patriotism, the true sons of the motherland. Yet the overwhelming success achieved by the Germans in 1941 invites some kind of explanation of what had happened. Grossman's response—one assumes it is Grossman's—suggests some aggressive editorial interference:

> What was the cause of the Red Army's retreat and the severe, tragic failures in the first months of the war? They were caused by the fact that the German troops by the time of the outbreak of war were already fully mobilized and that the 170 divisions, which were moved up to the borders of the Soviet Union by Hitler, were in a condition of complete readiness, awaiting merely the signal for the attack, whereas at that time Soviet troops were not sufficiently supplied with modern equipment and were not prepared for the idea of an inevitable and evident assault from fascist Germany, and they still had to be mobilized and deployed toward the border. One of the reasons for the Red Army's failures consisted in the absence of a Second front in Europe against the German-fascist armies, which had still not been opened. The Germans, considering their rear in the West secure, were able to move all their troops and those of their allies against our country. Finally, the reason for the Red Army's

failures in the first period of the war consisted in insufficient tanks, aircraft, and artillery.[53]

The journal version (1952) specifically cites Stalin. With references to Stalin omitted in later editions, we are left with a totally different impression. Taken at face value, the various explanations raise more questions than they purport to answer. Why were Soviet forces not properly mobilized? Nor is it accurate to say that Soviet troops had to be deployed toward the border. One reason why the German assault was so devastating was because Soviet troops were deployed too far forward and were easily overwhelmed and outflanked. Why were Soviet troops not supplied with modern equipment? This explanation is at odds with the boasts made during the prewar period.[54] If the war with Germany was perceived as "inevitable and evident," why were the necessary countermeasures not taken? Given the Non-aggression Pact between Germany and the Soviet Union, the absence of a Second front before 22 June 1941 is hardly an excuse. Moreover, the fact that the Soviet Union could conceive of a Second front launched by Britain against the Germans prior to 22 June 1941, so as to alleviate the pressure on the Red Army, can only mean that the Soviet high command (that is, Stalin) was aware of a real, impending threat from the Germans. That being so, the failure to take the necessary measures—modern equipment and sound tactical deployment in the border regions—is all the more inexplicable. Nor does the excuse that the Red Army had insufficient aircraft, tanks, and artillery withstand scrutiny. Quantity was not a problem; the crucial failings were poor quality and inept handling.

Within the confines set by Soviet censorship, Grossman uses his historical-strategic chapters to explain Hitler's rise to power and the nature of his grip on Germany. In chapter 30, a long, detailed chapter in part 2, which was added for the book publication of the novel, Grossman examines the phenomenon of Hitler and the rise of the Nazis. In places, this is a very insightful chapter, a mixture of standard Soviet positions and Grossman's own interpretations that nevertheless does justice to the theme. One way to read this Hitler chapter is to see it as the foundation of the fuller exposition of ideas that are presented in Life and Fate.

Germany, argues Grossman, wounded and humiliated in the aftermath of defeat in World War I, longed for a politician of the Hitler type: "Defeated in the imperialist war, Germany looked for Hitler, and she found him."[55] According to Grossman, Hitler's success stemmed from the many failings in his personal life: his lack of ability as a student, the frustration of his artistic ambitions, his lack of success with women. These failings drove him, fueling an insatiable desire for revenge against the circles that had rejected him. Grossman's analysis of the Hitler phenomenon is also of interest for the light it casts on the Soviet Union and Stalin, for a large part of the shortcomings that Grossman identifies in Hitler and his policies are readily applicable to the Soviet state—the moral and intellectual relativism of the Nazi state, repeatedly referred to, being one obvious parallel. The German officer Colonel Forster is ordered to Berlin to meet Hitler. Not the first officer to succumb, he is overwhelmed by the force of Hitler's personality. On his return to the front, the plane flies over the site of a death camp. Forster, still under Hitler's spell, reflects upon Hitler's intentions: "He started to perceive that the Führer in his striving toward world domination had lost ordinary, banal notions. At such a cold altitude, there was no longer good or evil. Suffering meant nothing. There could be no mercy, no reproaches, no conscience."[56]

If "all is permitted" in the name of race war, then such war finds its murderous analog in the class-based relativism initiated by Lenin and pursued by Stalin. Grossman's portrayal of life in Germany under Hitler must have caused a few Soviet heads to nod. Consider the comments made by a dissenting German.[57] One wonders what the discerning Soviet reader made of such transparently Aesopian interpolations:

> You know, submissiveness, not thinking about things, and timeserving are the high point of civil valor for a Berliner. Only the Führer has the right to think, but he just prefers intuition to thinking. Free, scientific thought, the titans of German philosophy—have all gone to hell. We have renounced general categories, universal truth, morals, and humanity. All philosophy, science, and art begin with the empire and end with the empire. There is no place in Germany for bold and free minds. They are sterilized like Hauptmann, or they fall silent like Kellerman. You see, the most powerful minds—Einstein and Planck—have risen and flown away like birds.[58]

The Nazi rejection of Einstein and the general comments on the state of intellectual life in Nazi Germany are also applicable to the Soviet Union. Returning to such remarks from the standpoint of *Life and Fate*, we see a specific adumbration of Viktor Shtrum's struggle for intellectual and moral autonomy.

Nor is Grossman's discussion of Hitler's fascination with the Nietzschean superman entirely one-sided. Grossman argues that "the superman is born of the despair of the weak, not the triumph of the strong."[59] In *Life and Fate*, Grossman coins the term "superviolence," which is one of the main weapons in the intellectual and physical arsenal of the totalitarian state. His comments regarding Hitler's fascination with violence are also germane to the Soviet state. And if Nazi Germany sought to perfect the superman through the application of eugenics programs, then communist states pursued their own vision of the superman, *Homo sovieticus*, with the same zeal. Idealized in the grotesque statues of muscle-bound factory workers and tractor drivers, the Soviet supermen (and -women) were to be the vanguard of the new class-based elite. Physical destruction of the class enemy was an obligation imposed by history and sanctified by the party. Grossman's categorical rejection of Hitler as a "true historical personality" cannot but include an outright rejection of Lenin, Stalin, Mao, and their swarms of imitators.

It seems to me that Grossman identifies something utterly profound for our understanding of totalitarianism, indeed of any form of power that involves the use of violence, and not just physical violence. "Ordinary, banal notions"—here Grossman anticipates "the banality of evil," a term coined by Hannah Arendt[60]—stem from the remoteness of the Führer from the deeds he makes possible (and let us not forget Stalin and Mao). Grossman suggests that there is a moral and bureaucratic threshold that, when crossed, makes mass killing all the more likely, and that this threshold is more easily reached and crossed the more remote the Führer (or Stalin or Mao) is. On the killing fields of Ukraine and Belorussia or in the crematoria, the mass murderers must believe that murdering millions of peasants and their children, as in the Terror-Famine, or gassing millions of Jewish men and women, little boys and girls, as in the Holocaust, is morally justified. The sense of purpose that enables them to carry out these gruesome deeds comes from Hitler. It matters not that in Germany and in the Soviet Union there were individuals who saw through this perversion. What matters is that sufficient numbers will obey—and did obey—on the basis that "all is permitted." Here we find one of the levers of totalitarianism, its satanic essence unflinchingly foreseen by Dostoyevsky, by means of which the

Führer, Vozhd', and the Great Helmsman commanded and manipulated the loyalty of their ideologically driven killers.

Battle scenes are one of Grossman's specialties. Three stand out in *For a Just Cause*: Tolia Shaposhnikov's artillery duel with the Germans; the huge German air raid on Stalingrad, which followed the pattern of Warsaw and Rotterdam; and the wiping out of Filiashkin's battalion, a unit of Rodimtsev's division, in Stalingrad. All three scenes show courage as a resource found in the most unlikely people, a courage that can be stimulated by a sense of duty, anger, or overwhelming compassion and concern for people in one's care. The destruction of Filiashkin's battalion deserves especially close attention.

Describing the course of the battle, Grossman leaves us in no doubt that the men of Filiashkin's battalion are driven by duty and patriotism. The battalion contains sinners and saints: a penal section and ordinary Russians, exemplified by Vavilov, whose moral authority grows as the battle progresses. Their task is to fight and die. Russia shall be saved, and all the sins of the past shall be wiped away.

Grossman's description of a night attack—matched only by Nekrasov's—is superb and conveys the ferocity and sickening fear of the fighting:

> At two o'clock in the morning in complete darkness something new, terrible, and completely unfamiliar began: a night attack.
>
> The Germans didn't use flares. They crawled in from all four sides. The killing went on all through the night. No stars could be seen; they were obscured by cloud, and it seemed that the blackness had come so that people could not glance into one another's frenzied eyes.
>
> Everything was used: knives, and shovels, and bricks, and metal heels of boots.
>
> In the blackness, you could hear screams, hoarse voices, pistol shots, the individual crack of a rifle, the short burst of automatic fire.
>
> The Germans crawled in groups and overwhelmed the defenders by sheer weight. Everywhere where there was noise, a fight, they appeared in tens against one or two. In the blackness, they struck out with knives, their fists. They went for the throat. They were seized by bestiality.[61]

The portrait of bravery and endurance under the relentless German attacks is made all the more credible by the fact that Grossman does not gloss over human weakness. Among the defenders are cowards. In the middle of the battle, a Soviet soldier lies in his trench crushed by fear. There is no summary execution, just contempt on the part of his former comrades, a response that may not be entirely realistic in the light of Order № 227 but that fits with Grossman's view that Russian patriotism was the rock on which the Nazi war machine was shattered.

Blinded by their success, the Germans seem unable to conceive that their fortunes could change. Here one can note Grossman's ax metaphor, which is conspicuously Tolstoyan:

> So, probably, an ax that was accustomed to splitting a log free of any knots would be inclined to overestimate the weight and sharpness of its edge and to underestimate the forces of cohesion in a thick-set, wooden trunk. And, well, an ax that would cut deeply into a knotty trunk would suddenly stop, seized fast by the forces of the tense wood. And it seems that the whole black earth, which experienced ferocious frosts, was beaten by heavy rains and scorched by fires, and which had come to know the meaning of terrible July storms and the dry autumns, transferred its strength, which had been sucked up by its deep roots, to this trunk.[62]

By showing the Germans despoiling and defiling the Russian dead in the aftermath of the battle, Grossman sharpens the readers' appetite for the inevitable retribution. The scene dehumanizes the German victors, not the Russians. The Russians are dead; the Germans are damned.

The prolonged agony of the battalion's destruction buys time for the rest of Rodimtsev's division, and indeed for the whole Soviet defense. In the immediate aftermath of the Soviet victory, there was bitter rivalry between Chuikov's and Rodimtsev's supporters, each side claiming that their general had saved Stalingrad at the last moment. Grossman devotes a great deal of time to Rodimtsev's division; as with Berezkin, Novikov, and Darenskii, the experience of 1941 is all-important. On the other hand, the depiction of Chuikov is respectful but restrained. Emotionally, we feel, Grossman belongs to the Rodimtsev camp.

Any discussion of Grossman's novels is perforce a discussion of censorship in Russian literature. Regarding *For a Just Cause*, the problem is of an order different from that which affected *Life and Fate*. As demonstrably brutal and pervasive as the institution of Soviet censorship was, it is probably overstating the case to cite it as the sole cause of all the omissions and supplements that can be identified. Some are innocent enough, part of the editing process that all writers go through. That said, consistent patterns emerge from the detailed process of comparing the journal and book versions and, given the obvious ideological importance that they have for Soviet war literature, and especially for a writer such as Grossman, the demands of the censor and the whole poisonous atmosphere engendered by Stalinism must be regarded as the main culprits.

In the various changes that Grossman makes, we can see that he is one of the first Soviet writers to address the impact of the purges on military and industrial performance, and indeed on Soviet society as a whole. In the journal version, we learn of the difficulties faced by Aleksandra Vladimirovna Shaposhnikova's son, Dmitrii, before the war. "Before the war" (*do voiny*) and "unpleasant matters" (*nepriiatnosti*) are codes that alert the reader, as Grossman perhaps intends, to the fact that Dmitrii has fallen foul of the organs. By the time we get to the book, Grossman confirms what we have suspected: Dmitrii has become another victim of the Great Terror. An addition to his mother's biography that Grossman makes for the later version—that she had lived in Switzerland and spoke German—almost certainly works against her hapless son, who is accused of conspiracy and of contact with "enemies of the people." In the journal we see that Colonel Darenskii, one of the future stars of *Life and Fate*, had his "difficulties" before the war. The way in which this situation is presented in the journal is misleading. It suggests that the arrests of officers such as Darenskii were isolated incidents that occurred because of the machinations of rogue individuals rather than being part of a state-sponsored terror campaign of class war.

In the later version, Grossman hints at the judicial lawlessness and the random, capricious violence of 1937, which is exposed and condemned in *Life and Fate*. In another chapter (28, part 1), which was added to the novel later, Grossman provides details of Liudmila Shtrum's first marriage to Abarchuk. One of the Bolshevik student fanatics who helped to purge the universities of students with politically and socially incorrect origins in the 1920s, Abarchuk is himself arrested as an "enemy of the people" a decade later. The arrests of Abarchuk in *For a Just Cause* and Krymov in *Life and Fate* confirm the adage that the revolution devours its children.

Many of the changes made for the new version reduce the overall importance and role of Stalin. Chapter 41 (part 2) in the journal portrays Stalin as the man who inspired bravery and determination as the crisis deepened. The entire chapter was omitted from the book. We find examples in the book where "Stalingrad" is omitted and "Volga" used in its place. In the transition from journal to book, "Supreme Commander" frequently gives way to "Supreme Command," thus emphasizing the collective nature of the leadership. Although this change quite properly helps to weaken the grotesque personality cult surrounding Stalin, it unfortunately obscures some of Stalin's incompetence. The removal of Stalin's speeches from the book version raises the question of why they were included in the journal. The most likely reason is one of the many "suggestions" made to Grossman before the journal was published. Once Stalin was dead, there was no pressure to cite the Father of All Strategists, so the ideological ballast could be jettisoned.

As Stalin's presence in the novel version of *For a Just Cause* is weakened by omissions and editing, so Hitler's is strengthened. Two chapters added to the novel (28 and 30, part 2) examine the importance of Stalingrad for Hitler and the Hitler phenomenon in twentieth-century German history. The significance of these chapters is twofold. First, they are serious attempts to try to understand the factors that made possible Hitler's rise to power and his subsequent military career. Given Grossman's own personal misfortune, the pan-European Jewish catastrophe that he had witnessed and helped to document from 1943 onward, and the Soviet lens through which so much regarding Hitler had to be focused, they are remarkably objective, demonstrably superior to what we find in Stadniuk's *War*. Second, as with other aspects of *For a Just Cause*, both journal and book redactions can rightly be seen as veiled and not-so-veiled attacks on Stalin and Stalinism, and so, once again, they prepare the way for what is to come in *Life and Fate*.

Regarding the war theme, the book version of *For a Just Cause* that emerges from the editing and additions is an improvement on the journal version, though the differences are slight. The additions made to the early chapters in which Vavilov is introduced—for example, the marked contrast between Vavilov, the dedicated patriot, and the essentially corrupt collective farm chairman and Vavilov's willingness to help people in distress when others would turn away enhances one of the major characters. By the time we get to Stalingrad and the final battle, Vavilov's stoicism in adversity is utterly convincing. If only Grossman had retained that enigmatic, apparently perplexing, yet ultimately optimistic epitaph: "So ended the battle of the rifle battalion on the Volga. Who was the victor therein?" On the downside are the many cuts made in the exchanges of ideas between Chepyzhin and Shtrum, though they emerge in a slightly different form in *Life and Fate*.

In spite of the censorship and the exhausting reediting schedule imposed on Grossman, *For a Just Cause* retains his voice. Even allowing for the various concessions that Grossman appears to have made for the first publication, he sets a standard that only a few Soviet writers have surpassed. In many ways, *For a Just Cause* is ahead of its time.

Hot Snow (1969)

Unlike the other major Soviet-Russian novels that deal with Stalingrad and are set in the city, concentrating on the street fighting, *Hot Snow* deals with the ultimately successful Soviet task of preventing Manstein from smashing a corridor through to the surrounded 6th Army. In keeping with the author's other work, *Hot Snow* draws upon his experience as an artillery officer. Despite the fact that many of the themes addressed by Bondarev are hot spots in Soviet-Russian war literature—desertion, the role of the NKVD, Vlasov, and Stalin's leadership—they are dealt with in a way that is by no means anti-Soviet. Indeed, in some ways Bondarev seems too conformist and too willing to pull his punches. By the time of his writing *Tishina* (Silence, 1964) and *Hot Snow*, Bondarev had softened the harsh tone that characterized *The Battalions Request Fire Support* and *The Final Salvoes*.

Evidence of softening some of the harsher realities can be seen in the way Bondarev deals with the theme of desertion. One of the soldiers in Kuznetsov's platoon, the orderly Chibisov, has spent time in German captivity. When surrounded by German tanks, the commissar shot himself, and Chibisov and the others surrendered and were taken prisoner. Kuznetsov asks what Chibisov did with his weapon, the implication being that Chibisov and the rest should have followed the lead of the commissar. There is no mention of time spent in NKVD filtration units or any judicial persecution. In other ways, the picture is contradictory. Chibisov says that "there's not the fear that there was before,"[63] yet there are references to cases of self-inflicted gunshot wounds (*samostrel*), which suggest that Soviet morale is not quite what Bondarev would have us believe, even with signs that the tide is starting to turn against the Germans.

The outcome of another incident is inconsistent with the harsh disciplinary regime of the Red Army. En route to the Stalingrad area, the column comes under attack from the Luftwaffe. Ukhanov, one of the gun-team commanders, is absent after the attack. Looking for Ukhanov, the platoon commander, Kuznetsov, bumps into the divisional commander, Bessonov. Informed that Ukhanov is missing, Bessonov touches on an important theme in the work: "In the rear, as you realize, Lieutenant, there's no such thing as those disappearing without a trace. . . . In the rear those disappearing without a trace have one name: deserters."[64] Eventually Ukhanov turns up, having called in at some village. The absentee receives a mild ticking off, though in the climate of the time he would have been liable to execution for desertion. Yet another example of unusual and hardly credible leniency occurs as Bessonov proceeds to the main Soviet defensive line, where Manstein's tanks must be stopped. Bessonov encounters a group of Soviet tanks. He accuses the tank commander of cowardice and orders him back into the fray, giving him a second chance to prove himself. What makes these examples of leniency especially unconvincing is Order № 227, which hung over the head of every soldier and commander, something of which Bondarev would have been only too well aware. Commanders who failed to show the necessary ruthlessness were themselves liable to punishment. We can speculate that Bondarev is perhaps trying to expose the inadequacies of such measures, since the pressure to be ruthless, regardless of circumstances, meant that innocent men were punished.

In the Soviet scheme of things, Bessonov's own biography is not without blemish, which makes his subsequent appointment by Stalin to command the defensive operation against the Germans all the more surprising. We learn that Bessonov's son was serving in the Second Shock Army, commanded by General Vlasov, and did not escape from the German encirclement. The full details emerge in chapter 6, which, anticipating Bogomolov, But, and Vladimov, serves as Bondarev's Stalin chapter. This chapter is rather crude historical revisionism. Bondarev's Stalin is no capricious tyrant; the pictures of Suvorov and Kutuzov in his office are intended to suggest that Stalin follows in their footsteps. There is no mention of the purges of the military, though, interestingly, Rokossovskii, who was arrested and then released, is the one who recommended Bessonov to Stalin. Nor does Bondarev make any attempt to explain Stalin's failure to heed intelligence warnings of a German invasion and thus his role in the summer defeats of 1941 and 1942.

Stalin, sounding out Bessonov's understanding of the situation at Stalingrad, mentions that the aim was to encircle the Germans at Moscow as well but that this was not possible due to lack of men. This remark suggests some rewriting of history, implying that the Red Army was planning this encirclement at Stalingrad all along, waiting for the moment rather than reacting to a perceived opportunity. In other words, the long retreat to the Volga was part of a deliberate strategy to ensnare the Germans. Bondarev cannot resist the historical comparison with Cannae while avoiding the obvious Cannae-like victories achieved by the Germans in their summer campaigns.

Given that Bessonov's son was taken prisoner along with Vlasov, it is remarkable that Stalin even considers Bessonov for the post. The attempts to denigrate the character and achievements of Vlasov conveniently ignore the fact that he distinguished himself in the Moscow battle and that he was singled out for praise in *Pravda*. Much of what Bondarev writes about Vlasov is based on Soviet sources that never gave an honest assessment of Vlasov after he was captured. Nor is Bondarev's Stalin convincing on this theme: "It is known that this political adventurist of average abilities"—Stalin started to speak with irritation—"has entered the service of the Germans. This shy general is to blame for the deaths of six thousand soldiers from his army and the disappearance of eight thousand. In my opinion, Comrade Bessonov, it is politically and morally weak elements that get captured. Those who are in some way dissatisfied with our system . . . With some exceptions . . . Agreed?"[65]

Again, by laying all blame on Vlasov, the aim is to avoid any discussion of large-scale disaffection among the rank and file:

> There are cases of treachery, cowardice, betrayal of armies, handing over secret documents in all wars. Vlasov's treachery in June 1942 was not an act of betrayal by the army, which had fought to the last man in the area of the village, Spaskaia Polist'—the remains of the divisions fought their way out of the ring. Vlasov's treason was the cowardly betrayal of one general who secretly abandoned his headquarters at night and went to the village of Piatnitsa, occupied by the Germans, with words of fear and humiliation, and said, "Don't shoot, I am General Vlasov." He saved his own life, which from that moment became death, for every act of treachery is spiritual death.[66]

That may well be Bondarev's view of the situation, but the Soviet state under Stalin took a completely different view, and Bondarev knew it, as did his readers. Stalin tells Bessonov that his son, IAkov, disappeared without a trace, which is not true because he was captured, and the Germans let the world know that they had captured him. Stalin means that IAkov became an unperson.

The Vlasov theme emerges again in the sudden appearance at Bessonov's battle headquarters of Colonel Osin, head of counterintelligence at army headquarters. Osin begins his meeting with Vesnin, the representative of the army council, by pointing out that it would be better if Bessonov moved to a position of greater safety, that is, from the divisional observation point to the one at army headquarters. Osin hints that two officers (Generals IAtsenko and Golubkov) at Bessonov's headquarters are informers. What appears to be concern for Bessonov's security turns out to be something quite different. Then Osin hints at the real reason why he has come, mentioning the "fateful events" in connection with the Second Shock Army. Osin hands Vesnin a German propaganda sheet that shows a picture of Bessonov's son in a German hospital. Osin assures Vesnin that the photograph is genuine. According to the sheet, the son is critical of his training and equipment. He says he has been well treated by the Germans and that the claims that Russians are badly treated are nothing but "Soviet-commissar propaganda."[67] The son is also reported as saying, "Here, in hospital, I have had time to understand. The Germans are a highly civilized and humanitarian nation which wants to establish freedom in Russia after the overthrow of Bolshevism."[68] It emerges that the sheet is dated 14 October 1942, which suggests that Stalin knew about it at the time of Bessonov's appointment. Bondarev seems to be implying that Stalin was not vindictive; that the fact of the general's son being in German captivity had no bearing on the appointment. Again, this notion is unconvincing. That the son was a prisoner would be held against both son and father, the latter now being deemed unreliable, tainted in the Soviet scheme of things. Moreover, an appointment of this kind would have been conspicuously at odds with Order № 270, which provided, among other things, for the families of deserters and those who had surrendered to the enemy to be arrested and even to be deprived of state assistance and benefits.

Life and Fate (1988)

In an age of personal computers, freedom of information, and access to worldwide sources of data and information via the Internet it requires a leap of imagination to conceive of a time when censorship was a major factor in Russian literature. Yet it was so, and not that long ago. One of the blackest days in Russian literature's long battle against Soviet censorship was the "arrest" of Vasilii Grossman's Life and Fate manuscript on 14 February 1961. Some time after this personal catastrophe, Grossman managed to secure an interview with Mikhail Suslov, the party's chief ideologue. Grossman tried to persuade Suslov to return the manuscript on which he had worked for over ten years. Suslov refused but conceded that publication might be possible in another 200 to 250 years. Two factors worked against Grossman. The first was the recent scandal that had arisen from the publication of *Doktor Zhivago* abroad and the subsequent award of the Nobel Prize to its author, Boris Pasternak. The second and decisive factor was the nature of *Life and Fate* itself.

Life and Fate is an encyclopedia of the Soviet state in war and peace, a compendium of relentless physical and psychological violence directed at individuals and whole nations. Almost as remarkable as the novel is the intellectual and moral transformation of the author, a process that involves his moving from a position of convinced Marxism-Leninism through cautious skepticism to outright heresy and rejection of the Soviet regime and doing so in a way that is fearless, explicit, pitiless, and uncompromising. IUrii Zhivago's musings are tame by comparison.

Pasternak views the revolution, the ravages of the Civil War, the NEP, and the onset of Stalinism with the jaundiced but penetrating eye of a man who has lost everything. Redolent of nineteenth-century literature's superfluous man, Zhivago scorns the revolutionary fanaticism unleashed by 1917, preferring to write poems and womanize. Soviet critics could have done a fairly good job of showing that someone like Zhivago, coming from a bourgeois background, would react that way to the forces of class war that had destroyed his comfortable world forever. In any event, the response to the publication of *Doktor Zhivago* was badly handled by the Soviet literary establishment. Despite the strident claims of literary freedom in the Soviet Union and elsewhere in the Soviet empire in Eastern Europe, the campaign against Pasternak underlined the repressive nature of censorship and the dangers associated with attacking official Soviet taboos. Whereas one Soviet critic dismissed *Doktor Zhivago* as "a stinking little thing,"[69] Suslov was in no doubt that *Life and Fate* posed an altogether greater ideological threat to the Soviet Union's standing than Pasternak's novel. *Life and Fate* was, he told Grossman, an atomic bomb: Publication could destroy the Soviet Union.

Had Grossman confined himself to a harsh portrayal of life at the front, punctuated with various allusions and asides to some of the darker aspects of the Soviet state at war, something along the lines of Vasil' Bykov's *The Dead Feel No Pain* or *A Page from the Front*, it is conceivable that *Life and Fate* would have been published in the 1960s. However, publication was precluded by Grossman's far-ranging analysis of the war and Soviet society and his readiness to deal explicitly with all kinds of awkward questions. *Life and Fate* is not concerned just with the outcome of the Battle of Stalingrad. Using the battle as his base, Grossman offers a moral assessment of the Soviet state, a strategic overview from its founding to its struggle to build "socialism in one country" under Stalin to its attempt to survive the German invasion to the consequences of victory for postwar Soviet society and Eastern Europe. In doing so, Grossman attacks nearly every sacred tenet of the Soviet state. *Life and Fate* is one of the first Soviet novels to attack Soviet censorship directly and to explore its impact on intellectual life. In the misery and humiliation inflicted on Viktor Shtrum, the Jewish physicist, censorship threatens to undermine Soviet attempts to obtain the atomic bomb. Soviet censorship is pervasive and severe, as the "arrest" of the manuscript itself demonstrates.

Nor are party and people one. On the contrary, the party is a state within a state and does not hesitate to place its own ideological or quasi-ideological or merely selfishly banal interests before those of the people. A state that was supposed to eradicate exploitation has instead built a super-monopoly backed up by secret police, spies, organized lying on an industrial scale, informers, and a massive chain of death and labor camps. Super-violence is one of its major tools. The Terror-Famine, which claimed more dead—some 11 million—than did the Nazis in their *Vernichtungslager*, and even now is still one of the twentieth century's forgotten holocausts, demonstrated Stalin's capacity for bloodletting. After Stalin had murdered peasants in millions, he turned on the party, the bureaucracy, the intelligentsia, and the officer corps. This period, the Great Terror, is also notorious for its carefully orchestrated show trials.

Then there is the Holocaust, in which Grossman's own mother perished, a victim of one of the early mass machine-gunnings used before the Nazis had fully developed and tested the infrastructure of gassing and crematoria. Although we are obliged to remember that Jews were not the sole victims of the Nazi camps, the infrastructure of mass murder built at Treblinka, Belzec and Sobibor (Operation Reinhard), and Auschwitz-Birkenau was intended primarily to exterminate Jews. For a whole host of reasons, Soviet officials wanted to understate the special nature of Jewish suffering at the hands of the Nazis. One reason after 1945 was that it drew attention away from the huge numbers of Soviet victims; even here we were to understand that the main victims were Russian. In *Life and Fate*, Grossman reconciles his own demand, issued in *Treblinskii ad* (The Hell of Treblinka, 1944), that those who have seen the full horrors of the Holocaust must tell the truth with his deep love of Russia. Jews, he insists, were singled out for extermination, but he argues that he is no less a Russian patriot for pointing out that truth, and that he feels the pain of Mother Russia no less acutely. Nor does Grossman's rediscovery of his own lost Jewishness, which the Nazis and then Stalin forced on him, blind him to the slaughter caused by forced collectivization. In both *Life and Fate* and even more so in the later work, *Forever Flowing*, Grossman examines these two separate examples of twentieth-century mass murder, concluding that they have much in common and thus help to explain certain facets of red and brown totalitarianism.

Through various Aesopian allusions in *For a Just Cause*, Grossman had hinted that the Soviet state was the mirror image of the National Socialist state. In *Life and Fate*, allegory is abandoned, and Grossman sets about making explicit parallels between the two states. At the center of this malevolent universe, in which two equally odious regimes compete for the domination of Europe, lies Stalingrad. In making these comparisons, Grossman removes any possibility, as far as Suslov is concerned, that *Life and Fate* would be published in the Soviet Union in the twentieth century. Grossman also poses a stiff challenge from an unexpected and unwelcome quarter to Western scholars who argued that there was little to choose between the West and the Soviet bloc, or that the West, and the Soviet Union were converging politically and economically. Grossman rightly describes the Soviet state as "totalitarian," as many other Russians did from the mid-1980s onward, thus rejecting another shibboleth of Western political science. Grossman, then, is an outsider from the point of view both of Soviet orthodoxy and of Western scholars who were trying in the latter half of the Cold War, somewhat tortuously, to reconcile the existence of two political systems—liberal democracy and Communism—by steadfastly ignoring, among other things, exceptionally severe and pervasive censorship, mass murder, a huge network of slave-labor camps, and the obvious failures of an economy based on the public ownership of the means of production.

Regarding the essence of Soviet totalitarianism and its affinity with National Socialist Germany, the meeting in *Life and Fate* between Liss, a senior SS officer, and a Soviet prisoner, the Bolshevik commissar Mostovskoi, is crucial. This meeting more than anything else in *Life and Fate* led to the arrest of the manuscript and to Suslov's 250-year prohibition. Liss, the supreme psychologist, acknowledges Mostovskoi's hatred yet also recognizes their common ground: "When we look into each other's face, we not only look into a face that we hate, we look into a mirror. In this there is the tragedy of the epoch."[70] "We are your deadly enemies, yes indeed. But our victory is your victory. Do you understand?"[71] Liss confronts Mostovskoi with the realities of Soviet Communism: that it fights not for the good of humankind but, like its Nazi rival, for supreme power.[72] Mostovskoi's reaction to Liss's challenge reveals a fundamental affinity with his SS interlocutor of which he is hardly aware: "Mostovskoi studied Liss's face, and it seemed to him that this pale face with its high forehead ought to be placed at the very bottom of the anthropological table, and that evolution would move upward from there to the woolly-clad Neanderthal man."[73] Such visceral race hatred is, to put it mildly, at odds with the commissar who laments the abolition of the Communist International (Comintern) and preaches the brotherhood of man. But it certainly imitates Nazi propaganda's use of the Untermensch. In Mostovskoi's own language, Liss is a nedochelovek. Mostovskoi, the red Nazi, condemns himself.

Grossman uses the biography of the German officer Lieutenant Peter Bach, the son of social-democrat parents, to explain the origins and growth of the Nazi state. This analysis is less convincing than that offered to explain the rise of the Soviet state, one likely reason being that Grossman lacked an intimate familiarity with Germany and Weimar politics. Grossman ignores, or is not aware of, the major role played by the German Communist Party (KPD) in destabilizing the Weimar Republic. The German communists made common cause with the Nazis against the moderate left parties, which they labeled "social fascists." Moreover, once the Nazis had achieved power—and Grossman passes over the spectacular electoral successes of the Nazis—many of the rank and file of the KPD were accepted into the Nazi Party.

One obvious flaw in the Nazi-Soviet comparison offered in Life and Fate—one that can be observed throughout Soviet war literature, its secondary literature, and other areas of Soviet historiography and beyond, particularly in Western scholarship and journalism—is the indiscriminate use of the term "Fascism" rather than National Socialism to describe Hitler's Germany. The trend of using the word "fascist" to discredit opponents, whether fascist or not, was first used by communists before and after World War II, and this vulgar use is how most people, ignorant of the origins of the word and the state it describes, now employ it. Hence, National Socialist Germany was rarely referred to as "Nazi" but almost always, incorrectly, as "fascist."[74]

An excellent example of this deliberate blurring, so clearly revealing its propagandistic intent, is to be seen at the time of the Nazi-Soviet Non-aggression Pact (itself an illustrative example of the deep affinity between these two systems). Throughout most of the 1930s, the Soviet media always referred to Hitler's Germany as "German-fascist" (*nemetsko-fashistskii*). In breaking news of the pact, *Pravda* dropped the reference to "fascist," using the less common Russian adjective for German, *germanskii*.[75] When the Germans invaded on 22 June 1941, the "German-fascist" label returned immediately to service, and there it has remained ever since.

There are, as far as one can see, two reasons for this deliberate misuse of the "fascist" label. First, "Nazi," being an acronym of Nationalsozialistische Deutsche Arbeiterpartei (NSDAP), the National Socialist German Workers' Party, underlined the party's entirely justified claim to be a socialist party and the sole advocate of the interests of the working class. This claim posed real problems for the KPD in its propaganda war with Goebbels. By calling their enemies "fascists" instead of Nazis, the communists hoped to be able to divert attention from their opponents' socialist component. Indeed, this considerable socialist element was the source of serious internal tensions within the Nazi party, which Hitler finally resolved in a night of violence, the Night of the Long Knives, on 30 June–1 July 1934. Referring to Nazi Germany as a fascist state removed the link in propagandistic terms between nationalism and socialism, which in the Nazi party found expression in the so-called Strasserite wing. Again, this suited the propagandistic purposes of the Soviet state. Designating Nazi Germany "fascist" was also intended to emphasize differences between the allegedly progressive Soviet Union and Nazi Germany. Even the use of the "Nazi" acronym served Soviet propagandistic purposes because it does away with any hint of "socialist." Second, "fascist" put Moscow's two main ideological opponents—Germany and Italy—together so that fire could be concentrated on both. An attack on fascist Italy and Spain was also an attack on "fascist" Germany. That Italy and Spain were exemplars of fascist states served to enhance the veracity of the propagandist's claims. To the general reader, these distinctions may seem something of a red (or brown) herring, yet they deal with serious differences that, to the extent that the use of the word "Fascism" hides and blurs them, are important. Fascism as it existed in Spain, Portugal, and Italy was a milder form of statist control than either National Socialism or Communism.

Grossman frequently refers to the Hitler state as fascist or national socialist, suggesting that these two terms define the same kind of state (see, for example, chapter 2 in part 1). Again, in chapter 42, part 1, the inconsistent use of Fascism and National Socialism tends to undermine the parallels between Nazi Germany and the Soviet Union. On the one hand, Grossman argues that the eschatologies of race and class are as bad as one another, but on the other hand, he argues that Fascism (National Socialism), were it to triumph, would drown the world in blood. Grossman cannot quite bring himself to acknowledge the greater amounts of blood spilled by communist states, and not just the Soviet Union. Later this view appears to be amended. Shtrum makes the explicit connection between race war and class war; that is, the Germans kill on the basis of race; the Soviets and their communist allies kill on the basis of class.[76] And in a summary and linkage of the war and postwar periods Grossman makes a case that very little separated Nazi Germany from the Soviet Union:

> There was the great uprising in the Warsaw ghetto, in Treblinka and in Sobibor. The massive partisan movement that raged in the dozens of countries enslaved by Hitler. The post-Stalin Berlin uprising in 1953 and the Hungarian uprising in 1956, the uprisings that gripped the Siberian and Far Eastern camps after Stalin's death, and the Polish go-slows that occurred at that time, the student movement of protest against the suppression of freedom of thought that swept through many cities. The strikes in many factories showed the indestructibility of the striving for freedom that is innate in man. It was suppressed, but it survived.[77]

With regard to the specific origins and growth of Soviet totalitarianism, then, many of the parallels drawn between Nazi Germany and the Soviet Union in *Life and Fate* explain a great deal: the meeting between Liss and Mostovskoi, the recollections of Abarchuk and Chernetsov, and the attempts by the party to break Shtrum. We have, though, to wait for Grossman's last work, *Forever Flowing*, for his devastating attacks on socialism and the view that Lenin, not Stalin, was the architect of Soviet totalitarianism and its imitators. *Life and Fate* is a step in that direction.

For example, the idea that "freedom is innate in man" penetrates nearly all of Grossman's work and nourishes the moral, intellectual, and practical rejection of the superstate and its coercion that we find in the testament of

Ikonnikov-Morzh (part 2, chapter 16), a copy of which is given to Mostovskoi by Liss. In many ways, this testament is an elusive and impenetrable document: either a suppressed scream in a seemingly endless night of horror and misery, the ravings of an unhinged mind, or a hymn of courageous stoicism speaking to us from the depths of hell.

The uniqueness of the individual is unflinchingly asserted in Ikonnikov-Morzh's testament. The conformity of the camp barracks is inhuman and justifies Grossman's warning in the opening pages of *Life and Fate* that "life perishes where violence strives to wipe out its distinctiveness and peculiarities."[78] Having lost his faith in God, Ikonnikov-Morzh, the former Tolstoyan and witness to the horrors of forced collectivization, now rejects the state and its coercive powers completely. "Where," he explains to Mostovskoi, "there is violence, grief reigns and blood is spilled. I saw the massive sufferings of the peasants, but collectivization was carried through in the name of the good. I do not believe in the good. I believe in goodness."[79]

These opening exchanges culminate in the meeting between Liss and Mostovskoi. Mostovskoi has no real answers for his ideological tormentor. Intellectually confused and spiritually broken, he is in no-man's-land between the cold-blooded ideological consistency of Liss and the self-sacrifice of Ikonnikov-Morzh. For all the common ground of the two antagonists that Grossman relentlessly lays before the reader, the Liss-Mostovskoi meeting leaves us with the impression that something truly satanic about Liss separates him from Mostovskoi. Ideologically, Liss is in control. Only Ikonnikov-Morzh has the spiritual resources and honesty to resist Liss, to look the devil's disciple in the eye. His testament is in effect the answer to Liss that Mostovskoi cannot provide. Mostovskoi is not just irredeemably compromised by his earlier work for the party. He believes, like Krymov and Abarchuk, that the party is always correct, that the latest line must always be followed, wherever it leads. If that means that millions of peasants must be exterminated like insects, then so be it. Heeding Lenin's call for democratic centralism, he has surrendered the capacity of a free man to decide for himself so that he lacks the moral and intellectual resources to resist Liss's malevolent and deeply wounding jibes. Mostovskoi is too much the party flunkey.

Ikonnikov-Morzh has penetrated to the ideological core of both Mostovskoi, the representative of the secular-teleological, and Liss, the articulator of the demonic-apocalyptic. At the summit of the demonic-apocalyptic stand Hitler and Stalin, but in *Life and Fate*, its purest embodiment is represented by

Liss. Liss is the true and ghastly reflection of Mostovskoi's secular official with his ideological justification of class or race war. Liss is the SS demon who works for the apocalypse promised by his master, Hitler.

The psychology of the secular-teleological appeals to a certain type of intellectual who fully accepts the need for planned violence if historical destiny is to be realized. The growth of collectivist ideologies, with their explanations of historical progress, is the single most important reason for this massive seduction and ensnaring of a group that prides itself on its ability to interpret the complexity of historical, social, and economic trends; to "see things as they really are"; or to "deconstruct the hegemonic discourse" and expose its hidden agenda. The intellectual gangster, a familiar figure of the twentieth-century landscape, is the offspring of historicism. No sooner has the belief in the laws of history seduced the intelligentsia—who as a group must bear an enormous responsibility for Hitler and Stalin—than it is but a short step to demand that social, economic, and even racial policies take these laws into account. The stage is set for the great plan, in the words of Friedrich Hayek, "the deliberate organisation of the labours of society for a definite social goal."[80] In the twentieth century, the great plan had various names: "Die Endlösung der Judenfrage"(the Final Solution of the Jewish Question); "god velikogo pereloma" (the year of the great crisis, or break); collectivization (the Terror-Famine); and more recently "The Great Leap Forward," "The Year Zero," and "The Great Proletarian Cultural Revolution."

Mass societies are, in the absence of any strong liberal-democratic tradition with a respect for the individual, highly vulnerable to promises of social and economic progress based on some distant or narrowly defined notion of "the good." Any narrow definition leads to what Alain Besançon has termed "the falsification of the good."[81] The greater the promised good, the more restrictive the nature of the plan and the more harshly it will be implemented. National Socialist Germany and the Soviet Union are the apotheosis of the superstate and the superplan. The horrors of the twentieth century—the Jewish Holocaust and Stalin's and Mao's Terror-Famines—were the direct result of the ideologically based belief that socially and racially distinct groups had to be exterminated in order to bring about the new world.[82]

Inspired by his secular-teleological mission, the party intellectual insists on total loyalty to the plan. Here too is the justification for the suppression of individual conscience and of the very idea of human individuality. One of the clearest statements of what was entailed can be found in Arthur

Koestler's *Darkness at Noon* (1940). Rubashov's first interrogator, Ivanov, chides him for his sentimentality and the growth of conscience:

> The principle that the end justifies the means is and remains the only rule of political ethics; anything else is just chatter and melts away between one's fingers. . . . If Raskolnikov had bumped off the old woman at the command of the Party—for example, to increase strike funds or to instal an illegal press . . . the novel with its misleading problem would never have been written, and so much the better for humanity.[83]

Koestler's portrait of History's executor and of the methods he must use is a perfect match of Liss, Mostovskoi, and Krymov in *Life and Fate*.[84] The party strives to penetrate the mind and soul of the people because it can never be absolutely confident that the collectivized conscience will always be obeyed. Consequently the party is ever watchful for the growth of individual conscience, doubt, and skepticism.

Ikonnikov-Morzh rejects the secular-teleological interpretation of history. Any form of good that entails large-scale social engineering must make huge assumptions about the nature of progress and the future. Ikonnikov-Morzh's attack lacks the intellectual rigor of other opponents of this idea, most notably Sir Karl Popper in *The Poverty of Historicism*, but the Russian's arguments and personal experience lead to similar conclusions: History has no meaning waiting to be discovered by political scientists and party ideologists; hence the ideas that are vital weapons in the party's intellectual arsenal are null and void. This conclusion is implicit in an early part of Ikonnikov-Morzh's testament when he laments the misery caused by those in pursuit of the good: "The good of the sect, class, nation, and state all strive to arrogate to themselves a false universality in order to justify their struggle against anything they consider to be evil."[85] All-embracing theories of social and economic behavior—in the twentieth century we would have used the word "ideology"—help to legitimize the struggle for the greater good. Their historical precedents are bad enough, as noted by Ikonnikov-Morzh:

> Byzantium's iconoclasm; the tortures perpetrated by the Inquisition;
> the struggle against heresies in France, Italy, Flanders, and
> Germany; the struggle between Protestantism and Catholicism; the
> treachery of the monastic orders; the struggle between Nikon and

Avvakum; the many centuries of repression visited on science and freedom; the Christian destroyers of the heathen population of Tasmania; the evil people who set fire to Negro villages in Africa: All this has brought about far greater suffering than the evil acts of brigands and evil people who perpetrated evil for the sake of evil.[86]

Ikonnikov-Morzh's final point is a fitting reply to Koestler's interrogator, Ivanov. Raskolnikov's idea is a thousand times more dangerous than the hedonism and sadism of a Svidrigailov. When the rulers of a modern state are seduced by the Raskolnikov idea, then the intellectual and ethical justification for Kolyma, "Auschwitz without the crematoria," in the words of Georgy Demidov,[87] and the Nazi death camps themselves is already present and waiting to be used. The individual pursuing his dream of the good (or bad) life will harm or benefit few other than himself. The notion of the collectivized good based on the idea of the "universal good" (*vseobshchee dobro*) is all too often the road to hell. It is, observes Ikonnikov-Morzh, "the invincible strength of the idea of the social good"[88] that drives the party in the campaign to collectivize the peasantry, to initiate a famine, and to root out the imaginary heretics of 1937.

It is, however, not enough to say, as Ikonnikov-Morzh does, that history's misery is due to a nation's or a sect's pursuing its own policies at the expense of others. Sects and nations have always behaved that way, and probably always will. Even the religions that Ikonnikov-Morzh rightly cites as the cause of much misery are limited in their ability to cause evil. The most zealous inquisitor must take note of God the witness while nevertheless committing atrocities in His name. No such spiritual authority inhibits the commissar or *Gauleiter*. He is driven by "the great and radiant idea of the social good."[89] His authority is either the iron law of historical materialism or the law that justifies any measures to ensure the survival of the master race.

The asserted universality of a particular good—that it marches shoulder to shoulder with a chosen group—could not function without the prescriptiveness of ideology. In the growth and power of ideology, we find a peculiarly twentieth-century evil and ultimately the main cause of the horrors recorded in Ikonnikov-Morzh's testament and elsewhere in *Life and Fate*. Ideology is more than a set of beliefs or principles with a hint of dogmatism. In this it differs from philosophy; it is altogether more grandiose in conception and design. Unlike history's other perpetrators of mass violence and suffering, Soviet and Nazi (and Maoist) tyrannies would not or could not recognize any external authority. To do so would be to abandon their claims of uniqueness that set them apart from the bourgeois democracies despised by both systems. It is this displacement of all traditional moral and ethical considerations that so sharply, and so catastrophically for their millions of victims, distinguishes the Soviet and Nazi (and Maoist) systems from anything previously known. Thus, the historical continuity depicted by Ikonnikov-Morzh—the struggle against heretics, the persecution of scientists by the church, and the growth of colonial empires—that finishes with the Soviet and Nazi terror should be interpreted with caution. Viktor Shtrum, whose struggle for moral and intellectual autonomy in many significant respects mirrors those of Grossman himself, seems to recognize the essential difference, his idiosyncratic use of "Fascism" notwithstanding: "Fascism renounced the concept of the individual, the concept of the person, and functions with huge aggregates."[90] It is at this juncture that the Soviet and Nazi systems break with the past. The removal of God and the secularization of the historical process lead us in strange and unexpected directions. The destruction of religious and moral hierarchies does not lead to the abandonment of all hierarchies. They are "merely" replaced by hierarchies, based not on humankind's capacity for good and goodness, and offering at least the possibility of controlling human bestiality, but on something clearly unanticipated. The path for the demonic to assert itself is now clear, as we see in Dostoyevsky's The Devils.

Embodying, perhaps, Jünger's concept of "the soldier of the idea," Ikonnikov-Morzh dies because he refuses to work on the foundations of a gas chamber. He rejects the world of the demon. His death is a symbolic reaffirmation of the absolutes of good and evil in a world ruled by moral relativism. His death also attacks the idea of the ideologically inspired good from another, unexpected direction. The great leap forward that is the basis of so much utopian social engineering makes enormous assumptions about what is possible and fails for many reasons, perhaps above all because it assumes that human behavior and morality can be conditioned infinitely. Ikonnikov-Morzh's decision to choose death rather than to submit to the dictates of a godless world, or perhaps a world ruled by the devil, poses insuperable obstacles for those who believe in the possibilities of wholesale moral reeducation. Regression as much as progression is implicit in social systems, as Ikonnikov-Morzh seems to understand when he tells Mostovskoi that "the world has not risen higher than the truth uttered by that Syrian Christian who lived in the sixth century . . . condemn the sin and forgive the sinner."[91]

Conclusion

"What a society gets in its armed services," wrote the British general Sir John Hackett, "is exactly what it asks for, no more and no less. What it asks for tends to be a reflection of what it is. When a country looks at its fighting forces it is looking in a mirror; the mirror is a true one and the face that it sees will be its own."[92] Can the same be said of a nation's war literature? And if so, what do the Stalingrad novels of Nekrasov, Simonov, Bondarev, and Grossman tell us?

The answer to the first question is affirmative, accompanied by the qualification that the mirror's surface may not be as smooth as possible, but nevertheless it provides some recognizable image. In *Days and Nights*, *In the Trenches of Stalingrad*, and *For a Just Cause*, we see a nation reeling from multiple disasters and defeats that, no matter what the censors wanted, could not be hidden. Russia's fate will be decided by the likes of Saburov (*Days and Nights*); Kerzhentsev and Chumak (*In the Trenches of Stalingrad*); and Berezkin, Darenskii, Vavilov, Ershov, Grekov, and Novikov (*For a Just Cause* and *Life and Fate*). Published well after Stalin's death, *Hot Snow* is the least convincing, mainly because of Bondarev's rather clumsy attempts to give Stalin all the credit for the Soviet victory. Consistent with Hackett's thesis, this answer provides us with a truth about Soviet war literature, specifically that a certain facet of Russian nationalism was prepared to ignore Stalin's failings.

One of Grossman's themes in *Life and Fate* is Russian nationalism without Stalin. In the belief that it was a hard core of individual soldiers that saved the day, in spite of Stalin, Nekrasov and Simonov are much closer to Grossman than to Bondarev.

6 NKVD Reports from Stalingrad, 1942–1943: Blocking Detachments, Deserters, Executions, and Morale

From now on the iron law of discipline for every commander, Red Army soldier, and political worker must be the demand—not a step backward without the order of a superior commander.
—Stalin, Order № 227, 28 July 1942

Declassified top-secret reports and dispatches compiled by the NKVD's Special Section during the course of the Battle of Stalingrad provide detailed information on the role of military censors, Red Army morale, blocking detachments, and ideological and moral disaffection as well as the number of soldiers arrested and executed. The raw data and reports make compelling reading for any historian of the battle and, in addition, provide valuable insights into the inner workings of the Soviet state at war and into one of its most secretive institutions. The documents reveal a wide spectrum of attitudes among soldiers toward the Soviet state, complicating our assessment of the motivation of the Stalingrad defenders and, with regard to the human factor in war, the overall Soviet victory on the Eastern front.

Introduction

Between 1941 and 1945, the Soviet regime prosecuted two separate yet interconnected wars. The first, now a byword for everything that defines the horrors of twentieth-century total warfare, turned decisively in favor of the Soviet state after the Stalingrad victory in February 1943. Less well known, though many blank spots are now being filled in, was the war against internal enemies—in essence a continuation of the ideological struggle that was pioneered by Lenin before the birth of the Soviet state and then institutionalized after 1917. This second war, unlike the first, did not end in 1945.[1]

The war against Germany widened the scope and definition of this ideological struggle. The tasks that now came within the remit of the NKVD and eventually, after April 1943, the newly created SMERSH,[2] were many and varied: countering rumors; the interrogation of Soviet soldiers who had escaped from the Germans; monitoring soldiers' criticisms of the conduct of the war; postal censorship; and the arrest and frequently the execution of deserters and those accused of spreading panic as well as the more conventional operations of counterintelligence. Informers were vital, and a large network was recruited in all branches of the army by NKVD and SMERSH handlers.

New operational requirements on top of the NKVD's existing roles generated a vast amount of reports, memoranda, analyses, and raw data, much of which has yet to be properly evaluated. For example, a collection of declassified Soviet documents on which this chapter is largely based illuminates in great detail the modus operandi of the NKVD during the battle of Stalingrad.[3] Revealed clearly are the day-to-day workings of the postal censors, who processed thousands of soldiers' letters from the front. Detailed reports based on content analysis—with particular attention being paid to attitudes among the rank and file—were compiled for front headquarters. Likewise, informer-based reports were drawn up by the NKVD and closely examined for attitudes among soldiers toward various orders, such as № 227, better known as the "not a step backward" order, and in October 1942 the news that the institution of commissars had been abolished. High levels of desertion accompanied the poor military performance of the Red Army, and the documents specify numbers detained, arrested, and executed. The figures are startling and suggest an army on the brink of cracking, which in turn only serves to complicate the issue of trying to understand the nature of Red Army resistance. Attitudes toward the Soviet state and the Communist Party were also a high priority for the network of informers. Their reports must have been deeply alarming for the NKVD and the Soviet high command.

Postal Censorship and Informers

The sheer scale of postal censorship was impressive. In one report to Viktor Abakumov,[4] the head of the Directorate of NKVD Special Sections, dated April 1942, it was noted that the military censor's section attached to the Special Section of the NKVD at the 57th Army (Southern front) had dealt with a total of 130,084 items in the postal system. Particular attention was paid to any material in German or of German origin. For example, German postcards, landscape photos with text in German, and German topographical maps were all confiscated by the NKVD; so were unofficial reports about casualties. No indication is given of what happened to the writers of these letters. In this particular batch, 9,286 letters were deemed to be of a "positive character." Another 7,023 letters were deemed to contain "information unsuitable for publication." Others contained "negative utterances."[5] Again, over the period 9–20 September 1942, a total of 74,667 letters from troops of the 66th Army (Don front) were processed by the censors, a vast expenditure of administrative resources.[6]

Postal censors dealt with letters in one of three ways. Letters deemed to be free of secrets or sensitive information were stamped "inspected by the censorship" (*prosmotreno voennoi tsenzuroi*) and sent on their way. Parts of letters containing information deemed to compromise military secrecy were "blacked out" (*podvergali zatushevke*). Letters in a third category were confiscated. It is safe to assume that the originators of confiscated letters attracted the further attention of the NKVD and in some cases were put before a military tribunal. Likewise, the intended recipients of such letters—parents, wives, and other relatives—would have fallen under suspicion.

One of the striking anomalies revealed by the NKVD censors' reports is the enormous risk run by soldiers expressing patently anti-Soviet views in letters that they all knew would be read by the censor. Solzhenitsyn, the system's most famous victim, was arrested on just such a basis in 1945 (he exacted his revenge on Abakumov, the head of SMERSH, in *First Circle*). Confronted with the likelihood of a violent death, soldiers, one assumes, lost their fear of the *osobist*. The following extract typifies what the censors describe, using the standard jargon, variously as "negative utterances" or "anti-Soviet sentiments" in confiscated letters:

> Yes, dearest mother, the battle here from 18 to 20 September [1942] was a big one, and even now it is still going on. On this front, the battle started on 18 September, and the meat-grinder was in good form. A great deal of flesh was hacked up over these 2–3 days, and much blood was spilled. And for what purpose? For the glory, power, and wealth of a small group of people. But as the Russian people's saying goes: "An eye for eye, a life for a life" and "You reap what you sow." For all this human suffering, for all the spilled blood, for the widows, the orphans, the organizers of this slaughter will pay with their heads and, as they used to say of old, the vengeance of the Lord will be at hand. Well, dearest mother, the few days that I have spent here, some 15–20 days or so, have, as they say, completely transformed me. I have changed completely from what I used to be. Only now have I understood the politics of this war, for what and for whom we are spilling our blood and laying down our heads, and what all our loans, collections, sacrifices, and taxes were spent on.

All this money has been spent to take our lives, to spill our blood; it has not been spent on building up our motherland. May I be damned if, when I get home, I donate so much as a kopeck to a loan, or other demands. I will sooner drink it all or give it to beggars or throw it down the toilet, but I'll never let it go to a loan. I ask you, go to the church for me, pray for me . . . and put a few candles in front of the icon. Pray to God for a speedy end to the war, pray for our long-suffering Russian people, for a new world.[7]

This particular soldier's fate is not recorded. On the other hand, letters written by Cossack volunteers serving in the German army, which were found by Soviet units after a German withdrawal, would have had disastrous consequences. The letters reveal satisfaction with the way the Cossacks are being treated by their German masters. In an obvious reproach to the Soviet high command's indifference to the well-being of its own troops, the Cossacks write that they are well fed and clothed. Left for dispatch within the German postal service, the letters are addressed to wives and relatives, thus laying an easy trail for NKVD and SMERSH operatives to follow and inflict retribution. In the discovery by Soviet troops of these Cossacks' letters we see the genesis of the vast tragedy that would eventually unfold around General Vlasov and all those who abandoned the Soviet state, which still causes so much bitterness in Russia today.

Letters to and from the front highlight one of the paradoxes of totalitarianism. Exercising exceptionally tight control over the means of expression, the state's functionaries have to expend vast efforts to ascertain what the citizens and soldiery really think. Did the NKVD, however, need informers or postal censorship to assess the hopes and fears of the civilian population and the mood of soldiers or the dire military situation in the summer of 1942? No matter; as the Germans advanced, the Soviet bureaucracy of spying and informing went about its business with indefatigable zeal. In a report to Beria dated 5 July 1942, Senior Major Selivanovskii began thus: "Recently, in connection with the withdrawal of units and formations of the Southwestern front to new lines, a number of anti-Soviet, defeatist, and traitorous utterances on the part of several service personnel have been noted."[8] Many of these "utterances" reveal a deep cynicism about the regime and its assurances. From Sergeant-Major Privarov: "We have been persuaded over and over again, loads has been written, that the war will be over in six months, and in actual fact the end of the war is not in sight. The situation at the front is just the same as it was at the beginning. People are thrown into this slaughterhouse, turned into cannon fodder. And there is nothing to show for it."[9] From Red Army Soldier Soprykin we have evidence of Soviet military incompetence: "So in the Kharkov sector 75,000 of our brothers lie dead, and nothing was achieved. And I can assure you that if we are not victorious by the time autumn comes, the soldiers of the Red Army will desert to the Germans and will not fight."[10] Similar sentiments were expressed by Red Army Soldier Nizovtsev, who underlined the scale of desertion to the Germans: "Once the hard fighting starts, then the Germans will be victorious and will capture the Donbass. Wait, you'll see the Germans fighting and their equipment. I personally saw our troops retreating in the Smolensk sector. Just think, one soldier deserted, and there's a real stink about it. I saw whole regiments surrendering with their equipment."[11] A recurring theme in both informers' reports and letters is the hatred of collectivization. Red Army Soldier Makagonov: "If everyone were to turn their weapons against the commissars and commanders, the war would be over in ten minutes and individual peasant holdings could be reestablished and there would be food aplenty."[12] On collectivization and life in the occupied territories, the remarks of gun-team commander Prokopenko are the stuff of utter heresy:

> The Germans are behaving completely correctly by dropping leaflets. What they say in these leaflets is all correct, and they are also right when they say that our government has run away. That the land will be distributed to individual peasants is true because Germany does not need all this land. My mother lives in the occupied territory and lives well and is waiting for me. They write in the papers, and the commissars go on about it, that there is no food in Germany. It's the other way around. German soldiers eat tinned food, chocolate, jam, and other good stuff. This can be seen from the dumps that they have abandoned. Things with us are much worse. We're fed on porridge and water and then not much of that. There's no truth in the papers.[13]

The fate of all these soldiers is recorded by Major Selivanovskii. Privarov is charged. Soprykin is to be arrested once the facts have been documented. Nizovtsev is arrested and placed under investigation. Makagonov is arrested and put before a military tribunal. Prokopenko, recommends Selivanovskii, should be arrested.[14]

While the Soviet press was blaming the Soviet retreat in the summer of 1942 on the failure of the British to open a Second front, the NKVD set about finding out how the soldiers had reacted to the press campaign. Junior Political Instructor Tishkevich, commenting on the recent treaty of cooperation signed by Britain and the Soviet Union, tactlessly summoned up the ghost of another treaty that had had disastrous consequences for the Soviet Union: "This is no treaty. It's just a piece of paper, a deception, something to soothe the people. Britain has never helped us and never will. One must not pin any hopes on a Second front being opened. We already had a treaty with Germany in 1939, and Germany let us down very badly, deceived us and prepared the way for invading the USSR."[15] Nor was Red Army Soldier Nikitin impressed. In a report dated 4 February 1943, immediately after the Soviet victory, Nikitin, who was charged and arrested in December 1942, is quoted as follows: "I read Churchill's statement, and he said clearly that the Second front would not be opened in 1943. Soviet papers write the whole time about the opening of the Second front, that it will soon be opened. In reality they are deceiving people. People believe this, and they are spilling their blood for nothing."[16]

Remarks similar to those expressed by Prokopenko—"There's no truth in the papers"—are quite common. Thus, from Kolesnikov, a clerk: "Our papers don't tell the truth. In the papers they keep going on about how we are beating the Germans. In actual fact it's the other way around."[17] And from Quartermaster Fingerut: "I no longer believe the papers or the radio when they give out information about the situation at the front. I somehow have more faith in foreign reports."[18] A medical officer offers a more sophisticated analysis of the same problem: "If, based on the reports from the information bureau, one estimates how many German planes have been shot down, how many tanks knocked out, and how many soldiers killed, then the German army would have been smashed long ago. But it is still on the offensive. They don't write the truth in the papers. The supreme command has no idea of the true situation at the front."[19] Soldiers knew that they were being lied to and resented it. The prewar censorship regime had not produced only unthinking, docile workers. On the contrary, at all levels in the rank structure we encounter hostility to party propaganda, which seems to induce indifference and despair; the realization that all efforts are fruitless; even the feeling that death would be preferable to the ubiquitous fear, hunger, uncertainty about the future, and exhaustion.

Extracts of confiscated letters—the report to Abakumov is dated 8 August 1942—show an almost total collapse in military and civilian morale, a resignation that the worst is upon them.[20] From Umnov, a soldier at army headquarters: "We have experienced and are experiencing days full of tragedy, as we head towards our own dear homes."[21] Chechkov's letter to his wife and children is especially moving: "Katia, my dear wife, and my little ones, it's difficult to stay alive; whatever happens we're all going to die here. We have been pushed right up to the Volga. Now we'll either drown or the enemy will destroy us on the bank or we'll all be taken prisoner. There'll be much slaughter around the city of Stalingrad-Tsaritsyn."[22] Pakomut, a submachine gunner, writes of the unbearable pain of separation: "Natasha, I can't live any longer without you and the children. Even if living means living with a wound, then at least we'll live together. I really want to see you and my children, and then die, but I don't want to die at this moment, but the chances are I will anyway."[23] Wives wrote equally harrowing letters to husbands. From inside Stalingrad, M. Perel'man points to a breakdown of law and order, hinting at that periodic recrudescence of anti-Semitism that seems to grip Soviet—and post-Soviet—Russia in times of crisis:

> I feel sorry for the children. They're full of life, without any cares, and totally unprepared to meet their deaths. We'll not die from bombs; we'll die at the loathsome hands of the local population. They're not human beings; they are beasts. Shurik has gone off to the day nursery. IUrik and Zhenia are sitting on the floor and playing. I find it very hard to write to you, knowing that we can't get away from here.[24]

N. R. Lapko provides evidence that some were more equal than others:

> My darling, it seems to me that the end of my life is approaching. I'm living in a location where you can't flee the enemy. There is no transport, and the enemy is not far away. If I can't get away and this bloody executioner comes, then I'll not remain on desecrated land, I'll throw myself and the children in the river. Everything that I can do, I have done. The regional bosses have already sent their wives away in cars.[25]

These brutally honest and moving summaries support the view that Soviet propaganda, based on its Leninist assumptions, actually helped to create panic and flight instead of the universal and unflinching resistance to the German invasion claimed by the party. Grandiose lying and boasting about Soviet success and, correspondingly, German shortcomings—the lies all too obvious to those at the front—were part of the problem, not of any solution. Consider, for example, the report's preamble: "Recently, in connection with the failures of our troops in individual sectors of the front and the dissemination by the enemy of various counterrevolutionary, fascist leaflets, evidence of very low morale among the troops has been noted in unit positions."[26] One wonders whether the compilers of these documents really believed that civilian and army morale had been subverted by counterrevolution. It is clear that a horrible blindness existed among Soviet leaders, induced by a fateful combination of wishful thinking and their own propaganda, which, developing the thesis of Barbara Tuchman's study, might well be referred to as the folly of ideology.[27]

In the various anti-Soviet sentiments recorded by the collators, there is a noticeable absence of any explicitly hostile remarks directed at Stalin, other Soviet leaders, or even the party. In the desperate circumstances in which many of these soldiers found themselves—human beings in extremis tending to look for scapegoats—this silence seems extraordinary. The absence of such remarks suggests the bowdlerization of informers' reports, in effect, another layer of censorship. The most likely reason for this measure was that it was intended to insulate the highest levels of the party and military leadership from what was being said about them. In any event, this would have been a sensible precaution for the censors and collators. It is one thing to circulate remarks about how bad things are at the front, quite another in the paranoid world of internal Soviet informing and spying to circulate remarks explicitly critical of Stalin and other senior Soviet leaders. To have done so would have been to risk incurring accusations of ideological sabotage and counterrevolution. We might perhaps see this as further evidence that censorship tends to attack the system it is designed to protect.

Reports dealing with German morale—somewhat negative at a time when the German army was sweeping all before it—encourage the belief that the NKVD collators told the Soviet leadership what it wanted to hear. A report from Abakumov to Shcherbakov claims to have found signs of a breakdown in discipline in the German army. The report is dated no later than 15 August 1942.[28] With the fall of Stalingrad looking imminent and German success reinforcing the belief in that outcome among the Germany army, Abakumov's report seems overly optimistic. For, as Alan Clark notes, "This period was the high peak of *enjoyment* for the German soldiery. The war was exciting and victorious" (emphasis in the original).[29] On the other hand, even if overstated, these early signs of disaffection are not insignificant. Especially ominous for the future of Paulus's 6th Army was the growing rift between the Romanians and the Germans, noted in the report. Also mentioned was the fact that German soldiers were cursing Hitler. That the report notes the hostile remarks directed at Hitler, at a time when the German army's fortunes seemed altogether more favorable reinforces the suspicion that Soviet censors and collators were quite deliberately cutting any hostile remarks aimed at Stalin. Or are we to believe that Soviet soldiers in that second dreadful summer of the war did not curse Stalin?

Order № 227

Promulgated on 28 July 1942 by the people's commissar for defense (Stalin), the "not a step backward" order, № 227, added new urgency to NKVD activity at the front.[30] Against the background of the desperate military situation, Stalin, in language remarkably free of the standard ideological clichés, berated those troops on the Southern front who had abandoned Rostov and Novocherkassk "without offering serious resistance and without any orders from Moscow and had covered their regimental banners with shame."[31] Turning to specific measures to restore the situation at the front and immediate operational rear areas, Stalin orders that cowards and those spreading panic be "exterminated on the spot."[32] Commanders at all levels and their commissars who withdraw without authority are to be regarded as "betrayers of the Motherland."[33] The psychology of retreat is to be eradicated through counterpropaganda. Penal battalions are to be formed for soldiers suspected of cowardice and other military crimes, so as "to give them the opportunity of expiating in blood their crimes against the motherland."[34] An especially ruthless measure was the formation of blocking detachments. Stalin ordered army commanders to "form in the framework of an army three to five well-armed blocking detachments (up to 200 men in each), place them in the immediate rear of irresolute divisions, and require them in the event of panic and a disorderly withdrawal of the division's units to execute on the spot cowards and those spreading panic, so assisting the divisions' loyal soldiers to discharge their duty to the motherland."[35]

Reactions to Order № 227 were collected and reported to the highest levels with an even greater assiduity than normal. The manner in which these reactions were collated and presented suggests that the party and the NKVD are concerned not solely with morale and "defeatist sentiments" but with the possibility of armed mutiny at the front. Three reports, dated 14 August 1942,[36] 14–15 August 1942,[37] and 19 August 1942,[38] all note "negative and at times anti-Soviet utterances of individual soldiers and commanders."[39] Really critical remarks are categorized as "counterrevolutionary."[40]

Medical Officer Ol'shanetskii saw the order as the "final scream of despair at a time when we no longer have the power to stand up to the Germans. It makes no difference. Nothing will come of this measure."[41] Chastised for a lapse in discipline, Red Army Soldier Zhiviakov threatened his superior officer with the Soviet equivalent of "fragging": "You want to establish discipline on the basis of the Stavka order. We'll sort people like you out on the front line."[42]

But it was the creation and deployment of blocking detachments that aroused the greatest resentment in the Red Army. Major Selivanovskii, one of the NKVD officers involved in compiling the reports, identified this as a major theme:

> The measures envisaged in the order are assessed as a sign of weakness on the part of our army, on the strength of which the supreme high command has resorted to extremes.
>
> Hostile elements are trying to exploit the creation of blocking detachments and the resort to repressive measures with regard to cowards and those manifesting panic and battlefield deserters, with the aim of inducing unstable soldiers to go across to the enemy or to surrender to the Germans.[43]

Some soldiers saw an altogether more sinister purpose to the order, one divorced from the threat of the Germans. Medical Instructor Demchenko stated, "This order is aimed solely at the destruction of the people, and nothing will come of it, as we have retreated, so we will continue to do so."[44] Red Army Soldier Vikhrev echoed the same sense of despair: "If you advance, the Germans will kill you, and if you run backward, your own side will have a go at you. So it makes no difference; we're all done for."[45] Red Army Soldier Dubovik took a more sarcastic view: "The organization of blocking detachments, that's the Second front. On the front line we'll be shot by the Germans, and from the rear by the blocking detachments."[46] Red Army Soldier Kizhankin saw them as actually helping the Germans: "These blocking detachments will shoot the soldiers from behind, the Germans from the front. As a result of this, there will be an armed confrontation between our units and the blocking detachments. The enemy will exploit this and may be able to smash us all."[47] Once their anti-Soviet statements have been documented, notes Major Selivanovskii, Demchenko, Vikhrev, Dubovik, and Kizhankin are to be arrested.

Blocking Detachments, Desertions, and Executions

Consequent upon the order, three blocking detachments totalling 600 men were formed in the 4th Tank Army. In the report dated 14 August 1942, we find the first details of blocking-detachment operations within the 4th Tank Army. By 7 August 1942, 363 soldiers had been detained by barrier detachments, of whom 187 were returned to their units, 43 were held in a reserve-replenishment section, 73 were sent to an NKVD special camp, 27 were sent to penal companies, 2 were brought before a medical commission, 6 were arrested, and 24 were shot in front of their units.[48] The various categories in which the NKVD placed detained soldiers are by no means clear-cut and tend to obscure the fate of the detainees. By the middle of October 1942, the number of soldiers being detained jumped dramatically, and with it the proportions of those arrested and shot.[49] With such numbers involved, the distinctions between the various categories assume greater importance.

This importance can be appreciated by examining a detailed report on blocking-detachment operations for the period 1 August–15 October 1942.[50] Of wider interest for the war on the Eastern front as a whole is the fact that a total of 193 blocking detachments have been formed in the Red Army on the basis of Stalin's order. Stalin's original allocation of 200 men per detachment indicates that a total of 38,600 men are involved in blocking-detachment operations. Sixteen detachments are operational on the Stalingrad front (a total of 3,200 men); another 25 are operational on the Don front (a total of 5,000 men).

Over the period 1 August–15 October 1942, 140,755 soldiers have been detained on all fronts of the Red Army, men who, in the words of the document, "ran away from the front line."[51] Among those detained, the breakdown of punishments is as follows: 3,980 arrested, 1,189 executed, 2,776 sent to penal companies, 185 sent to penal battalions, and 131,094 returned to their units or to transit centers.[52]

For the Don and Stalingrad fronts over the same period, the breakdown of punishments is as follows: on the Don front, 36,109 detained, 736 arrested, 433 executed, 1,056 sent to penal companies, 33 sent to penal battalions, and 32,933 returned to their units or to transit centers.[53] On the Stalingrad front, 15,649 detained, 244 arrested, 278 executed, 218 sent to penal companies, 42 sent to penal battalions, and 14,833 returned to their units or to transit centers.[54] Executions on the two fronts over this period amount to 60 percent of all executions in the Red Army at that time.

The number of soldiers detained on the Stalingrad and Don fronts— 51,758 (37 percent of the Red Army total)—bears witness to a severe breakdown in command and control and unit morale. It must also have been a huge strain on military resources at a critical juncture in the battle to have to process all these soldiers. Though the NKVD distinguishes those soldiers "detained" (zaderzhannyi) from those "arrested" (arestovannyi), the report nevertheless refers to all 140,755 soldiers detained as "having run away from the battlefield." Given the exceptionally harsh disciplinary measures introduced as a result of Stalin's Order № 227—shooting on the spot for deserters—all the soldiers detained were, under the provisions of this order, technically liable to execution for having abandoned the front line. No distinction is made between being detained for a routine document check and being arrested where there is evidence to justify arrest. There is, in other words, an explicit presumption on the part of the Special Section of the NKVD that all soldiers who are detained in its dragnet are guilty until proven innocent. In the hysteria of the time and given the extreme ruthlessness that it helped to engender, we must presume that large numbers of innocent soldiers were executed or otherwise punished for no reason other than the breakdown of command and control structures over which they had no power.[55] Presumably even the Special Sections of the NKVD recognized that shooting 140,755 men was not possible, so they concentrated on what they regarded as particularly egregious cases of desertion. Again, this focus implies a considerable level of arbitrariness as to who got executed, arrested, or sent to a penal unit. In the sort of conditions that obtained at the front, proper investigations were not possible, and the NKVD executioners simply made snap judgments.[56]

The information provided in this report does not explain what happened to those arrested. How many, for example, were subsequently executed? And what of the fate of those sent to penal units, a punishment tantamount to a death sentence? Those detained and returned to their units could expect to be regarded with extreme suspicion, ostracized, and given particularly dangerous assignments. In the language of the reports, they would be required to "expiate their guilt." Included in the figure for those returned to their units are soldiers sent to transit centers. No precise figure is given.

Knowing, however, what these days might be called the mission statement of the NKVD, we are right to assume the worst. The NKVD's dispatch of an unspecified number of soldiers to transit centers points to the hidden or delayed wrath of the agency. The transit center was either a stay of execution or possibly the beginning of the long and grueling journey to the gulag.

The scale of executions at Stalingrad can be grasped by bearing in mind that in World War I, the British Army executed 346 soldiers for crimes of cowardice and desertion.[57] We must also bear in mind that all the figures cited relate to the period from 1 August to 15 October 1942. Three and a half months of attrition warfare still remained. Some idea of what happened in the period leading up to the final Soviet victory is provided in a memorandum written by Colonel Kazakevich dated 17 February 1943.[58] Kazakevich states that in the period from 1 October 1942 to 1 February 1943, "mass desertion by service personnel from the battlefield [Don front] and the withdrawal of units without orders from commanders were isolated incidents."[59]

An obvious response to this assertion would be to point out that it is inconsistent, at the very least, with the huge numbers of soldiers absent from their units and detained by the NKVD's blocking detachments on the Don front up to 15 October 1942 (36,109 soldiers in all). The sort of psychological instability and fear indicated by these numbers would not disappear immediately. Although we can reasonably assume that the numbers would decline in the period from the beginning of October 1942 to the beginning of February 1943 as the situation turned in favor of the Red Army, the data provided in an earlier report (dated 15 October 1942) indicate that we could expect the numbers of soldiers detained (after having "run away from the battlefield") to remain at high levels—certainly higher than Kazakevich states.

Referring back to the report dated 15 October 1942, we see that the total number detained (all categories) on the Don front was 36,109, of whom 433 were executed, a ratio of 83 detained (all categories) to every execution. On the Stalingrad front, for the same period, the total number detained (all categories) was 15,649, of whom 278 were executed, a ratio of 56 detained (all categories) to every execution. The higher rate of executions on the Stalingrad front, which included Chuikov's 62nd Army, is consistent with the severe fighting in the city and the harsher measures taken to impose discipline.[60]

Applying a ratio of 83 detained (all categories) to 1 execution to Kazakevich's own data for executions in the armies of the Don front for the period

October to December 1942, a total of 79 executions, we get a total of 6,557 detained (all categories). This is a steep drop overall when compared with the figures for 1 August–1 October 1942, but it still represents a large number. Applying a ratio of 56 detained (all categories) to 1 execution to Kazakevich's own data for executions in the 62nd Army (Stalingrad front) for the months of September (195), October (68), November (41), and December (21), 325 executions in all, we get a total of 18,200 detained (all categories) for the period from September to the end of December. This large figure, subject to the caveat of the ratio's remaining constant, does not support the contention that desertion and panicking were isolated instances. The ratio of 56 detained (all categories) to 1 execution does, of course, reflect the greater chaos and volatility of the battlefield from the period 1 August–15 October 1942. Nevertheless, even if one reduces, arbitrarily, the ratio of detained (all categories) to executions by 50 percent and confines the calculation to the two months for November and December, the low period for executions, the figure of detainees (all categories)—1,736—would still be high—again, higher than Kazakevich would have us believe.[61] The potential flaw in this arithmetic is the assumption that the ratio of detained to executions remains constant, whereas the ratio may not actually be a reliable indicator of those detained. Another consideration is that the numbers of executions might bear no relation to the numbers of those detained, which would suggest an execution regime operating completely out of control or one that was based on no obviously rational criteria, however ruthless.

With all the difficulty in arriving at precise figures for those detained, Kazakevich's own report underpins the view that numbers continued to be high in the latter half of the battle. He cites a number of serious incidents of desertion that occurred in October, November, and January. The incidents involve large units—companies and battalions—abandoning the battlefield. Thus, in a fifteen-day period in October, one operational group of the NKVD returned 800 soldiers, other ranks and officers, to the battlefield. Of the 800 detained, 15 were executed (a ratio of 53 detained to 1 execution, which is very close to the ratio of 56:1 noted earlier). Even after the Soviet counteroffensive, Operation Uranus, was launched on 19 November 1942, incidents of desertion and cowardice remained high. Antony Beevor has argued that the number of Red Army deserters still trying to reach the German army after the launch of Operation Uranus can be explained "mainly through a mixture of ignorance and mistrust."[62] This is an acceptable explanation until one realizes that the German Army, no less than the Red

Army, believed in observing normal security precautions before initiating major operations on the need-to-know principle. Yet it never suffered anything like the mass defections of the Red Army. The ignorance and mistrust that Beevor cites should rather be seen as a reflection of the fundamental nature of the Soviet state itself, not just of the conditions at Stalingrad. Years of organized Soviet lying and propaganda created that ignorance and mistrust, and in the rubble of Stalingrad, it nearly proved fatal to the regime and, more importantly, led to hundreds of thousands of Red Army soldiers' being sacrificed in the name of the party's policies.[63] Red Army deserters trying to reach the German lines were also victims of these policies.

The desperate nature of the NKVD's struggle to impose order can be seen in the countermeasures themselves. Kazakevich writes:

> In order to put a stop to cowardice and panic in the units, all Special Section branches in operational formations and the agent-informer network in the forward units were mobilized. Army blocking detachments and battalion detachments were brought in as well, and they, through the Military Councils of the armies, were set the task of conducting blocking operations immediately behind the combat formations of the units so as not to allow panic and mass desertion of service personnel from the battlefield.[64]

In some cases, notes Kazakevich, cowards and those spreading panic were dealt with on the personal initiative of NKVD operatives: "In individual cases, properly instructed agents themselves dealt with cowards and panic-mongers on the spot."[65] Numbers of men eliminated in this way are not given.

Kazakevich goes on to cite extracts in which officers confess to cowardice and desertion. On 24 September 1942, the Germans broke through the defenses of the 42nd Independent Rifle Brigade and reached the banks of the Volga. In the course of the NKVD's investigation, battalion commissar Lukin, according to Kazakevich, acknowledged his guilt: "In the intense fighting, I did not take the necessary decisive steps towards those soldiers who arbitrarily abandoned the battlefield, and I myself abandoned the brigade without any order from the army's command."[66] Lukin was sentenced to "the highest measure of punishment" (execution by shooting, *rasstrel*). In another example of a damning self-indictment, so appreciated by the NKVD, Junior Political Instructor Shilkin stated, "I confess that I deserted the battlefield, leaving the soldiers on the defense line. I deserted because I lacked confidence in the strength of the soldiers' resistance in my platoon. It seemed to me that they would not stand up to the pressure of the Germans and would run away. But it turned out differently. The soldiers stood their ground, and I behaved like a coward and ran away."[67] Shilkin was shot in front of the unit. Given the interrogation methods favored by the NKVD, the pressure to get results, and a presumption of guilt, there must be grave doubts as to the reliability of these confessions. Nor is there any evidence that the army interceded on behalf of arrested and accused soldiers and officers or that any proper defense was permitted to be mounted. Those arrested on accusations of cowardice and desertion—whatever the evidence—became outcasts and were abandoned to their fate.

Compiling top-secret reports whose circulation was restricted to the highest levels of the Soviet political leadership, NKVD officers were uniquely placed to promote themselves and their organization at the expense of the Red Army. Evidence of a partisan approach to its own activities can be seen in an NKVD dispatch to Beria and Abakumov dated 16 September 1942. The ubiquitous and zealous Selivanovskii records that between 13 and 15 September 1942 1,218 men were detained by the blocking detachment of the Special Section of the 62nd Army.[68] Of those detained, 21 were executed (a ratio of 58:1). The majority of the troops detained belonged to the 10th Rifle Division NKVD and the signals regiment of the 399th Rifle Division, which would imply that some of those executed were serving in the 10th Rifle Division NKVD. Yet the report specifically highlights the executions of the commander and commissar of the signals regiment of the 399th Rifle Division. In a later report, one example of the execution of an NKVD soldier, a private, is noted, suggesting perhaps that this was an isolated case and that the unit as a whole was ideologically sound.[69] The fact that large numbers of those troops detained were from the 10th Rifle Division NKVD is inconsistent with the glowing report to Beria about this division's military performance dated 13 October 1942.[70] The first line of the report reads, "Based in Stalingrad, the 10th Rifle Division NKVD has played an exceptional role in the defense of the city."[71] Recommended immediately for the Order of the Red Banner and promotion to the status of a guards (*gvardeiskii*) unit, the division was also awarded the Order of Lenin on 2 December 1942.

Again, in a report to Abakumov dated 21 September 1942, one can detect the tendency to highlight the apparently exemplary role played by the NKVD while stressing the poor combat performance of the Red Army. Guns, abandoned by the 92nd Rifle Brigade because of a lack of means to move them, were found by the NKVD, which then loaded them onto vehicles. This episode could highlight an example of battlefield incompetence on the part of the brigade commander, but it might also be taken as evidence of favorable treatment enjoyed by the NKVD, allowing it to procure vital equipment in short supply.[72] Reading these reports, we are left with the impression that but for the NKVD and the heroic blocking detachments, the whole front line would have collapsed—even indeed that the unacknowledged saviors of Stalingrad were the NKVD, not the Red Army. Among the returns for executions and desertions we find the telltale signs of the same sort of institutional rivalry that existed between the various bureaucracies of the SS and the Wehrmacht in the Nazi state.[73]

One final comment needs to be made on the numbers of executions. High as they are by Western standards, the figures cited in these documents are much lower than the 13,500 referred to by John Erickson and cited by Antony Beevor.[74] The total number of executions on the Stalingrad and Don fronts for the period 1 August–15 October 1942 is given as 711, which for the two-and-a-half month period is a monthly average of 284. Assuming the rate of executions remained at that level until the end of January 1943, we can calculate a total of 1,704 executions for the duration of the battle. That other index of morale, the number detained, remained high, 15,649 on the Stalingrad front alone between 1 August and 15 October 1942, a monthly average of 6,260. Again, it should be stressed that those detained are classified in the report as having run away from the battlefield. They were therefore liable to summary execution.

Abolition of the Institution of Commissars

During the course of the battle, the party made a number of what appeared to be high-profile concessions to the army. One was the abolition of the institution of commissars, announced in a order issued on 9 October 1942. Three reports, two collating soldiers' reactions on the Stalingrad front (dated 14 and 16 October 1942) and a third collating soldiers' reactions on the Don front (dated 17 October 1942) were sent to Abakumov.

The reports show that for all the relentless propaganda of partnership and mutual respect, a standard theme of Soviet-Russian war literature, commissars were, for the most part, barely tolerated and frequently loathed.[75] Constant among the complaints is the accusation that they lacked proper military training and that this prevented the discharge of professional command and control, which had disastrous consequences. In the words of Artillery Lieutenant Shul'man: "The failures at the front were the consequence of the commissars' military illiteracy."[76] "Now," responded Vereskun, a cipher operator in the 8th Air Army, "we'll spend less time on politics and more on fighting."[77] Nor was Colonel Selivanov, Hero of the Soviet Union and an air navigator serving in the 8th Air Army, exactly sad to see the commissars go: "At last, there'll be no more of these parasites in the air force. What did a commissar do at air force headquarters? Nothing."[78] Selivanov's sentiments were echoed by Pinut'ev, head of coding at the headquarters of the Soviet 6th Army: "They have done the correct thing in getting rid of commissars in the army. We had a commissar at headquarters, a loafer. He did nothing at all. And when he was removed and replaced by another, the replacement turned out to be no better. Generally, commissars are not needed in the army."[79] In remarks that the report classifies as "anti-Soviet," Captain Rutskii declared, "It's a good thing that these commissars have been driven out; it should have been done ages ago. They go about snooping, and because of them you can't do things in your own way." And for good measure, unconcerned about informers, Rutskii added, "And it is still necessary to drive out these Special Sections as well."[80]

Their colleagues on the Don front felt much the same. Colonel Cherkasov, who, it is noted in the report, crossed himself, thus compounding the felony, expressed himself thus: "Thank God for that; for twenty-four years this confusion has existed whereby the commander takes a decision, the commissar disagrees, and the paperwork starts."[81] Again, we find further accusations of laziness from Captain Akhunov at 66th Army headquarters: "The correct decision because our commissars are rotten snakes. With all their evasions, all they do is to gnaw away at the soldiers and officers and subvert the discipline of the Red Army. This lot can only talk and loaf about and get on the nerves of the command staff. They do nothing."[82] And finally, to quote Lieutenant Colonel Timoshenko:

> This order should have been issued ages ago. Just imagine, yesterday I went to the commander to get some documents signed. He had signed everything, so it seemed. Then, however, it was necessary to go chasing about all over the place after Katkov, the brigade commissar, so as to get him to countersign the documents. But we should not have to go through this. And now things will much easier. The commander is the one. We ought to appoint these commissars as assistants in the admin unit and let them muck about there.[83]

The institution of commissars enjoyed a strong revolutionary tradition and party affiliation, so its abolition appears highly significant.[84] Much, indeed, has been made of its abolition in discussions of party policy toward the Red Army. However, one question that now seems relevant in the light of these NKVD documents is whether the abolition of the office of commissar really amounted to any concession at all. In view of the pervasive influence of the Special Sections and the *osobisty* in the Red Army, did the party really need the commissars as ideological auxiliaries? One officer, Captain Rutskii, whose comments have already been quoted, seems to have been aware of this potential deception, arguing that the logical step would be the abolition of the Special Sections. The battlefield lapses of commissars, reported frequently and with some relish by the NKVD, cannot have done them any good in the bureaucratic turf wars. We might see the removal of commissars from the Red Army as a measure paving the way for the creation of SMERSH in April 1943 and as a new, more ruthless phase in the struggle against counterrevolution as the Red Army began to recapture territory from the Germans and the work of rooting out spies, wreckers, and collaborators, especially Vlasov's men, began in earnest.

Morale and Patriotism

The commander's skill, the experience and courage of the troops, and their patriotic spirit are, Clausewitz instructs us, the principal moral components of an army.[85] How then are we to assess Soviet resistance and combat performance at Stalingrad when so much of the declassified NKVD material leaves us with the impression that the Red Army was all too vulnerable to uncontrolled retreat and a collapse in discipline?

Take the question of patriotism. True, the censors encountered letters expressing pro-Soviet feelings, which should not be conflated with Russian patriotism, and ones that the NKVD considered to be politically correct. The trouble is that the number reflecting marked anti-Soviet sentiments, indifference to the outcome of the battle, and panic are numerically significant and continued to be so throughout the course of the battle. This poses a problem for interpreting what exactly happened in September and October 1942, when the Red Army just managed to contain the German offensive. If one agrees with Grossman that it was Russian nationalism and love of the motherland (Rodina) that supported the soldiers so that they found the inner resources to fight to the death, the NKVD documents suggest that these soldiers were not an overwhelming majority, that there was a sizeable minority that was not similarly inspired.

The numbers of Soviet soldiers executed by their own side, arrested, and sent to penal companies support this argument. Recall the number of troops detained in the period 1 August–15 October 1942 on the Stalingrad and Don fronts by the NKVD's Special Departments: 51,758. Stripped of so many troops, certain frontline units must have had their operational efficiency, already perilously low, severely degraded, to the point that they played no useful role. Another factor that takes the shine off the patriotic thesis was, obviously, Stalin's "not a step backward" order and the formation of blocking detachments. If all ranks of the Red Army contained a majority of patriotic, ideologically committed, and competent soldiers, then such orders and the blocking detachments would not have been necessary. Measures to restore discipline say a great deal about unit morale and do not sit easily with the views of another famous student and practitioner of war: "For with war a subtle change happened to the soldier. Discipline was modified, supported, even swallowed by an eagerness of the man to fight. This eagerness it was which brought victory in the moral sense, and often in the physical sense, of the combat."[86]

Though full payment be delayed, results matter. The Germans were prevented from taking the city and forced to surrender. Does this, in the final analysis, vindicate the patriotic thesis? Not exactly. The presence of a large minority, not entirely committed to the battle but rather to merely staying alive, undoubtedly acted as a drag on Red Army performance. This fact is recognized by Generals Rokossovskii, Trubnikov, Malinin, and Zhadov.[87] In an astonishing display of contempt for his soldiers, Trubnikov is reported by an informer as saying, "The problem here is not with the air force; the fact is, our infantry are useless; the infantry won't fight, and that's the whole problem."[88] Equally dismissive was Malinin: "Our infantry are useless. . . . The artillery is doing its job, keeping the enemy's heads down, but the infantry won't stand up and push forward."[89] And Zhadov complained that the "infantry, particularly the new divisions, are not trained, don't know how to fight, and aren't capable of carrying out their assigned tasks."[90] Nor was Rokossovskii, the Don front commander, impressed by the Soviet infantry's *Daraufgängertum*. With a marked lack of solidarity with his own men, this former prisoner of the NKVD, who in 1937 was "beaten senseless and dragged off to prison,"[91] displayed no reluctance

in deploying against his soldiers the same organization that had once arrested and interrogated him. "Rokossovskii," according to the informer,
"insisted that the blocking detachments follow after the infantry units and
by force of arms compel the infantry to go into the attack."[92] Rokossovskii
and his generals do not seem to have considered the possibility that the
state of field rations, or absence of them, may have been a powerful contrib-
utory factor to the poor physical performance and lack of fighting spirit of
their men. So bad, in fact, was the supply situation that cases of soldiers'
eating raw horse meat were reported, and in units of the 66th Army, a formation under Rokossovskii's command, a total of thirty-two cases of death
by starvation were recorded, a scandalous state of affairs when so much
was demanded from the Soviet infantry in subzero temperatures.[93]

Even if patriotic, committed troops constituted a majority in the Red
Army, but not necessarily a massive one, they bore a disproportionately
heavy burden of the dangers at the front. They had to make up for the shortcomings of their less dedicated comrades. As junior officers, noncommissioned officers, and ordinary soldiers, they took the extra risks and, correspondingly, suffered heavier casualties. This is doubtless true for all
armies, but the problem appears to have been especially acute in the Red
Army. As the more dedicated Soviet soldiers were killed and wounded in
greater numbers than their less committed comrades, so the Soviet high
command was continually required to find reserves to fill the gaps, and,
once again, in disproportionately large numbers so as to ensure that the
critical mass of dedicated soldiers and officers was present. Where the reserves could not be deployed, the most expedient solution was to resort to
ever harsher disciplinary measures. The price of Soviet victory was therefore exceptionally high. The Stalingrad meat grinder resulted in higher casualties overall, and especially among the dedicated.[94] Clausewitz's observations on the deployment of reserves and its relation to morale strikes one
as being profoundly relevant to the Soviet defense of Stalingrad:

> The faster one's own reserves have shrunk in relation to the enemy's,
> the more it has cost to maintain the balance. That alone is palpable
> proof of the enemy's superior morale, and it seldom fails to cause
> some bitterness in a general—a certain loss of respect for the forces
> he commands. But the main point is that soldiers, after fighting for
> some time, are apt to be like burned-out cinders. They have shot off
> their ammunition, their numbers have been diminished, their

strength and morale have been drained, and possibly their courage
has drained as well. As an organic whole, quite apart from their loss
in numbers, they are far from being what they were before the action;
and thus the amount of reserves spent is an accurate measure on the
loss of morale.[95]

Desertion, executions, and other signs of soldierly disaffection revealed
in NKVD documents not only cast a shadow over the patriotism of Soviet
troops but also raise questions regarding this theme in Soviet war literature
generally, and particularly in Grossman's two major Stalingrad novels, For
a Just Cause and Life and Fate.[96] More than other writers, Grossman has promoted the patriotic thesis in his novels. This explanation of final victory reveals itself most clearly in the actions and thoughts of Vavilov, Berezkin,
Grekov, Ershov, Novikov, and Darenskii. Grossman's heroes are dedicated
military professionals who love Mother Russia, and he intends that the moment of victory and aftermath of the battle shall belong to them, the survivors of 1941 who have endured so much, rather than to Stalin and his secret police and the odious bureaucrat-commissars Getmanov and
Neudobnov. This may explain why Grossman more or less ignores Order
№ 227 and the role of the NKVD. Unfortunately, as the NKVD documents
reveal only too clearly, executions, desertions, and blocking detachments
were a reality. Nor did such things escape the notice of the intelligence officers of the German 6th Army, who, for obvious reasons, were interested in
Soviet morale. German military intelligence carefully noted the numbers of
Soviet deserters—Überaüfer—and, like the NKVD, tried, though with less
success, to evaluate the impact of Stalin's decrees on Soviet morale. German officers correctly interpreted Order № 227 as a desperate measure,
even a gamble.

Grossman covered the battle for Red Star and would have been well aware
of the provisions of Order № 227 and the fact that soldiers were being executed and that there were Soviet deserters. This knowledge is readily confirmed by Grossman's own wartime notebooks, the final parts of which
were published in 1989. The notebooks cover the period from August 1941
(Central front) to May 1945 in Berlin. There are numerous observations regarding desertion, panic, executions of soldiers, miscarriages of justice,
and dispatch to penal units. In a particularly gruesome case, a soldier is
stripped of his clothing, shot, and buried. Somehow he survives and returns to his unit, covered in blood, whereupon the executioners complete

their task.[97] Grossman also provides evidence that mistakes were made and that innocent soldiers were condemned. In a notebook entry made while he was on the Southwestern front in the winter of 1942, Grossman records that Red Army Soldier Ignat'ev was separated from his unit and detained by the NKVD. In the subsequent military tribunal hearing, he was sentenced to death as a deserter. Surviving the execution attempt because the officer's pistol misfired, Ignat'ev escaped. Eventually he returned to his unit, and a commissar who could vouch for the fact that he had not deserted interceded on his behalf; the death sentence was rescinded, but only after the case went all the way to the army commander.[98] Chuikov's words, recorded by Grossman, leave little doubt about the basis of the Red Army's disciplinary regime: "If you retreat, you'll be executed. If I retreat, I'll be executed."[99]

Despite the failure to attack the provisions of Stavka Order № 270 and Stalin's Order № 227, Grossman alludes to both in *Life and Fate*. "Not a step backward" crops up in a conversation between Darenskii and another officer about the crushing burden of Soviet bureaucracy.[100] The date cited—1941—is wrong, but it is possible that Grossman confuses Order № 270, issued in August 1941, with the later Order № 227. Neudobnov, one of Stalin's creatures, who is attached to Novikov's unit, alludes to Order № 270 when he says that "our material" is the "apple of our eye," an echo of Stalin in Order № 270.[101] Grossman's conspicuous failure to discuss the implications of both orders in *Life and Fate*, far more striking and obvious than in *For a Just Cause*, detracts from the novel's realism.

In *For a Just Cause*, there are references to the executions of soldiers. The theme of panic among the civilian population is touched upon (the book version is more explicit in this regard than the original publication), and the presence of an NKVD division at Stalingrad is acknowledged. Immediately before Rodimtsev's men are deployed, Grossman records that the order of the Military Council—"to stand to the death"—is read out to the troops. As the situation deteriorates, Eremenko makes it clear that "for unauthorized crossing of the Volga to the left bank, the penalty is the firing squad."[102] During the battle in which Filiashkin's battalion is destroyed, Grossman also cites a specific example of cowardice and desertion. The reference to the Military Council's order to stand to the death is slightly misleading because it implies that the council itself ordered this desperate measure, whereas it is merely filtering Stalin's earlier Order № 227. Here we have another example of Stalin's presence being reduced in the book version of *For a Just Cause*.

Significant in this respect is the fact that the short and only chapter in the journal version (chapter 62, part 1) that alludes to Order № 227 is omitted from the later book edition. Krymov, who has just arrived in Stalingrad, calls on the brigade commander:

> Read this, comrade commissar,—he said and withdrew a piece of rice paper folded in two from his map case. It was an order of Stalin's.
>
> Krymov read the harsh words that were addressed to the retreating army. They burned in their bluntness, calling for a bitter struggle. With a shattering directness, they spoke of mortal danger; they announced that any further retreat would spell doom, and that means there is no greater crime in the world than retreat: the fate of the country and its people, the fate of the world, would be decided in the days ahead.
>
> There was not only sadness and anger in these words, there was also faith in victory. . . .
>
> Well, it has been said,—uttered Krymov and took the order in both hands and handed it to the brigade commander. It seemed to him that the alarm bell was booming.[103]

The omission of this chapter from the book version of *For a Just Cause* and the lack of any prolonged analysis of Order № 227 in *Life and Fate* may not be unrelated. Convinced that Russian patriotism saved the day, Grossman, I suggest, finds it intolerable, maybe psychologically insuperable, to consider the possibility that Stalin's harsh, even savage, disciplinary measures made any difference other than to weaken and destroy morale and to waste lives. For if, as Grossman claims in *Life and Fate*, "the flame of Stalingrad was the sole flicker of freedom in the kingdom of darkness,"[104] how can there be a place for Stalin and his orders among the Stalingrad brotherhood? The very idea is blasphemous. Grossman is fully aware that not all Soviet soldiers behaved honorably—and for Grossman that meant above all patriotically—but there were many who did, and it was their leadership at the moment of crisis that made the difference. For example, Vavilov, Novikov, and Berezkin set a standard of the leadership and moral behavior, not Stalin acting through the NKVD.[105]

The essence of this Russian patriotism was that it came from within a man's heart, from the very depths of the soul, nurtured and sustained over the centuries. One recalls Grossman's ax metaphor and the tree that cannot be broken. Or the effect of sighting the Volga on foe and friend alike: for

Weller, the German general, the end of the Russian lands, the beginning of Asia, the promise of final victory; for Lieutenant Bach, the triumph of Nietzsche over good and evil; for the Soviet soldiers, the end of Russia. Patriotism was not conceived and coerced by Stalin's decrees: To admit this possibility would be to reduce its power, to sully its purity.

The high point of this theme in *For a Just Cause* is the destruction of Filiashkin's battalion. All past differences are gone; there is no future. All are doomed to die. Dodonov's punishment is not to die in accordance with Order № 227—to be executed on the spot—but to become an outcast who has forfeited the comradeship of his fellows. With the Judas cast out, the elect, Grossman's Spartans, make ready to meet their heroic end. Such is the cruel winnowing of war. Even here Grossman rebels against the spirit of Order № 227. Stalin demands that soldiers and officers found guilty of cowardice and unsteadiness are the ones to be drafted into the penal units. Yet the penal component of Filiashkin's battalion is innocent of such military crimes. Rather they are the victims of the Soviet system, and what inspires them to fight and to die is not any desire to expiate nonexistent crimes but the desire to show themselves to be worthy Russian patriots, true sons of the motherland.

Conclusion

The documents cited and discussed in this chapter reveal a war that was far removed—in more than geography alone—from the one fought by the Western Allies against the Germans in North Africa, Italy, and Normandy. Under the harsh provisions of Order № 227, Stalingrad became a giant laboratory in which different punitive regimes were tested and refined, as if coping with the ferocious German assault were not enough. Waged behind the scenes with utter ruthlessness, this was a dirty war, barely hinted at in official statements and in the press.[106] The scale of NKVD and later SMERSH spying on and punishment of Soviet troops has no parallel in the Allied armies.

If, as Hew Strachan asserts, students of both world wars "need to take cognisance of the possibly positive consequences of punitive procedures for combat motivation,"[107] then the limits of such policies must also be explored. Can one, for example, posit a relationship between the NKVD's executing Soviet troops and the willingness of Soviet troops to defect to the German army, even in the later stages of the battle and war? Collectivization, one reason for these mass defections, has already been noted.

It goaded large numbers of Ukrainians, Russians, and Belorussians into collaborating with the German army. Where the hatred of the Soviet state was overwhelming or the sense of alienation and apathy great, then the firing squad was not necessarily a deterrent. The same holds for censorship. Faced with imminent death, soldiers wrote from the heart, "I'll write and be damned."

When combined with deliberate lying, suppressing the truth has real dangers for a regime facing a crisis. A recurring theme in soldiers' "anti-Soviet" statements is that the state media, print and radio, are not telling the truth. To the extent that it failed to give an honest picture, one could argue that Soviet propaganda created uncertainty, encouraged rumors and panic, and thus helped to magnify the effects of German military success, inflicting great damage on morale. The more intelligent soldiers felt insulted, which encouraged cynicism and even hostility toward the regime, hardly a desirable outcome.

If, however, results are what matter, at whatever price, then it could be said that the whole NKVD apparatus of censorship, rooting out dissenters, blocking detachments, tribunals, executions, and agitprop succeeded.[108] From this perspective, one that many patriotic Russians will find too awful to contemplate, the NKVD might be entitled to claim some credit for the Soviet victory. Where the NKVD failed, like its successors, was in encouraging the party to abandon efforts at reform and not to make any concessions. Consequently, final victory in 1945 was a stay of execution for the Soviet state, not a guarantee of long-term survival.

In the next chapter, I assess three works published in the 1990s in which the authors, unconstrained by censorship, offer a far harsher portrayal of the NKVD and SMERSH than would have been possible during the Soviet period.

7 The Russian War Novel of the 1990s: A Final Reckoning?

And I sat there and I thought: if the first tiny droplet of truth has exploded like a psychological bomb, what then will happen in our country when whole waterfalls of Truth burst forth?

And they will burst forth. It has to happen.

—Alexander Solzhenitsyn, *The Gulag Archipelago*

The celebrations in the 1990s to mark the fiftieth anniversary of the end of World War II were unique. For the first time since 1945, critics, historians, and writers were able openly to discuss the war. The subjects of this chapter are three outstanding war novels that were published in Russia in the 1990s: Viktor Astaf'ev's The Damned and the Dead, Georgii Vladimov's The General and His Army, and Vladimir But's Heads—Tails. The Damned and the Dead is, in the first instance, a work dedicated to the memory of Russia's fallen. Within this framework of remembrance, we find an apocalyptic interpretation of Communism and the war, one point of reference being Old Belief, which, it is argued, Astaf'ev exploits to portray Communism as the reign of the Antichrist and the German invasion as retribution. Vladimov's theme in The General and His Army is the fate of General Vlasov. Sixty years after the end of the Great Patriotic War, the collaboration of Soviet citizens with the German invaders continues to ignite controversy. This is especially true with regard to the large numbers of Soviet soldiers who fought against their own side after being captured. Vladimov suggests that notions of treachery are conceptually and morally inadequate as explanations of the large-scale defections to the German enemy. The appropriate conceptual framework, argues Vladimov, is civil war. Heads—Tails is a relentless and harrowing exposure of military incompetence and the responsibilities involved in exercising military command. The complicating factor—one unique to the Soviet army—was the role of the NKVD, SMERSH, and other ideological functionaries that inhibited and frequently punished the discharge of competent, professional leadership. Heads—Tails casts new light on a major theme in Soviet-Russian war literature and, the specific Soviet-Russian features notwithstanding, supports the general conclusions of Norman Dixon's classic study of military incompetence.

Introduction

During the Soviet period, the anniversaries of the great battles—Moscow, Stalingrad, Kursk, and Berlin—were commemorated in the main journals with articles and reminiscences from survivors. Many of these articles were accompanied by contributions from leading prose writers and poets expressing their views on the state of the war literature genre, a tradition that has continued in the post-Soviet period. For example, two surveys

were undertaken by the editorial board of *Znamia*, one in 1995,[1] as part of
the celebrations to mark the fiftieth anniversary of the end of the war, and
another in 2000.[2] Though not large enough to meet the strict criteria of statistical significance, the samples nevertheless reveal some useful insights
into the status of war literature in Russia after 1991.

In the 1995 survey, respondents were asked to consider what the Great
Patriotic War meant for them: Was it merely a state-sponsored myth, or was
it a reality? In addition, did they think there was such a thing as war prose
(*voennaia proza*)? A majority of those surveyed were favorably disposed toward Astaf'ev, Vladimov, Grossman, and Bykov. Interestingly, IUrii Buida
bemoaned the fact that there was nothing comparable in Russian war literature to Norman Mailer's *The Naked and the Dead* (1948), Joseph Heller's
Catch-22 (1961), or James Jones's *From Here to Eternity* (1951).[3] This plaint is
akin to a British or American admirer of Solzhenitsyn bemoaning the absence of anything comparable to his work in Western literature. The Russian construction of the title notwithstanding, *The Naked and the Dead* was
made in the USA. Mailer's novel reflects the unique features—or some of
them—of U.S. society at war. As soon as the war was over, it was business
as usual. As far as most Americans are concerned, the books of Mailer,
Heller, and Jones are not war literature in the sense perceived by Buida; they
are entertainment. Whatever else it is, Soviet and now Russian war literature has never been entertainment, and whatever their ideological differences, Soviet and Russian writers have approached the war with solemn
moral purpose.

In the survey of writers conducted in 2000, the impact of changes in the
media, above all television and the growth of the Internet, along with the
ongoing Chechen conflict and even the possibility that readers were no
longer interested in the 1941–1945 war, was evident. Vladimir Berezin identified two changes in media consumption habits. First, he argued that the
documentary or pseudodocumentary book is more efficient in terms of
finding a publisher and reaching a target audience than the traditional
novel. This has given rise to a new type of *rasskaz*: reportage written by eye-
witnesses.[4] Second, telejournalism has replaced written literature, a view
shared by Aleksandr Kabakov, who believes that since the first Gulf War
(1991), "all armed conflicts, whether we want it or not, are above all television shows, a terrible and repulsive picture on the domestic screen. War
has lost its uniqueness and become part of the daily roundup of news,
among which it is not always the most important."[5]

This later survey included the thoughts of Vasil' Bykov and Grigorii Vladimov, two stalwarts who were well placed to judge both the Soviet period and the first post-Soviet decade. As uncompromisingly honest as he was during the Soviet period, Bykov argued that it was not just censorship and the dogmatism of socialist realism that disfigured the literature on war but a willingness on the part of people to collude in the dissemination and acceptance of Soviet myths:

> One such beloved myth was the immortal one about the leading role of the party, about the feats of arms of commissars, political instructors, to which were later added the Chekists and SMERSH operatives. These and other similar myths suited everyone, including readers who had been at the front, whose personal experience, it goes without saying, contradicted the beauty of these heroes which only existed on paper. . . . Truth about the war in society's eyes became disadvantageous, barely decent, even amoral. The slightest overstepping of the generally accepted standards was regarded as having stepped on the holy of holies—the struggle for, and independence of, the Soviet motherland.[6]

War literature, Vladimov asserted, is nourished by a society that values honor, self-sacrifice, and valor. As these values fade away, the basis for war literature is eroded. The success of The General and His Army would seem to vitiate its author's bleak view of Russian society. In the middle of what appeared to be Russia's moral meltdown in the 1990s, The General and His Army celebrated honor, self-sacrifice, and valor. A society in which all respect for these virtues had been lost or marginalized would have found the novel incomprehensible. Or maybe Vladimov is right: We can enjoy reading about honor and other such qualities as long as we ourselves are not expected to behave too honorably.

The Damned and the Dead: Sons of the Soviet Apocalypse

In war a nation reveals to itself and to the world the essence of its nationhood, that primordial, enduring self, the will to survive. For Soviet Russia, this will to survive culminated in the costly victory at Stalingrad, the beginning of the end of the Nazi empire in Eastern Europe. Well before Vasilii Grossman bore witness in Life and Fate to what he believed was the role of Russian nationalism, Viktor Kravchenko had identified it as a decisive factor in the miracle on the Volga: "At the core of a nation there is a hard, eternal and unconquerable element—it was this that was bared in Stalingrad, that survived bloodletting and disaster on a horrifying scale. It had nothing to do with Karl Marx and Stalin."[7] War, especially the total wars of the last century, is, then, the time of absolute trial, in Churchillian rhetoric, the time of "blood, sweat, and tears." Not surprisingly, the two apocalypses described in the Bible—in The Book of Daniel (7) and The Revelation of St. John the Divine, in the Old and New Testaments, respectively—are, given the place of the Last Judgment in Western religion, a ready and endlessly adaptable source of themes and imagery to which even the hardened atheist can repair in search of an interpretive framework when confronted with total war and other calamities.

Apocalypticism is pervasive in all genres of war literature.[8] Some of Siegfried Sassoon's most powerful poems invoke the end of the world and the final judgment, for example, "The Investiture" (1917), "To the Warmongers" (1917), "In the Church of St Ouen" (1917), "Enemies" (1917), "They" (1916), "Christ and the Soldier" (1916) and "The Redeemer" (1915–1916), and "Golgotha" (1916).[9] Among British writers in World War II there was a brief resurgence of interest in the apocalyptic theme in art centered round a number of writers known, collectively, as the New Apocalypse. The movement's main theorist was the Scottish poet J. F. Hendry, who edited two collections of prose and poems. According to Hendry, the New Apocalypse was "concerned with the study of living, the collapse of social forms and the emergence of new and more organic ones."[10] Unlike English literature in the seventeenth century, when thoughts about the Day of Judgment amid religious fervor and political turmoil were discussed with deadly seriousness, the New Apocalypse appears somewhat artificial and contrived, too theoretical and removed from the invaders and the invaded of continental Europe.

Returning to Russian literature, history, and thought, we find that they are deeply imbued with apocalyptic themes, are perhaps inconceivable without them: Such themes inhere in the response of the early Russian chroniclers to the Tartar conquest;[11] they form the basis of the doctrine of the Third Rome; they are central to the religious fervor occasioned by the Nikonian reforms of the seventeenth century; and they inspire Dostoyevsky's Legend of the Grand Inquisitor and the idea of Russia's divine mission. Last, but not least, they are at the heart of Vladimir Soloviev's Tri razgovora (Three Conversations, 1901), the final section of which is "A Short Story of the Antichrist." Even the avowedly secular philosophy of

Marxism-Leninism bears the stamp of Russian culture's obsession with the Day of Judgment (strashnyi sud). The Damned and the Dead[12] clearly draws upon this long-established philosophical, literary, and theological tradition of apocalypticism: The devil rides out; man slaughters his fellow man; God is a spectator, sometimes a reluctant participant. The Damned and the Dead is not for the faint of heart. Conforming to another well-established Russian tradition, the novel is also a magnificent sermon, aimed at a generation emerging from seventy years of Communism. In a foreword, added to the book edition of part 1 of The Damned and the Dead, Astaf'ev apostrophizes Russia:

> Oh, motherland of mine! Oh, life! Oh, people of mine! What are you? What more must be done so that you recover your sight, that you be resurrected, so that you do not fall into oblivion, so that you do not cease to exist? And if you still exist, my people, then perhaps you will heed the prophetic words of a modern, persecuted poet: "And perhaps, through the torments of hell, across all its bloody paths, you will understand that no one must be blindly believed and that the lie must not be cited as the truth."[13]

Communism, Astaf'ev argues, was alien to Russia, a malevolent virus of the mind that pitted brother against brother. Communism and the German invasion are the two poles of the novel's apocalypticism, the alpha and omega, as it were. Only through the suffering of war can Russia cleanse itself of communism and become whole again.[14] Writing in the early 1990s, with Russia bearing more than a passing resemblance to Weimar Germany of the 1920s, Astaf'ev, one feels, has a distinct message for contemporary Russia.

There are, in effect, two separate novels under one title. We have the conventional war novel, elements of which are to be found in both "The Devil's Pit" and "The Beachhead."[15] By conventional I mean consistent with the standards set by Grossman, Bykov, Vladimov, Solzhenitsyn, and Baklanov. Within this larger war-novel framework, sometimes part of it and at other times occupying its own discrete framework, we find Astaf'ev's discourse on Russia's suffering.

The war novel per se begins in Siberian training camps. The time is late 1942. The battle of Stalingrad is nearing its climax. In book 2, "The Beachhead," we encounter many of the same recruits as they are about to force a major river, possibly the Dnieper. The river is crossed under heavy fire with massive loss of life (the forcing of the river and the ensuing bloodbath bear an uncanny resemblance to the opening scenes of Bloody Omaha's capture in *Saving Private Ryan*).[16] There follows a ferocious battle to gain and to retain the beachhead. After much mutual slaughter, the Germans are forced to retreat, and the westward advance of the Red Army continues. Astaf'ev's themes are familiar: the training regimen of the Soviet recruits; the competence or otherwise of the Soviet leadership; and the role of the political officers/commissars, with an especially nasty twist for the theme of memory at the end.

The stupefying cruelty and indifference of the Soviet military leadership toward its own troops, both in training and in combat, cannot be explained entirely by incompetence. Rather, it is a Russian version, at times specifically Soviet, of hell, so the first part, or book, of the novel, "The Devil's Pit" (*chertova iama*), is aptly named: "Everything is at the level of a modern cave, hence the cavelike existence, the cavelike life."[17] The troglodyte regimen endured by the recruits and the brutal treatment to which they are subjected suggest the early persecution of the Christians and their martyrs living in the catacombs. A particularly strong identification can also be made with Isaiah (24:22): "And they shall be gathered together, *as* prisoners are gathered in the pit, and shall be shut up in the prison, and after many days shall they be visited."

Even in basic training, we sense the presence of the beast, perhaps the pale rider of Revelation, in search of victims. The arrival of the train bringing the next batch of raw recruits—the novel's opening scene—is a scene of impending doom and unrelieved menace:

> Penetrating cold and damp surrounded the train on all sides. The space in which the train had stopped was wrapped in a stagnant mist. Hardly discernible, sky and earth merged into cold, impenetrable blackness. Over everything, literally everything . . . there reigned an unrelieved alienation, a supernatural emptiness in which scratched a weakening paw, some sharpened claw of unknown creatures breathing their last. The enveloping blackness was penetrated by short clicks and rattles, reminiscent of some final consumptive cough, becoming a barely audible wheezing of the departing soul. Such was the likely sound of the winter forest surrounded by frost, breathing and fearful of the slightest careless movement, any deep inhalation or exhalation, from which the wooden flesh would be torn to the very core.[18]

Here and elsewhere, Astaf'ev is an outstanding evocator of mood and atmosphere. Portents of the respiratory plagues that ravage the bodies of the recruits—bronchitis, tuberculosis, and asthma—possess a symbolism that resonates beyond the camp. We might see them as a collective metaphor of Stalin's Russia, in which the very breath of life cannot be taken for granted. More ominously, the train, the setting, the end of the line, literally, highlight the role of the train as the indispensable servant of twentieth-century totalitarianism. It was, after all, the *eshelony*—the slow-moving freight trains—that took the hapless *kulaks* to die in the wastes of Kolyma and the Jews to be exterminated in Auschwitz.

From the manner of their arrival and treatment, very little separates one day in the life of a Soviet recruit from a day endured by a *zek*. In Astaf'ev's parallel universe, the recruits live in squalor, and in the struggle to secure even the most basic creature comforts—extra food, an upper bunk, or a place close to the stove—it is everyone for himself. This is a new world unlike anything the men have previously experienced. Some will prosper; some will succumb. The same brutal induction process can be seen in James Clavell's *King Rat* (1962), an account of life in a Japanese prisoner-of-war camp: "For the men, Changi was more than a prison. Changi was genesis, the place of beginning."[19]

The *zeks* must endure slave labor, the recruits exhausting and pointless exercises designed and run by incompetents. Starvation rations are the norm, and in both groups, the *zeks* and the recruits, we find the thieves and other dreadful parasites of the system who prey on their fellows, often with the collusion of the camp authorities: "The thieves, gamblers, and former prisoners had a much better time of it in the training camp than back home. They formed small groups and in alliances with one another stole and plundered on a brazen scale and lived well in the crowded, gloomy shelter."[20] These are observations that we expect to find in Varlam Shalamov's *Kolymskie rasskazy* (Kolyma Tales, 1978) or Solzhenitsyn's *The Gulag Archipelago* (1973, 1975, 1978), but not in a war novel.

Disease is rampant, the military authorities largely indifferent to the consequences. Like the respiratory illnesses, the progressive loss of night vision, induced by poor diet, that affects the recruits has metaphorical implications: the inability or refusal on the part of senior officers to see the true situation. It is a descent into darkness and confusion. The recruits are not being converted into good soldiers but, through criminal incompetence, squalor, malnutrition, and wretchedly barbarous living conditions, most certainly are being converted into a stinking, starving mass. The whole purpose—though it happens more by incompetence and laziness on the part of the leadership than by design—is to reduce healthy, able-bodied young men to scrofulous, pediculous, apathetic wretches. The terror inspired by the obligation to believe, publicly at least, in Stalinist agitprop exerts a malign influence on the administration of the training camps. Senior officers, recalling Stalin's boast that "never before have we had such strong support in the rear of the front,"[21] are frightened to report the incompetence and squalor lest they be suspected of spreading "anti-Soviet propaganda." Agitprop itself induces blindness.

Astaf'ev's use of camp slang, such as *dokhodiaga* (goner) to describe soldiers who, crushed by the conditions, have lost all will to live, is another conspicuous parallel with the world of the *zeks*.[22] The way the goners, hapless young soldiers, are treated by their fellows marks a further spiral downward into bestiality, a coarsening of spirit and behavior. The weaker they are, the more they are beaten:

> Becoming ever more brutalized, Poptsov's fellow soldiers beat him. All the goners were beaten, and every day the numbers of goners kept on rising and rising. In the lower bunks, tightly huddled together, lay up to ten contorted, whimpering bodies. Someone, it was none other than Buldakov, had come up with the idea of taking out the steps from the bunk columns so that the goners could not reach the upper bunks. But if they climbed up there, in the morning, occupying the upper bunks while the company was on its military exercises, they were mercilessly dragged down, onto the floor. And the ill offered no resistance. They merely whined helplessly, wiping the tears and snot from their faces.[23]

A disturbing aspect of Poptsov's eventual death from exhaustion, implies Astaf'ev, is that responsibility cannot be entirely borne by the company commander who pushes the recruit too far. Poptsov was, after all, beaten and abused by his fellow recruits. Beaten themselves, they beat their weaker fellows. We might see Poptsov's death as a sacrifice to propitiate the system or even the pale rider. In this semipagan ritual, which every army knows to some degree or another (known as *dedovshchina* in contemporary Russian military slang), the weak are persecuted, driven out, or killed by the tribe. We are confronted by the disconcerting idea, given the universality of this sort of treatment, that it may reflect some kind of biological imperative—our selfish genes, perhaps—in which the weak are driven out before the enemy is confronted so that the group's chances of survival are enhanced.

Many of Astaf'ev's soldiers remain aloof from this ritual barbarism and are truly inspiring characters. Their survival imperatives are not merely biological; they resist the beast in their own hearts, not succumbing to the gratification of violence. As a result, they resist the beast in others, providing some hope in the devil's pit. Among Astaf'ev's Siberians, Vaskonian, an Armenian, emerges as an unlikely hero. As a result of his getting the better of the commissars, whose ignorance and posturing about humanism he exposes during political instruction classes, Vaskonian is brought before the battalion commander, who, it turns out, is no friend of the Special Section. He puts Vaskonian in the picture: "In the trenches, there's complete freedom of thought and speech. Your mind is not overloaded. One thought constantly gnaws away at your heart and head: How will I manage to survive today? Perhaps I'll be lucky tomorrow. . . . Off you go! And don't upset these idiots for the lads, don't get on their nerves. It's not the time or the place. Now, clear off!"[24]

That Vaskonian the learned has been cast into this seething mass of frightened, ignorant humanity is not perhaps the punishment it seems. The same learning that exposed the posturings and struttings of ignorant political Pharisees, and for which his fellow soldiers beat him because they lost the chance to sleep in the hour of political instruction, carries, Astaf'ev seems to imply, a burden toward his fellow men, an obligation that becomes obvious after the war-weary battalion commander, Vnukov, has warned him. Vaskonian, the storyteller, is the bearer of at least some light, a thousand times more valuable to his fellows than the mind-numbing agitprop sessions:

> The children of workers, the children of peasants, of those resettled during collectivization, of proletarians, scoundrels, thieves, murderers, and drunkards, who had not seen anything humane, let alone beautiful, in their lives, they imbibed the fairy tales of a luxurious world with a sense of reverence, firm in their belief that things were just as they were written in the books and could be found in some place or other, but for them, the children of their time, and, as Kolia Ryndin asserted, of a country damned by God, all this was beyond their reach, for them whose life was ordained according to God's command and rules.[25]

The recruits' response to Vaskonian's stories recalls Dostoyevsky's assertion that the world, with its damned, insulted, and injured, will be saved by beauty. Within the novel-as-religious-allegory, Vaskonian, the conspicuous outsider, first rejected and then accepted, appears as an apostle of Christ, whose stories are to be heard as parables. We might also see Vaskonian as the promised visitor who acts in accordance with God's wish in Isaiah (42:7): "To open the blind eyes, to bring out the prisoners from the prison, *and* them that sit in darkness out of the prison house."

Two incidents during training provide additional examples of the injustices meted out to soldiers by the political class of soldier-bureaucrats. The first concerns what Soviet officialdom calls a *pokazatel'nyi sud*, a show trial or exemplary trial, the aim of which is to demonstrate what happens to malingerers and violators of military discipline. For some relatively minor disciplinary offense, the irrepressible Zelentsov is to be tried. The trial backfires on officialdom, and the victim, refusing publicly to be cowed, argues his case with passion and conviction. (I shall return to this scene later because it appears to be significant within the religious interpretation of the novel.) The aim of sentencing one in order to intimidate a hundred fails. Zelentsov is given the death sentence, which is commuted to service in a penal battalion, a variation on the death sentence. We are left in no doubt that Soviet justice is that of the devil and leads to precisely the situation of which Paul, cited by Astaf'ev at the start of *The Damned and the Dead*, warns: "But if ye bite and devour one another, take heed that ye be not consumed one of another" (Galations 5:15). In the macropolitical arena of Soviet Russia, this is an obvious reference to the Great Terror, of which the *pokazatel'nyi sud* is but one minute cog.

The second incident is much worse. Two brothers who left the barracks without permission to acquire food for their hungry comrades are executed by firing squad. Intended to serve as an example, an act of exemplary discipline, the execution results in a catastrophic decline in morale and a deepening of the sullen resentment toward military authority. It is to God, not to the political officer, that the young men turn to express their grief and to find solace. Even the platoon's battle-hardened second in command, IAshkin, who initially intended to dismiss the execution as unimportant in the Soviet scheme of things, is overwhelmed by faith and the need to give religious expression to it. As he tells the political officer, who is disgusted by such outpourings of faith, "There [at the front] the wounded cry for God or their mothers, not for the political officer."[26]

The harsh, inflexible treatment of these simple peasant lads, carried out for the most part by incompetent and cowardly officers, is the same hysterical treatment meted out to soldiers at the front. IAshkin recalls the summer rout of 1941 and the desperate attempts of some retreating Russians to cross a river before the advancing Germans:

> Some of the crews who had survived, together with some of the infantry, threw themselves into the autumn river in an attempt to ford it. Many drowned, and those who managed to reach the far bank of the river were executed personally by some enraged regimental or brigade commander, dressed in new black tank overalls, with flashing evil eyes and foaming with anger. Half dead with drink, he screamed, "Traitors! Sons of bitches, cowards!" and he kept on firing and firing, barely able to replace the pistol clips, which were handed to him by lackeys, who were also prepared to despise and to shoot the retreating soldiers in such a righteous manner.[27]

IAshkin's recollections compare the judicial murder of the Snegirev brothers with the panic-induced murders of Soviet soldiers in the summer of 1941: "For every soldier who actually fights, there are two to three educators, what we politely call spies."[28] These are the same educators and ideological vigilantes who murder retreating soldiers. IAshkin's calculated, and potentially suicidal, insolence toward the political officer reminds us of any number of Grossman's soldier heroes in *Life and Fate*, such as Grekov, Ershov, and Novikov, who stand up to the commissars. The source of this inner confidence and resistance stems from their having endured and survived the debacle of 1941. Tempered in this crucible, they find nothing so terrible thereafter.

In "The Beachhead," the conflict between the soldiers and the political officers and commissars resurfaces at numerous critical points in the narrative. A particularly unsavory character is Musenok, the divisional political officer, who, we are told, established his career alongside Mekhlis, denouncing army officers in 1937. Zarubin's musings on Musenok highlight the gulf that separates professional Russian soldiers from the party bureaucrats:

> "Where's this Musenok off to?" thought Zarubin in some confusion, still not understanding that as far this individual was concerned, this safe haven on the other bank was the front line, the front itself, the

most dangerous place, the heart of the war. Here, for days and
nights, Musenok fought the enemy, creating a feat of arms on behalf
of the party, pestering and preventing people from carrying out their
military duties. Along with his dear party, Musenok had talked
himself into believing that in the war there was nothing and nobody
more important than the party. A lofty word, military rhetoric, was
more terrible than all the most terrible guns put together.[29]

At a crucial moment in the battle, with communications severely dis-
rupted, Musenok insists on using the sole operational link across the river
to the beachhead to make political speeches, at a time when it is desperately
needed to pass corrections to the artillery so that fire can be brought down
on the enemy. Later, Captain Shchus', one of the officers fighting to retain
the beachhead, castigates Musenok for his interference. The stage is set for
Musenok to seek revenge for this publicly administered humiliation.

The Musenok-Shchus' showdown comes after the battle for the beachhead has been won, when the former tries to discipline Shchus' in the presence of his fellow officers. Almost immediately afterward, Musenok is
killed in a mine explosion. Shchus' is responsible, and Astaf'ev hints
strongly that Musenok's brutal end is no more than he deserves, condign
retribution for the misery and suffering he has inflicted on soldiers before
and during the war. His funeral is a grossly disproportionate response to
this one death. Whereas thousands of Russian soldiers who fell in battle are
buried in mass, anonymous graves with no act of remembrance, this party
functionary is accorded a lavish burial replete with a military band. Perhaps
the greatest insult to the fallen is the fact that the grave becomes the main
memorial around which the postwar acts of remembrance will be celebrated in this part of Russia.

In a perceptive article published in 1995, Vakhitova makes the connection between Dostoyevsky and Astaf'ev, noting the predilection of both
writers for the extreme, the absence of any middle ground:

> In Astaf'ev's prose it is as if the tradition of Dostoyevsky, which in its
> search for the truth strives for the absolute and final point, is revived.
> But whereas Dostoyevsky strives to resolve the contradictions at the
> level of ideas and philosophical disputes, Astaf'ev appeals to actual,
> historical existence, day-to-day life of the people, and as if to the
> natural, bodily existence. . . . Astaf'ev places his heroes in the

situation of the "insulted and the injured," forcing his readers to
suffer their torments. Despite the coarse, vulgar manner of writing,
the soldier's theme in the novel is reproduced in a sentimental tone
by the buildup of negative details and individual moments, by the
desire to show the "whole truth."[30]

There is something to this criticism of Astaf'ev's use of gruesome, natu-
ralistic detail. It overwhelms and numbs the reader. However, its main effect is to induce a sense of powerlessness and frustration. Why, the reader
asks, do Astaf'ev's soldiers allow themselves to be treated in this way? And,
as important, what is the source of this dreadful contempt for their lives?

A far harsher response to Astaf'ev and his novel comes from a former
veteran in an article published, significantly, in Nash sovremennik, a journal
that would have been the natural home for most of Astaf'ev's work. Bitterly
offended by The Damned and the Dead, Zelenkov lays into Astaf'ev for what he
regards as the false and empirically inaccurate basis on which army life is
portrayed in the novel. Zelenkov objects to the depiction of troops used to
bring in the harvest (this, he argues, relates to the Brezhnev era); claims
that too many of the characters are unconvincing (Shchus', IAshkin, Shpator, Ryndin, and Mel'nikov); argues that Astaf'ev fails to attach sufficient
weight to Stalingrad; and questions whether the conditions in which the recruits lived were as bad as those Astaf'ev depicts.[31] To bolster the last point,
he cites letters from soldiers to their parents that were published in 1992:
"The letters contain no complaints about arbitrary behavior or any bitterness about the conditions of service or poor food."[32] Given the nature of Soviet military censorship, the absence of any complaints tells us very little.
Zelenkov's response also betrays a sense of genuine perplexity at The
Damned and the Dead and at what he regards as Astaf'ev's espousal of Western literary trends. Thus, he praises Astaf'ev for having resisted the pressure to conform throughout the Soviet period but accuses him of succumbing to one of the fashionable isms—new realism, postrealism, new
naturalism, retro realism, or postmodernism—that have entered the Russian literary world since 1991. "In my opinion," asserts Zelenkov, "this is reverse socialist realism, but with a clear mixture of unbridled naturalism,
malice, and aggressiveness."[33] Some idea of the extent to which Astaf'ev is
now regarded as having sold out by former admirers can be seen in the editorial note included at the end of Zelenkov's article in Nash sovremennik. The
editorial board—"on the basis of reliable sources"—claims that on Eltsyn's

orders, two billion rubles have been allocated to a fifteen-volume edition of Astaf'ev's collected works. This, it is implied, is Astaf'ev's reward.[34]

Now, to begin my discussion of the explicitly religious digressions and themes in The Damned and the Dead, I might consider the presence of Old Belief, whose settlements and devotees are to be found in Siberia and other remote parts of Russia. That many of Astaf'ev's soldiers profess Old Belief or come from regions of Siberia where there are many adherents to it, and also that they are the source of much trenchant opposition to the Soviet state strikes me from the very outset as significant for interpreting The Damned and the Dead.

Old Belief rejected the reforms introduced by Patriarch Nikon in the 1650s, among which were a new psalter and an order to make the sign of the cross with three fingers instead of two (the traditional way).[35] Opposition to these reforms also served as an outlet for other grievances, specifically to Western influences in Russia, to serfdom, and to the increasing intrusiveness of the state bureaucracy. In fact, it has been argued that the Nikonian reforms were merely a catalyst that sparked a number of deepseated grievances.[36] Importantly, the Old Believer communities that arose in opposition to Nikon were founded on apocalyptic expectations. To quote Robert Crummey, "Clearly, in the eyes of the Old Believers, Nikon's reforms were the first act in the apocalyptic drama described by St. John the Divine and St. Cyril of Jerusalem. The real significance of the first act was clear; Antichrist's reign had begun. . . . Whether or not they expressed their feelings in the language of the Apocalypse, the Old Believers shared their attitude that the Russian state was Antichrist."[37] And in the first half of the twentieth century, Russian writers once again turned to Revelation to interpret Russia's fate. At a time when collectivization was tearing the countryside apart, Nikolai Kliuev wrote his epic poem Pesn' o velikoi materi (The Song of the Great Mother, 1930–1931), with its alternative title "The Last of Russia." Brought up in Old Belief by his mother, Kliuev prophesies a dreadful fate for Russia under Communism. "When he turned to the Soviet era," notes Vitalii Shentalinskii, "Kliuev depicted it uncompromisingly as the Apocalypse, the reign of the Antichrist, fating the Russian soul to perdition."[38] And in one of the many interrogations to which he was subjected, Kliuev made clear his absolute opposition to collectivization: "I regard collectivization with mystic horror, as a devilish delusion."[39]

One consequence of their rejection of the state church as corrupted by Antichrist was that the Old Believers had to do without their own priestly class—or at least some did. One solution, adopted by the *popovtsy*, as they became known, was to accept priests from the state church who rejected the Nikonian reforms.[40] Another group, the *bespopovtsy*, rejected this solution and remained, as their name suggests, priestless. Pressure from the state to renounce Old Belief frequently led to the Old Believers' preferring martyrdom—often whole communities would commit self-immolation— to sacrificing their faith. So savage were the initial state campaigns against the Old Believers that even harboring an Old Believer was regarded as a crime against the state. The Old Believers were, in the language of Stalin's Russia, "enemies of the people."

This brief summary shows that certain themes and allusions in *The Damned and the Dead* appear to extend beyond the military theme. For example, we might reconsider the recruit Poptsov, whose name has an obvious resonance with the *popovtsy* Old Believers. Exhausted and starving, Poptsov collapses and dies, a victim of the squalid training regimen. His name, the manner of his dying, and Astaf'ev's characterization of the death as an act of martyrdom imply that his death has religious significance. Poptsov is a Christlike figure in the heart of darkness who, even though he is victimized by his fellow recruits, dies to propitiate their common tormentors, a similar role to that played by Ikonnikov-Morzh in *Life and Fate*. The leitmotif of martyrdom is also apparent in the execution of the Snegirev twins, the innocents. Sergeant Major Shpator's last request is to be buried next to the "martyr, Poptsov" or to the "slaughtered lambs—the Snegirev brothers."[41] Cast as the "slaughtered lambs" (*agnus Dei*), the brothers are an allusion to Revelation (5 and 6) and the opening of the seven seals, the very nature of the Apocalypse.

Zelentsov's trial may also refer to an important incident in the history of the Old Believers: the debate between Andrei Denisov, the leader of the Vyg Old Believers, and the state church. Representatives of the state church were convinced that the debate would be a mere formality, that the Old Believers would be exposed as superstitious and ignorant, unable to hold their ground. The reverse was true. Far from being cowed, Denisov put together a devastating counterargument, which became known as the *Pomorskie otvety* (The Pomorskii Responses), which in turn became the seminal document of Old Belief.

The apocalyptic vision is at its most compelling in "The Devil's Pit." Even though this is a training camp, the presence of the four horsemen is more powerfully felt than in the frontline scenes on the beachhead. In fact, war is almost a release from the hell of the training camp. Subsequent to the crossing are seven days on the beachhead, each day being the subject of a single chapter. There is an obvious reference to Genesis; that is, the act of creation comes after the defeat of Satan and his being bound for a thousand years. The battle for the beachhead, then, represents part of the eternal cycle of life and death, the paradoxical realization perhaps that war is indeed the "father of all things." This paradox forcefully intrudes with the citation from the Sermon on the Mount in Matthew (5:21–22) at the beginning of "The Beachhead": "Ye have heard that it was said by them of old time. Thou shalt not kill; and whosoever shall kill shall be in danger of the judgment." God weeps as His children slaughter one another. This is man's folly, not God's, even if Astaf'ev, Joblike, berates his master:

> Dear God, what's it all for, why hast Thou chosen these people and cast them down into this infernal cauldron, created by them? Why hast Thou turned away Thine countenance from them and abandoned them to be lacerated by Satan? Surely the whole guilt of mankind has not fallen on the heads of these unfortunates, driven by another's will to their destruction? *You see, many of them have not even managed to sin. Hear Lord, Thy name which like a groan moves across the dead, cold river. Here in this place of slaughter, answer, why dost Thou punish these innocents? Blind and terrible is Thy judgement. The arrow of Thy vengeance smites the innocents and not those who deserve to be smitten. Blind is Thy eye and poorly dost Thou watch over the order created by Thee, tormenting not the devil, but Thy children.*[42]

At its most basic and brutal, the battle between good and evil is waged between individuals, between simple, god-fearing soldiers, such as Kolia Ryndin, or between dedicated professional officers and the party bureaucrats of the political sections. The political instructors, the commissars, the Special Sections, and the NKVD are rightly seen by Astaf'ev as the soldier's enemy. They are the caste apart, who have abandoned God and serve the devil. Despite their lack of formal education, many of these recruits, especially the Old Believers, are well able to resist the ideological vacuities of the commissars. Thus, Kolia Ryndin, an Old Believer, refuses to bow to the agitators: "He submitted only to God in prayer; this was his positive example to his brother soldiers in the unhappiness of the barracks."[43] Denial of God, argues Ryndin in argument with Mel'nikov, the political officer, leads to "this terrible camp and bestiality."[44] The commissars, he argues, bear a special responsibility, for which they shall be punished: "They shall head the column of those being driven into hell, the first rank; their red breeches will be taken from them; indeed they will be whipped with hardened twigs."[45] More than just an allusion to Communism and war, the color symbolism of red also suggests "the scarlet colored beast" on which the mother of harlots rides "arrayed in purple and scarlet" in Revelation (17:4). And in his sustained attack on Revelation, as it has been traditionally interpreted, D. H. Lawrence points out that red is "the colour of evil in the cosmic creatures or gods."[46]

Now, it is an article of faith in *The Damned and the Dead* that humankind's destiny is inextricably linked with the land, with the production of bread; that human labors directed to these ends are fulfilling divine destiny; that all else is the work of the devil. This belief receives its most powerful expression in the novel in the painfully brief interlude in which the recruits help local peasants to bring in the harvest. That their physical and psychological well-being improves merely serves to highlight the mutilations of body and soul that they have had to endure in the devil's pit. This is paradise after hell.

Astaf'ev's obsession with the spiritual and physical theme of bread reveals most fully the nature of the plague that has ravaged Russia in the twentieth century. There was, Astaf'ev suggests, a time when the tiller of the soil plowed the land, "thinking his thoughts of the land and God."[47] Then came war and conflict between the tiller of the soil and the warrior class, "the wild and half-wild tribes" who plundered Russia's lands from the east. No matter; these tribes were like a steppe fire out of which new life emerged. Russia's twentieth-century enemies have proved far more dangerous because they have "humiliated history and reason."[48] The revolutionaries have taught men to forget their past, to worship the false gods of "progressive ideas."[49] Astaf'ev echoes the warning given by Paul in his epistle to the Colossians: "Beware lest any man spoil you through philosophy and vain deceit, after the tradition of men, after the rudiments of the world, and not after Christ" (Colossians 2:8). The revolutionaries bring a different type of fire, a fire that destroys men's minds, that sends them mad. And it is not just Russia that suffered from this disease of the mind and soul: It is universal. Communism, the creed of the godless, destroys the peasant's link with the land so that he loses the meaning of his existence: "Osipov's cornfields, ruined and dead, like our fatherland now in the grip of terrible troubles, laid waste by the storms of revolution, from transformations, from civil war, from the sterile reason of self-assured bosses, who have nurtured neither ideological nor any real grain of bread, since nothing grows on blood or on tears."[50] Such, Astaf'ev suggests, was the absolute catastrophe of collectivization, when the party's mechanized barbarians broke the peasant's love for the land, using "the fornication of false words" to persuade brother "to take the bread from his brother."[51] "The fornication of false words" alludes to Revelation (17:2 and 4), when the prophet speaks of the mother of harlots and "the wine of her fornication," which has bewitched the kings of the earth. Again, in what seems a deliberate echo of Kliuev's warning of environmental destruction, we are reminded of the poet's "The Song of Gamaiun" from "Destruction," a cycle of unpublished poems:

> Dark clouds the tidings brought:
> Silt and shallow the blue Volga,
> In Kerzhenets fell men did fire
> Green fortresses of fir and pine,
> And rotting, Suzdal's wheat fields gave
> Birth to lichen and tree roots tangled.[52]

The communists are the destroyers of nations, the ones who, Kolia Ryndin, in an allusion to the title, assures his fellows, "will be damned and destroyed by God."[53] Driven by men who are inspired by modernity's promises of mastery over nature and possessed by the illusory certainties of Communism, Russia is a land in which the devil struts his stuff. Astaf'ev suggests that the denial of the teachings of Christ, as demanded by the atheist, secular ideology of Marxism-Leninism, destroys the means and will to live: "Harsh authority and sciences have imposed on them an eternal struggle, a deadly struggle for victory over dark forces, for a radiant future, for a scrap of bread, for a place in the bunks, for, for . . . the struggle day and night."[54] The "harsh struggle and sciences," the "radiant future," the "scrap of bread" are allusions to the real enemy of Russia: not the German army but Communism, the teachings of the Antichrist. Hunger, war, death, and pestilence justify the warnings of Kolia Ryndin that they are in "the dwelling of the Antichrist, the demon's amphitheater."[55]

Explicit in the Osipov interlude is the miracle of life, rebirth, and hope. For the apocalypse is a beginning as well as an end: "Wars pass; the fields are forever" and "Osipov's fields shall be resurrected."[56] Even in darkness there is light, the mutual devotion of man and woman, which, the author asserts with complete conviction, is the path to salvation. Love, it seems, is the all-conquering miracle, one of God's gifts—maybe his supreme gift to man and woman. As the author notes in an earlier work, The Shepherd and the Shepherdess, "There is only one holy truth on earth, the truth of a mother, who gives birth to life, and the tiller of the soil who feeds her."[57] Amid the carnage and mayhem, The Damned and the Dead is a devotional exegesis of man's love of woman (obvious biblical allusions being the books of Ruth and The Song of Solomon). One of the great evils of war, Astaf'ev suggests, possibly the greatest, is that it tears man from woman, violating the sanctity of home and hearth.

Astaf'ev's belief in rebirth, the possibility that Russia can recover from the moral ravages of Communism, is relayed in a scene of extraordinary beauty and calm in which exhausted soldiers—the benighted sons of the Soviet apocalypse—find some relief from their misery when confronted with the mystery of being amid the Siberian winter landscape and its white silence:

> A pure silence reminiscent of a Christmas tale lay across the land. In quiet prayer the earth waited for the birth of the Son of God. Ahead lay the Christmas festival, and with it would arrive the customary, but always new time with its promise of a long, bitter winter and the full, unhurried life under roofs weighed down with snow. Many of the lads tramping to the barracks had never managed to learn anything of peasant life; they did not know that the great holy day was approaching because a godless force, a corruption, had fallen upon them and had pressed them toward a cold wall. As children, together with their parents, they had been driven from their homes into some meaningless, infernal, and unceasing whirlwind, into workers' camps, long journeys by train, into prisons, barracks, yet something alerted them to some recent memory, which caused something to stir, something to shudder in their hearts. Out of that pure white vista the arrival of the miracle was awaited, the miracle which was able to change all this repellent life, to deliver people from agony and suffering. A world of such divine light, shining in its greeting, which until recently was called His world, cannot be bad, indifferent and empty toward everything and everyone because that would mean eternal, intense, active evil. Not for that, you see, was this world conceived and created.[58]

Like Nikolai Kliuev, Astaf'ev laments the destruction of rural life, in which he sees God's plan for Russia. He manifestly rejects grandiose social and economic engineering. Russia, in order to be cured of Communism, requires a long period of soul-searching and quietist reflection, free from foreign adventures and political messianism. The preceding passage is, arguably, the artistic and philosophical culmination of The Damned and the Dead, revealing the author's faith in Russia and the possibility of its being reborn. It also demonstrates a powerful belief in divine purpose. For even when he is berating God, one senses that Astaf'ev believes in God's love for His creation. To quote Bernard McGinn, "The apocalyptic view of history is structured according to a divinely-predetermined pattern of crisis, judgement and vindication. God's control over history, conceived of as a foreordained and unified structure, is more evident to believers the worse things are imagined to be."[59]

In purely military themes, The Damned and the Dead does not break new ground, something that would be extraordinarily difficult to do after Grossman, Nekrasov, Vladimov, and Bykov. Nevertheless, some of the battle scenes are of astonishing power and virtuosity, certainly on a par with the very best in the works of Jünger, Remarque, Heinrich, and Grossman. On the specific question of any affinity with Remarque, it seems to me that Vakhitova is wrong to claim that The Damned and the Dead is closer to the "lost generation" of Hemingway and Remarque than to Tolstoy.[60] The Damned and the Dead goes beyond any boundaries established by Western writers. What gives The Damned and the Dead its unique Russian ethos, while recognizing some of the universals of war and captivity, is that no other nation—with the possible exception of China under the communists—has suffered so dreadfully in the twentieth century. This is one of the novel's main themes. Vakhitova recognizes that Astaf'ev, unlike Grossman in his first wartime story, is painfully aware that "the people are mortal and can be destroyed."[61] The main danger is internal, as Vakhitova acknowledges: "Not only Fascism, but above all one's own people, that totalitarian machine, which without conscience and reckoning destroyed the Russian peasant or forced him on his knees during the revolution, collectivization, and the war."[62] Hemingway's writing leaves one with the impression that war, killing, and hunting are all a game, an adventure that you are not required to embark upon in the first place and from which you can retreat if necessary. A visit to Spain in the 1930s was an essential part of any respectable writer's curriculum vitae. However well written Hemingway's work, it has a fundamental insincerity when compared with The Damned and the Dead. Nor is the kinship with Remarque particularly strong. There is nothing in Remarque that is remotely comparable to the religious theme in Astaf'ev's novel. In the twentieth century, Russia nearly perished, and it is this brutal fact that places *The Damned and the Dead* in a completely different moral universe than the works of Hemingway and Remarque.

As a war novel, *The Damned and the Dead* represents a different order of achievement from that of Vladimov's *The General and His Army* or the earlier works of Grossman, Baklanov, and Bykov. Soviet myths about the war had been effectively destroyed by these writers well before 1991; Astaf'ev has moved on. Astaf'ev's portrayal of war is never too far removed from the primeval or the supernatural, and this is the bridge that crosses over into new territory.

The biblical perspective promised in the title, a promise that is delivered, means that *The Damned and the Dead* emerges as something much greater, more profound, than a mere work of remembrance or just another war novel. One might say that the author, having set out to acknowledge the debt of the living to the dead, ends up writing an inspired work of religious devotion. *The Damned and the Dead* can be seen as veneration of Russia's fallen, a quasi-mystical, religious tract that explores suffering and good and evil. We can also see *The Damned and the Dead* as a judgment on Russia's Time of Troubles in the twentieth century; it may also be a plea to postcommunist Russia to rediscover a sense of the sacred and, at long last, to emerge from the long night of Soviet Communism.

The General and His Army: The Ghost of General Vlasov

In the course of World War II, large parts of Western Europe—Belgium, Holland, Denmark, Norway, and France—endured German occupation. In the East, Poland and Czechoslovakia were occupied for over five years, and parts of the Soviet Union were occupied from June 1941 until April 1944. In the soul-searching that followed the German collapse, the extent to which citizens of these states had collaborated with the occupiers became a major issue. Paradoxically, as it turns out, occupation by enemy troops for what in historical terms are very short periods poses a far more severe challenge to a nation-state's collective self-esteem, identity, and even its very existence than do prolonged occupation and eventual assimilation.

In France, occupied from June 1940 until liberation by the Anglo-American armies in late 1944, questions of collaboration and occupation have given rise to especially bitter and prolonged counterarguments. By the time of de Gaulle's death in 1970, a definite backlash against the Gaullist myth of implacable resistance to German occupation, so powerful after 1945, was under way. In *Le Chagrin et la Pitié* (The Sorrow and the Pity), a documentary drama made for French television in 1969 but not shown until 1981, the point was made that only an exceptionally small minority of the French were active against the Germans. *Bleubite* (The Raw Recruit, 1975), *Les Combattants du petit bonheur* (Fighters for a Little Happiness, 1977) and *Le Corbillard de Jules* (Jules's Hearse, 1977), three novels by former resistance fighter Alphonse Boudard, consolidated this challenge, with, according to one scholar, catastrophic consequences for the Gaullist myth.[63] In Paul Werrie's two novels, *La Souille* (The Dirt, 1970) and *Les Chiens aveugles* (The Blind Dogs, 1972), the hero is an unrepentant collaborator. By the middle of the decade, a real collaborator, Lucien Rebatet, published *Les Mémoires d'un fasciste* (The Memoirs of a Fascist, 1976), a sign of just how much things had changed.[64]

Problems of collaboration have arisen even in Germany. General Seydlitz, one of a number of German generals who collaborated with the NKVD-sponsored Committee for Free Germany, after being captured at Stalingrad, was given a very frosty welcome on being repatriated home. That he had collaborated with the communist enemy, even against Hitler, was held against him in postwar West Germany. The evidence, then, from those states occupied by the Germans, and the German reaction to similar situations, suggests that collaboration is to be expected in any protracted struggle and that it will remain a contentious issue long after the cease-fire. Such issues, it is also clear, go to the very core of a nation's being.

In the case of the former Soviet Union, the problem is of a much greater order of magnitude, for the German invasion of the Soviet Union exposed a lack of allegiance on the part of large numbers of Soviet citizens toward their leaders that has no parallel in the history of war. Even with the obvious advantages of vast spaces and strategic hinterlands, limitless human and material resources, this lack of allegiance very nearly proved catastrophic for the Soviet Union. It can be reiterated that had the Wehrmacht and SS units not been so blinded by notions of their own racial superiority, had they adopted a more pragmatic approach to the demonstrable and massive signs of hatred of Stalin's Russia, the outcome of the war on the Eastern front might well have gone irreversibly in Germany's favor. As it is, the war on the Eastern front was very nearly won by Hitler's army. Had the liberator-from-communism card been part of Nazi strategic thinking from the outset instead of a belated reaction to military defeats (Stalingrad and

Kursk, for example), Hitler's boast to his generals that the structure would come tumbling down might well have been vindicated. This, naturally, remains one of history's what-ifs, but it is not outrageously speculative. At various times in the summer of 1941 and in the summer of 1942, after the German army had recovered from the setback at Moscow, Soviet Russia came close to military collapse.

Hitler was defeated. The Soviet Union emerged victorious from a long and bloody war. Decades later, however, the collaboration of Soviet citizens, whether coerced or willing, remains the most painful and viciously contested of all the memories and injuries that survive in Russian recollections of the German invasion and occupation, 1941–1945. In Western Europe, only France's obsession with the *années noires* comes anywhere close.

So sensitive was the theme in the former Soviet Union that any examination largely fell to prose writers—among them Anatolii Kuznetsov, Vasilii Grossman, Alexander Solzhenitsyn, Il'ia Palkin, Tat'iana Vasilieva, and Vasil' Bykov—rather than to historians.[65] And nowhere are the arguments and counterarguments conducted more ferociously than with regard to the former Soviet general Andrey Vlasov, a major theme, among others, of Georgii Vladimov's Booker Prize–winning novel, *The General and His Army*.[66]

The circumstances of Vladimov's own life have a certain resemblance to those of Vlasov. Vladimov, a Russian writer in German exile, like many exiled writers, became an official unperson, a "literary Vlasovite," yet he continued to write on Russian themes and was able to reach the Soviet Union via the broadcasts of Radio Free Europe/Radio Liberty. For his part, Vlasov, a captured Soviet Russian general in exile, made a pact with the devil, as it were, to serve—or so he hoped—the Russia he still loved. One detects the author's uneasy feeling that he too, cut off from Russia, must justify, if only to himself, his time in German exile. Heavy is the burden of Russian letters; heavier still is the burden of love for Russia. *The General and His Army* is more than just an exploration of the theme of political loyalty. It explores the much deeper questions of love of country and the nature of reciprocal obligations, not just in the context of war but also in the wider and unique context of Soviet Russia, with the memories of the Great Terror and forced collectivization.

Biographical details for Vlasov are sketchy. Prior to the German invasion, he was a military adviser to the Chinese. As commander of the Soviet 37th Army, he fought his way out of encirclement. Summoned to assist with the defense of Moscow, he distinguished himself in the Soviet counterattack.

The Russian Liberation Army (Russkaia Osvoboditel'naia Armiia, or ROA), supposedly led by General Vlasov, did not in point of fact exist. It was the creation of certain enlightened Abwehr officers who, understanding the depth of dissatisfaction that existed toward Stalin's regime, hoped to bring about a change of policy on the part of the German high command. To quote Catherine Andreyev, "a unified military formation, such as this [the ROA], remained a desire, not a reality, despite widespread use of the term ROA."[67] More correctly, one should talk of the military and civilian opposition to Stalin as the Russian Liberation Movement (Russkoe Osvoboditel'noe Dvizhenie, or ROD). Misleading too was the term "Vlasov movement" because, as Andreyev has also pointed out, opposition to Stalin and his regime was evident well before Vlasov was captured in the second week of July 1942.[68]

Vladimov is by no means the first Russian writer to take up the Vlasov case. As we have seen, Bondarev in Hot Snow is hostile, tending to repeat the standard Soviet line that Vlasov was a second-rate officer and traitor for whose betrayal there are no mitigating circumstances. Writing in exile, Viktor Nekrasov adopted a somewhat neutral position: "I do not have the right to condemn the Vlasovites—I did not run into them; there's much I do not know—but had they ended up on our path, we would have shot at them."[69]

Grossman tends to be ambiguous, perhaps reflecting his own uncertainty. In Life and Fate, he mentions that some Soviet prisoners of war are ready to join Vlasov's army, yet he does not really explore why this willingness exists. Nor does he explore in any depth what it means to "betray one's country" in the context of the Soviet Union, failing to consider that Tartars, Ukrainians, Cossacks, and Russians might well have good reasons for joining the ranks of Vlasov's army. Grossman seems to be implying that no matter what Stalin does, a Soviet citizen does not have the right to go over to the enemy. In Life and Fate, Chernetsov, the émigré who left Russia after the revolution, tells a Soviet Russian prisoner who is on the verge of joining Vlasov that this is no time to settle scores. This is a curious position to adopt because the would-be Vlasovite could point out that Lenin and the Bolsheviks had no sense of loyalty to tsarist Russia during World War I and actively sought every opportunity to subvert the Russian army at a time of dire national peril, encouraging disaffection and desertion and undermining military discipline. If Lenin and his party could use these methods to destroy tsarist Russia and impose a totalitarian regime— which Grossman condemns in absolute terms in Life and Fate and in Forever Flowing—then shouldn't those who suffered so terribly under Bolshevik totalitarianism and its superviolence use the same methods to destroy this illegitimate regime in the hope that life might be better after the war? This question remains unanswered.

Ershov is another of Grossman's soldiers whose response to Vlasov is perplexing and not entirely convincing. Ershov's family are victims of collectivization, the father and daughters having been deported to a life of misery and slavery in Siberia. He himself is denied a place in the military academy despite passing all the necessary exams. He visits his father in Siberia, which leads to his being thrown out of the army. Yet he seems curiously blind to any understanding of how people who, like himself, have suffered so much because of Stalin could work with Vlasov to destroy Stalin:

> Sometimes he asked himself why he found the Vlasovites so hateful. In the appeals of the Vlasovites, they wrote what his father had said. He knew it was the truth. But he knew that this truth in the mouths of the Germans and the Vlasovites was a lie.
>
> He felt—to him it was clear—that in fighting the Germans, he was fighting for the life of a free Russia; that the victory over Hitler would also be a victory over those death camps where his mother, sisters, and father had perished.[70]

Solzhenitsyn harbors no doubts about Vlasov's behavior, submitting the whole question of mutual loyalty in the conditions of the Stalin state to a searching examination in the first volume of *The Gulag Archipelago* (see chapter 6, "That Spring"). Solzhenitsyn condemns the Soviet high command's abandonment of Vlasov's Second Shock Army after the attempt to lift the blockade of Leningrad failed. Stalin, Solzhenitsyn argues, was the architect of this disaster and was himself guilty of treachery. He explains, "Treason does not necessarily involve selling out for money. It can include ignorance and carelessness in the preparations for war, confusion and cowardice at its very start, the meaningless sacrifice of armies and corps solely for the sake of saving one's own marshal's uniform. Indeed, what more bitter treason is there on the part of a Supreme Commander in Chief?"[71] Lost in an encirclement that should have been avoided, Vlasov's army suffers the same fate as Samsonov's in World War I. Solzhenitsyn defends Vlasov's men, arguing that they were driven to do what they did by a regime that demanded total, uncompromising loyalty yet treated its soldiers and citizens as disposable commodities, as raw material to be expended.[72] The desperate plight of these Russian soldiers, faced with starvation and death from slave labor or the chance of survival in German uniform, is something unique in the annals of warfare, as Solzhenitsyn asserts.[73]

If Solzhenitsyn's eleventh commandment is "Thou shalt not live by the lie," then for Vladimov's General Kobrisov it is "Russian shall not smite Russian." It is this hope that he can somehow mitigate the killings of Russians in German uniforms that convinces Kobrisov that he must return to the bridgehead. So begins the epic journey, the opening lines of *The General and His Army*, to Moscow and then back to the bridgehead, a mission to save Russia, as it were, which suggests Gogol's famous image of Russia as a carriage in search of her destiny:

> It appears, hurtling out of the murk of rain, tires whining, along the broken surface of the road, the jeep, king of the roads, chariot of our victory. Bespattered with mud, the tarpaulin cover flaps in the wind, the windscreen wipers flying to and fro, smearing the half-transparent screen, a whirlwind of slush flies behind it like a tail and settles with a hissing sound. And so it surges ever onward under the constant rumble of Russia's warring skies—whether the thunder of an approaching storm or a far-off cannonade—this ferocious little beast with its blunt snout and flat forehead, which wails in its spiteful eagerness to cover the distance, to push on to its unknown, mysterious destination.[74]

Here, in this Homeric simile, Vladimov poses the same question as Gogol: "Oh, Russia, whither goest thou?"—and answers it with brutal bathos. Kobrisov's epic quest to the "unknown destination" leads not to the glorious liberation of Russia, not to its salvation from internecine strife, but to the artillery ambush that Major Svetlookov of Counterintelligence (SMERSH) arranges for him and his men.

Though much of the life and fate of Vladimov's fictional General Kobrisov mirrors that of Vlasov—service in the Far East, the recognition that his division was the outstanding one, the breakout of encirclement—Kobrisov is nevertheless a separate creation, which permits the author room for maneuver so that wider themes can also be examined and some distance between Kobrisov and Vlasov can be maintained.[75] Yet these two generals (and their armies) remain brothers in arms, though they pursue their ends in different ways. Both officers exemplify to an unusual degree what Solzhenitsyn writes of Vorotyntsev in *August 1914*: "The only sentiment the masculine heart can fittingly cherish is love of country."[76]

Love of Rodina rather than of *partiia* or *gosudarstvo* is a threat to the party. The party state thus saw the much older nation, its history and folkways, as a mortal enemy, but one that cannot be vanquished, that has to be co-opted for the purposes of the party state. From this demand arises the need for the party, in its own words, "to exterminate the *kulaks* as a class," to wage perpetual war against Russia in the name of Russia. The grotesque demands for loyalty made by the party state, even as it was killing and crushing its own, must be understood as a battle to possess the idea of the nation, to wrest it from the grip and the love of the Russian people and their true defenders (Vlasov, Kobrisov), only to turn it against them. The war against the Germans is straightforward. It is the civil war, covert and overt, explicit and tacit, and utterly pitiless, being prosecuted by Russians against Russians, with the Russian-German war as the backdrop, that Vladimov wants us to follow. As Vatutin, who himself will die from the bullet of a Ukrainian separatist, poignantly notes, "We fight our own more than we do the Germans. Were we not fighting each other, we would have been in Berlin long ago."[77] Herein lies the terrible tragedy, the moral apocalypse, that has wrought such devastation on Russia and that, in the words of Solzhenitsyn, perhaps its greatest interpreter, "revealed to us that the worst thing in the world was to be a Russian."[78]

Kobrisov's prewar recollections of Vlasov suggest that the renegade general has the makings of a national leader, a theme that emerges during Kobrisov's own breakout of encirclement. During the summer battle of 1941, Vlasov stands out among the generally poor Soviet generals. He defended Kiev, then successfully withdrew his army out of the cauldron. Of Vlasov's generalship, Kobrisov has no doubt:

> To give up towns, as Vlasov conceded Kiev, to avoid the pincers of Guderian and Von Kleist, meant letting one's own people and the enemy know that not all the best commanders had been eliminated in the prewar purges, that there remained some on whom hopes could be placed. The second occasion when he imposed his authority was in the Moscow area, and Kobrisov could not help but appreciate the daring beauty of his aggressive decision to surge forward in a confident leap, without any reconnaissance, in a snowstorm, at random, having taken another's brigade. Had it all ended in failure, he would have been put up against a wall without any mercy. And most of all it was that surge that saved Moscow rather than the

Siberian divisions maintained by the high command, which were not battle-experienced, but which for some reason were supposed to be more combat-effective than the frontline soldiers who had retreated.[79]

Vlasov's decisive role in saving Moscow can be seen as Vladimov's contribution to the polemic first initiated by the author of *War and Peace*, regarding the great-man-of-history theme. Vladimov's fictional Kobrisov himself can be seen as an exemplar, since his bold and imaginative stroke in crossing the river Dnieper, taken without consultation with Vatutin and Zhukov, seizes the initiative from the Germans and achieves a notable victory with minimum loss of life. A follow-up airborne operation, however, goes disastrously wrong, as we see from the interrogation of the Russian paratrooper conducted in the presence of Svetlookov.[80] No matter; decisive action taken by individuals can change the course of a battle. Other twentieth-century Russian writers, most notably Solzhenitsyn and Grossman, take a similar position on this matter. In *August 1914*, the bold, aggressive, and opportunistic tactical maneuvers of General François are contrasted with the inept grasp of modern warfare shown by Ludendorff and Hindenburg and by the Russian general staff, especially Samsonov, the direct outcome of such Russian incompetence being the catastrophic defeat at Tannenberg. On the prosecution of the war with Germany, Solzhenitsyn notes, "We might look for consolation to Tolstoy's belief that armies are not led by generals, ships are not steered by captains, states and parties are not run by presidents and politicians—but the twentieth century has shown us only too often that they are."[81] In *Life and Fate*, Novikov, on his own initiative and against the orders of his superiors, delays the advance against the Germans at Stalingrad. That the delay leads to victory and reduced losses counts for nothing. Novikov is recalled to Moscow, almost certainly to face arrest and execution. Vorotyntsev, Solzhenitsyn's roving military eye, avoids execution, but his forthright exposure of Russian military incompetence is punished with professional oblivion.

A specific challenge to Tolstoy's thoughts on the art of war and the question of generalship comes, interestingly, not from Kobrisov but from Heinz Guderian, the outstanding German tank general. Vladimov's Guderian is no blinkered Nazi fool. He is the outstanding practitioner of Blitzkrieg, the supreme tactician, and a general who is well aware of the obvious historical parallels between the French and German invasions of Russia. I suspect that Vladimov's favorable and sensitive portrayal of Guderian explains a great deal of the hostility toward *The General and His Army*, especially from Vladimir Bogomolov. Guderian, reading *War and Peace* at the author's desk in IAsnaia poliana, rejects many of Tolstoy's views as those of an amateur. It is the mark of the military professional, which Napoleon most certainly is, that he discerns a pattern to the course of the battle and imposes his will or is able to recognize opportunities that, if taken, can decide the outcome of the battle, as do Vlasov and Kobrisov. The warning for the invader in *War and Peace*, which Guderian sees as he nears Moscow, is the staggering capacity for self-sacrifice shown by the Russian troops. As Guderian notes,

> While paying due tribute to Russian soldiers, their courage and their quiet readiness to lay down their lives, at the same time he also firmly believed that they, unlike the Germans, lacked initiative, were fearful of any uncertainty, and behaved unpredictably even to themselves. So, having submitted to an inexplicable fear, they would surrender in a sheeplike herd or run helter-skelter, and then suddenly a desperate bunch of them would hold to the death a piece of ground, which was not worth a drop of blood, let alone their lives.[82]

This is an enemy that does not wage war according to the doctrines of Carl von Clausewitz.

Kobrisov, in reviewing Vlasov's Soviet career, notes that it was pure chance that Vlasov was captured—yet what, he asks, was the source of the anti-Soviet grievance? Unlike some other prominent Soviet generals (Rokossovskii and Gorbatov, for example) Vlasov had not been "repressed" during the purge of the military. Vlasov's subsequent motives and behavior appear to be more opportunistic than noble. He bears the stamp of the pretender, driven more by personal ambition than altruism. Moreover, in the murky world of Nazi politics and the equally murky world of Russian emigrants, with their competing agendas and personal rivalries, Vlasov was fighting a different war, which he was not equipped to win. "He was," in Kobrisov's words, "a player, but became a plaything."[83] Vlasov's "fateful error,"[84] as Kobrisov sees it, was that he allowed himself to be identified, if only briefly, with Russia's German executioners and tormentors (that he married the widow of an SS officer in Germany did not help his case). Moreover, the various appeals of the ROD came after the battle of Stalingrad and the Kursk salient—too late, in other words, to bring about decisive change. Vlasov's legacy was not the Smolensk Declaration or the Prague Manifesto, though both documents adumbrate a Russia without the Bolsheviks and are historically important, but that he saved Moscow. In Vladimov's words, "And so one minute of his resolution and an hour of weak will determined Moscow's fate. And although what came after did not depend on him alone, history shall always know him as the savior of the Russian capital, the very same capital to which four years later, he would be taken to be judged and put to death; but no matter what efforts be made, his name shall never be separated from the name of Moscow."[85] Had Vlasov been captured and turned by the Germans before his name as a competent general had been made, his critics would have found it much easier to erase him from the historical record.

Temptation, political and moral, which confronts both Vlasov and Kobrisov, is one of the central themes of *The General and His Army*. Two important episodes in the novel examine this question with regard to Kobrisov: his symbolically significant forty-day period of imprisonment before the German invasion and the period spent in avoiding German encirclement and the return of the men and equipment under his command to the Soviet lines. In the Lubianka, Kobrisov is subjected, in effect, to two quite different interrogations. The first is the formal, preposterous one in which the NKVD interrogator tries to coerce a confession that tanks under Kobrisov's command that stalled in front of the Mausoleum during the May Day parade in 1941 represented a plot to assassinate Stalin. The second is the lengthy, indirect examination of his motives by his fellow prisoners and the strengthening of his resolve to serve Russia. A fellow prisoner, a literary scholar, arrested for his interpretation of Voltaire (one of Kobrisov's favorite authors), sees a special role for Kobrisov in the forthcoming war with Germany. Kobrisov, whose talents and moral strength he perceives, must, he tells him, survive so as to be able to serve and to save Russia. It is here, I think, that a major difference emerges between Kobrisov and Vlasov. If service to Russia means service to Stalin, so be it. Of course, how Kobrisov would have behaved in German captivity remains unanswered.

Breakout from German encirclement in the summer of 1941 is the vehicle by means of which Vladimov tries to reexamine the same fateful period in the life of Vlasov. As far as Kobrisov is concerned, collaboration with the Germans is not an option. He is, however, subjected to a different form of temptation. In Kobrisov, Kirnos, the commissar, sees Russia's savior, urging him to become a military dictator, a people's president, with the obvious requirement of a final reckoning with Stalin: "Oh, you know who I'm talking about . . . he must be deposed. That's the first thing that must be done! And then put him on trial for the whole people to see. He must answer for all his crimes."[86] These speculations from Kirnos point toward what might have happened in Russia had the generals collectively refused to cooperate with Stalin and raise the question as to why Stalin was not removed from power on, or very soon after, 22 June 1941. Indeed, one might even argue that these speculations are an implicit criticism of the Soviet generals, who, in the period from 22 June to 3 July 1941, when Stalin was by all accounts in a state of nervous collapse, had a unique window of opportunity to overthrow him. At least it could be said that the German generals—or some of them—tried to get rid of Hitler. From Stalin's point of view after he had weathered these critical eleven days, the purges, the physical extermination of perceived rivals, and the psychological crushing of the army's spirit and subsequent total subjugation to the will of the party, even if it meant unparalleled military defeats—even the threat of total defeat—must have seemed justified. This period also justified his contempt for the generals: They could have removed him, but they did not do so. From that moment on, Stalin, unlike Hitler, could do with his generals as he wished.

There is an enormous conceptual gulf between the loyalty demanded by Stalin and the Soviet state and that which would be expected in the West (with the exception of Nazi Germany). It may be, as Grossman has argued controversially in *Forever Flowing*, that the origins are to be found in Russia's long history of brutal and arbitrary rule, unconstrained by civil society. In pre-Soviet and Soviet Russia, absolute loyalty is the tribute demanded by the ruler. The merest hint of skepticism can readily be construed as treachery. Again as argued by Grossman and gruesomely indicated in episodes in *The General and His Army*, this state of mind manifests itself in one of two ways: submission/masochism or domination/sadism. And if the slave does rebel against his master, it is only to use the same methods. Indeed, even as he is advocating a special role for Kobrisov in liberating Russia from Stalin, Kirnos sees nothing wrong in another round of executions: "The firing squad in the name of mankind, the most widespread and cruel, well, I'm for it. But for the very last time!"[87] Kirnos's belief in the efficacy of violence as a way of perfecting Russian society shows he has learned nothing from Lenin's and Stalin's experiments. It justifies the depressing view expressed to Kobrisov by one of his fellow prisoners in the Lubianka: "God has abandoned this country; all hope is on the devil."[88]

Major Svetlookov, the SMERSH officer, is one of Russia's demonic tormentors. He is the symbol and substance of the nation killer, the corrupter of loyalty and friendship, the zealous protector and promoter of party interest, the destroyer of heresy and its bearers. He is a familiar type in much Soviet Russian war literature: the cynical and ruthless bureaucrat-cum-murderer, securing his own self-interest on the backs of others. As befits his occupation, his machinations are everywhere; in particular they are aimed at Kobrisov, his driver, orderly, and chief of staff.

In chapter 1, appropriately titled "Major Svetlookov," we see the recruitment of Kobrisov's staff by SMERSH. At this stage, it is not exactly clear why Svetlookov wishes to be kept informed of Kobrisov's moods and intentions. Ostensibly he fears for the general's well-being, worried by his reckless disregard for his own safety, his habit of traveling up to the front line without an adequate guard. There is a suggestion, no more yet, that Svetlookov is concerned that Kobrisov, arrested before the German invasion, will try to defect—not, as becomes clear later in the novel, to the Germans but to the Russians in German uniform opposing his river crossing. That Kobrisov is under suspicion is also strongly implied by one of Svetlookov's more successful recruitments, Zoechka, the telephonist. She expounds Svetlookov's cynical manipulations to Kobrisov's driver:

> The major has opened up avenues for me that just make your head spin, honestly. You just cannot imagine how many hidden enemies there are in our ranks, how the majority of people really feel, those who have an incorrect attitude and those who are hostile. Sometimes even very highly-placed persons with high ranks and a chest full of medals. For the time being they are fighting, fulfilling their duty, and as a result we can't fully occupy ourselves with them. Still not the time.[89]

For the time being the party needs the professional military to win the war. Once that is over, there will be a reckoning, the completion of unfinished business. Vladimov takes up one of the central themes of Life and Fate, namely, that fanatical Russian resistance to the Germans merely saved Stalin's regime and prolonged Russia's agony. Wartime concessions and tacit assurances that the terror of the 1930s would not be repeated were tactical ploys to buy time.

Svetlookov's recruitment of Sirotin plays on the driver's desire to find a less gung-ho general, one who does not have a death wish. In the case of Major Donskoi, the general's chief of staff, the weak spot is injured pride, a festering grievance that the general did not put him forward for a medal for his part in the forcing of the river Desna. There is also another reason, one more central to the novel. Donskoi is present when a number of Russian prisoners wearing German uniforms are executed. He fails to intervene, apart from a feeble protest that two of them are wounded. Wounded vanity—he resents being undermined by a junior officer—seems to be the source of his discomfort, not the fact that his countrymen have been executed. Of the three members of the general's entourage, Donskoi is the least congenial. Svetlookov achieves no real success with Kobrisov's orderly, Shesterikov, who saves the general's life in the winter battles for Moscow and becomes part of the general's family. Yet, despite his resistance to Svetlookov, there is a hint that simply by his meeting with Svetlookov, the deep bond of friendship and love that exists between him and the general has somehow been weakened or tainted. It is perhaps significant that the shell that strikes the general's lend-lease jeep kills his three staff members while he survives—and, of course, that they die because of Svetlookov's intrigues. We might see this, on one level, as condign retribution for the three soldiers' meeting with Svetlookov.

But Svetlookov's work amounts to much more than recruiting spies inside Kobrisov's headquarters and elsewhere. He is the party's witch-finder general, who seeks to root out all heresies while manifesting a sadistic pleasure born of the knowledge that the Russian captives before him are defenseless. It is not enough for the Soviet state to own the bodies of its citizens; it wants their minds. Ever fearful that the compliant masses simulate devotion, the state, personified by Svetlookov, must compel devotion by unimaginable cruelty. Kobrisov understands this:

> And why was he [Svetlookov] needed? So as to trap them, to enslave them, to force them to their knees, to bend those guilty heads to the ground that they had "betrayed"? That Vatutin, normally so cautious, had said, "We fight our own more than we fight the Germans." What was that? It came out involuntarily; what was on his mind? Well, he was chief of staff of the Kiev military district, served alongside Vlasov; he could not but have thought about him. Moreover, he's not the only one who has concluded that there is nothing more terrible than civil war since you are fighting your own. . . . And in actual fact, the spite one feels toward captive Germans soon fades, but how the feeling of cruelty toward one's "own" hardens. In pleasurable

anticipation of the "holy retribution," a green fire would start to
sparkle in Svetlookov's eyes. Truly, there is no more intoxicating
work in the whole of Russia![90]

This institutional sadism, a grotesque parody of military discipline,
reaches its apogee in the loathsome General Drobnis (almost certainly
based on Lev Mekhlis), Stalin's "watchdog,"[91] his faithful Russian, as it
were. Drobnis's sadism, as is frequently the case, masks cowardice—here
of a particularly repulsive kind, a willingness, maybe a craving, for total
submission. Thus, having been largely responsible for losing the Crimea to
Manstein, Drobnis can expect no mercy from his master, yet he earns a re-
prieve "on his knees, groveling and crying before the Supreme One that
they can take his life, but they cannot take away his devotion to his beloved
master, and that death itself is not so terrible for him as the thought of
being parted prematurely from the object of his devotion."[92] Such fanatical
debasement—redolent of Grossman's Lev Mekler in *Forever Flowing*—demands its payment: Drobnis slowly and with great relish shoots one of his
staff, Major Krasovskii, to death. In this gruesome carnival of sadism, the
victim cannot be helped, indeed does not wish to be helped. As the broken
Krasovskii tells Kobrisov,

> Does it not seem to you, Comrade General, that you are interfering in
> things that do not concern you? It is for Leonid Zakharovich
> [Drobnis] to decide the appropriate punishment for me. And how it
> is to be carried out. . . . So don't poke your nose in, understood? If I
> am guilty, I will die by the hand of Leonid Zakharovich, but, excuse
> me, I don't want to hear your thoughts on the matter![93]

This extreme denial of the self, the total surrender to another, or more
accurately to the party, so that one is no longer capable of individual action,
paralyzes the will until neither flight from, nor violent reaction to, one's ex-
ecutioner is possible. Equally, as Kobrisov realizes, contempt for one's own
life results in contempt for the lives of others. The message for Russia is a
truly dreadful one: There can be no social contract, no rule of law, no civilization, only the endlessly savage whims of the ruler and the ruled, the latter colluding in and perpetuating the eternal agony. If Kobrisov recoils in
horror, unable to comprehend Krasovskii's collusion in his own physical
torture and psychological annihilation, then the reader, especially a
Westerner, is bound to question it or to be equally perplexed—maybe

even repelled in equal measure by the apparent pusillanimity of the officers, among them Kobrisov, who are released from interrogation and assigned commands at the front.

To win battles against troops led by the caliber of officers such as General Guderian and Kleist, let alone to contain the rampaging German army,
Soviet commanders must show initiative, must, in other words, lead. Slaves
cannot lead. Only free men can do this, and thus Soviet military disasters
must be seen as a function of the total slavery demanded by the Vozhd' in
the Kremlin. Even as Russia was being overrun by Nazi hordes, this angry,
insecure, and cowardly god continued to demand his blood sacrifice.

In the corridors of the People's Commissariat for Defense, Stalin and
Beria confront a number of officers waiting to receive their orders:

> Among the garbled words and the guttural, fragmented phrases,
> Kobrisov could clearly distinguish "Cowards, traitors, why have they
> been released; no one can be trusted. . . ." This was the sort of
> spiteful abuse that one could hear in a dog's barking or the cawing of
> a crow. To hear and see this was terrible, and so lacking in restraint,
> shameful for a soldier to behave in such a way, or even an ordinary
> man, but not the boss! For the thing which stood in front of him,
> pockmarked, crushed, and babbling, was Stalin.[94]

This scene resonates throughout the entire novel. In terms of the liter-
ary-historiographical task Vladimov has set himself, it is the crux of *The General and His Army*. Here is one of the more important variations on the theme
of Vladimov's title: Stalin as murderous and incompetent "general," sacrificing his army. After such an assault upon Kobrisov's personal and professional dignity, "collaboration" with the Germans would not have been unforgivable. In his own way, though, he does what one of his fellow
prisoners predicts: "When the terrible hour comes for our poor motherland, you, my general, shall show yourself to be a knight, and you shall protect her."[95] Soviet Russia, with its legions of Svetlookovs, Berias, and Stal-
ins (not to mention Drobnises and Krasovskiis) cannot pass judgment on
Vlasov, Kobrisov's brother in arms, the talented, erudite, politically naive
soldier who, when the gamble failed, declined to accept an offer of safe passage to Franco's Spain, returning instead to challenge his accusers, and
met a gruesome end.[96] In defending Vlasov, Vladimov is also defending
other disgraced Soviet generals and their armies who were condemned as
traitors and cowards, one being General Ponedelin, whom Kobrisov recalls

in connection with Vlasov's fall from grace. Ponedelin was singled out for attack in Order № 270, which was effectively his death sentence: "Ponedelin did not demonstrate the necessary persistence and will to victory, gave in to panic, behaved in a cowardly fashion, and surrendered to the enemy. He deserted to the enemy, so committing a crime in the eyes of the motherland, as someone who broke his military oath."[97]

In spite of Stalin, Vlasov is, for many Russians, still a traitor who carries the mark of a *predatel'*. A serious attempt to make the accusation of *predatel'stvo* stick to Vlasov and any Soviet soldier or citizen who collaborated with the Germans has been made by Leonid Reshin in a lengthy, detailed article published in *Znamia*.[98] Reshin draws a distinction between those who through no fault of their own were captured by the Germans and, after the war, found themselves the victims of lengthy interrogations, long periods in slave-labor camps, loss of livelihood, exile, and execution and those such as Vlasov and others who actively collaborated with the Germans. This distinction is reasonable but fails to provide a satisfactory answer as to why former Soviet prisoners of war were subjected to such brutal and arbitrary treatment after their repatriation to the Soviet Union. Presumed guilty of treachery by the mere fact of having been captured, these Soviet soldiers, among them Vlasov, well aware of what awaited them on their return, had no incentive to remain loyal to Stalin. Vital here are the provisions of Order № 270, for, as Mikhail Nekhoroshev has correctly pointed out, the essence of the order was clear: "We don't have the term 'prisoner of war,' but there is the word 'traitor.' And over the course of this war, according to the most modest calculations, there were no less than *four million* such traitors."[99]

We should not, Reshin argues, look to political considerations, such as dissatisfaction with Stalin's regime, to explain why vast numbers of Soviet soldiers surrendered to the German army. He explains, "Military failures, lack of experience and incompetence on the part of the command structures, mistakes, miscalculations, and the crimes of the party-state leadership must be held responsible for the fact that at the very least one and a half million Soviet soldiers fell into captivity in the first days of the war."[100] Granted, these factors explain why the bulk of the Soviet Army—there were some exceptions—was simply overwhelmed by the Wehrmacht, but the list also hides a great deal. What was the source of this incompetence? What was the nature of these mistakes, and why did they occur? And what were the crimes of the party-state leadership? We look above all to Stalin for an answer to these questions.

Stalin decapitated his high command at a time when Nazi Germany was becoming an obvious threat to the Soviet Union. Dual command—the system according to which political commissars, often woefully ignorant of military matters, had a say in tactical decision-making—was a crippling handicap in the type of highly mobile tank warfare pioneered by the Germans, in which a premium is placed on the initiative of commanders (*Auftragstaktik*). And there is plenty of evidence, certainly as late as 1994, when Vladimov's novel was published, to show that Stalin simply ignored thoroughly reliable intelligence from many sources—including his own agents—that a German invasion was imminent. The Soviet response to the German invasion in the first hours of 22 June 1941 was completely inadequate, for which Stalin, with his determination to avoid "provoking" the Germans (as if they needed to be provoked), must be held responsible. Psychologically unable to take initiative, one of many serious consequences of the purges and Soviet military training, senior commanders awaited orders that never came or that were irrelevant in a rapidly changing tactical situation. Overwhelmingly, in a totalitarian state such as the Soviet Union, political, or rather ideological, considerations were paramount. As a consequence, the incompetence, the inertia in the face of mounting and obvious danger to the Soviet Union, and the crushing of all independence in the military made these early defeats all the more likely.

Reshin's essay contains no mention of collectivization and the Terror-Famine, an important omission, and one identified by Vladimov in his rejoinder essay. In the words of Vladimov:

> In Reshin's entire essay one does not find the word "*kulak*" or "*raskulachennyi*"; there is no discussion of the families of the repressed, of those who had survived the famine in the Ukraine, and such people comprised the heart of the anti-Soviet formations and as such had every reason to surrender in such numbers: either so as not to have to serve in the Red Army and leave their beloved homelands unprotected, or to take their revenge on someone or other for all the horrors of collectivization.[101]

In the light of collectivization, the purges and the brutality routinely deployed against people in the 1930s, the charge of *predatel'stvo* against ordinary Soviet citizens, driven to despair by such treatment, is untenable and unjust.[102] Moreover, the numbers of Soviet citizens who fought against the Soviet Union or who remained passive render any accusation of *predatel'stvo* grossly inadequate, both conceptually and morally. On such a scale, this is rebellion, even civil war. V. Kardin notes,

> The Patriotic War threatens to turn into a civil war. Without formulating this directly, Vladimov immerses himself in the psychology of the people who in some degree are involved with a tragic turning point of history. In this novel about war there are no battle scenes, no images from the prisoner-of-war camps. But their weight lies unseen on the shoulders of the protagonists and is perceived by those of us reading about the generals and their armies. *The artistic truth corroborates the truth of history, which in this respect has not been examined by our literature.*[103]

Reshin nevertheless insists that Vlasov was "a traitor, not to Bolshevism but to the motherland."[104] Now, this distinction also lacks cogency. In the Stalin state, no distinction could be made between the two because the party had co-opted the nationalist tradition and sentiments for its own ends. This, as we have seen, is one of the main themes of *The General and His Army*, about which Reshin is curiously silent. SMERSH and the NKVD were deeply suspicious of all forms of Russian nationalism and, indeed, of any manifestations of nationalism in the Soviet republics. And Russian nationalist sentiment that was independent of the party was viewed as a species of counterrevolution.[105] So by the time of Stalingrad, Russian nationalism, love of Rodina, and the party had all become fused together, and it had become impossible to remain loyal to the motherland but disloyal to Stalin or the party. The hapless Soviet citizen had to accept them all or "betray" them all. Discussing *The Damned and the Dead*, Ivan Esaulov makes a similar point. In defending the Soviet system, soldiers—Christian soldiers—were forced to violate their conscience. The confrontation between patriotism in its Soviet variant and the Christian conscience during a defensive war had not been dealt with before in Russian literature. "Astaf'ev's novel," he writes, "may perhaps be the first novel about this war written from a Russian orthodox position and with the full awareness of the tragic collision."[106] Once captured and free of the psychologically crushing atmosphere of Soviet Russia, it is not surprising that large numbers of Soviet citizens viewed Stalin's Russia differently. That this deep, latent hostility toward Stalin could achieve its fullest expression only in German captivity and was exploited by the Germans in no way means the loathing of Stalin was any less genuine or was somehow self-seeking or unjustified.[107]

Reshin is also conspicuously silent about the role and the ubiquity of SMERSH and the NKVD in the narrative of *The General and His Army*. Thus, when Kobrisov manages finally to extricate his men from German encirclement, he is met by an NKVD reception party, which, with a German assault on Moscow likely, demands that Kobrisov's troops hand over their weapons (the preliminary to their being arrested, filtered and interrogated, and punished). Militarily suicidal with the Germans pressing so hard, this demand yet again bears witness to the extraordinary ideological vendettas being pursued by the organs at a time when every able-bodied soldier was surely needed for the desperate defense of Moscow. And what of the NKVD itself? Thousands of well-armed and -organized NKVD troops were deployed against their own side—to shoot any Soviet troops attempting to retreat from the front—instead of joining the defense. The presence of the NKVD in the area immediately to the rear of the front was well known to the frontline troops, as it was intended to be. And we have to ask: Are accusations of *predatel'stvo* really credible when Soviet soldiers, sacrificed by incompetent commanders to achieve tactically irrelevant ends, deserted to the enemy rather than be shot down by NKVD troops outside the immediate danger area?

One important connection, which, as far as I am aware, has not been made by Russian critics, is that *The General and His Army*, with its positive appraisal of Vlasov and overwhelmingly negative view of the NKVD and SMERSH, is at least in part a calculated riposte to Vladimir Bogomolov's *In August 1944*. The two novels have conspicuously similar beginnings: In Bogomolov's novel, we see the SMERSH trio traversing the countryside; in Vladimov's novel, Kobrisov and his crew are hurtling back to the front. Even the choice of transport reflects the ideological rivalry between Bogomolov and Vladimov: The SMERSH crew drives a Soviet-made GAZ, whereas Kobrisov and his retinue drive an American lend-lease jeep.

Bogomolov himself seems to recognize the significance of *The General and His Army* for *In August 1944* because in 1995, to mark the fiftieth anniversary of the war's end, he wrote an exceptionally lengthy, detailed critique of Vladimov's novel.[108] Of immediate relevance, however, is that in his lengthy, detailed reply to Bogomolov, Vladimov made a specific reference to *In August 1944*:

> Some twenty years ago we got the Western *In August 1944*, a work that stood out and, without any cavilling, slandered the Polish Armia Kraiova. In it the language of official protocol, reports, and

operational documents served to provide a fascinating background to this detective story. For this the author needed a sense of taste and balance. Somewhat later we found out that in the SMERSH operative Tamantsev he was describing himself as a young man; that the book was read and esteemed by members of the KGB; that is, by competent people, who found themselves lauded as worthy; that he was a favorite of Chebrikov, of his deputies and assistants; that he frequently spoke at informal meetings; that he gave signed copies away. Everything was cozy and on first-name terms. Several generations of KGB men were brought up on In August 1944. They themselves acknowledge this with gratitude. However, not only does the writer make the book, but the book the writer. It seems to me that at that time, something happened to Bogomolov, and not only with his language but also with his view of the world.[109]

Bogomolov reacts vigorously, among other things, to Vladimov's very sympathetic portrayal of German general Heinz Guderian, the pioneer of the Blitzkrieg, and to the role assigned by Vladimov to General Vlasov. To begin with, Bogomolov is offended by Vladimov's portrayal of Guderian as the representative of a higher culture, with the implication that Russia is backward and requires the firm, even harsh, civilizing hand of the Germans. Guderian is the scholar general, not only the pioneer of a devastating new way of waging war but one who enjoys Russian literature.

Bogomolov is surely correct in pointing out that Guderian, whatever his scholarly and moral qualities and whatever his allegedly hostile attitude toward Hitler, was a thoroughly professional soldier and senior officer in an invading army.[110] At this stage of the war, his one ambition was to take Moscow. Again, Guderian, whatever he thought about Hitler, refused to have any dealings with the anti-Hitler faction in the German army. In an essay published in 1994, just after the publication of The General and His Army, Vladimov heaps further praise on Guderian, regretting the fact that Guderian did not meet and form an alliance with Vlasov.[111] Guderian's plan then, according to Vladimov, would have been to open the Atlantic front to the Anglo-American armies, having removed Hitler, and to transfer all German troops to the Eastern front for a final reckoning with Stalin's Russia. This Guderian-Vlasov coalition would, Bogomolov insists, have been just as rapacious as any army under the control of Hitler: "Guderian at the head of Hitler's Wehrmacht and General Vlasov with his ROA divisions, without any interference on the part of the USA, UK, and France, would have fallen upon Russia with their combined forces. Just think how many more of these *Untermenschen*, *Homo sovieticus*, and Eastern subhumans would have been buried!"[112] Bogomolov has a point, but his indignation would be more convincing and consistent had he recalled Alekhin's contemptuous attitudes toward Poles and Belorussians in the earlier *In August 1944* before writing his response to Vladimov. Again, Bogomolov avoids an explicit reference to the main victims of Nazi genocide in the East: the Jews.

On the particular issue of the exaggerated role that Vladimov ascribes to Guderian, Bogomolov's sense of wounded national pride is almost certainly a factor in his response. Like the Poles and Belorussians whom Alekhin dismisses as "Westerners," Vladimov is a writer who looks to the West for answers to Russia's ills, whereas Bogomolov appears to occupy a position somewhere between traditional Slavophilism, with its spiritual rejection of the West, and secular Russian nationalism.

Another inconsistency can be seen in Bogomolov's apparent sympathy for the Poles and his attack on Guderian for his role in the suppression of the Warsaw uprising. The Germans did suppress the uprising with utter ruthlessness, yet Bogomolov sidesteps the problem that most Poles, certainly including those who were fighting the Germans, considered Soviet Russia to be a threat to Polish independence as well; he ignores the protocols of the Nazi-Soviet Non-aggression Pact, the sources of so much misery for Poland, as well as the Katyn massacre. In 1995, with literary censorship a thing of the past, Bogomolov had a chance to plug some of these important historical lacunae identified in his thriller *In August 1944*. That he elected not to suggests that we have to look to factors other than the censorship regime that obtained in 1974 to explain these historical omissions. As Vladimov argues, perhaps something in Bogomolov's worldview did indeed change.

Nowhere in *In August 1944* do we find any sympathy for the Poles' striving for independence. Quite the reverse, in fact: The Polish Home Army, *Armiia Kraiova*, which was the backbone of resistance to German and Soviet rule, along with Ukrainian, Belorussian, and Lithuanian nationalists, is shown as an implacable enemy of the Soviet Union—which it was—and a puppet of the Polish government-in-exile in London. Bogomolov's citing of Guderian's role in the suppression of the Warsaw uprising—and the undeniable compendium of sadistic German army and SS violence that went with it—is a purely tactical concession designed to discredit Vladimov, an admirer of

Guderian, in the eyes of Russian readers. The plight of Poland is of little concern to Bogomolov.

The same approach is adopted with regard to Vlasov, whom Bogomolov tries to discredit as a weak, vain opportunist. Even allowing for some of the less attractive sides to Vlasov's character, some of which are surely irrelevant, he showed himself to be a cut above the average Soviet commander at Kiev. Nor can his role in saving Moscow in the winter battles of 1941–1942 be denied. Bogomolov blames Vlasov for the fate of his 2nd Army when the real culprit was Stalin and his unrealistic expectations. In some ways, Vlasov is a distraction from something far more fundamental already referred to, namely, the sheer numbers of Soviet citizens who welcomed the Nazis and those who were willing to wear the uniform of the enemy. Also, the willingness with which hundreds of thousands of Soviet soldiers surrendered to the Germans does not suggest that loyalty to the Soviet regime was deep-rooted.

Finally, with regard to criticism of Vladimov's novel, one cannot exclude the possibility that the timing of publication was significant. After all, The General and His Army was published and the author honored with the Booker Prize during the period of the first Chechen War (1994–1996). At a time when the Russian army was being humiliated by its failure to bring a swift conclusion to the war, nothing could have been better calculated to antagonize Russian nationalists, the military, and what one might call the more conservative elements in the Russian Federation than Vladimov's sympathetic portrayal of a Soviet general, Andrei Vlasov, who, taken prisoner by the Germans in 1942, assisted his captors. The award of the Booker Prize, a prize of Western origin, in December 1995 would in some quarters have readily been construed as further evidence of a Western-inspired information war, the aim of which was to undermine the Russian Federation.[113]

The real challenge posed by The General and His Army is not whether Vlasov and others were guilty of predatel'stvo. The extraordinarily brutal conditions that obtained in Soviet Russia and the extent of the resistance to Stalin render any such accusation largely untenable, in my opinion. If guilt is to be apportioned, it is, possibly, to some of Vlasov's military colleagues close to Stalin who did not take their chance very soon after 22 June 1941. Even later there were opportunities, and Kobrisov himself reads the leaflets dropped by the Germans announcing the formation of the ROA as "a mild reproach aimed at those who understood everything but took no part in the disastrous enterprise."[114] The enterprise was doomed because so few senior

Soviet officers supported it. In this respect, it is curious that the German generals, who were far more tightly bound by the traditions of the Prussian officer corps and their *Militäreid*, and who have been collectively indicted for failing to remove Hitler, nevertheless tried, albeit late in the war, to assassinate him. No such attempt to assassinate Stalin was ever made, as far as I am aware. Yet no taint of moral cowardice hangs over the achievements of Zhukov, Rokossovskii, Vatutin, Konev, and others like them.

In his remarkable novel, Vladimov attempts to understand—if this is indeed possible—why citizens at all levels of Soviet society did remain loyal to a regime that treated them so abominably and, equally, compelled them to treat others in the same manner. One possible explanation has been noted: the exceptionally powerful collectivist ethos that predates Communism's arrival in Russia. In conditions of Communism, this collectivist grip on the individual becomes even stronger, especially for the party member. Confronted with the possibility of expulsion, party members collapsed. This was an essential weapon in the armory of the NKVD interrogators in the 1930s, and one that was used with spectacular effect against Bukharin and other senior party members in Stalin's theater of judicial terrorism.

Reasonable enough, perhaps; the trouble is that Russia's titanic struggle against Nazi Germany is an essential part of its national identity, and it is this that makes the Vlasov theme arguably the most painful memory of the war. In the mid-1990s, at a time when too many Russians were looking back with nostalgia to communist times, when the sense of Russian nationhood seemed so fragile, *The General and His Army* touched a very raw nerve indeed.[115]

Heads—Tails: Leadership and Conscience

Of the many memories of the Great Patriotic War that assailed Russian national pride during the Gorbachev years, Soviet military competence has proved to be one that intractably refuses to transform itself into any kind of consensus among historians and writers. The failure of the Red Army to stem the German invasion for nearly eighteen months; the huge losses in land, matériel, and prisoners; and the catastrophic failure to act on intelligence are some of the issues that still exercise the minds of writers and survivors.

Ultimately such memories and the questions they raise—perhaps all questions that belong to this period—must return to Stalin, the central figure on the Soviet side. As is often the case in Soviet Russian war literature, and the literature that followed in the 1990s, what appears to be an argument in the narrow field of personal recollections of war is essentially about something much bigger and more fundamental. Certainly this is the case with Vladimir But's *Heads—Tails*,[116] an exceptionally powerful and well-crafted war story with two primary themes—the responsibility of command and conscience and the nature of trust—that both lead directly back to Stalin and his state apparatus designed to monitor individual and collective behavior.

Set in the late autumn of 1943, *Heads—Tails* chronicles the disastrous Soviet attempt to secure and hold a bridgehead on the Crimean coast. The focus on the small bridgehead and small group, desperately hanging on against a powerful and determined enemy, cut off from the supporting Soviet armies and compelled to rely on its own resources, harks back to the narrative device favored by Grigorii Baklanov, IUrii Bondarev, Vasil' Bykov, Emmanuil Kazakevich, and Viktor Nekrasov. But, like Remarque, is one of very few Russian writers who has forced his readers to confront the casualty evacuation station on the battlefield, which he does in chapter 9, through the eyes of a junior nurse:

> Tucked away in a corner, behind a groundsheet, the hellish kitchen in which human bodies were carved up did its work. Living flesh was cut, there was not a drop of chloroform, the screams of those being tortured bit into one's nerves. As they regained consciousness, the badly wounded would start to groan. Those who had the strength to move would sit up, resting on their arms. . . . From the cellar came a constant, deafening howl. Tos'ka had never had the strength to take a look behind the groundsheet. Forcing herself, she was merely able to stand and wait for the bed curtain to be turned up and take the zinc buckets from the hands of the operating sister. Trying not to look at what was in the buckets, she carried them out of the cellar and emptied the contents into a pit that had been dug nearby and was full of bloody stumps.[117]

But also shares Remarque's fascination with fate—the flip of a coin, as the title suggests. Many of the various strands of the fate theme in But's work seem to lead back to, or emanate from, Taman. At times this port town seems to take on the role of a protagonist, somehow influencing the outcome of the battle on the beachhead. Frequently the associations appear negative, even sinister. But's description of the loading of men and matériel portends doom, and the manner in which army headquarters at Taman responds as the situation becomes desperate is capricious, almost indifferent.

Taman is the place where Selivanov, the officer in charge of the raid, appears to succumb to temptation. And the description of the small fishing harbor, where the survivors hope to get evacuated to safety, recalls Pechorin's better-known description of Taman in Mikhail Yuryevich Lermontov's *Hero of Our Time* (1839–1840) and that author's fascination with fate, specifically in the simile of the spider's web. The final throw of the dice with which the story ends sees a small group of survivors setting off for Taman on a hastily improvised raft as the Germans close in (perhaps another allusion to Lermontov's novel as the smugglers escape under cover of darkness).

Graphic detail from battlefield hospitals, the emphasis on fate, and his remorseless criticism of Soviet military competence would appear to justify classifying But as a neo-Remarquist. What sets But and earlier Soviet Russian writers apart from Remarque, however, is that, bloody though the war is, they believe in the justice of their cause. The Soviet Union has been invaded, and the country must be defended, even if that means defending Stalin. Remarque's novel owes much to a sense of guilt and aimlessness, which, post-1918, arises from his reevaluation and rejection of Wilhelmine Germany. In addition, his war was fought in France, not in his native Germany. The title and the whole ethos of Remarque's novel would likely have been quite different had the war been waged on German soil and had Germany been subjected to the ravages of total war.

The bridgehead setting in *Heads—Tails* lends itself particularly well to an exploration of the work's supporting themes and digressions: the ubiquitous SMERSH and the NKVD; the blocking detachments; the role of the *shtrafniki*, or penal troops; the theme of fate; and even ideological and moral temptation.

But, in common with Astaf'ev, Bykov, and Vladimov, has much to say about the role of the NKVD and SMERSH detachments.[118] In the aftermath of the first landing attempt, it emerges that many of the survivors are *shtrafniki*. In the confusion of the landing, ordinary soldiers are mixed with them, which suggests that in one sense they are all penal troops. Death does not discriminate between the two categories, so the distinction and the stigma break down. There are no consistent reasons why some soldiers end up in penal units and others do not: one, the platoon commander, a former colonel, because he shot a sergeant who raped a female signaler; another, a party official who waved away flies at a party meeting. It is all too often a question of chance. One camp inmate who volunteers for the front is chosen by the simple expedient of tossing a coin.

One of But's characters, Len'ka, finds himself separated from his fellow defenders on the beachhead and wanders into an NKVD blocking detachment. At this first encounter between a frontline soldier and the organs, the privileged status of the NKVD is evident:

> Len'ka stood up. Some five meters immediately in front of him, peering out from behind the shield of a Maxim machine gun, was a stranger wearing a forage cap with a crimson cap-band. To the left and right soldiers stared at him from out of hastily dug trenches. Soldiers such as these Len'ka had not seen before: rosy-cheeked, well fed, looking as if they had been fed on good food, well kitted out in new helmets, and, which particularly set them apart from ordinary frontline soldiers, wearing wide waterproof groundsheets—a luxury not available to most officers.[119]

This encounter is the prelude to the familiar and nightmarish ordeal of identification and interrogation.[120] But's main SMERSH character is Vorozhetskii, who is unimpressed by the ideas of a "presumption of innocence or the insufficiency of relying on a defendant's confession to secure a guilty verdict."[121] On the contrary, he considers "every individual guilty, if he is unable to prove his innocence."[122] Another soldier, a *shtrafnik*, summoned to support Len'ka's story, denies ever having seen him before. But hints strongly that some kind of deal has been struck between Vorozhetskii and this less than convincing witness—the promise of a transfer from the penal battalion, perhaps—to persuade the latter to deny any knowledge of Len'ka. At this moment, Len'ka is rescued by the timely appearance of Selivanov, the senior army officer and the focal point of the command and conscience theme, who accepts his account of what has happened. A further rejection of SMERSH and NKVD prerogatives occurs when Len'ka is ordered by Selivanov to return to conduct a reconnaissance of that part of the beachhead overrun by the Germans. They return with the body of Kondrat'ev, the demoted colonel, who, on Selivanov's orders, is given a proper military funeral with recognition of his former rank and achievements. Selivanov's decision involved considerable personal risk because he publicly honors an officer deemed to be an "enemy of the people" by the secret police.[123]

Soviet audiences had to wait until the late Gorbachev years before anything like an open discussion of the role of penal troops was possible. The icebreaker was Lev Danilov's documentary *Shtrafniki*, shown in 1990.[124] In a subsequent article on the film and the wider question concerning the use of penal troops, Viacheslav Kondrat'ev conceded that harsh disciplinary measures were probably necessary in the summer of 1942 (a reference to Stalin's Order № 227) but that this exacerbated the war's inherent brutality, creating plenty of leeway for the professional sadists to exploit a dire military situation. For example, Kondrat'ev recalls one incident when a soldier in his platoon lost his way, which, in the hysteria induced by Stalin's decree, was taken to be an attempt to desert to the Germans. The soldier was executed.[125] Kondrat'ev's article drew a furious response from a number of senior officers. Danilov's film, they insisted, was of the same order of lying and propaganda that characterized a Goebbels production. The generals were particularly sensitive to the ratio of Soviet to German dead cited by Kondrat'ev because the discrepancy suggested further incompetence on the part of the Soviet high command.[126]

While on the subject of penal troops, some mention must be made of Kondrat'ev's *Iskupit' krov'iu* (To Pay in Blood, 1991).[127] The story exposes the cruel interference of the Special Section and examines the behavior of soldiers who find themselves caught between orders (however senseless) and a sense of duty to one another. *To Pay in Blood* is a study of Soviet military discipline that regards ruthlessness as its supreme virtue, regardless of tactical circumstances. The title alludes to the expression used by Stalin in Order № 227, that those in penal units "expiate their crimes before the motherland in blood." Kondrat'ev's contention is that the main crime is the fanatical insistence on obeying orders, not individual acts of cowardice. Discipline is a military virtue, but when all other factors are ignored, it can itself become a crime and make the commander a criminal. It is, however, not the commanders who pay in blood but the rank and file.

Two controversial characters in *To Pay in Blood* are an *osobist* and Seryi, a professional criminal, who uses the army to evade capture by the civil authorities (his name, appropriately, suggests the gray man). Alarmed that the Germans have dropped leaflets calling on Soviet soldiers to desert, the *osobist* insists that all remaining leaflets in an area under fire from the Germans be recovered. The order is disobeyed, but a soldier who retains a leaflet for cigarette paper is arrested, thus beginning a chain of events that leads to the *osobist* being shot by his own side in revenge for the soldier's arrest. Seryi is also interested in the *osobist*, or rather his uniform and documents, because he too plans to kill him, assume his identity, and desert. Kondrat'ev suggests that not much separates the *osobist*, a trusted member of the Soviet military's inner circle, and Seryi, the total outcast. Both live by a code that is largely indifferent to the virtues of the surrounded Soviet soldiers. The *osobist* and Seryi fight for their own self-interest.

Yet there is no real explanation of why the soldiers tolerate being treated as if they were cattle for the slaughter, why the remnants, having been surrounded and nearly overwhelmed by the Germans, make it back to their own lines only to be condemned as traitors and ordered under pain of execution to "pay in blood," that is, to make yet another attempt to oust the Germans. The company commander tells a soldier that the power of the organs is "a sort of infernal irrationality,"[128] even worse than the Germans and the fear of death. In that case, is Seryi—the brutally honest, self-interested killer—the hero, or are the real heroes the Soviet infantry with their limitless capacity for suffering? And if so, is the secret of this resilience to be found in the simple statement of a soldier: "I'm fighting for Mother-Russia. Understood?"[129] Will, to coin a phrase, the divine irrationality of Russian patriotism save Russia from its enemies?

Clausewitz's statement that "everything in war is very simple, but the simplest thing is difficult"[130] is a suitable starting point from which to approach the command problem highlighted by But in *Heads—Tails.* The Soviet plan is straightforward: to attack across the widest part of the straits under cover of darkness. Yet the inevitable "friction in war,"[131] to quote Clausewitz again, disrupts the plan of operations. Severe gales delay the loading and departure schedule, and Selivanov, the divisional commander, concludes that the operation should be delayed:

> Selivanov contacted army headquarters and outlined the situation. After a long pause he heard: "Your considerations will be reported to the commander. . . ." Straightaway in this initial reaction, he understood one thing: He'd get no support here. He could just imagine how his suggestion would rush to the higher levels of command, causing nothing more than dissatisfaction and irritation. No references to "unfavorable weather conditions" or to "stormy seas" would work. Things would turn against him, against anyone who after him would start reporting through the chain of command: against the army commander—at front headquarters—against the front commander—in the general staff, against the general staff officers. An assault landing on such a scale cannot but be coordinated with the Stavka, and that means with HIM. And HE will not tolerate the slightest deviations from any agreed plan of any military action whatsoever,

even more so when it comes to postponing the schedule. He knows that in the event of a failure, that could serve as a pretext, as a rule, for the most unexpected and disastrous changes in one's fate. Fears of this kind have long taken precedence over any considerations of common sense. The matter would get nowhere near the Stavka, thought Selivanov; front headquarters is as far as it will get. Everything will be decided there and quite emphatically: "Get on with it!"[132]

The advantages accruing from a postponement are obvious. The landing would have been concentrated in time and space, and a far more powerful blow would have landed on the German defenders than the disparate and confused landings arising from blind adherence to a schedule rendered ineffective by inclement weather. The landing proceeds, and the not unexpected disaster, hinted at in the mood among the naval infantry, occurs. The boats hit mines; those laden with vital antitank guns are lost. Only a small fraction of the assault troops land, and many are pushed overboard by sailors desperate to make the return trip to safety as quickly as possible. In one of the many brutal examples of peripeteia that characterize this work, the order is received that the landing is to be aborted and the ships are to return to Taman. The handful of troops who land are nearly overwhelmed by the Germans. A second landing attempt is made and succeeds, only to be denied the necessary support; those troops are abandoned to their fate.[133]

All the signs show that Selivanov has discharged his duty in both spirit and substance. He reported his concerns to his superiors, only to be told to proceed regardless, and he can draw some cold comfort from the fact that the first landing was aborted, thus vindicating his professional judgment. Gradually, however, as the fate of the bridgehead becomes clear, But seems to suggest—the dreadful moral and psychological pressures applied by the party apparatus notwithstanding—that commanders cannot entirely evade responsibility for what has happened, even in the conditions that obtained in the Red Army. As the commander demands that sacrifice of blood and life from his men in carrying out their mission, so the willingness of the men to lay down their lives imposes a reciprocal burden on the commander to sacrifice himself as well. In essence, this means the commander's must be willing to refuse to carry out orders that he, as a senior and experienced officer, knows and judges to be criminally negligent and irresponsible, and to accept the consequences. The chain of command that stretches from Selivanov to Stalin is not based on professional, military considerations. Its links are forged through fear and the destruction of military judgment. The links are strong only as long as the fear that they inspire is able to over-power the professional judgment of the officers (is this the "infernal irra-tionality" noted by Kondrat'ev?). The commander who refuses to be intimi-dated and breaks ranks weakens the authority of the party apparatus, the spell of HIM (Stalin, in uppercase, as used by But).

Although the clash between political and military considerations as-sumes a grotesque form in the Stalin state, it was by no means confined to the Soviet political and military establishments. Hitler frequently interfered in military decision-making, often with disastrous consequences. Yet by comparison with their Soviet counterparts, German generals and com-manders exercised a degree of professional freedom that was unheard of in the Red Army, even after the Red Army had wrested the strategic initiative from the Wehrmacht in 1943. Again, in a way that would have been incon-ceivable in the Red Army, German officers did disobey Hitler's orders. For example, Generals Hans Speidel and Dietrich von Choltitz both refused to carry out Hitler's orders to destroy bridges and other installations in Paris in August 1944 as the Anglo-American armies were about to liberate the city. Nor was the problem confined to the two totalitarian states of World War II. Thousands of British soldiers were sacrificed by incompetent gen-erals in the battles of World War I.[134] In both world wars, Churchill loved nothing better than to cajole and lecture his senior officers on what they should do. Field Marshal Montgomery's biographer, Nigel Hamilton, men-tions a clash of wills between Montgomery and Churchill that took place some three months before D-Day. Montgomery refused to allow the prime minister to interfere with the preparations, insisting that it would under-mine the men's confidence in him, the commander in chief, at such a late stage.[135] More recently Neil Sheehan's study of the Vietnam War highlights the curious and often deadly blindness that often afflicts very senior officers and other policy-makers.[136] The determination to win a war brings with it the risk of being insensible of, or indifferent to, information that threatens the war-winning plan. It is always much easier to shoot the messenger or to reject him as being mentally unstable.[137] These non-Soviet examples—many more could be cited—suggest that what But portrays in Heads—Tails can be seen as an exaggerated form of a universal problem: The very nature of military organizations and their hierarchical structure, though a neces-sary ingredient of military success, nevertheless paradoxically predisposes them toward military incompetence. Or rather, that to which we refer as incompetence reflects the brutal and unavoidable realities of war.[138] The memorable sentence with which Lawrence begins his account of the Arab rebellion, *Seven Pillars of Wisdom: A Triumph* (1935), comes to mind: "Some of the evil of my tale may have been inherent in our circumstances."[139]

Selivanov's own thoughts on the nature of command and the course of the war show that he fully understands the predicament of command in the Red Army. Frequent flashbacks to an earlier, disastrous series of attacks on the village of Grebennikov are also illuminating. The village has no tactical or strategic significance, yet poorly equipped Soviet troops are sacrificed in pointless attacks—pointless, that is, from any tactical or strategic perspective. The standard fallback position, again by no means confined to the Red Army, is that orders are orders; that, as Selivanov's chief of staff tells him, "The higher-ups see things better."[140] These words are interpreted by Selivanov as a form of ritual evasion: "They liberated one from the burden of thought, from responsibility, from any guilt toward those who died in vain."[141] In fact, it is to nonmilitary considerations that one must turn in order to understand the rationale for these attacks. The key factors are trust and the ideological suspicions of the party. The units launched against Grebennikov comprised personnel who until recently had lived under German occupation. In the Soviet universe, this raises the suspicion that they have collaborated with the German occupiers and thus merit special treatment:

> There exists, as Selivanov soon understood—and this explained a
> great deal to him—the pejorative word "occupied," which came into
> use in the course of the terrible events of 1941 and 1942. Somehow
> this word deleted a person from the ranks of the living. The terrible
> thing here was not the tragic essence of what had happened but
> above all the mark of Cain, hanging over people who had been in the
> occupied territories.[142]

Senseless attacks of the kind ordered at Grebennikov are a test of loyalty, a redemptive blood sacrifice, that has to be paid by those bearing the taint of occupation in order to earn trust. The question that is so baffling to non-Russians, and possibly to Russians as well, is how to account for this apparent collapse in rational norms. The origins of this mentality, argues Selivanov, go back much further than the disasters of 1941 and 1942. It is a manifestation of the new class morality that extolled absolute pitilessness and that so stupefies the rational faculty that military disasters are not only likely but inevitable. One confused political officer, admitting that he did not know how to reply to questions from his men about the number of prisoners seized by the Germans, is told by Lev Mekhlis that even asking such a question warrants the firing squad. "There are," Mekhlis tells him, "no Soviet prisoners of war; there are just traitors."[143]

As the situation on the beachhead deteriorates, Selivanov speculates that they have been sacrificed to some higher strategic end. Despite the withdrawal of artillery support and the inadequate supply system, they will still be expected to fight in the knowledge that it is futile. Is, he ponders, their fate "an absurd play of chance? Or have we simply lost our grip and allowed things to develop as they have? Have we fallen into a whirlpool of universal mistrust?"[144] Trust or the lack thereof is perhaps the key issue, and it begins and ends with Stalin:

> Trust moves merely upward, from below upward, not the other way. . . . And there, at the very top, what is there? The highest judge? The holy preacher? The divine? . . . Selivanov had never seen HIM in the flesh, just portraits, in photos and cinema images. . . . No, a man like any other. And with some surprise he discovered that he did not experience toward HIM anything resembling that which others felt, or gave the impression that they did. This bowing and scraping always struck him as unreal and forced. Something akin to shame stirred in his soul when he saw people, supposedly normal people, bowing down to such a thing.[145]

Below Stalin is a cowardly and ruthless theocracy, administered and represented by the likes of Lev Mekhlis. Mekhlis occupies a special place in the annals of Red Army catastrophe, especially in the Crimea in the spring of 1942, and despite his portrayal of Stalin, one suspects that Mekhlis is But's real bête noire:

> In him GOD's manic suspicion, his distrust of people found its zealous apostle. Imagining himself to be a seer, blessed with supersight in the uncovering of enemies, this patriarch of GREAT FEAR made it his life's task not to trust anyone. He began his role as the Stavka's representative by the completely unnecessary and unjustified purging of the military cadres. He removed General Tolbukhin from his post as chief of staff, replacing him with a complete nonentity, but one who was "trusted." He trampled Kozlov, the front commander, underfoot. An absolute ignoramus in military matters,

he "amended" and countermanded orders, accusing commanders of having a defensive mentality and of cowardice: "All we have here are moles who just want to bury themselves in the ground!"—he roared at staff conferences.—"There is no point in weakening the forward echelons by withdrawing the combat units into the reserve! Forward! Only forward! The Germans do not know how to advance; they are twice as weak as us! . . ." And when in May the catastrophe occurred, he was the first to report to his master that he and only he had considered the question of defense. It is to him, to Mekhlis, that Manstein, the commander of the German 11th Army is in no small measure obliged for the fact that more than 150,000 of our soldiers and their equipment fell into a deadly trap. And what then? This bankrupted, supervigilant custodian was merely removed from his post as deputy people's commissar and briefly reduced in rank. . . . GOD, you see, needed to rely on someone.[146]

The GREAT FEAR is but one element. Independent action must be preceded by independence of mind, and everything in the Soviet state conspires to destroy that facility. Independence of mind, But suggests, is nourished by conscience. To destroy or to weaken a man's conscience is to undermine his moral and intellectual independence. For both the Nazi and the Soviet states, the problem is critical, and Selivanov's reference to *Mein Kampf* explicitly compares the two states:

> You finished the military-political academy; I dare say you were given *Mein Kampf* to browse through. Do you remember: "I'm freeing you from the humiliating illusion known as conscience"? He is not the fool we portray him as. He understood only too well the psychology of the Bavarian brewers, butchers, and tradesmen. This formula was well suited to his character; you know yourself what's being done on our territory. But we're not tradesmen. But does it not seem to you somehow that someone really wants to free us from this "humiliating illusion"?[147]

The conscience theme leads back to 1937, the year in which the Red Army was the target of Stalin's purges. Selivanov and others remained silent when people were falsely accused of spying and denounced as "enemies of the people." This particular point is addressed to the divisional commissar: "I simply believe that if someone is truly a human being, then you cannot take away his conscience. . . . And were you, you son of a bitch, silent when your brothers in arms were branded as enemies and their heads were cut off? . . . And what about 1941 and how we ended up on the Volga, and what about our assault?"[148]

Selivanov's implied assertion that the commissars alone were guilty of silence allocates blame in a way that is not entirely reasonable or equitable. Senior army officers also failed to speak out when their colleagues were accused of bizarre plots, and many went to their deaths in silence (recall the episodes in July 1941). This problem has exercised Solzhenitsyn a great deal. Why did so many soldiers who demonstrated such bravery on the battlefield allow themselves to be bullied and maltreated by the NKVD and SMERSH? Why, in fact, were rebellions not more common?

With the order to break out from the beachhead given, it is Selivanov who must decide the fate of the wounded. His dilemma is the very essence of the loneliness of command:

> According to all the norms of human morality, the sole thing that could save them would be a base act that bordered on dishonor. Nobody wanted to be the first to say this. That had to be done by someone much stronger, by someone who bore the stamp of authority to dispose of others' lives, by someone who had to free them from their sordid deal with the devil, who would take upon himself the shame of having made this decision of "salvation." In silence, they all looked at Selivanov.[149]

We come back to Hitler's remarks cited by Selivanov on conscience, highlighting a very uncomfortable paradox. Military success demands discipline and obedience, yet initiative is required in the light of changing circumstances on the battlefield. Selivanov's junior officers are glad that they will not have to make the decision whether to abandon the wounded or to carry them to safety.

The lengthy, detailed presentation of the conscience theme and Selivanov's specific request to his commissar that in the event of his being killed in the breakout the operation not be portrayed as a triumph hint at some kind of dramatic showdown between Selivanov and his superiors. Selivanov prepares himself for a reckoning:

> He would summon up his courage and on arrival at front headquarters tell them straight: You all know perfectly well that

there can be no question of talking about the fulfilment of the
mission, no talk of the assault's "success." I am no hero; I left nearly
eight hundred badly wounded men to be tortured by the Germans. I
am reviled by hundreds of soldiers abandoned in Burunnyi to the
whims of fate.[150]

Indifferent to the losses of men, the Soviet high command requires that
Selivanov play the hero, not the honest critic of a disaster. Propaganda
comes first. At precisely the moment when Selivanov appears to be contem-
plating suicide, fate in the shape of his adjutant intervenes to inform him
that he has been promoted to general (thoughtfully bringing the general's
shoulder boards with him). This represents the denouement of the novel,
where the temptation of professional advancement clashes with the need to
speak out. By now the stage is set, we have been led to believe, for Selivanov,
the dedicated professional, But's *honnête homme*, who cares for his men and
at some personal risk has checked the power of the SMERSH officers in his
division, to hold forth with a magnificent Solzhenitsyn-like sermon against
the party, a glorious antiparty finale. It does not happen. Selivanov rationalizes that as a general, with his considerable experience, he has the chance
to make a difference in the fighting that lies ahead. If he rejects the promotion, he will be dispatched to a penal unit, to be sacrificed in suicidal and
useless military operations. If he accepts, he can do some good—or so he
reasons. Recent history—the calculated waste of life at Grebennikov and
the latest fiasco across the straits—suggests otherwise.

Selivanov realizes that he is no hero, that the operation was a disaster.
He arouses contempt in those soldiers whom he has abandoned. He must
act the part; he must uphold, to borrow Neil Sheehan's phrase, "a bright
shining lie." In so doing, he destroys something in himself. He buys time,
only because the same machine that finds it expedient in the Soviet scheme
of things to broadcast failure as success and to sacrifice so many soldiers in
incompetently planned operations is of course entirely arbitrary. Tomorrow Selivanov can be crushed if the "hellish mechanism"[151] demands it. His
own fate is governed by the same law of "heads or tails." In a story full of
capricious and malign twists of fate, Selivanov's bowing down in the House
of Rimmon at the very moment when we expect an emphatic demonstration of moral and professional resistance is a painful and depressing,
though perhaps realistic, conclusion.

Conclusion

Had Viktor Astaf'ev, Georgii Vladimov, and Vladimir But written their novels before the advent of glasnost and submitted them to a Soviet journal for publication, the manuscripts would likely have been seized by the KGB, and the authors would have incurred harsh administrative and penal sanctions. Censorship of this kind can protect the regime from immediate harm, but the less obvious damage is longer lasting. One consequence of Soviet censorship, especially with regard to the Great Patriotic War, that has not been fully explored is whether it impeded or even prevented the process of national cultural grieving and revival. To the extent that the classical Russian literary tradition has been founded on a devotion to truth and the great questions, and the fact that the party attempted—not always with success—to impose its own interpretation of the war, censorship undoubtedly distorted the process whereby the nation could face its past. Until Gorbachev's policy of glasnost, this process took place in fits and starts, which may help to explain what many Westerners consider an unhealthy Russian obsession with the war—self-pity or even worse, a deliberately orchestrated cult of death worship. The novels of Astaf'ev, Vladimov, and But are far removed from self-indulgence or even self-loathing. The past still matters: How can such a terrible war not matter? Yet the novels of Astaf'ev, Vladimov, and But published in the 1990s represent that final move to some kind of normality.

But the man who can most truly be accounted brave is he who best knows the meaning of what is sweet in life and of what is terrible, and then goes out undeterred to meet what is to come.
—Thucydides, *History of the Peloponnesian War*

I love the smell of napalm in the morning . . . the smell, you know that gasoline smell. . . . Smells like victory.
—Lieutenant Colonel Kilgore, *Apocalypse Now*

In this final chapter, I return to the question of truth in war literature, examining the claim made by Grigorii Baklanov that the best war novels are opposed to war. I discuss (briefly) some recent Russian films and the responses to them for the light they cast on the ongoing debate in the Russian Federation on the theme of the Great Patriotic War. I also discuss the impact of intellectual relativism on the search for the truth in war literature.

The War Experience: Some Final Observations

In 1995, the fiftieth anniversary of the end of World War II, Grigorii Baklanov wrote a short essay in which he considered some of the fundamental questions about war and war literature. Baklanov's essential point is that the best war books and novels are concerned with the truth and that they are against war: "For all their differences the best books about war have a common hero, the truth, and a common trend, the rejection of war."[1] In order to make his case, Baklanov refers to some of the better-known writers on the subject: Lev Tolstoy (*War and Peace*); Erich Maria Remarque (*All Quiet on the Western Front*); Vasilii Grossman (*The Hell of Treblinka* and *Life and Fate*); Viktor Nekrasov (*In the Trenches of Stalingrad*); and the diaries of Anne Frank and the Leningrad child diarist, Tania Savicheva.

The point about truth, a nod in Tolstoy's direction, is indisputable. In this regard, Baklanov, Astaf'ev, Grossman, and Bykov have all done their duty. However, the second claim is far from being robust. One of the main obstacles to seeing *War and Peace* as an antiwar novel is that it would implicitly condemn the Russian people for having resisted the French-led invasion. Should the Russians have offered no resistance to Napoleon and stood by as their country was plundered and desecrated? As for Grossman, the war against the Germans is something of a holy war, a sacred cause:

Mother Russia must be protected; the Nazi menace must be defeated. This is what drives his fictional heroes: Grekov, Darenskii, Novikov, Berezkin, and Ershov. Both Grossman and Nekrasov understand the costs and suffering of war but also that there are times when home and hearth must be left because duty calls. Nor does it seem to me that the works of Bykov or Astaf'ev could be described as being antiwar. Disturbing and distressing they certainly are: Bykov is obsessed with the unpredictable ways men and women behave in war—with, among other things, the contrasts between duty and desertion, treachery and loyalty—whereas Astaf'ev's heroes are convincingly imbued with a sense of duty whose origins are to be found in Russia's past and spiritual traditions. In one sense, war may even serve divine purposes in *The Damned and the Dead* because the Germans appear as agents of retribution for Russia's descent into atheism.

The apparently compelling evidence against war in *War and Peace* and *All Quiet on the Western Front* is always the wounded and the dead. They are to be taken as the irrefutable evidence in the prosecution's case against war. Such, however, has been the longevity of war, its prevalence and ubiquity, that the only conclusion must be that war for all its undoubted horrors and suffering is part and parcel of the wide spectrum of human behavior in all its forms: the good, the bad, and the ugly. War is not some beast that emerges adventitiously from nowhere to wreak havoc and mayhem. War arises from the behavior of human beings; its bestiality is human. Long before Tolstoy initiated his vendetta against Napoleon in *War and Peace*, Thucydides identified the three reasons that determine why men wage war: fear, honor, and interest.[2] The Thucydidean analysis explains why wars are unlikely to disappear from the range of options open to states and to nonstate prosecutors of war.

The real target of antiwar novels, especially *All Quiet on the Western Front*, is not war per se but human nature and the ease with which all apparently rational objections to waging war and all appeals to refrain from killing are brushed aside. All over Europe in 1914, declarations of war were accompanied by popular approval, as if entering a war were the start of a great adventure. Ernst Jünger's own account of reactions to the start of the war confirms the sense of excitement and expectation: "Brought up in an age of security, we all felt the longing for something out of the ordinary, the longing for great danger."[3] In *August 1914*, Solzhenitsyn recounts that Russia, soon to suffer the disaster at Tannenberg, reacted in much the same way. Workers of the world did not behave in accordance with the script written by Marxists. In this regard, Lenin completely fails to grasp the power of national allegiance, dismissing it as a device to enslave the masses.[4] In 1914, workers hastened not to cast off any illusory chains but to take up rifles so that they could kill their fellow proletarians. That the killing impulse trumps any class solidarity is also the conclusion drawn by Reinhard Goering in *Seeschlacht* (Sea Battle, 1917). At a critical moment in the play, one of the sailors instructs his comrades, "I know that what we are doing is madness and a crime, and for this reason alone because there are things between man and man which are a far holier duty to accomplish toward man than any battle."[5] The play ends with the same sailor acknowledging the failure of his earlier position and explaining why he and the others have not mutinied, despite the fear, the stress, and the appalling conditions: "I would have mutinied very well! And? But shooting was much closer to us? And? It must indeed have been much closer to us?"[6]

In the case of writers who have actually served in wars, there may well be a strong sense of self-disgust, even shame. Consider what Astaf'ev has to say in a passage added to a post-1994 version of *The Damned and the Dead*: "The main and pernicious effect of war consists in the fact that mass death, which one encounters head on and sees with one's own eyes, becomes an everyday occurrence and gives rise to a submissive acceptance of it."[7] It seems to me that these trends are particularly strong in Remarque's novel. Both Remarque and Baklanov provide some confirmation of this position. I have already noted the contradictory behavior of Remarque's hero toward the French soldier whom he stabs and then tries to save—there is a similar scene in *Life and Fate* (part 2, chapter 23)—yet there is another compelling incident in the novel. While guarding Russian prisoners of war, the central character, Paul, is deeply moved by the wretched state of these prisoners. He recognizes that he has much in common with them: "Every NCO is for the recruit and every senior teacher is for a pupil a worse enemy than they are to us. And nevertheless, were they free they would shoot at us and we would shoot at them."[8] Paul's response to this reality of war is itself revealing: "I am shocked: At this point I ought not to consider this matter further."[9] The rational response to a paradox of war is suppressed or rather overwhelmed by something instinctive, even primordial. The modern term to describe this soldier's state of mind might be "cognitive dissonance" or the Orwellian neologism "crimestop."

For his part, Baklanov recalls the lines from a German soldier's letter written in Stalingrad. Baklanov ponders the writer's fate: "Perhaps he was not killed on the Volga but ended up as a prisoner and survived. I wish him this in spite of everything that he in his blindness has done. But back in the war, when I was a soldier myself, I would not have wished him that."[10] Baklanov's point that he would have behaved differently as a soldier is explicit recognition that war imposes its own order, laws, and regime and that Baklanov, like Tolstoy and Remarque, submitted to them, obeying not just the formal orders of superiors but the ancient summons of war. Baklanov could, of course, properly defend his position by arguing that Mother Russia had to be defended from the German invaders, but this argument concedes that there are times when it is right to wage war. Whether waged out of defensive or offensive considerations, war remains war. Baklanov clearly recognizes this position: "Of the things undertaken by man, war belongs to the most inhuman. This Great Patriotic War was forced upon us. We beat off the enemy's attack and rescued our people from collapse and from systematic extermination."[11] Baklanov's use of "inhuman" to describe war as something extraneous, something extrinsic to human behavior, should not be permitted to mislead us. The horrors of war are horrible, apart from anything else, because of their uniquely *human* provenance. Human beings wage the organized violence known as war. To be against war must therefore commit any person holding such views to be against the people who wage war and the institutions they create so that they can prosecute war. In other words, the men who create and train armies, who formulate and study doctrine; the men who fully accept the implications of the maxim enunciated by Flavius Vegetius Renatus—*Igitur qui desiderat pacem, praeparet bellum*—are somehow suspect, not to be trusted. Where does this leave the men, including Baklanov and his generation, who in every age and time have volunteered to take up arms? Are they to be regarded with suspicion as well?

The sternest challenge to Baklanov's view about war novels and accounts of war—and I believe that it is an insurmountable challenge—is the experience and writing of Ernst Jünger. Jünger's personal experience and his willingness to seek out danger clearly repudiate Baklanov's assertion that "those who maintain that war is inherent in man's nature do not fight themselves but send others to fight, mainly young, immature men who are so easy to kill."[12] Jünger served all through World War I, leading from the front. Even if one grants that Jünger is something of an anomaly and that his reactions to war are not representative of the way the majority of former soldiers have reacted to war, it does not follow that those who claim that war is inherent in human nature are making a false claim or disseminating a lie merely because they send others to war. The nature of organized violence—war—mandates hierarchy, organization, discipline, obedience, order, duty, and symbols; all the things that the antiwarriors and much of our contemporary world find so disturbing. War also requires sacrifice, and that burden typically falls most heavily on young men. Recall that in *The Dead Feel No Shame* (see chapter 2) Baklanov instructs us that "others pay in blood for those who spare themselves in battle. That is the law of war." Baklanov recognizes that sacrifice is inevitable and necessary. That final sentence, written in the 1960s, comes back to haunt Baklanov in 1995 because the very notion of being a "law of war" requires the recognition that although war may involve killing and destruction, it is indeed inherent in, and subject to, humankind's biological and cultural constitution: There is a time to kill and to be killed.

Baklanov seems aware of this predisposition but cannot bring himself to accept that some former soldiers could have enjoyed the experience of war, that to some the smell of napalm in the morning is indeed intoxicating. On a trip to the United States in the 1980s, at the start of the glasnost campaign, Baklanov came across an article published in *Esquire* that was written by William Broyles Jr., a former U.S. Marines officer who recalled his time in Vietnam.[13] The Broyles view of war has much in common with what we find in Jünger. Broyles acknowledges that "war is ugly, horrible, evil, and it is reasonable for men to hate all that."[14] Yet he recognizes that "part of the love of war stems from its being an experience of great intensity. . . . War stops time, intensifies experience to the point of a terrible ecstasy."[15] Baklanov was drawn and repelled in equal measure by Broyles's reminiscences and his admission that he missed the war and even found some beauty in it. If the Broyles view of war is not an aberration but represents part of the war experience that is only very rarely confronted, does this imply that Baklanov is unable to confront his own demons; that perhaps there exists a deeper truth about war that he prefers to ignore? Von Moltke is famous for declaring that eternal peace was a dream and that without the pressures of war, the world would descend into materialism. Von Moltke may be right about eternal peace, but comfortable and prosperous societies can drive men to seek out danger rather than submit to the eternal, material pleasures of life in Arcadia.

I suggest that what detaches Baklanov's claim about the best war novels from, say, Grossman is that in pursuing the particular truth about the Great Patriotic War, Grossman, in *Life and Fate*, also asserts some fundamental, general truths about the nature and the permanence of war that Baklanov wants to disavow. One of those truths, love of country, is evoked in Viktorov's

long training flights over Russia's remote forests as he prepares to take part
in the Soviet counteroffensive at Stalingrad: "This forest, these lakes breathed
the life of ancient Russia";[16] we see another in Grekov's reasons for fighting:
"I want freedom. That's what I'm fighting for."[17] Simonov's writing, most famously in the case of the poem "Zhdi menia" (Wait for Me, 1941), is rich in
themes of love of Rodina inspired by the great danger facing Russia.

The Ongoing Struggle in Russia to Own the Truth

The truth about the Great Patriotic War, and especially the manner in
which the war has been portrayed in Russian documentaries and television
serials since the mid-1990s, provides evidence of a bitter cultural divide.
One article, which may be regarded as symptomatic, illustrates this trend
particularly well. In the preamble to an essay written by General Makhmut
Akhmetovich Gareev, which was first published in *Voenno-istoricheskii zhurnal* (Military-Historical Journal) at the end of 2005 and republished on the
web site of the Ministry of Defense of the Russian Federation, the editors
point out that positions regarding a whole range of questions on the war
are now more polarized and entrenched than ever before. For Gareev, the
fault lies with a new generation of revisionists: "As far as our own homegrown 'new interpreters' of the Great Patriotic War are concerned, whose
numbers have multiplied over recent years (so a form of political competi-
tion has taken shape), then, for many of these people our Victory sticks in
their throat."[18] Gareev's remarks contain an unmistakable echo of Stadniuk's jibes at 1970s-style revisionists, which I discussed in chapter 4.

Attacks on the achievements of the Red Army and the status of the Great
Patriotic War are prompted, according to Gareev, by a desire to eradicate
what is perceived to be the last bastion of conservative forces, the remnants
of the old Soviet Union. To this end, Gareev cites an unnamed commenta-
tor: "Without the debunking of this victory, we will not be able to justify
everything that has occurred since 1991 and the ensuing years."[19] This, according to Gareev, explains "the widespread campaign of lies and falsification of the Great Patriotic War."[20]

Over the past fifteen years, insists Gareev, hardly any films, apart from
older ones produced and shown during the Soviet period, have portrayed
participants in the war with any truth or warmth. Gareev is especially hostile to *Poslednii mif* (The Last Myth, 1999), *Enemy at the Gates* (2001), and
Shtrafbat (The Penal Battalion, 2004). These films, he asserts, manifest
nothing but hatred toward the country's past. Given that *The Last Myth* owes

much to the thesis of former GRU officer, defector, and author Viktor Suvorov, that Stalin was planning to attack Germany, and that Hitler's invasion was a preemptive strike, it is unlikely ever to receive a fair hearing from senior army officers. The film, officially at any rate, will always be regarded as having been sponsored by those hostile to Russia. *Enemy at the Gates* also attracts heavy fire from Gareev: "And in the film *Enemy at the Gates*, this battle [Stalingrad] is presented in an exceptionally distorted and repulsive form when untrained reserves, newly arrived at the front, are sent into battle without any weapons. In the film one sees no army commanders; only the 'cruel' commissars are in charge."[21] The fact of the matter is that the commissars (until the institution was abolished in October 1942) did wield power and influence beyond, in most cases, their abilities. They were regarded by the troops as ideological attack dogs and a hindrance to effective command. The declassified material examined in chapter 6 puts this matter beyond doubt.

The Penal Battalion raises themes that go far beyond the purely military-historical aspects of the Great Patriotic War. First shown on Russian television in 2004, the eleven-part series highlights the dreadful plight of Soviet soldiers who, like the *kombat* (battalion commander), Captain Tverdokhlebov, the main character, are captured by the Germans in 1941 and manage to escape. On returning to Soviet lines, they are regarded as having committed some unspeakable crime or suspected of having been recruited as German agents. One punishment is the penal battalion. Whenever this happens, we hear the wording used in Stalin's Order № 227: Soldiers must "expiate their crimes before the motherland in blood." In one scene, we see NKVD blocking detachments gunning down Soviet soldiers who have retreated. Throughout much of his ordeal, the *kombat* remains psychologically as well as militarily loyal to the Soviet state despite the way he is treated (a distinctive theme in its own right). He demonstrates exemplary leadership, and the *shtrafniki*, many of them hardened criminals and deeply cynical, are won over by his example, undoubted personal courage, and competence. The other target in the Soviet hierarchy—and this cannot have endeared the film to Gareev—are senior Red Army officers who fail to stand up to the *osobisty*. Nor do the filmmakers pull their punches with regard to the horrors of collectivization and the party's war against the peasants.

The film was criticized for its lack of attention to military and historical detail. However, its portrayal of the way the Special Sections behaved, the role of blocking detachments, the impact of Order № 227, the filtration (interrogation) of Red Army soldiers who escaped from German captivity, and the role of penal units is certainly consistent with much of what we encounter in the works of Grossman, But, Vladimov, Bykov, and Astaf'ev. Historically these specific features of the Soviet military regime are beyond dispute. Viewed as a purely historical documentary, The Penal Battalion is flawed, but not irrevocably so. The film's great strength is the religious theme that emerges in the final episodes. A Russian Orthodox priest attaches himself to the battalion. During a German tank attack, we see him carrying ammunition for the antitank guns. In the last episode, the battalion is ordered to force a river and occupy a bridgehead. Moving among the damned and abandoned, the priest brings solace and comfort to those who are about to be slaughtered. Before the operation begins, he blesses the soldiers, including Tverdokhlebov, accompanying them on their final journey. Amid the carnage of the war, the themes of repentance, forgiveness, and a sense of the spiritual begin to emerge. Mother Russia—eternal Russia—asserts herself and, critically, is being rediscovered by those deemed to be outcasts. In this part of the film, the influence of The Damned and the Dead is unmistakable; the intensity of the spiritual message—men kill one another but God loves them all—is overpowering.

In contrast to Gareev, I see nothing in this film that could give rise to hatred of Russia's past (though it could cause pain and distress without a doubt). What the film does do—and I suspect that this is what angers Gareev—is highlight the arbitrary behavior of the Soviet state toward its own soldiers. In this regard, The Penal Battalion is certainly bleak and unyielding, which is not the same thing as being anti-Russian or hostile to the motherland or intended to denigrate the achievements of the Soviet victory. Toward the end of the series, the plot rises above ideological and historical disputes, placing the mysteries of life, love, and death at center stage. Another point I take from the film is that rational and empirical tools do not seem to be entirely adequate as a means of understanding the dreadful, ineffable suffering of the Great Patriotic War. One must use one's heart and soul as well as one's mind. This is the great achievement of The Penal Battalion that the film's detractors either ignore or fail to grasp. Astaf'ev, whose novel The Damned and the Dead played, I suspect, a prominent role in inspiring the film, leaves us in no doubt that, as far as he is concerned, men cannot fully apprehend the nature of war: "I repeat: The whole truth about the war and indeed about our lives is known only unto God."[22]

The striking feature about Gareev's article—and many others adopting a similar position—is the remarkable degree of consistency and continuity it shares with the attacks leveled at Remarquist writers, or those deemed to be, in the 1960s. Gareev is concerned that the heroic nature of the Great Patriotic War is being deliberately undermined, along with the significance of the victory and the achievements of the soldiers. He identifies this process as *degeroisatziia*, which might be translated as "the destruction of the heroic ethos," a term that was also used to target Baklanov and Bykov in the early stages of their careers.

One clear consequence of these attacks, at least as identified by Gareev, is a weakening of the Russian Army's morale, and in order to deal with this threat, Gareev concludes his article with a profoundly relevant and acute insight taken from Aleksandr Andreevich Svechin, a leading military thinker of the early twentieth century. I cite Svechin in full:

> Whatever the attitude of the people to the last war [World War I], it must have due regard to the efforts, stubbornness, and self-sacrifice and to the memory of those who, without counting the cost, have scattered their small, modest graves all over our western borders. For any government that shall continue to require armed forces and shall again summon the people to make sacrifices, the setting up of a monument to the fallen in the form of an official history is inevitable. Martial valor needs a cult, and the cult of martial valor is required in order to secure victory.[23]

The cult of martial valor not only sustains the army, steeling soldiers to make the ultimate sacrifice, but also serves to ensure that their sacrifice will not be forgotten (precisely the all-important point made by Nathaniel Fick and cited in chapter 1). Anything that attacks, demeans, or is perceived to demean that sacrifice in whatever genre—film, literature, and documentaries—can only arouse fierce emotions, even hatreds. These arguments will, of course, be nothing new to Western viewers of *The Deer Hunter* (1978), *Apocalypse Now* (1979), *Platoon* (1986), and *Black Hawk Down* (2001).

Gareev's recourse to Svechin's undoubted wisdom and insight suggests an inconsistency in his hostility to the three films mentioned. Any official history of Russia's participation in World War I—what Svechin sees as the monument to the fallen—could not avoid a detailed analysis of the role played by the Bolsheviks and Lenin in undermining the cult of the warrior in the tsarist army. Morale and discipline were subverted, and patriotism was ridiculed. Every defeat and setback inflicted on the tsarist army by the Germans was welcomed as another step toward the seizure of power. If "martial valor needs a cult, and the cult of martial valor is required in order to secure victory," then the record of the party in creating and nurturing this cult in the Red Army is not a good one. Commissars were introduced to spy on former tsarist army officers (in the system of dual command) with disastrous effect, and in 1937 Stalin murdered some of his most talented commanders, who, had they lived, would have made a big difference in the summer of 1941.

Western Influences

Throughout the period 1941–1991, the main threat to Soviet writers and historians seeking to write about the Great Patriotic War was the official Soviet ideology of Marxism-Leninism, which was more or less recognized to be dead by the mid-1980s and formally declared dead by history in 1991. However, while Marxism-Leninism was on the way to extinction, new threats to interpreting literature and history were emerging in the West. Known variously as deconstuctionism, structuralism, and postmodernism, these ideologies' central thrust was the aggressive assertion that truth can never be known; that at any given moment in history truth (often "truth") is the product of the ruling class and serves its needs. Wrongly accusing Astaf'ev of succumbing to a whole host of imported Western ills—postmodernism among them—Zelenkov (see chapter 7) nevertheless identifies the threat posed to a traditional view of Russian literature.

Now, I readily concede that what I have presented in this volume is necessarily circumscribed and properly subject to the age-old philosophical caveats about knowledge, perception, and arguments about truth, but this concession should not in any way be interpreted as indicating acceptance of postmodernism's relativism: that there are no privileged perspectives, that truth is a matter of perspective, or indeed that truth is a social and political construct. Though these ideas are intended primarily to undermine the Judeo-Christian and Greco-Roman foundations on which the West is based, they have unintended consequences: They provide ready weapons and comfort to those who wish to deny or to play down the enormity of Nazi and Soviet crimes, especially the pan-European Jewish catastrophe, the Holocaust, and Stalin's Terror-Famine. If truth is a mere social and political construct, where does this claim leave Grossman's eyewitness accounts of the Holocaust in the German-occupied territories, *Chernaia kniga* (The Black Book, 1980 and 1991), which he compiled with the assistance of Il'ia Erenburg? Are they rendered irrelevant? And what of Solzhenitsyn's accounts of the Soviet forced-labor camps? Are these, together with Grossman's reportage, to be dismissed as mere social and political constructs with little or no relevance for new readers and historians other than to expose the social and political biases of Vasilii Grossman and Alexander Solzhenitsyn? Truth denied or redefined to suit some ideological agenda must necessarily affect what we are to understand by the lie. Given that lying is intellectually hostile to the truth, lying ceases to exist if the truth falls or is deemed to be fugacious. In the absence of any distinction separating the truth and the lie, our epistemological compass is deactivated, and history, to quote Henry Ford, is indeed more or less bunk.

As a further example of what such doctrines can mean for interpreting the war experience and history generally, and where this pyrrhic skepticism can lead, I cite the approach to truth recorded by Milos Stankovic, a former British army officer who served as an interpreter and carried out liaison duties during the Bosnian War in the 1990s:

> I learnt one very valuable lesson in the Balkans. There is no Truth. There is only Perception. This book does not claim to be an accurate portrayal of what was true and what was not true in the Balkans—no book can be, despite the best efforts of the author to convince the reader that he or she is the sole guardian of Truth. *Trusted Mole* is therefore a true story based on my *perceptions*.[24]

If there is "no Truth," then what is there, and what credence can be attributed to what Stankovic has to say? Indeed, a great deal of truth (or Truth) can be established concerning the Bosnian War, the obvious truth being that the war was in Bosnia. Other obvious truths are that Stankovic served there, that General Rose was the officer to whom he reported, that people were killed, and that Stankovic wrote a book about his experiences. If there is only "Perception," is the assertion that there is only "Perception" itself a perception, and if so, what status does it have? Again, if *Trusted Mole* is not an "accurate portrayal," then what is it? Can the author be trusted? To press the point: Are we expected to doubt whether Germany invaded the Soviet Union on Sunday, 22 June 1941?

Somewhere in Stankovic's intellectual confusion there nevertheless lurks a serious point: The extent to which truth depends on perception means, given the nature of human perception, that we have to exercise caution about drawing conclusions. These difficulties notwithstanding, we can still establish some fundamental truths about war. Moreover, the extent to which these truths are recognized by others as a truthful or perhaps an accurate account of the war experience enhances the standing of a particular observation: It becomes statistically and socially significant. For example, a war novel in which the author claimed that soldiers never knew fear would rightly be regarded with some suspicion because it would be inconsistent with the experience of war that has been recognized and recorded since at least the time of Thucydides. Perceptions can therefore be tested against known experience, and gradually it becomes possible to make statements about war that, although not recognized as Absolute Truth, do for all their imperfections bring us closer to the essence of war. Not all perceptions, then, are of equal merit. The very best writers in Soviet and Russian war literature—Vasil' Bykov, Viktor Astaf'ev, Vasilii Grossman, Georgii Vladimov, and Grigorii Baklanov—are not only true to the classical Russian literary tradition but also, and because of that, offer a truer picture of war, and one generally, but not universally, recognized to be so.

Max Hastings, responding to the general criticisms of war correspondents and war reportage made by Philip Knightley in The First Casualty (1975),[25] indicates another problem that has a bearing on assessing truth in war and in war literature: "One is seeking to assemble a jigsaw, from which most of the pieces are missing. The choice for the war correspondent is not between retailing truth and falsehood, but between reporting a fragment of the reality or nothing at all. All journalists must compete with official deceit, in war and peace."[26]

"Official deceit" lies at the very heart of Soviet war literature, creating another layer through which light must be refracted before anything can be seen. Those Soviet writers who had the moral and intellectual strength to see, who refused to be blinded, were feared. When KGB officers seized the manuscript of Grossman's Life and Fate in 1961, they knew what they were dealing with. Likewise, when Solzhenitsyn refused to remain silent, the Soviet Politburo panicked and ordered his expulsion. Suslov and his colleagues recognized the truth and tried to crush it, supporting the belief that the best liars know the truth.

Russian War Literature and Five Ways of the Warrior

Soviet war literature and its Russian successor reflect the entire range of human experience in twentieth-century warfare. There are the universals of war: courage; death; betrayal; fear; moral and physical cowardice; exhaustion; horror; ugliness; incompetence; brutality; human depravity; sublime behavior in the presence of evil; and dreadful, unimaginable suffering. It is the peculiarly Russian aspects—the cluster of Vlasov-related themes—that are so baffling: the behavior of the NKVD and SMERSH; the capacity of Russians for self-sacrifice on behalf of an odious totalitarian regime; the willingness of Soviet commanders to squander the lives of their soldiers; the party's expectation of total loyalty, no matter how soldiers and civilians were treated—and that was one's own side, never mind the *Vernichtungskrieg* prosecuted by the Nazis with utter relentlessness.

In chapter 1, I located war literature and the responses to war in five main categories: (1) pacifism (war is evil and to be avoided in all circumstances, the view of many pacifists in the 1930s even as the Nazi threat was becoming clear); (2) Remarquism (war is futile and senseless, yet the call to arms is still obeyed, exemplified in *All Quiet on the Western Front*); (3) heroic pragmatism (if good men do not take up the cudgels, evil will triumph, summed up by Edmund Burke); (4) the just war (certain wars are inherently just and must be fought, as argued by Sir Winston Churchill); and (5) Jüngerism (war is destiny, ecstasy, the father of all things, to be pursued for its own sake, as derived from the experience and articulated in the diaries and novels of Ernst Jünger). So where does Soviet-Russian war literature and its immediate successor stand in relation to the war literature and experiences of non-Russians?

Isolated Soviet authors come close to espousing pacifist sentiments—for example, Okudzhava's *Take Care, Schoolboy*—but they are rare and do not represent the majority. Certain writers could be said to be very close to Remarque, Genatulin, for example, and there are undoubtedly Remarquist themes in the work of Baklanov, Bondarev, Vorob'ev, and Kurochkin. Maybe Okudzhava is closer to Remarque than to Tolstoy. Jüngerism at the other extreme is totally absent; the only other belligerent nation of World War II that could reveal something similar would be Japan, where a combination of militarism and fanatical Shintoism exalted and advocated Bushido—literally, the way of the warrior—which led to Japan's final and total collapse. The bulk of Soviet and Russian war literature would appear to fall between heroic pragmatism and the just war part of the spectrum. The Soviet Union was attacked, and it was the duty of every citizen to defend the state from the German invaders (see Baklanov, as discussed earlier).

For the Soviet Union, however, there was a whole raft of complicating factors: the Soviet state's lack of legitimacy for very large numbers of people in Ukraine, the Baltic states, Belorussia (in which an insurgency was waged against the Red Army until the early 1950s), and Russia itself; the Non-aggression Pact with Hitler, which provided for the partition of Poland by Nazi Germany and the Soviet Union; the murder of just under 22,000 Poles at Katyn and other sites in 1940 by the NKVD (a direct consequence of the Molotov-Ribbentrop Pact and only officially acknowledged by Gorbachev in 1991); the complicity of a substantial number of Soviet citizens in the Nazi Endlösung der Judenfrage; the legacy of collectivization and the purges (major themes in the work of Grossman, Astaf'ev, Bykov, and Baklanov); Vlasov and the scale of collaboration; Stalin's competence as supreme commander (especially in the period leading up to and after 22 June 1941); and an arbitrary regime of executions and the callous treatment of Soviet prisoners of war by the NKVD and SMERSH (direct consequences of, among others, Orders № 270 and 227).

One requirement to wage the just war rests on there being a properly constituted authority. For a large number of Soviet citizens, the regime was nothing of the sort. Consider that in the early 1930s, Stalin and the Communist Party declared war on the peasants, as a consequence of which millions of peasants were exterminated by starvation, shootings, and cold. Do we remember these victims? Soviet claims to have waged a just war thus expose a cruel dilemma: How is it possible to wage a just war against Hitler *and* on behalf of Stalin and his regime? This is, arguably, the central theme of *Life and Fate*, and to a lesser extent of *The Damned and the Dead* and many of Vasil' Bykov's accounts of partisan warfare. Despite all the bravery and sacrifices of the Red Army, the Soviet Union in 1945, in terms of physical destruction and the profound moral questions arising from its totalitarian behavior before and during the war, had far more in common with the vanquished of World War II than with the victors.

In our technical ability to depict war, we have come a long way from the time when our remote ancestors etched the outcome of a hunt or some battle on rocks and on cave walls. In other ways, nothing has changed. The technological narrative changes, but the essential need of the survivors and chroniclers to make sense of the realm of fear, uncertainty, and chance remains unchanged. War literature is the warrior's confession and a memorial to the fallen. When all else fails, war remains the instrument to which states will resort in order to defend vital interests. Fear, honor, and interest—the Thucydidean triad—still rule. That being the case, Plato's apocryphal remark—only the dead have seen the end of war—has lost none of its force: War literature is a story without end.

APPENDIX A
ORDER OF THE HEADQUARTERS OF THE SUPREME COMMAND OF THE RED ARMY № 270, 16TH AUGUST 1941

To All Members and Candidate Members of the Central Committee of the All-Union Communist Party (Bolsheviks).
To All Secretaries of *oblast* committees, *krai* committees.
To the Central Committees of the Communist Parties of the Union Republics.
To the Chairmen of the *oblast*, *krai* executive committees, to the Council of People's Commissars of the Republics.
To all secretaries of district and town committees, to all chairmen of district and town executive committees.

Not for publication

Order
of the Headquarters of the Supreme Command
of the Red Army
№ 270
16 August 1941

Not only our friends but also our enemies are compelled to acknowledge that in our war of liberation against the German-fascist invaders the vast majority of the units of the Red Army, their commanders and commissars are conducting themselves irreproachably, courageously, and at times, to be frank—heroically. Even those units of our army that find themselves unexpectedly cut off from the army and surrounded are maintaining their courage and steadfast spirit. They are not surrendering themselves into captivity and they endeavor to inflict as much damage on the enemy as possible and to escape encirclement. It is well known that individual units of our army that find themselves encircled by the enemy are exploiting all possible means in order to defeat the enemy and to break out of encirclement.

Deputy commander of the troops of the Western Front General Lieutenant Boldin, finding himself surrounded by German-fascist soldiers in the area of the 10th Army near Belostok, organized detachments from those units of the Red Army that remained in the enemy's rear and in the course of 45 days fought in the enemy's rear and broke through to the main forces of the Western Front. They destroyed the headquarters of 2 German regiments; 26 tanks; 1,049 light, transport, and headquarters vehicles; 147 motorcycles; 5 artillery batteries; 4 mortars; 15 mounted machine guns; 3 submachine guns; 1 plane on an aerodrome; and a dump of aviation bombs. More than 1,000 German soldiers and officers were killed. On 11 August General Lieutenant Boldin attacked the Germans from the rear, broke through the German front line, and having joined up with our troops, extricated 1,654 armed Red Army soldiers and commanders, of whom 103 were wounded, from encirclement.

The commissar of the 8th Mechanized Corps, Brigade Commissar Popel, and the commander of the 406th Rifle Regiment, Colonel Novikov, led 1,778 armed men out of encirclement in a fighting withdrawal. In the fierce battles with the Germans the Novikov-Popel group covered 650 kilometers, inflicting massive losses on the enemy's rear echelons.

The commander of the 3rd Army, General Lieutenant Kuznetsov, and member of the Military Council Army Commissar of the second rank Biriukov fought their way out of encirclement, leading 498 Red Army soldiers and commanders of units from the 3rd Army, and organized the withdrawal from encirclement of the 108th and 64th Rifle Divisions.

All these and other numerous, similar facts bear witness to the steadfastness of our troops, to the high morale of our fighters, commanders, and commissars.

However, we cannot hide the fact that several shameful episodes of surrendering to the enemy have recently taken place. Individual generals have set a bad example for our troops.

The commander of the 28th Army, General Lieutenant Kachalov, finding himself and the headquarters group of his troops encircled, demonstrated cowardice and surrendered to the German-fascists. Kachalov's headquarters group escaped encirclement, and units of Kachalov's group broke out of encirclement. But Kachalov preferred to surrender. He preferred to desert to the enemy.

General Lieutenant Ponedelin, who commanded the 12th Army and was encircled by the enemy, had every opportunity to break through to his own side, as was done by the overwhelming majority of units in his army. However, Ponedelin did not demonstrate the necessary persistence and will to victory, succumbed to panic, behaved in a cowardly fashion, and surrendered to the enemy. He deserted to the enemy, so committing a crime in the eyes of the motherland as someone who broke his military oath.

The commander of the 13th Rifle Corps, General Major Kirillov, instead of fulfilling his duty to the motherland and organizing the units entrusted to him to repulse the enemy and escape encirclement, when finding himself encircled by German-fascist troops, deserted the battlefield and surrendered to the enemy. As a result of this, units of the 13th Rifle Corps were destroyed and several of them surrendered to the enemy without offering serious resistance.

It must be noted that in all the incidents of surrendering to the enemy indicated above members of the armies' military councils—commanders, political instructors, Special

Section officials—who were also surrounded demonstrated impermissible confusion and shameful cowardice and did not even attempt to prevent Kachalov, Ponedelin, Kirillov, and others who had taken fright from surrendering to the enemy.

These shameful episodes of surrendering to our accursed enemy bear witness to the fact that in the ranks of the Red Army, steadfastly and selflessly defending our Soviet motherland from the foul invaders, there are unreliable, fainthearted, cowardly elements. And these cowardly elements are to be found not only among the ordinary ranks of the Red Army but also among the command personnel. As is well known, several commanders and political instructors by their behavior at the front not only do not set an example of courage, steadfastness, and love of the motherland for Red Army soldiers but, on the contrary, hide in their slit trenches; waste time in their offices; do not see or observe the battlefield; and at the first serious difficulties in battle fall before the enemy, remove their badges of rank, and desert the battlefield.

May one tolerate cowards in the ranks of the Red Army who desert to the enemy and surrender or such fainthearted commanders who at the first setback at the front remove their badges of rank and desert to the rear? No! One must not! If we allowed these cowards and deserters to have their way they would corrupt our army and kill off our motherland in the shortest possible time. Cowards and deserters must be destroyed.

Is it possible to consider such commanders to be proper battalion and regimental commanders if they hide in their slit trenches during a battle and do not see the battlefield, if they do not observe the course of the battle on the battlefield and nevertheless imagine themselves to be battalion and regimental commanders? No! It is not! These are not battalion and regimental commanders but impostors. If one allows such impostors to have their way, they would in a very short time turn our army into one giant office. It is necessary to remove these impostors from their posts immediately, remove them from their posts and reduce them to the ranks. Where necessary they must be executed on the spot, and bold and courageous people from the ranks of the junior command staff or from the rank and file must replace them.

I ORDER:

1. Commanders and political instructors who remove their badges of rank during a battle and who desert to the rear or who surrender to the enemy shall be considered malicious deserters whose families shall be subject to arrest as families of those who have broken their military oath and deserted their motherland.

All senior commanders shall be required to execute on the spot similar deserters from the ranks of the command personnel.

2. Units and subunits who have been surrounded by the enemy shall fight selflessly to the very last. They shall look after their equipment as something precious and shall

break through to their own forces through the enemy's rear echelons, inflicting damage on the fascist dogs.

Every soldier shall be required, regardless of his military status, to demand of a superior commander, if his unit is surrounded, to fight to the very last in order to break through to one's own forces. If such a commander or a unit of Red Army soldiers, instead of making an attempt to repulse the enemy, prefers to surrender, they are to be destroyed with all means, both on the ground and from the air, and the families of Red Army soldiers who have surrendered shall be deprived of state benefits and assistance.

3. Divisional commanders and commissars shall be required immediately to remove battalion and regimental commanders from their posts who hide in their slit trenches during battle and who are afraid to manage the course of a battle on the battlefield, to remove them from their posts as impostors and to transfer them to the ranks, and where necessary to execute them on the spot, promoting to their positions bold and courageous people from the junior command personnel or those from the rank and file who have distinguished themselves.

This order shall be read out in all companies, cavalry squadrons, batteries, air squadrons, commands, and headquarters.

HEADQUARTERS OF THE SUPREME COMMAND OF THE RED ARMY:

Chairman of the State Defense Committee	I. Stalin
Deputy Commander of the State Defense Committee	V. Molotov
Marshal of the Soviet Union	S. Budennyi
Marshal of the Soviet Union	K. Voroshilov
Marshal of the Soviet Union	S. Timoshenko
Marshal of the Soviet Union	B. Shaposhnikov
General of the Army	G. Zhukov

Source: "Prikaz Stavki verkhovnogo glavnogo komandovaniia Krasnoi armii, № 270, 16 avgusta 1941 goda'," *Voenno-istoricheskii zhurnal* 9 (1988): 26–28.

APPENDIX B
ORDER OF THE PEOPLE'S COMMISSAR FOR DEFENSE OF
THE USSR, № 227, 28TH JULY 1942

Not for Publication
Order of the People's Commissar for Defense of the USSR
№ 227
28 July 1942
Moscow

The enemy is throwing in ever new forces at the front and regardless of his losses, which are huge, is moving forward, breaking into the depths of the Soviet Union, and seizing new regions, laying waste and ruining our cities and villages. The enemy is raping, plundering, and killing the Soviet population. There are battles in the region of Voronezh, on the Don, in the south at the gates to the northern Caucasus. The German occupiers are forcing their way toward Stalingrad and the Volga. They want to seize the Kuban and the northern Caucasus, with their oil and grain riches, at any price. The enemy has already seized Voroshilovgrad, Starobelsk, Rossosh, Kupiansk, Valuiki, Novocherkassk, Rostov-on-Don, and half of Voronezh. A unit of troops from the Southern front, following panicmongers, abandoned Rostov and Novocherkassk without serious resistance and without orders from Moscow, staining their regimental colors with shame.

The population of our country, which regards the Red Army with love and respect, is beginning to become disillusioned with it and starting to lose faith in the Red Army. Many of them curse the Red Army for the fact that it is abandoning our people to the yoke of the German oppressors while it itself flees to the east.

Some stupid people at the front console themselves with talk about the fact that we can continue to retreat to the east because we have much territory and lots of people, and that we will always have reserves of bread. By this they want to justify their shameful behavior at the front. But such conversations are utterly false and mendacious and are of use only to our enemies.

Every commander, Red Army soldier, and political worker must understand that our resources are not limitless. The territory of the Soviet state—this is not a desert but human beings—workers, peasants, the intelligentsia, our fathers, mothers, wives, brothers, and children. The territory of the USSR that has been seized by the enemy and that he continues to seize—this is the bread and other food produce for the army and rear, the metal and fuel for industry, the factories and plants that supply the army with weapons and ammunition, and the railways. After the loss of Ukraine, Belorussia, the Baltic, Donbass, and other regions, we now have much less territory. Accordingly, we now have fewer people, bread, metal, factories, and plants. We have lost more than 70 million of our population, more than 800 million poods [1 pood = 16 kilograms] of grain a year, and more than 10 million tons of metal a year. Already we no longer enjoy a superiority over the Germans in people or in our reserves of bread. To retreat further is to destroy ourselves and to destroy our motherland as well. Every new piece of territory abandoned by us will strengthen the enemy to the utmost and weaken our defense and our motherland to the utmost.

Therefore, it is necessary to put a stop to conversations along the lines that we can retreat indefinitely, that we have lots of territory, that our country is large and rich with a big population, and that there will always be plenty of bread. Such conversations are mendacious and harmful. They weaken us and strengthen the enemy, because if we do not stop retreating we will be without bread, without fuel, without metal, without raw materials, without factories and plants, and without railways.

From this it follows that the time has come to stop retreating.

Not a step backward! Such, now, must become our main slogan. It is necessary stubbornly, to the last drop of blood, to defend every position, every meter of Soviet territory, to cling to every scrap of Soviet land and defend it to the very last.

Our motherland is living through terrible times. We must stop and then push back and destroy the enemy, no matter what it costs. The Germans are not as strong as it seems to those spreading panic. They are harnessing their last forces. To withstand their blows now, and in the next few months, means that we shall secure ourselves victory.

Will we be able to withstand the enemy's blow and then throw him back to the west? Yes, we can, since our factories and plants in the rear are now working superbly and the front is receiving ever more and more planes, tanks, artillery, and mortars.

What are we short of?

There is insufficient order and discipline in the companies, battalions, regiments, divisions, tank units, and air squadrons. That now is our main shortcoming. We must establish the severest order and iron discipline in our army if we want to save the situation and defend our motherland.

No longer is it possible to tolerate commanders, commissars, and political workers whose units and formations willfully abandon their combat positions. No longer is it possible to tolerate a situation where commanders, commissars, and political workers allow a few panicmongers to determine the situation on the battlefield and encourage other soldiers to retreat and open the front to the enemy.

Panicmongers and cowards must be exterminated on the spot.

From now on the iron law of discipline for every commander, Red Army soldier, and political worker must be the demand—not a step backward without the order of a superior commander.

Company, battalion, regimental, and divisional commanders, their corresponding commissars, and political workers who retreat from their combat positions without being ordered to do so from above are traitors of the motherland. And it is necessary to deal with such commanders and political instructors as traitors of the motherland.

Such is the slogan of our motherland.

To carry out this order means that we shall defend our land, save our motherland, exterminate and conquer the hateful enemy.

When, after its winter retreat and under pressure from the Red Army, discipline among German troops was weakened, the Germans, in order to reestablish discipline, took several harsh measures that had favorable results. They formed more than a hundred penal companies made up of soldiers who had been found guilty of violating discipline because of cowardice or irresolution, placed them on the dangerous sectors of the front, and ordered them to expiate their guilt with their own blood. Further, they formed about ten penal battalions made up of commanders who had been found guilty of violating discipline because of cowardice or irresolution, deprived them of their awards, placed them on the more dangerous sectors of the front, and ordered them to expiate their guilt. Finally they formed special blocking detachments, placing them behind the unsteady divisions, and ordered them to shoot panicmongers on the spot in the event of an attempt at unauthorized abandonment of positions and in the event of an attempt to surrender. As is known, these measures had their effect, and now German troops are fighting better than they fought during the winter. And so it turns out that German troops have better discipline, though they do not have the noble aim of protecting their homeland, but merely one of plunder— of conquering a foreign land. Our troops, who have the noble goal of defending their violated motherland, do not have such discipline and as a consequence of this are suffering defeat.

Should we not learn in this matter from our enemies, as our ancestors learned from our enemies in the past and were then victorious over them?

I think we should.

The Supreme High Command of the Red Army orders:

1. The military councils of the fronts and above all the front commanders shall:

a) unconditionally eliminate the defeatist sentiments among the troops and put a stop with an iron hand to the propaganda that we allegedly can and must retreat further eastward, that from such a retreat there will allegedly be no harm;

b) unconditionally remove from their posts army commanders who permit the unauthorized withdrawal of troops from occupied positions without an order from the front and send them to headquarters to be put before a military court;

c) form within the framework of the front from one to three (depending on the situation) penal battalions (up to 800 men within each) to which shall be sent middle- and senior-ranking commanders and their corresponding political workers of all arms who have been found guilty of violating discipline because of cowardice and irresolution and place them on the more difficult sectors of the front in order to enable them to expiate their crimes against the motherland in blood.

2. The military councils of the armies and above all the army commanders shall:

a) unconditionally remove from their posts corps and divisional commanders and commissars who permit the unauthorized withdrawal of troops from occupied positions without an order of the army command and send them to the front military council to be brought before a military court;

b) form in the framework of an army 3 to 5 well-armed blocking detachments (up to 200 men in each), place them in the immediate rear of irresolute divisions, and require them in the event of panic and a disorderly withdrawal of the division's units to execute on the spot cowards and those spreading panic, so assisting the divisions' loyal soldiers to discharge their duty to the motherland;

c) form within the framework of the army from 5 to 10 (depending on the situation) penal companies (from 150 to 200 men in each) to which shall be sent private soldiers and junior commanders who have been found guilty of violating discipline because of cowardice or irresolution and place them in difficult sectors of the front in order to enable them to expiate their crimes before the motherland in blood.

3. Corps and divisional commanders and commissars shall:

a) unconditionally remove from their posts regimental and battalion commanders who have permitted the unauthorized withdrawal of units without an order from a corps or divisional commander and remove their awards and medals and send them to the front military councils so that they can be brought before a military court;

b) render all assistance and support to the blocking detachments of the army in the task of strengthening order and discipline in the units.

This order is to be read out in all companies, cavalry squadrons, artillery batteries, air squadrons, commands, and headquarters.

People's Commissar for Defense   I. STALIN.

Source: "Prikaz Narodnogo komissara oborony Soiuza SSR, № 227, 28 iiulia 1942 g.'," Voenno-istoricheskii zhurnal 8 (1988): 73–75.

APPENDIX C
STATUTE CONCERNING THE MAIN COUNTERINTELLIGENCE DIRECTORATE OF THE PEOPLE'S COMMISSARIAT OF DEFENSE ("SMERSH") AND ITS AGENCIES IN THE PROVINCES, 21ST APRIL 1943

"I CONFIRM"
Chairman of the State Defense Committee I. Stalin
21 April 1943

Top Secret
of special importance

STATUTE

concerning the Main Counterintelligence Directorate
of the People's Commissariat of Defense ("SMERSH")
and Its Agencies in the Provinces

I. General Provisions

1. The Main Counterintelligence Directorate of the People's Commissariat of Defense ("SMERSH"—Death to Spies), formed on the basis of the former Directorate of Special Sections of the NKVD USSR, shall be part of the personnel of the People's Commissariat of Defense.

The head of the Main Counterintelligence Directorate of the People's Commissariat of Defense ("SMERSH") shall be a deputy of the People's Commissar of Defense and shall be directly subordinated to the People's Commissar of Defense and shall fulfil only his instructions.

2. The agencies of "SMERSH" constitute a centralized organization: At the fronts and in the districts the agencies of "SMERSH" (the Directorates of "SMERSH" of the People's Commissariat of Defense, and the sections of "SMERSH" of the People's Commissariat of Defense of armies, corps, divisions, brigades, military districts, and other formations and other institutions of the Red Army) shall be subordinated only to its higher agencies.

3. "SMERSH" agencies shall inform the Military Councils and the commanders of respective units, formations, and the institutions of the Red Army on questions of its work concerning the outcome of the fight against the enemy's agent network; about those anti-Soviet elements that have penetrated army units; about the results of combating treason to the motherland; and about treachery, deserters, and cases of self-inflicted wounds.

II. The Tasks of "SMERSH" Agencies

1. "SMERSH" agencies shall assume the following tasks:

a) combating espionage, sabotage, terrorism, and other subversive activity carried out by foreign intelligence agencies in the units and institutions of the Red Army;

b) combating anti-Soviet elements that have penetrated the units and institutions of the Red Army;

c) taking the operational, counterespionage, and other measures (via the command structure) that are necessary in order to create conditions at the fronts eliminating the possibility of enemy agents passing through the frontline with impunity, and to make the frontline impassable for spies and anti-Soviet elements;

d) combating treachery and treason to the motherland in the units and institutions of the Red Army (desertion to the enemy, hiding agents, and generally to prevent any assistance to the work of the latter);

e) combating desertion and self-inflicted wounds at the fronts;

f) processing service personnel and other persons who have been in enemy captivity or in encirclement;

g) carrying out the special tasks of the People's Commissar of Defense.

2. The agencies of "SMERSH" shall be free of any other work that is not directly connected with the tasks specified in the present paragraph.

III. The Rights and Obligations of "SMERSH" Agencies

1. In order to implement the tasks specified in the second section the Directorate of Counterintelligence of the People's Commissar of Defense ("SMERSH") and its agencies in the provinces shall have the right:

a) to recruit agents and informers;

b) to conduct, in accordance with the procedure established by law, seizures, searches, and arrests of Red Army personnel and, additionally, any member of the civilian population connected with them who is suspected of criminal activity;

Note: The procedure for the conduct of arresting service personnel is set out in Section IV of the present Statute.

c) to conduct the investigation of arrestees' cases with the subsequent handing over of the cases for coordination with the prosecutor's office in order that they be examined by the respective judicial agencies or the Special Session attached to the People's Commissariat of Internal Affairs of the USSR;

d) to employ various special measures with the aim of uncovering the criminal activity of agents run by foreign intelligence services and of anti-Soviet elements;

e) to summon, in the event of operational necessity and for purposes of interrogation, members of the rank and file and members of the command personnel without any prior agreement of the Red Army's high command.

IV. The Procedure for the Conduct of Arrests of Red Army Personnel by the Agencies of "SMERSH"

1. The agencies of "SMERSH" shall conduct arrests of Red Army Personnel in the following manner:

a) Arrests of the rank and file with agreement of the prosecutor.

b) Arrests of the middle-ranking command staff in agreement with the commander and formation or unit prosecutor.

c) Arrests of the senior command staff in agreement with the Military Councils and prosecutor.

d) Arrests of the high command staff, with the sanction of the People's Commissar of Defense.

V. The Organizational Structure of "SMERSH" Agencies

1. The staff of the Main Counterintelligence Directorate of the People's Commissar of Defense ("SMERSH") shall consist of the following:

Assistants of the head of the Main Directorate (according to the number of fronts) with groups of operational officers attached to them who shall be responsible for the running of the "SMERSH" agencies' work at the fronts.

First Section—agent-operational work throughout the agencies of the Red Army—and Directorates of the People's Commissariat of Defense.

Second Section—work among the ranks of service personnel who are of interest to the agencies of "SMERSH," the checking of Red Army personnel who have been in enemy captivity or encirclement.

Third Section—combating enemy agents (parachutists) dropped behind our lines.

Fourth Section—counterintelligence work behind the enemy's lines with the aim of uncovering the channels used by the enemy's agent network to penetrate the units and institutions of the Red Army.

Fifth Section—administering the work of "SMERSH" agencies in the military districts.

Sixth Section—investigative work.

Seventh Section—operational inventory and statistical analysis.

Eighth Section—operational equipment.

Ninth Section—searches, arrests, installations, and overt surveillance.

Tenth Section—"S" work on special tasks.

Eleventh Section—ciphered communications.

Cadres Section—the selection and training of cadres for "SMERSH" agencies, the formation of new "SMERSH" agencies.

Administrative-Financial and Supply Section—the provision of financial and supply services to the directorate, the command structure.

Secretariat

2. The following "SMERSH" agencies shall be organized in the provinces:

a) Front Directorates of Counterintelligence of the People's Commissar of Defense ("SMERSH");

b) Counterintelligence sections of the People's Commissar of Defense ("SMERSH") of armies, districts, corps, divisions, brigades, reserve regiments, garrisons, reinforced regions, and the institutions of the Red Army.

3. The structure of provincial agencies of "SMERSH" shall be established in conformity with the structure of the Main Counterintelligence Directorate of the People's Commissar of Defense ("SMERSH") and shall be confirmed by the People's Commissar of Defense.

4. In order to secure the operational work, escort duty, guarding of arrestees, and detention centers by "SMERSH" agencies in the provinces the following shall be detached from Red Army units:

a) to the "SMERSH" front directorate—a battalion;

b) to the "SMERSH" army section—a company;

c) to the "SMERSH" corps, division, and brigade sections—a platoon.

VI. "SMERSH" Agencies Personnel

1. "SMERSH" agencies shall be staffed at the expense of the operational personnel of the former Directorate of Special Sections of the NKVD USSR and from a special selection of service personnel drawn from the command and political stratum of the Red Army.

2. The training of cadres for "SMERSH" agencies shall be provided through the creation of special schools and courses attached to the Main Counterintelligence Directorate of the People's Commissar of Defense ("SMERSH").

3. Staff of "SMERSH" agencies shall be granted the military ranks established in the Red Army.

4. Staff of "SMERSH" agencies shall wear the uniform, shoulder boards, and other insignia of rank established for the respective arms of service in the Red Army.

VII.

In carrying out their work "SMERSH" agencies are, as far as it is necessary, to maintain close contact with the corresponding agencies of the NKGB USSR, NKVD USSR, and the Intelligence Directorate of the Red Army's general staff and shall exchange information and operational analyses.

VIII.

Alterations of any kind to the present Statute are only to be made on the order of the State Defense Committee.

Source: Rossiiskii Gosudarstevennyi Arkhiv Sotsial'no-Politicheskoi Istorii, Fond 644, Opis' 1, Delo 108, listy 152–157.

APPENDIX D
THEMATIC REFERENCE FOR WORKS AND CHARACTERS

For the works of authors that are discussed in this book, I include below a list of fictional and historical characters under each author's name and works. This list is intended to be a quick thematic reference linking a character with a theme or themes, and for that reason no page numbers are cited.

Viktor Astaf'ev, *The Damned and the Dead* (1992–1994)
IAshkin: autonomy, hostility to party, military professionalism, the summer of 1941
Leshka: collectivization and its savagery, extreme hardship
Mel'nikov: party propaganda
Musenok: memory, military incompetence, NKVD, party
Poptsov: *dedovshchina* (*see* glossary), living conditions in Red Army
Ryndin: love of Russia, moral absolutes, Old Belief
Shchus': autonomy, military professionalism, hostility to party, revenge
Shpator: faith, Mother Russia
Snegirev twins: executions, Order № 227 (*see* glossary), Revelation, starvation
Vaskonian: intellectual rebellion, the outsider, the storyteller
Zelentsov: penal troops, show trial

Grigorii Baklanov, *South of the Main Blow* (1958), *The Dead Feel No Shame* (1961), and *July 1941* (1965)
Belichenko/*South of the Main Blow*: duty, ruthless professionalism, sacrifice
Bogachev/*South of the Main Blow*: *okruzhenie* (*see* glossary), professional autonomy
Ishchenko/*The Dead Feel No Shame*: cowardice, dereliction of duty
Mostovoi/*The Dead Feel No Shame*: filtration, German captivity, *okruzhenie*
Vasich/*The Dead Feel No Shame*: duty, loyalty, truth
Broval'skii/*July 1941*: moral and physical courage, purges
Emel'ianov/*July 1941*: influence of Stalin on Soviet society, moral courage, purges
Lapshin/*July 1941*: military incompetence, purges
Shalaev/*July 1941*: ideological orthodoxy, military incompetence, the purges, Special Section/NKVD
Shcherbatov/*July 1941*: military professionalism, purges
Sorokin/*July 1941*: military incompetence, purges

Vladimir Bogomolov, *In August 1944* (1974)
Alekhin: ideological orthodoxy, SMERSH
Anikushin: hostility to SMERSH, Red Army, summer retreat 1942
Pavlovskii: German agent, *Volksdeutsche* (*see* glossary)

Polish woman: Marshal Pilsudski, Polish nationalism, Warsaw uprising
Stalin: great military leader, omniscience, saviour of the Soviet Union
Tamantsev: extreme professionalism, ideological orthodoxy, SMERSH

IUrii Bondarev, *The Battalions Request Fire Support* (1957), *The Final Salvoes* (1959), and *Hot Snow* (1969)

Ermakov/The Battalions Request Fire Support: deserters, Order № 270 (*see* glossary), ruthless professionalism, sacrifice, treatment of collaborators
Iverzev/The Battalions Request Fire Support: ruthless professionalism
Novikov/The Final Salvoes: ruthless professionalism, *okruzhenie*
Bessonov/Hot Snow: duty, Order № 270, Vlasov
Stalin/Hot Snow: far-sighted leader
Ukhanov/Hot Snow: desertion

Vladimir But, *Heads—Tails* (1995)

Kondrat'ev: duty, penal troops
Len'ka: duty
Mekhlis: cowardice, military incompetence, purges, party
Selivanov: conscience, friction in war, ideological temptation, military professionalism
Stalin: propaganda construct as the omniscient, infallible war leader
Vorozhetskii: informers, NKVD, SMERSH

Vasil' Bykov, *The Dead Feel No Pain* (1966), *Sotnikov* (1970), *The Obelisk* (1972), *The Wolf Pack* (1974), *The Sign of Misfortune* (1983), *The Quarry* (1986), and *The Great Freeze* (1993)

Gorbatiuk/The Dead Feel No Pain: military tribunals, SMERSH
Katia/The Dead Feel No Pain: dedication, Red Army, role of women in war, self-sacrifice
Sakhno/The Dead Feel No Pain: military tribunals, SMERSH
Vasilevich/The Dead Feel No Pain: devastation of Belorussia, memory, Red Army, truth
Rybak/Sotnikov: changing nature of loyalty, collaboration, envy, moral thresholds, weather
Sotnikov/Sotnikov: duty, honor, illness, loyalty, partisan warfare, summer of 1941
Cain/The Obelisk: collaboration, moral relativism, partisan warfare, treachery
Moroz/The Obelisk: Dostoevsky's moral teaching, duty, following orders, intellectual independence, memory, moral teaching, partisan warfare, self-sacrifice
Tkachuk/The Obelisk: memory, partisan warfare, truth
Klava/The Wolf Pack: partisan warfare, sexual betrayal, treachery
Kudriavtsev/The Wolf Pack: partisan warfare, sexual betrayal, treachery
Levchuk/The Wolf Pack: devastation of Belorussia, honor, memory, partisan warfare
Guzh/The Sign of Misfortune: collaboration, revenge of the dispossessed
Petrok/The Sign of Misfortune: collectivization, dispossession of the peasants, German occupation, private property
Stepanida/The Sign of Misfortune: collaboration, collectivization, dispossession of the peasants, German occupation, private property, role of party in countryside

Ageev/*The Quarry*: collaboration, Dostoevsky's moral teaching, German occupation, God, love, memory, moral relativism, nationalism, partisan warfare, Sovietization of Belorussia, summer of 1941

Baranovskaia/*The Quarry*: God, memory, patriotism

Azevich/*The Great Freeze*: collaboration, collectivization, cold, illness, nationalism, repentance

Vasilii Grossman, *For a Just Cause* (1952) and *Life and Fate* (1988)

Abarchuk/For a Just Cause and Life and Fate: forced labor camps, ideological orthodoxy, intellectual cowardice, loss of self

Bach/For a Just Cause and Life and Fate: Nietzsche, beyond good and evil, love, redemption

Berezkin/Life and Fate: duty, freedom, leadership, love of Russia, summer of 1941

Chepyzhin/For a Just Cause and Life and Fate: individualism, intellectual and moral freedom, science

Chuniak, Khristia/Life and Fate: collectivization, compassion and forgiveness, maternal love

Darenskii/For a Just Cause and Life and Fate: freedom, love of Russia, military professionalism and initiative, purges, summer of 1941

Ershov/Life and Fate: freedom, initiative, love of Russia, loyalty to family

Filiashkin/For a Just Cause: love of Russia, penal troops, sacrifice

Getmanov/Life and Fate: new party type, purges, ruthless self-seeking

Grekov/Life and Fate: initiative, freedom, military professionalism

Hitler/For a Just Cause and Life and Fate: allegory of the Soviet state, propinquity with Stalin

Ikonnikov-Morzh/Life and Fate: evil, good, moral absolutes, self-sacrifice

Katsenelenbogen/Life and Fate: end justifies the means, hatred of self, loss of self, moral relativism

Krymov/For a Just Cause and Life and Fate: devotion to communism, ideological orthodoxy, loss of self and intellectual and moral independence, Old Bolshevik

Lenin/Life and Fate: destroyer of Russia's freedom, founder of totalitarian state

Leonard/For a Just Cause and Life and Fate: beyond good and evil, informer, the theme of decline

Levinton, Sof'ia/Life and Fate: Holocaust, maternal love

Liss/Life and Fate: apocalypse, moral relativism, National Socialism, SS

Mostovskoi/Life and Fate: ideological orthodoxy, loss of self and intellectual and moral independence, Old Bolshevik

Neudobnov/Life and Fate: party bureaucrat, ruthless self-seeking

Osipov/Life and Fate: party bureaucrat

Novikov/For a Just Cause and Life and Fate: freedom, love of Russia, military professionalism and initiative, summer of 1941

Semenov/For a Just Cause and Life and Fate: collectivization, Red Army soldiers in German captivity

Shtrum, Liudmila/Life and Fate: maternal grief and maternal love

Shtrum, Viktor/Life and Fate: craving for intellectual freedom, Holocaust, Jews in Russia, sense of belonging, scientific enquiry, *Zhdanovshchina* (*see* glossary)

Shtrum's mother/*Life and Fate*: her letter as symbol of truth, Holocaust (Berdichev ghetto), maternal love

Stalin/For a *Just Cause* and *Life and Fate*: completes the destruction of Russia's freedom, perfects the totalitarian state founded by Lenin, saved by the victory at Stalingrad

Zhenia/For a *Just Cause* and *Life and Fate*: artistic and individual freedom, conscience, loyalty

Emmanuil Kazakevich, *Star* (1946) and *Two Men on the Steppe* (1948)

Mamochkin/*Star*: fate, retribution, supernatural

Travkin/*Star*: duty, fate, SMERSH

Ogarkov/*Two Men on the Steppe*: arbitrary nature of Soviet military justice, duty

Siniaev/*Two Men on the Steppe*: betrayal, lack of moral courage

Viktor Nekrasov, *In the Trenches of Stalingrad* (1946)

Abrosimov: Order № 227

Chumak: independence, military professionalism

Kaluzkskii: dereliction of duty

Kerzhentsev: duty, shame, summer of 1941

Ivan Stadniuk, *War* (1970–1980)

Chumakov: military orthodoxy

Churchill: active hostility to Soviet Union, perfidious Albion

Glinskii brothers: hatred of Soviet Union, German saboteurs

Mekhlis: ideology, NKVD, orthodoxy

Pavlov: military incompetence (alleged)

Romanov: military orthodoxy

Stalin: outstanding leader, saviour of the Soviet state

Timoshenko: orthodoxy

Georgii Vladimov, *The General and His Army* (1994)

Drobnis: associated with Mekhlis, cowardice, loss and hatred of self, military incompetence, party

Guderian: duty, understanding of Russia

Kobrisov: *okruzhenie*, purges, Russian patriotism, summer of 1941

Stalin: incompetence, search for scapegoats, weakness

Svetlookov: informers, party, purges, SMERSH, retribution, sadism

Vlasov: battle of Moscow, collaboration, duty, Russian Liberation Army, Stalin's incompetence

NOTES

Preface

1. Lazar' Lazarev, *Pamiat' trudnoi godiny: Velikaia Otechestvennaia voina v russkoi literature* (Moscow: Druzhba narodov, 2000), 5.

2. Alexander Solzhenitsyn, *The Russian Question at the End of the Twentieth Century* (1994) (London: Harvill Press, 1995), 104. This magnificent philippic against Communism and its legacy in Russia was first published in the journal *Novyi mir* 7 (1994): 135–176.

Chapter 1. The Sword and the Pen

1. Epitaph of Simonides at Thermopylae, trans. by William Lisle Bowles; Nathaniel Fick, *One Bullet Away: The Making of a Marine Officer* (London: Weidenfeld & Nicolson, 2005), 72.

2. One of the sternest critics of Viktor Astaf'ev's *Prokliaty i ubity* (The Damned and the Dead) (Moscow: Veche, 1994) argued that the novel insults, rather than honors, the memory of the fallen: "By means of his novel, V. Astaf'ev has wounded not only true communists but all the frontline soldiers and turned a considerable number of young people against them, calling upon them to forget the fallen: If they are damned by God, then why remember them? . . . Not only frontline soldiers but also children, the grandchildren of the fallen, cannot but perceive the novel's title as a blasphemous subtitle to *The Books of Remembrance*." V. Zelenkov, "Komu voina, a komu mat' rodna. Podzagolovok k 'Knigam pamiati'? Zametki frontovika o romane V. Astaf'eva 'Prokliaty i ubity,'" *Nash sovremennik* 9 (1997): 82.

3. Georgii Vladimov, *General i ego armiia* (The General and His Army) (Moscow: Knizhnaia palata, 1997). This is the epigraph to chapter 3 of the novel.

4. Mikhail Bulgakov, *Master i Margarita* (Moscow: Khudozhestvennaia literatura, 1983), 279.

5. John Stuart Mill, *Utilitarianism* (1863) (London: Collins, Fount Paperbacks, 1982), 154.

6. Vasilii Grossman, *Povesti, Rasskazy, Ocherki* (Tales, Short Stories, Sketches) (Moscow: Voenizdat, 1958), 478.

7. Vasilii Grossman, *Zhizn' i sud'ba* (Life and Fate) (Moscow: Sovetskii pisatel', 1990), 494.

8. Quincy Wright, *A Study of War* (1942), abridged by Louise Leonard Wright (Chicago and London: University of Chicago Press, 1964), 355.

9. One can note the following distinction in this regard made by James Johnson: "While just war is the term used by tradition, a more exact term would be *justifiable* war." See *Just War Tradition and the Restraint of War: A Moral and Historical Inquiry* (Princeton, NJ: Princeton University Press, 1981), xxxiv (emphasis in the original).

10. Sun Tzu, *The Art of War*, edited and with a foreword by James Clavell (New York: Delacorte Press, 1988), 9. *Ping Fa* literally means "the way of the soldier," a title that is

much closer in its cultural and historical meaning to the Japanese concept of *bushido* (also derived from Chinese) than to modern notions of soldiers serving in regular, professional armies. Unlike *bushido*, which is a code of morals and ethics by means of which the warrior lives and dies, *The Art of War* is more a manual in intrigue than in soldiering. A more suitable translation might be *The Way of the Spy Master*. Certain elements in *The Art of War* retain their relevance for the prosecution of modern warfare— the emphasis on deception and spying, for example—but the book's contemporary value lies more in the valuable insights the author provides into the minds of his countrymen. *The Art of War* is as much the *Chinese* art of war as anything else. It is the art of the indirect riposte, in which the soldier must cultivate the skills of both the magician (the deceiver) and the tactician. The main weakness of Sun Tzu's treatise is that he occasionally seems more concerned with aesthetic considerations—with the *art* of war in itself—than with the awkward, abrasive substance that is the friction in war.

11. Carl von Clausewitz, *On War* (1832), ed. and trans. by Michael Howard and Peter Paret (Princeton, NJ: Princeton University Press, 1989), 69.

12. Peter Brock, *Pacifism in Europe to 1914* (Princeton, NJ: Princeton University Press, 1972), 3. In an earlier work, Brock had defined pacifism as "the movement which has grown up in our century, combining advocacy of nonparticipation in war of any kind or in violent revolution with an endeavour to find nonviolent means of resolving conflict." See Peter Brock, *Twentieth-Century Pacifism* (London: Van Nostrand Reinhold Company, 1970), v. For an exhaustive discussion of this theme, see Peter Brock, *Against the Draft: Essays on Conscientious Objections from the Radical Reformation to the Second World War* (Toronto, Ontario: University of Toronto Press, 2006). One of the best-argued cases against pacifism and peace studies, and the view that interstate wars are now a thing of the past, is to be found in Colin Gray's *Another Bloody Century: Future Warfare* (London: Weidenfeld & Nicolson, 2005). Gray readily concedes that moves to reduce the likelihood of war can sometimes succeed, but he believes that diplomacy and other such initiatives cannot always be guaranteed to overcome the three main reasons why states and other entities wage war, first set out by Thucydides: fear, honor, and interest.

13. Ernst Jünger, "Der Kampf als inneres Erlebnis" (Combat as an Inner Experience), *Sämtliche Werke*, Band 7, *Betrachtungen zur Zeit* (Stuttgart:Klett-Cotta, 1980), 40 (hereafter cited as KAE).

14. Alexander Solzhenitsyn, *Warning to the Western World* (London: The Bodley Head and BBC, 1976), 21. Sidney Hook, who debated nuclear issues with Russell in the 1950s, pointed out that there are other alternatives to "better red than dead": "Our slogan should be not 'Red or Dead' but 'Neither Red nor Dead,' and more positively 'Better free than Slave.'" See Sidney Hook, *Out of Step: An Unquiet Life in the 20th Century* (New York: Harper & Row Publishers, 1987), 570.

15. Andrew Rutherford, *The Literature of War: Five Studies in Heroic Virtue* (Basingstoke and London: Macmillan Press, 1978), 87.

16. Alistair Maclean, *HMS Ulysses* (London: Harper Collins, 1994), 17.

17. Ibid., 35. It is tempting to speculate that the captain's name is an allusion to Saint-Valéry, the place where the Scottish 51st Highland Division surrendered in the summer of 1940, that the choice of name is intended as an act of remembrance, a tribute

to Maclean's fellow Scots. The French place name and its anglicized equivalent not only suggest valor but also, in the case of the French, hint that there is something saintly about Vallery. Certainly Maclean creates that impression: "Among naval captains, indeed among men, he was unique. In his charity, in his humility, Captain Richard Vallery walked alone. It was a measure of the man's greatness that this thought never occurred to him" (35). Anticipating his death, Vallery tours the ship, stiffening the men's courage. He appears as a Christlike figure: "He had gone among them and made them almost as himself" (349).

18. Pirogov, a medical expert quoted in Amnon Sella, *The Value of Human Life in Soviet Warfare* (London: Routledge, 1992), 49.

19. This definition was used in a recent court case in which 2,000 British soldiers, claiming to be victims of Gulf War Syndrome, filed suit against the Ministry of Defense. Quincy Wright defines war as "*a violent contact of distinct but similar entities.*" See *A Study of War*, 5 (emphasis in the original).

20. Johnson, *Just War Tradition*, xxii–xxiii.

21. Ibid., xxix (emphasis in the original).

22. Jünger, KAE, 49.

23. *Marxism-Leninism on War and Army*, trans. by Donald Danemanis (Moscow: Progress Publishers, 1972), 88.

24. Jünger, KAE, 40.

25. For a discussion of Jünger, see Graf Christian von Krockow, *Die Entscheidung: Eine Untersuchung über Ernst Jünger, Carl Schmidt, Martin Heidegger* (Stuttgart: Ferdinand Enke Verlag, 1958); Gerda Liebchen, *Ernst Jünger. Seine Literarischen Arbeiten in den 20er Jahren. Eine Untersuchung zur gesellschaftlichen Funktion von Literatur* (Bonn: Bouvier Verlag, 1977); Karl Prümm, *Die Literatur des soldatischen Nationalismus der 20er Jahre (1918–1933)* (Kronberg Taunus: Verlag, 1974); and Roger Woods, *Ernst Jünger and the Nature of Political Commitment* (Stuttgart: Akademischer Verlag Hans Dieter Heinz, 1982).

26. Jünger, KAE, 11–12.

27. Heraclitus states that "war is father of all and king of all; and some he has shown as gods, others men; some he has made slaves, others free." See Charles H. Kahn, *The Art and Thought of Heraclitus* (Cambridge: Cambridge University Press, 1979), 67.

28. Jünger, KAE, 12–13.

29. Ibid., 37.

30. Ibid., 54.

31. Ibid., 74.

32. José Ortega y Gasset, *The Revolt of the Masses* (1930) (New York and London: W. W. Norton & Company, 1993), 75.

33. Ibid.

34. Zelenkov, "Komu voina, a komu mat' rodna," 80.

35. T. M. Vakhitova, "Narod na voine: Vzgliad V. Astaf'eva iz serediny 90-kh. Roman 'Prokliaty i ubity,'" *Russkaia literatura* 3 (1995): 114.

36. Viktor Astaf'ev, "Pastukh i Pastushka: Sovremennaia pastoral'," *Prokliaty i ubity* (Moscow: Veche, 1994), 370. The first version of *The Shepherd and the Shepherdess*, published in *Nash sovremennik* 8 (1971), was subjected to some severe cuts by the censors.

The novel was restored by the author between 1971 and 1989. Not all readers appreciated the love theme amid war. "Astaf'ev's story," notes Vakhitova, "was attacked for its 'banalities'; for its 'pacifism'; for being contrived; for its pastoral theme; for subverting the heroic; and for its romantic, unmilitary hero who dies from love." See Vakhitova, "Narod na voine," 119.

37. Nikolai Shpanov, *Pervyi udar, Povesti i Rasskazy* (The First Blow: Tales and Short Stories) (Moscow: Sovetskii pisatel', 1939), 13.

38. Ibid., 9.

39. Ibid., 21. Rejection of any kind of Western-style pacifism is a major theme in *The First Blow*. In expectation of a war against Germany, one pilot explains, "Our war will be the most just of all wars that mankind has ever known. Bolsheviks are not pacifists. We are active defenders. Our defense is the offensive. The Red Army will not remain on its borders for a single moment; it will not mark time but like an avalanche of steel surge onto the territory of the warmongers" (28).

40. Ibid., 21.

41. Ibid., 20.

42. Ibid., 41.

43. *Stalingradskaia epopeia: Materialy NKVD SSSR i voennoi tsenzury iz Tsentral'nogo arkhiva FSB RF, IA. F. Pogonii i dr.* (Moscow: Zvonnitsa-MG, 2000), 264.

44. Jünger, KAE, 55.

45. Sir Karl Popper, *The Open Society and Its Enemies: The Spell of Plato* (1945), vol. 1 (London: Routledge and Kegan Paul, 1993), 182.

46. The same desire to seek out war and find what it has to offer is evident in T. E. Lawrence's *Seven Pillars of Wisdom* (1935) (Harmondsworth, Middlesex: Penguin, 1988). There are passages in Lawrence's book that describe and analyze war in terms that would not have been out of place in the work of Jünger. Lawrence, like Jünger, submits to war, seeking to lose himself and reveling in the violence and the sensations of war.

47. Astaf'ev, "Pastukh i Pastushka," 374.

48. See, for example, Simonov's trilogy *Zhivye i mertvye* (The Living and the Dead, 1959), *Soldatami ne rozhdaiutsia* (Soldiers Are Not Born, 1963–1964), and *Poslednee leto* (The Last Summer, 1970).

49. Bulat Okudzhava, *Bud' zdorov, shkoliar* (Take Care, Schoolboy), Stikhi, vtoroe izdanie (Frankfurt: Possev-Verlag, 1966), 1.

50. For a detailed discussion of the themes of tragic guilt and innocence in *Killed at Moscow* with reference to classical precedents, see E. V. Volkova, "Tragicheskaia vina ('Ubity pod Moskvoi' Konstantina Vorob'eva)," *Voprosy filosofii* 11 (2001): 29–39. Volkova develops her discussion through the figures of Riumin and IAstrebov. One aspect of this article that could have been profitably pursued is whether the notions of tragic guilt and innocence apply to Russia at war and what this might mean for the Stalinist formula "to expiate one's guilt in blood."

51. War and sacrifice are major themes in the repertoire of the Russian rock band Liube. Two of its songs, "Soldat" (Soldier) and "Kombat" (The Battalion Commander), together with the videos that accompany them, portray war in a manner that is redolent of stories by Okudzhava, Vorob'ev, and Kurochkin.

52. "Over the course of many years," wrote Vasil' Bykov in 2000, "the incomplete truth and the straightforward lie about the war belittled the meaning and significance of our war literature (or antiwar, as is sometimes said). The excess of pompous heroism of all types did exactly the same thing." See "Literatura i voina," *Znamia* 5 (2000): 6.

53. Aleksandr Nekrich, *1941, 22 iiunia* (1941, 22 June, 1965), izdanie 2-e, dopolnennoe i pererabotannoe (Moscow: Pamiatniki istoricheskoi mysli, 1995), 255.

54. Ibid., 159.

55. Ibid., 158.

56. Ibid., 250.

57. Ibid., 263.

58. Ibid., 273.

59. Ibid., 278.

60. Erich Maria Remarque, *Im Westen nichts Neues* (All Quiet on the Western Front, 1929) (Köln: Kiepenheuer & Witsch, 1984), 236.

61. Rutherford, *The Literature of War*, 76.

62. Ibid., 3 (emphasis in the original). Correlli Barnett and Cyril Falls tend to agree with Rutherford that some measure of skepticism is merited regarding what the British war writers have to say. Barnett, for example, questions whether the outrage felt by the war writers was justified. He cites a number of objections: The writers were highly untypical of the British people (wealthy, comfortable); their idealistic upbringing rendered them less able to adapt to conditions; and they failed to note just how harsh life was for the rank and file in peacetime and, as a consequence, "this unbalanced impression, because of their literary powers, was accepted in a generalised way by British educated opinion as 'the truth' about the war. And whence derives, in my view, the long-term and catastrophic effect of the war literature on British history." See Correlli Barnett, "A Military Historian's View of the Great War," in Mary Stocks, ed., *Essays by Divers Hands: Being the Transactions of the Royal Society of Literature*, vol. 36 (London: Oxford University Press, 1970), 17. "The war," Barnett writes, "crippled Britain *psychologically*, and in no other way" . . . "the authors of our war literature played a crucial, if unwitting role" (18). Falls argues that the concentration of grim scenes distorts the portrayal of war: "But the falsest of false evidence is produced in another way: by closing up scenes and events that in themselves may be true. Every sector becomes a bad one, every working party is shot to pieces; if a man is killed or wounded his brains or entrails always protrude from his body; no one ever seems to have a rest. . . . Attacks succeed one another with lightning rapidity. The soldier is represented as a depressed and mournful spectre helplessly wandering about until death brought his miseries to an end." See Cyril Falls, *War Books: An Annotated Bibliography of Books About the Great War* (1930), with a new introduction by R. J. Wyatt (London: Greenhill Books, 1989), xvii.

63. Rutherford, *The Literature of War*, 77.

64. Ibid., 65.

65. Willi Heinrich, *Das geduldige Fleisch* (1956), trans. by Richard and Clare Winston, *Cross of Iron* (London: Cassell Military Paperbacks edition, 2002), 138.

66. Ibid., 139.

67. Ibid., 467. Although Heinrich's attempts to justify the invasion of the Soviet Union in terms of defending the West conspicuously ignore the nature of National Socialist Germany and its ambitions, another equally deplorable position is to deny that Germans suffered in World War II or even that Germans, especially civilians, merit the status of victim. So powerful has this taboo been in Germany since 1945 that it is only very recently that attempts have been made to write about Germany's forgotten dead. Two books can be noted: Günter Grass's Im Krebsgang (Moving Like a Crab, 2002) (Göttingen: Steidl Verlag, 2002), which deals with, among other things, the sinking of the Wilhelm Gustloff, and Jörg Friedrich's Der Brand: Deutschland im Bombenkrieg 1940–1945 (The Fire: Germany in the Bombing Campaign 1940–1945, 2002) (Munich: Propyläen Verlag, 2002), which takes a hard look at the Allied bombing of Germany and the losses inflicted on German civilians.

68. Vasil' Bykov, Kar'er (The Quarry), Druzhba narodov 5 (1986): 77.

69. Bykov, "Literatura i voina," 8.

Chapter 2. Return from the Front

1. Sun Tzu, The Art of War, edited and with a foreword by James Clavell (New York: Delacorte Press, 1988), 77–78.

2. Holger Klein, J. E. Flower, and Eric Homberger, eds., The Second World War in Fiction (London and Basingstoke: Macmillan Press, 1984), 140.

3. Emmanuil Kazakevich, Izbrannye proizvedeniia, vol. 1 (Moscow: Khudozhestvennaia literatura, 1974), 7.

4. Ibid., 9.

5. Ibid., 46.

6. Ibid., 52.

7. Ibid., 98.

8. Ibid., 106.

9. Ibid., 130.

10. Ibid.

11. Ibid., 131.

12. Grigorii Baklanov, "IUzhnee glavnogo udara" (South of the Main Blow), Voennye povesti (Moscow: Sovremennik, 1985), 355.

13. Ibid., 341.

14. Ibid., 365–366.

15. Ibid., 391.

16. Ibid.

17. Ibid., 403.

18. Ibid., 420.

19. Ibid., 414.

20. Grigorii Baklanov, "Mertvye sramu ne imut" (The Dead Feel No Shame), Znamia 6 (1961): 27.

21. Ibid.

22. Ibid., 28.

23. Ibid., 41–42.

24. Ibid., 48.

25. Ibid., 57.

26. Ibid., 47.

27. Ibid., 48.

28. Vasil' Bykov, "'Za rodinu! Za Stalina.' Tsena proshedshikh boev," *Rodina* 5 (1995): 34.

29. Ibid., 35.

30. Grigorii Baklanov, "Iiul' 41 goda" (July 1941), *Znamia* 1 (1965): 6.

31. Grigorii Baklanov, "Iiul' 41 goda," *Znamia* 2 (1965): 15.

32. Ibid., 16.

33. Ibid., 3.

34. Ibid., 4.

35. Ibid., 7.

36. Ibid., 9.

37. Ibid., 34.

38. Ibid., 37.

39. Ibid., 34.

40. Ibid., 57.

41. Ibid., 58.

42. Ibid., 63.

43. Ibid., 70.

44. IUrii Bondarev, "Batal'ony prosiat ognia" (The Battalions Request Fire Support), *Sobranie sochinenii v shesti tomakh*, vol. 1 (Moscow: Khudozhestvennaia literatura, 1984), 164.

45. Ibid., 161.

46. Klein et al., *The Second World War in Fiction*, 165.

47. Bondarev, "Batal'ony prosiat ognia," 135.

48. Ibid., 131.

49. IUrii Bondarev, "Poslednie zalpy" (The Final Salvoes), *Sobranie sochinenii v shesti tomakh*, vol. 2 (Moscow: Khudozhestvennaia literatura, 1984), 67.

50. Ibid., 91.

51. Ibid., 35.

52. Ibid., 84.

Chapter 3. Traitors, Wolves, and Infernal Cold

1. Lazar' Lazarev, "Na vsiu ostavshuiusia zhizn': Zametki o povesti Vasilia Bykova 'Kar'ep' i nekotorykh problemakh literatury, posviashchennoi Velikoi Otechestvennoi voine," *Novyi mir* 11 (1986): 233–234.

2. Vasil' Bykov, "Mertvym ne bol'no" (The Dead Feel No Pain), *Novyi mir* 1 (1966): 5.

3. Vasil' Bykov, "Mertvym ne bol'no," *Novyi mir* 2 (1966): 7.

4. Bykov, "Mertvym ne bol'no," *Novyi mir* 1, 30.

5. Ibid., 31.

6. Bykov, "Mertvym ne bol'no," *Novyi mir* 2, 22.

7. Ibid., 23.

8. Ibid., 24

9. Ibid., 16.

10. Ibid., 21.

11. Ibid., 49.

12. Ibid., 9.

13. Ibid., 10.

14. Ibid., 40.

15. Ibid., 13.

16. Bykov, "Mertvym ne bol'no," *Novyi mir* 1, 15.

17. Ibid.

18. Ibid., 46.

19. Ibid., 16.

20. Ibid.

21. Ibid., 18.

22. Bykov, "Mertvym ne bol'no," *Novyi mir* 2, 56. Siegfried Sassoon's poem "The Hero" (1916) deals with exactly the same problem. An officer comforts the mother of a fallen comrade who believes her son died a glorious death. In the final stanza we learn: "He thought how 'Jack,' cold-footed, useless swine/Had panicked down the trench that night the mine/Went up at Wicked Corner; how he'd tried/To get sent home, and how, at last, he died/Blown to small bits. And no one seemed to care/Except that lonely woman with white hair." *The War Poems of Siegfried Sassoon*, arranged and introduced by Rupert Hart-Davis (London: Faber and Faber, 1983), 49.

23. Vasil' Bykov, "Sotnikov," *Novyi mir* 5 (1970): 73.

24. Ibid., 66.

25. Ibid., 142.

26. Ibid., 143.

27. Bertolt Brecht, *Die Dreigroschenoper*, Act 2, in the song "Denn wovon lebt der Mensch?"

28. Bykov, "Sotnikov," 112.

29. Ibid., 127.

30. Ibid., 132.

31. Ibid., 89.

32. Ibid., 71.

33. Ibid., 98. Bykov uses the same metaphor in *The Dead Feel No Pain* to describe the crossing of the minefield.

34. Bykov, "Sotnikov," 90.

35. Ibid., 80.

36. Ibid., 82

37. Ibid., 84.

38. Ibid., 139.

39. Ibid.

40. Ibid., 148.

41. The themes of crucifixion and resurrection are brilliantly portrayed in *Voskhozhdenie* (The Ascent, 1976), Larissa Shepitko's film interpretation of *Sotnikov*. Other Bykov stories

that have been turned into films are *The Third Flare* (1963, directed by Richard Viktorov), *The Wolf Pack* (1975, directed by Boris Stepanov), *To Live until Dawn* (1975, directed by Viktor Sokolov and Mikhail Yershov), *The Obelisk* (1976, directed by Richard Viktorov), *The Sign of Misfortune* (1986, directed by Mikhail Ptashuk), *Kruglianskii Bridge* (1989, directed by Aleksandr Moroz), *The Quarry* (1990, directed by Nikolai Skuibin), and *In the Mist* (1992, directed by Sergei Linkov).

42. Bykov, "Sotnikov," 100.

43. Ibid., 153.

44. Ibid., 96.

45. Ibid., 68.

46. Ibid.

47. Vasil' Bykov, "Obelisk" (The Obelisk), *Novyi mir* 1 (1972): 23.

48. Ibid., 24–25.

49. Ibid., 27.

50. Ibid., 28.

51. *Sotnikov* also suggests an adaptation of the Cain-and-Abel parable. As Rybak becomes ever more irritated with Sotnikov's physical state and rationalizes his treachery, one can almost hear him posing to himself the question "Am I my brother's keeper?" In the prison cell, Sotnikov refers to Rybak as "brother," and we might see Rybak's eventual desertion as the spiritual murder of Sotnikov.

52. Bykov, "Obelisk," 39.

53. Ibid., 42.

54. Ibid., 43.

55. Ibid., 44.

56. Vasil' Bykov, "Volch'ia staia" (The Wolf Pack), *Novyi mir* 7 (1974): 31.

57. Ibid., 29.

58. Ibid., 39.

59. Ibid., 65.

60. Ibid., 66.

61. Ibid., 68.

62. Vasil' Bykov, "Znak bedy" (The Sign of Misfortune), *Sobranie sochinenii v chetyrekh tomakh*, vol. 4 (Moscow: Molodaia gvardiia, 1986), 9–10.

63. Ibid., 21.

64. Ibid., 63.

65. Ibid., 69.

66. Ibid., 97.

67. Ibid., 7.

68. Ibid., 100.

69. Ibid., 102.

70. Ibid., 62.

71. Ibid., 69.

72. Ibid., 114.

73. Ibid., 119.

74. Ibid., 120.

75. Ibid., 121.

76. Ibid., 122.

77. Ibid.

78. Ibid., 124.

79. Ibid., 127.

80. Ibid., 166.

81. Ibid., 144.

82. Alexander Solzhenitsyn, *The Russian Question at the End of the Twentieth Century* (1994) (London: The Harvill Press, 1995), 104.

83. Bykov, "Znak bedy," 6.

84. Ibid., 218.

85. Ibid., 248.

86. In a long article dedicated to a discussion of Viktor Astaf'ev's *The Damned and the Dead*, Igor' Dedkov considered the view—one of the most bitterly contested arising from Astaf'ev's novel—that the German invasion was retribution. Only "Astaf'ev and Bykov in *The Sign of Misfortune*," he concluded, "had posed this question with such clarity." See Igor' Dedkov, "Ob'iavlenie viny i naznachenie kazni," *Druzhba narodov* 10 (1993): 202.

87. Vasil' Bykov, "Kar'er" (The Quarry), *Druzhba narodov* 4 (1986): 48.

88. Ibid., 55.

89. Ibid., 73.

90. Bykov, "Kar'er," *Druzhba narodov* 5 (1986): 95. The relevant chapters in *The Brothers Karamazov* are 6 and 7 in book 4.

91. Bykov, "Kar'er," *Druzhba narodov* 5, 122.

92. Ibid., 94.

93. Ibid., 148.

94. Bykov, "Kar'er," *Druzhba narodov* 4, 6.

95. Ibid., 11.

96. Bykov, "Kar'er," *Druzhba narodov* 5, 139.

97. Ibid., 97.

98. Ibid., 142.

99. Vasil' Bykov, "Stuzha" (The Great Freeze), *Znamia* 11 (1993): 47.

100. Ibid., 45.

101. Ibid., 43.

102. Ibid., 40–41.

103. Ibid., 38.

104. Ibid., 41–42.

105. Ibid., 58.

106. Ibid.

Chapter 4. The Imperium Ripostes

1. Ivan Stadniuk, "Zametki ob istorizme," *Sobranie sochinenii v chetyrekh tomakh*, vol. 4 (Moscow: Molodaia gvardiia, 1985), 380.

2. Ivan Stadniuk, *Voina* (War) (Moscow: Sovremennik, 1977), 105. Book 1 of *Voina* was published in *Oktiabr'* 12 (1970); books 2 and 3 in *Molodaia gvardiia* 5, 6, and 7 (1974) and *Molodaia gvardiia* 5, 6, and 9 (1980), respectively.

3. Ibid., 20.

4. Ibid., 22.

5. Ibid., 170–171. Volkogonov's assessment of Stalin's performance as the catastrophe unfolds is somewhat harsher: "In the depths of his soul, Stalin increasingly understood that the prewar miscalculations, the poor management, 'the fear of provocations,' the inadequate training of the many newly promoted middle and senior commanders rendered the army and defense flabby, difficult to control and one which quickly lost faith in itself. The papers wrote—and how true!—about the heroism of Red Army soldiers, about the feats of the airmen, tank troops, about the fact that the country had risen to resist the enemy. All this was so. But at the front, and this could not be hidden from the people, catastrophe loomed. Stalin could feel that the country was looking at him, the boss, who so many times had assured the Soviet people together with Voroshilov that the Red Army was capable of destroying any enemy." See Dmitrii Volkogonov, "Triumf i tragediia: Politicheskii portret I. V. Stalina," *Oktiabr'* 7 (1989): 21.

6. Stadniuk, *Voina*, 75.

7. Ibid., 25.

8. Ibid., 26.

9. Ibid., 52.

10. Ibid., 56.

11. Ibid., 57.

12. Ibid., 507.

13. Ibid., 173.

14. Ibid., 175.

15. Ibid., 11.

16. Ibid., 41.

17. Ibid., 454. The Red Army conducted a very detailed study of methods and tactics in Spain and concluded that large armored formations should be broken up. In this regard, see IUrii Rybalkin, *Operatsiia "Kh": Sovetskaia voennaia pomoshch' respublikanskoi Ispanii (1936–1939)* (Moscow: AIRO-XX, 2000).

18. Stadniuk, *Voina*, 172.

19. Aleksandr Nekrich is surely correct when he notes the dire consequences of the TASS bulletin on Red Army morale in such a tense situation: "All Soviet military leaders unanimously confirm that the TASS declaration had a fatal, demoralizing influence on the army." See Nekrich, *1941, 22 iiunia* (1941, 22 June, 1965), izdanie 2-e, dopolnennoe i pererabotannoe (Moscow: Pamiatniki istoricheskoi mysli, 1995), 190. The vigilance of the troops was weakened at a time when maximum alertness was required: "It [the TASS statement] gave rise to the conviction that there were certain, unknown circumstances allowing our government to remain calm and confident in the security of Soviet borders" (ibid.).

20. Stadniuk, *Voina*, 268.

21. Ibid., 269.

22. Ibid., 170.

23. An assessment of Pavlov by one of his officers flatly rejects that offered by Stadniuk: "In Pavlov's operations and acts in the prewar period or in his conduct of difficult defensive operations, I personally see no wrecking, still less treachery. The front experienced failure not because of Pavlov's inefficiency but for a number of reasons, the most important of which were: the numerical superiority of the enemy; the surprise assault of the enemy; the delay in getting down to the start lines; and Kulik's illiterate interference in Boldin's and Golubev's orders, which led to an inglorious end for the front's mobile group." Quoted in Volkogonov, "Triumf i tragediia," 39–40.

24. Stadniuk, *Voina*, 69.

25. A revealing account of the confusion and professional incompetence that dominated Soviet military thinking in the period leading up to the German invasion can be found in General Vadim Matrosov's article published in *Krasnaia zvezda* in June 1991. Matrosov joined the border guards in 1938 and was on duty when the Germans invaded. Acknowledging the factor of surprise that assured the rapid German breakthrough, Matrosov nevertheless questions whether surprise alone could account for the Germans' dramatic successes. His article is important because he cites various reports and operational assessments submitted to Stalin by senior officers and officials, including Beria. Thus, in two interim memoranda (21 April and 20 May 1941) submitted to Stalin and Molotov by Beria, it was noted that between 1 April and up to 19 May 1941, border-guard units had established that 46 German divisions, of which 9 were armored and motorized, and 48 artillery regiments as well as aircraft and other equipment had arrived in the regions contiguous with the western borders of the Soviet Union and stretching from the Baltic Sea to the Black Sea. Further, between 1 January and 10 June 1941, Soviet border guards detained 2,080 people involved in border violations, of whom 183 were identified as German intelligence agents. On this, Matrosov comments that "a number of the incidents involved people who were armed, which led to exchanges of fire." No less aggressive in the pursuit of intelligence data were probes of Soviet airspace by German aircraft. Between October 1940 and 10 June 1941 there were 185 violations of Soviet airspace, 91 alone in the period 1–10 June 1941. And in the report cited by Matrosov, it is pointed out that the flights showed a specific interest in defensive installations. The huge increase in reconnaissance flights in the period 1–10 June 1941, nearly 50 percent of the total recorded since October 1940, should have alerted any competent counterintelligence service to the possibility that *something* was imminent. Consistent with the reasonable interpretation that the big increase in flights in June pointed to something important, German agents had been given a deadline of 20 June 1941 for passing on the latest information. Matrosov rightly draws attention to the response to General Golikov's report to Soviet leaders submitted on 20 March 1941 (Golikov was head of the intelligence directorate of the general staff). Having, according to Matrosov, laid bare the essential plans for Barbarossa, Golikov went on to claim that the evidence should be regarded as "disinformation." Similarly detailed information was reported by N. Kuznetsov (Soviet Navy) and Maslennikov (General Lieutenant I. I. Maslennikov, NKVD), but the conclusion that an invasion or some kind of attack

was imminent was not drawn. Commenting on these multiple intelligence failures by senior figures, above all Stalin, Matrosov makes an important observation: "Our unpreparedness for war, the striving on the part of the country's leadership to push back at any price its start, 'not to succumb to provocation, not to force the situation,' gave rise to a skeptical attitude toward intelligence information not only on the part of Stalin and his entourage but also on the part of the heads of intelligence themselves who, covering themselves, cast doubt upon important intelligence information." Matrosov adds, "Up to the very last moment he [Stalin] considered that Hitler would start a war no sooner than the summer of 1942." Stalin, having convinced himself, or rather hoping, that the Germans would not invade that year, created a situation in which senior intelligence officers told him what he wanted to hear, the high point of self-deception being the TASS communiqué issued on 13 June 1941. We must see this fear of incurring Stalin's wrath as a consequence of the purges. Stalin's persecution of initiative and independence would reap a grim harvest. Compared with Stalin's intelligence services, those of Nazi Germany played a masterful hand. Disinformation went hand in hand with the aggressive pursuit of information in the border areas. The weakness of this article is the failure to deal with the consequences of the purges on military effectiveness. See Vadim Matrosov, "Na pervom rubezhe voiny," *Krasnaia zvezda* (5 June 1991): 3.

26. Stadniuk, *Voina*, 302.

27. Ibid., 288.

28. Ibid., 290–291.

29. Ibid., 305.

30. Ibid., 397.

31. Ivan Stadniuk, *Voina* (Moscow: Voenizdat, 1980), 167.

32. Ibid., 169.

33. "Common sense" seems to have prevailed quite often, in contrast to what we find in other writers. One of several incidents in *War* in which soldiers and officers accused of desertion somehow survive involves General Lukin's brother, a colonel. As the fate of Colonel Lukin is being decided, Stadniuk informs us with breathtaking insouciance that "everyone must be equal before the law" (ibid., 53). The brother is reprieved and dies in battle.

34. Stadniuk, *Voina* (1977), 31.

35. General Lukin's views on the purges are largely uncritical as well: "There were periods of despair when he was mistaken about people, when he found out about the treachery of friends or was subjected to unjust punishments. But he never lost heart, never lost his faith, never weakened his will. And in the final analysis, truth and justice looked him in the face." Stadniuk, *Voina* (1980), 54.

36. Stadniuk, *Voina* (1977), 257.

37. Stadniuk, *Voina* (1980), 128.

38. Ibid., 205.

39. Ibid., 207.

40. Stadniuk, *Voina* (1977), 329.

41. Ibid. During the glasnost period, Stadniuk was attacked by, among others, Viktor Astaf'ev for being an apologist for Stalin. Undeterred, Stadniuk responded with the

publication of *Ispoved' Stalinista: Vospominatel'naia povest'* (The Confession of a Stalinist: A Tale of Recollection) (Moscow: Patriot, 1993).

42. *Ivan* was filmed as *Ivanovo Detstvo* (Ivan's Childhood, 1962) by Andrei Tarkovskii.

43. Vladimir Bogomolov's "V avguste 1944 goda" (In August 1944) was first published in *Novyi mir* 10–12 (1974) and has run to many separate editions. One spin-off is the cult film *Moment istiny* (The Moment of Truth, 2000). See also Bogomolov's short memoir "V Krigere" (In the Meat Wagon), *Novyi mir* 8 (1993): 94–114.

44. See, for example, Don Piper's chapter on Soviet war literature, "The Soviet Union," in Holger Klein, J. E. Flower, and Eric Homberger, eds., *The Second World War in Fiction* (London and Basingstoke: Macmillan Press, 1984), 131–172; and Arnold McMillin, "The Second World War in Official and Unofficial Russian Prose" in Ian Higgins, ed., *The Second World War in Literature* (London and Edinburgh: Scottish Academic Press, 1986), 19–31.

45. For example, Wolfgang Kasack's *Lexicon der Russischen Literatur des 20. Jahrhunderts: Vom Beginn des Jahrhunderts bis zum Ende der Sowjetära* (Munich: Sagner, 1992); and *Reference Guide to Russian Literature* (London: Fitzroy Dearborn Publishers, 1998). Nor do we find any discussion of *In August 1944* in Willi Beitz, ed., *Vom 'Tauwetter' zur Perestroika: Russische Literatur zwischen den fünfziger und neunziger Jahren* (Berlin: Peter Lang, 1994).

46. Of the spy genre in general and *In August 1944* in particular, Hedrick Smith has commented, "By the time the CIA was being roasted for domestic intelligence snooping, *New World* [*Novyi mir*], the most liberal of Soviet monthly magazines, was running an heroic novel about the campaign by SMERSH, the death-to-spies counterintelligence agency, to wipe out nationalist, non-communist Polish partisans fighting the Nazis in 1944. The magazine dedicated the novel: 'To the few to whom very many are indebted.' For something comparable in America, the *New Yorker* would have to run a serial romanticizing Allen Dulles [head of the CIA under President Eisenhower] and Richard Helms [a senior CIA officer]." Hedrick Smith, *The Russians* (London: Sphere Books, 1977), 388. In a recent study of the Russian media, Ivan Zassoursky also notes the cult of the spy: "The spy hero was one of the most recognizable images of the Brezhnev era." See Zassoursky, *Media and Power in Post-Soviet Russia* (Armonk, NY: M. E. Sharpe, 2004), 134.

47. The concept of the *Volksdeutsche* was formulated in National Socialist Germany. It applied to the citizens of foreign states who were of German or related blood, who spoke German, and who without compulsion recognized themselves to be part of the German cultural community. Under the slogan *"Heim ins Reich,"* German propagandists sought to mobilize the loyalty of the *Volksdeutsche* to Germany. See Gerhard Taddey, ed., *Lexicon der Deutschen Geschichte: Personen, Ereignisse, Institutionen. Von der Zeitwende bis zum Ausgang des 2. Weltkrieges* (Stuttgart: Alfred Kröner Verlag, 1979), 1246.

48. Bogomolov, "V avguste 1944 goda," *Novyi Mir* 10, 6–7.

49. Ibid., 6.

50. Some measure of the UPA's success and reflection of its leaders' desire to liberate Ukraine from all occupiers can be seen in its successful policy of assassinating senior officers among the current occupiers. Thus, in May 1943 the UPA assassinated General Victor Lutze, head of the Sicherheitsdienst (SD) in Ukraine during the Nazi

occupation, followed by the assassinations of Marshal Nikolai Vatutin, a well-known Soviet officer, in March 1944 and of the Polish minister of war, General Karol Swierc- zewski, in March 1947. The idea that the UPA was a fascist organization was the stan- dard line adopted by Soviet propagandists throughout the Cold War. It was standard procedure for both Nazi and Soviet propagandists to refer to the UPA as, respectively, *die Banderabewegung* and *Banderovtsy*, the name referring to Stepan Bandera, leader of the Organization of Ukrainian Nationalists. Yuriy Tys-Krokhhmaliuk correctly ar- gues, "The tacit collaboration between German National-Socialism and Russian Communism against the Ukrainians has yet to be properly evaluated in political and military literature. It demonstrates conclusively how dangerous for Moscow Ukrai- nian nationalism was and still is." See Yuriy Tys-Krokhhmaliuk, UPA *Warfare in Ukraine: Strategical, Tactical and Organisational Problems of Ukrainian Resistance in World War II*, trans. by Walter Dushnyck (New York: Society of Veterans of Ukrainian Insur- gent Army, 1972), 239.

51. Ibid., 228.

52. Bogomolov, "V avguste 1944 goda," *Novyi mir* 11, 15.

53. I suspect that something similar happens when the British viewer watches *Das Boot* (The Boat, 1981). Adapted from Lothar-Günther Buchheim's 1973 novel of the same name, the film never really explores the bigger picture, concentrating instead on the ups and downs—no pun intended—of life in a German submarine during the Bat- tle of the Atlantic. Even British audiences tended to identify with the captain and his crew, whose badly damaged submarine makes it safely back to La Rochelle harbor only to be sunk by the Royal Air Force.

54. Bogomolov, "V avguste 1944 goda," *Novyi mir* 11, 22.

55. Ibid.

56. Ibid., 82.

57. Ibid., 84.

58. Bogomolov, "V avguste 1944 goda," *Novyi mir* 12, 195.

59. Ibid., 196.

60. Ibid.

61. Ibid., 210.

62. Bogomolov, "V avguste 1944 goda," *Novyi mir* 11, 34. In the book edition, "intui- tion" has been replaced by "Hitler." See *Moment istiny: V avguste 44 goda* (Moscow: Olma-Press, 2000), 258.

63. In an editorial note accompanying an article by Vadim Matrosov, "Na pervom rubezhe voyny," *Krasnaia zvezda* (5 June 1991): 3, it was noted that the opinions of those border guards who had experienced the German invasion "made it possible to get to the heart of the events of that terrible time and to establish that moment of truth which for us today is so vital."

64. Bogomolov, "V avguste 1944 goda," *Novyi mir* 11, 35. The remarks were made by Churchill when discussing cover plans with Stalin at the Teheran conference: "In war truth must have an escort of lies." See Winston S. Churchill, *The Second World War*, vol. 5, *Closing the Ring* (London: Cassell & Co., 1952), 342.

65. Bogomolov, "V avguste 1944 goda," *Novyi mir* 11, 34.

66. Winston S. Churchill, *The Second World War*, vol. 3, *The Grand Alliance* (London: Cassell & Co., 1950), 316.

67. Pilsudski, who was revered by the Polish officer corps, regarded Russia as the main enemy of Poland. As Jan Ciechanowski points out, "Pilsudski was considered by many Poles, especially soldiers, to be Poland's redeemer, the embodiment of the Polish insurrectionary tradition. The Pilsudski legend rested mainly on his exploits and the services, real and imaginary, which he had rendered to the cause of Polish independence in the years 1914–20. His political ideology was strongly permeated by romanticism, insurrectionary traditions and a belief in the greatness of Poland." See Jan Ciechanowski, *The Warsaw Uprising of 1944* (London: Cambridge University Press, 1974), 73.

68. Bogomolov, "V avguste 1944 goda," *Novyi mir* 10, 83.

69. On Stalin's refusal to renew the offensive against Warsaw after 25 August 1944, which has been interpreted by many as indicating that his motives were sinister, Ciechanowski comments, "It is possible that, preoccupied with his offensive in the Balkans, which had begun on 20 August, he [Stalin] felt unable to pursue the offensive on two fronts. Again his motives for not advancing on Warsaw may well have been more sinister. It is possible, and it is often believed, that Stalin decided to abandon Warsaw to its own fate and thereby avoided a direct confrontation with the London Poles; that he left it to the Germans, his main adversaries, to crush his political opponents." Ciechanowski, *The Warsaw Uprising of 1944*, 251.

70. Bogomolov, "V avguste 1944 goda," *Novyi mir* 10, 48.

71. Ibid.

72. Bogomolov, "V avguste 1944 goda," *Novyi mir* 11, 45.

73. As the Red Army entered Germany, its soldiers were surprised by the much higher standard of living enjoyed by Germans even after five years of war. As Grossman noted in "On the Threshold of War and Peace," an article written in 1945 but not published until 1958 (*Povesti, rasskazy, ocherki* [Moscow: Voenizdat, 1958]), the vastly superior standard of living caused enormous problems for Soviet propagandists who, since Hitler's coming to power, had been painting a picture of material impoverishment and misery in Hitler's Germany. Citing an NKVD report, Antony Beevor notes that the NKVD was thoroughly alarmed by soldiers' talking about the obvious comfort of German civilians and "the politically incorrect conclusions." See Antony Beevor, *Berlin: The Downfall, 1945* (London: Viking, Penguin, 2002), 34.

74. The Katyn question was a running sore in postwar Soviet-Polish relations that was resolved only in the last years of the Soviet Union when Mikhail Gorbachev admitted Soviet responsibility for this dreadful crime. See Wojciech Materski, ed., *KATYN, Documents of Genocide, Documents and Materials from the Soviet Archives Turned over to Poland on October 14th 1992*, with an introduction by Janusz K. Zawodny, trans. by Jan Kolbowski and Mark Canning (Warsaw: Institute of Political Studies, Polish Academy of Sciences, 1993). For further documentation, see *Katyn: Plenniki neob"iavlennoi voiny*, in the series Rossiia. XX VEK, Dokumenty, Mezhdunarodnyi fond, "Demokratiia," Moscow, 1997.

75. For a comprehensive study of Ukrainian attitudes toward Soviet occupation and Sovietization, see Yury Boshyk, ed., with the assistance of Roman Waschuk and Andriy

Wynnyckyj, *Ukraine during World War II: History and Its Aftermath—A Symposium* (Edmonton: Canadian Institute of Ukrainian Studies, University of Alberta, 1986). Numbers of Ukrainian prisoners murdered by the NKVD before fleeing are cited in Orest Subtelny's essay from this book "The Soviet Occupation of Western Ukraine, 1939-1941: An Overview": "Major massacres occurred in the following places: in Lviv (about 1,500 victims), in Sambir (about 1,200), in Stayslaviv (about 2,500), in Zolochiv (about 800), in Chortkiv (about 800), and Dobromyl (about 500). These figures do not include the many small towns and villages where dozens of prisoners died. Thus, an estimated 10,000 prisoners were killed in Galicia. In neighbouring Volhynia, particularly in the towns of Rivne and Lutske, about 5,000 more were executed." Subtelny's source for these figures is the compilation of memoirs of the Soviet occupation edited by Milena Rudnytska, *Zakhidnia Ukraina pid bolshevykamy: IX 1939–VI 1941* (New York: Naukove t-vo im. Shevchenka v Amerytsi, 1958), 465–492.

76. Many of the writers discussed by Arnold McMillin preferred this option. See McMillin, *Belarusian Literature of the Diaspora*, Birmingham Slavonic Monographs, No. 34 (Birmingham: Centre for Russian and East European Studies, The University of Birmingham, 2002).

77. See Tys-Krokhhmaliuk, *UPA Warfare in Ukraine*. Even allowing for the fact that the author has a particular ax to grind, this book provides insights into the armed struggle—the war, in fact—that continued well after the official end of World War II in most of Europe. It was only with the death of General Roman Shukhevych, the UPA commander in chief, that Ukrainian military operations came to a halt. The Ukrainian Insurgent Army began by resisting the Nazi occupation, which it did with great effect. Tys-Krokhhmaliuk describes the UPA thus: "UPA (*Ukrainska Povstanska Armia*), the Ukrainian Insurgent Army, organized in Ukraine in 1942 for the purpose of waging a liberation struggle against Nazi Germany and Communist Russia and for achieving the freedom and independence of Ukraine" (p. 403).

78. Sun Tzu, *The Art of War*, edited and with a foreword by James Clavell (New York: Delacorte Press, 1988), 11.

79. See A. N. IAkovlev et al., eds., *1941 god v 2-knigakh*, in the series Rossiia XX Vek, Dokumenty, Mezhdunarodnyi fond, "Demokratiia," Moscow, 1998. For details of Pavlov's interrogation, see vol. 2, 455–468.

Chapter 5. The Hinge of Fate

1. Churchill resolved to call volume 4 of *The Second World War*, which covers the twelve months beginning in mid-January 1942, *The Hinge of Fate* because "in it we turn from almost uninterrupted disaster to almost unbroken success. For the first six months of this story all went ill; for the last six months everything went well." Winston S. Churchill, *The Second World War*, vol. 4, *The Hinge of Fate* (London: Cassell & Co, 1951), ix.

2. Ibid., 640.

3. Ibid., 638.

4. Such is the fascination with Stalingrad that during the early stages of the Anglo-American invasion of Iraq, some were expressing the opinion (maybe the hope) that

Baghdad would turn out to be a second Stalingrad. See "Letters to the Editor: Battle for Baghdad Is Not a Second Stalingrad," *Daily Telegraph*, 7 April 2003, 21.

5. Vasilii Grossman, "Volga—Stalingrad," in Grossman, *Gody voiny* (Collected Works) (Moscow: Pravda, 1989), 6.

6. AOK 6, Abt Ia. Lagemeldung, 24.09.1942, BA-MA/RH 20-6/213/120.

7. *Bericht über eine Fahrt nach Stalingrad*, 25.09.1942, BA-MA/RH 20-6/213/175.

8. *Dem Herrn Oberbefehlshaber der 6. Armee*, 27.9.1942, BA-MA/RH 20-6/214/89.

9. Ibid., BA-MA/RH 20-6/214/90.

10. Writing of Russian resistance to Napoleon, Clausewitz argues that "the Russians showed us that one often attains one's greatest strength in the heart of one's country, when the enemy's offensive power is exhausted, and the defensive can then switch with enormous energy to the offensive." See Carl von Clausewitz, *On War* (1832), ed. and trans. by Michael Howard and Peter Paret (Princeton, NJ: Princeton University Press, 1989), 220.

11. Quoted in Alexander Werth, *Russia at War 1941–1945* (1964) (London: Pan Books, 1965), 832. Werth speculates that de Gaulle, irritated by Stalin's remarks on the French army's performance in the summer of 1940, may have intended his assessment of the Wehrmacht as a riposte to Stalin.

12. Just how powerful can be seen from a revisionist Russian study of the battle published in 2003. Its author sees Stalingrad not just as a key battle in World War II but as one whose significance goes beyond purely military considerations. Some idea of the author's chiliastic fervor is reflected in the title of the second chapter: "Stalingrad—the Secret Boundary of the Social Evolution of the Nations of Russia, Europe, and All Mankind." See V. V. Pavlov, STALINGRAD: *Mify i real'nost'* (Moscow: Olma-Press, 2003).

13. A comprehensive bibliography of literary and academic works on Stalingrad up to the year 1992, which includes Soviet and Western sources, is K 50-letiiu. *Stalingradskaia bitva (17 iiulia 1942–2 fevralia 1943 g.). Katalog knizhno-illiustrativnoi vystavki* (Moscow: Gosudarstvennaia publichnaia istoricheskaia biblioteka, 1992). A very important publication is the collection of recently declassified NKVD documents in *Stalingradskaia epopeia: Materialy NKVD SSSR i voennoi tsenzury iz Tsentral'nogo arkhiva FSB RF, IA.* (Moscow: F. Pogonii i dr., Zvonnitsa-MG, 2000). See also V. V. Amel'chenko, *Stalingrad: K 60- letiiu srazheniia na Volge* (Moscow: Voenizdat, 2002). A major English-language studies is William Craig's *Enemy at the Gates: The Battle for Stalingrad* (New York: Reader's Digest Press, 1973), which was published during the Cold War. Craig's account has lost nothing in the quarter of a century since it was published. In fact, in some ways it has gained in value, for many of the participants interviewed by Craig are now dead. Craig's template regarding interviews and human interest anticipates Antony Beevor's approach in *Stalingrad* (London: Penguin, 1999). John Erickson's *The Road to Stalingrad* (London: Weidenfeld & Nicolson, 1975 and 1983) and Earl Ziemke's *Stalingrad to Berlin: The German Defeat in the East* (Washington, DC: Army Historical Series, Center of Military History, U.S. Army, 1968) are essential reading, as are the first two volumes in the David M. Glantz and Jonathan M. House trilogy: *The Stalingrad Trilogy*, vol. 1, *To the Gates of Stalingrad: Soviet-German Combat Operations April–August 1942* (Lawrence: University Press of Kansas, 2009) and *The Stalingrad*

Trilogy, vol. 2, Armageddon in Stalingrad, September–November 1942 (Lawrence: University Press of Kansas, 2009).

14. Vasilii Chuikov, Nachalo puti (The Beginning of the Road), izdanie tret'e, ispravlennoe i dopolnennoe (Volgograd: Nizhne-Volzhskoe izdatel'stvo, 1967).

15. A. M. Samsonov, Stalingradskaia bitva (The Battle of Stalingrad), chetvertoe izdanie (Moscow: Nauka, 1989).

16. Vasilii Zaitsev, Za Volgoi zemli dlia nas ne bylo: Zapiski snaipera (Beyond the Volga There Was No Land for Us: Notes of a Sniper) (Moscow: DOSAAF, 1971). The title of Zaitsev's memoir is taken from chapter 5 of General Chuikov's own account of the battle.

17. Less well known, presumably because it deals with the air war over Stalingrad, is Artem Anfinogenov's Mgnovenie—vechnost' (An Instant Is an Eternity), published in Znamia 8 (1982): 3–129 and Znamia 9 (1982): 3–96. For a discussion of this novel, see Lazar' Lazarev, Eto nasha sud'ba: Zametki o literature, posviashchennoi Velikoi Otechestvennoi voine, 2nd ed. (Moscow: Sovetskii pisatel', 1983), 349–358. See also the collection of stories by I. Arsent'ev, "Stalingradskie rasskazy" (The Stalingrad Stories), Znamia 11 (1982): 78–143.

18. Ziemke, Stalingrad to Berlin, 24.

19. Matthew Gallagher, The Soviet History of World War II: Myths, Memoirs and Realities (New York and London: Frederick A. Praeger, 1963), 108.

20. Grossman, "Volga—Stalingrad," 5. With its association with the Volga, the battle is, as far as Grossman is concerned, one of freedom, which is not necessarily how the party saw it.

21. In this respect, note the title of Boris Polevoi's article "Za Volgu-matushku" (For the Volga, Mother River), Pravda, 12 October 1942, 2, and the title of Gennadii Goncharenko's novel Volga—russkaia reka (The Volga Is a Russian River) (Moscow: Moskovskii rabochii, 1970).

22. Pravda, 29 August 1942, 1.

23. Pravda, 30 August 1942, 2.

24. Pravda, 24 August 1942, 3; 25 August 1942, 3; 26 August 1942, 3; and 27 August 1942, 3.

25. Vasilii Grossman, Zhizn' i sud'ba (Life and Fate) (Moscow: Sovetskii pisatel', 1990), 83. Alexander Werth points out that the play completely bypasses the purges and that Rokossovskii and other army officers did not care for it. See Werth, Russia at War 1941–1945, 389–392. More recently, Catherine Merridale treats the play and its author very lightly. See Ivan's War: The Red Army 1939–45, Faber & Faber, London, 2005, 139–140.

26. "1812—Borodinskaia bitva—1942 uroki istorii," Pravda, 7 September 1942, 3.

27. Pravda, 18 October 1942, 1.

28. See, for example, E. Tarle, "Koalitsionnye voiny" (Coalition Wars), Pravda, 9 October 1942, 4.

29. Vasilii Grossman, "Tsaritsyn-Stalingrad," Gody voiny (Moscow: OGIZ, 1946), 220.

30. Pravda, 23 November 1942, 1.

31. As Ziemke has pointed out, the new status of Soviet officers, manifested in the uniforms and other trappings of rank, was a desperate measure from the orthodox

party point of view that stressed a revolutionary tradition, not from that of Suvorov. See Ziemke, *Stalingrad to Berlin*, 35.

32. Nikolai Tikhonov, "Klassicheskii sluchai" (A Classic Episode), *Pravda*, 19 January 1943, 4. To which I add Ziemke's remarks on the subject: "Although the Russians claimed that Stalingrad had supplanted Cannae as the classic encirclement battle, they did not employ the double envelopment as frequently as did the Germans." Ziemke, *Stalingrad to Berlin*, 145.

33. One small but significant sign of which was the lengthy coverage given to the new badges of rank to be introduced in the army. See "Novye znaki razlichiia" (New Badges of Rank), *Pravda*, 19 January 1943, 1–2.

34. Konstantin Simonov, "Dni i nochi," (Days and Nights), *Sobranie sochinenii v shesti tomakh*, vol. 2 (Moscow: Khudozhestvennaia literatura, 1967), 8.

35. Ibid., 19.

36. Ibid., 47.

37. Ibid., 109.

38. Ibid., 110.

39. Ibid., 112–113.

40. Viktor Nekrasov, *V okopakh Stalingrada* (In the Trenches of Stalingrad, 1946), in Nekrasov, *Stalingrad* (Frankfurt-am-Main: Possev-Verlag, 1981), 15.

41. Ibid., 50.

42. Ibid., 265.

43. Ibid., 171.

44. Ibid., 92.

45. Ibid.

46. Ibid., 226. This exchange is inexplicably absent from the English translation, *Front-Line Stalingrad* (1962), trans. David Floyd (Glasgow: FontanaCollins, 1978), 195. In the following exchange, the italicized text is absent from the 1981 Russian-language Possev-Verlag edition: "Is it true that Hitler is only a corporal? That's what the political officer told us.—It's true.—How can that be? To be at the head of everything and only a corporal? *I thought the political officer was lying."* (*Front-Line Stalingrad*, 31). A lengthy passage comparing the merits of various soldiers in the English translation (pp. 49–50) is absent from the Russian edition (pp. 61–62). In a discussion of why France fell to the Germans, it is argued that France was betrayed by all those Petains and Lavals. Igor' says, "We don't have them. That's the main thing" (p. 93). In the English translation we find the interpolation "We finished them off" (p. 78). This interpolation implies that the purges were possibly prophylactic and justified. In the Russian, the delivery of some American barbed wire is noted with "Made in USA" (p. 217). This is absent from the translation (p. 188).

47. Nekrasov, *V okopakh Stalingrada*, 231.

48. Ibid., 289. Don Piper sees no optimism at all: "The novel ends not with a celebration of victory, but with a squalid episode in which men are killed so that absurd orders from above may be fulfilled." See Don Piper, "The Soviet Union," in Holger Klein, J. E. Flower, and Eric Homberger, eds., *The Second World War in Fiction* (London and Basingstoke: Macmillan Press, 1984), 142. I suggest that this assessment is based on a

misreading of Chumak's remarks. The failure to take those 200 yards surely refers to the failure of the Germans who, having come so far, could not dislodge Rodimtsev's guards.

49. Vasilii Grossman, *Za pravoe delo* (For a Just Cause) (Moscow: Sovetskii pisatel', 1989), 520.

50. Ibid., 89.

51. Ibid., 507-508.

52. Ibid., 189.

53. Ibid., 209.

54. In a secret speech given to graduates of the Red Army's academies on 5 May 1941 in the Kremlin, Stalin stressed that the Red Army—the infantry, artillery, and armored formations—had been thoroughly modernized. As far as I am aware, the text of this speech was first published in 1998. See "Vystuplenie general'nogo sekretaria TsK VKP(b) I. V. Stalina pered vypusknikami voennykh akademii RKKA v kremle," ed. by A. N. IAkovlev et al., *1941 god, v 2-knigakh*, in the series Demokratiia, Rossiia. XX VEK, Dokumenty, vol. 2 (Moscow: Mezhdunarodnyi fond, 1998), 158-162.

55. Grossman, *Za pravoe delo*, 383.

56. Ibid., 377.

57. Inside the Kessel rumors circulate concerning Leonard's machinations against fellow officers, which clearly and obviously anticipate what happens to Krymov and Shtrum in *Life and Fate*. Even though the context is Nazi Germany, the nod in the direction of the Soviet Union by Grossman is almost too obvious: "In a whisper they were informed that before the war, on the basis of his denunciation, two officers were arrested. He accused Major Schimmel of covering up the Jewish blood of his father, and regarding another, Hoffman, Leonard claimed to have uncovered a long history of secret links with internationalists who were incarcerated in a camp. It turned out that Hoffman not only corresponded with them but also, with the help of relatives living in Dresden, contrived to send them money from the army and parcels of goods" (ibid., 602). Leonard also appears in *Life and Fate*, where he sees the impending German defeat as an ominous confirmation of Spengler's decline of the West (*zakat evropy*). Grossman's Leonard is almost certainly a reference to the German physicist Philip Eduard Anton Lenard (1862-1947), who won the Nobel Prize for physics in 1905. Lenard was an ardent German nationalist who insisted on the purity of German physics and warned of the dangers of its being contaminated by Jewish influences, especially Einstein.

58. Grossman, *Za pravoe delo*, 381. Other coded attacks on the Soviet state in *Za pravoe delo* would be the report given by one of Shtrum's colleagues about life under German occupation in Czechoslovakia (part 1, chapter 36) and Chepyzhin's and Krymov's thoughts on the nature of Fascism (part 1, chapters 42 and 45, respectively). Moreover, Abarchuk's role in policing the class purity of the student intake before his arrest anticipates the policies excluding Jews from higher education in Nazi Germany (part 1, chapter 28).

59. Ibid., 385.

60. See Hannah Arendt, *Eichmann in Jerusalem. A Report on the Banality of Evil* (London: Faber & Faber, 1963).

61. Grossman, *Za pravoe delo*, 647.

62. Ibid., 358.

63. IUrii Bondarev, "Goriachii sneg" (Hot Snow), *Sobranie sochinenii*, vol. 2 (Moscow: Khudozhestvennaia literatura, 1984), 167.

64. Ibid., 190.

65. Ibid., 244.

66. Ibid., 246–247.

67. Ibid., 380.

68. Ibid.

69. A. IA. Krivitskii, quoted in D. Fel'dman, "Do i posle aresta," *Literaturnaia Rossiia* 45 (11 noiabria 1988): 16.

70. Grossman, *Zhizn' i sud'ba*, 300.

71. Ibid., 301.

72. In *Hot Snow*, a captured German officer gives Bessonov a brutally frank assessment of war that echoes, in part, Liss's remarks to Mostovskoi: "'You consider us to be evil and cruel; we consider you to be from the depths of hell. . . . War is a game that began in childhood. People are cruel from the cradle. Have you really not noticed, Herr General, how the eyes of youths sparkle at the sight of a fire in a city? And at the sight of any disaster? Weak people assert themselves through violence; they feel themselves to be gods when they destroy. This is a paradox, monstrous, but that's as it is. Germans, in killing, bow to the Führer. Russians also kill in the name of Stalin. No one considers that they are doing evil. On the contrary, murdering one another is raised to an act of good. Where, Herr general, shall we seek the truth? Who bears the divine truth? You, a Russian general, also order soldiers to kill. In any war there are none who are right. There is merely the bloody instinct of sadism. Is that not so?'" Bondarev, "Goriachii sneg," 498.

73. Grossman, *Zhizn' i sud'ba*, 299.

74. For a detailed analysis of the crucial differences separating Fascism, National Socialism, and Communism and the propagandistic use of the "fascist" label by communist regimes to discredit opponents, see Richard Pipes, *Property and Freedom* (London: Harvill Press, 1999), 217–225.

75. See *Pravda*, 21, 22, and 24 August 1939.

76. Grossman, *Zhizn' i sud'ba*, 436.

77. Ibid., 160.

78. Ibid., 15.

79. Ibid., 23.

80. Friedrich Hayek, *The Road to Serfdom* (1944) (London: Routledge, 1993), 42.

81. Alain Besançon, *The Falsification of the Good: Soloviev and Orwell*, trans. by Matthew Screech (London: The Claridge Press, 1994). Besançon's analysis concentrates on the work of George Orwell and Vladimir Soloviev and follows a line of argument that at times comes very close to Grossman's in *Life and Fate* and *Forever Flowing*, particularly the testament of Ikonnikov-Morzh.

82. To quote Besançon, "It is a fact that the greatest number of murders happened in areas where the most ambitious historical experiments took place. Both the Communist

NOTES TO PAGES 182-187   325

and Nazi movements tried to eradicate political and social evil once and for all. We can analyze their respective doctrines as a treatise on evil, on its causes, on its whereabouts, on how to reduce it, to get rid of it, and to purify the earth. Yet, during these undertakings, evil was more abundant than ever. What was held to be good and noble was the height of crime and villainy!" Ibid., 8.

83. Arthur Koestler, *Darkness at Noon* (1940) (Middlesex: Penguin, 1987), 127.

84. "[He] is thin, ascetic, a fanatical devotee of logic. He reads Machiavelli, Ignatius of Loyola, Marx, and Hegel: he is cold and unmerciful to mankind, out of a kind of mathematical mercifulness. He is damned always to do what is most repugnant to him: to become a slaughterer, in order to abolish slaughtering, to sacrifice lambs so that no more lambs may be slaughtered, to whip people with knouts so that they may learn not to let themselves be whipped, to strip himself of every scruple in the name of a higher scrupulousness." Ibid., 122.

85. Grossman, *Zhizn' i sud'ba*, 307.

86. Ibid.

87. Quoted in Vitaly Shentalinsky, *The KGB'S Literary Archive* (London: Harvill Press, 1995), 134. For uttering these words, Demidov received a second sentence in the camps in 1946.

88. Grossman, *Zhizn' i sud'ba*, 308.

89. Ibid.

90. Ibid., 72.

91. Ibid., 23. I have not pursued the matter of Grossman's sources here, but there are two likely ones: the *Philokalia*, a collection of texts written by the spiritual masters of the Orthodox Christian tradition between the fourth and fifteenth centuries, or *The Ascetical Homilies of St. Isaac of Nineveh*, sometimes referred to as *The Ascetical Treatises of St. Isaac of Nineveh*.

92. General Sir John Hackett, *The Profession of Arms* (London: Sidgwick and Jackson, 1983), 158.

Chapter 6. NKVD Reports from Stalingrad, 1942–1943

1. The internal continuance of the war can be seen in the manner in which various Soviet generals were treated. See two articles by A. A. Maslov, "Forgiven by Stalin—Soviet Generals Who Returned from German Prisons in 1941-45 and Who Were Rehabilitated," *Journal of Slavic Military Studies* 12, no. 2 (1999): 173-219, and "Tried for Treason Against the Motherland: Soviet Generals Condemned after Release from German Captivity," *Journal of Slavic Military Studies* 13, no. 2 (2000): 86-138.

2. SMERSH (*smert' shpionam*, "death to spies") was formed on the basis of a decree promulgated on 14 April 1943 and confirmed by Stalin on 21 April 1943.

3. IA. F. Pogonii, ed., *Stalingradskaia epopeia: Materialy NKVD SSSR i voennoi tsenzury iz Tsentral'nogo arkhiva FSB RF* (Moscow: Zvonnitsa-MG, 2000) (hereafter *Stalingradskaia epopeia*). The collection is the first in a series of monographs to mark the fify-fifth anniversary of the end of the Great Patriotic War. One of the more significant revelations about Stalingrad that has emerged only very recently concerns the existence of Dulag-205, nominally a transit camp but essentially a death camp, inside the Kessel. From

October 1942 to the end of January 1943, some 3,000 to 4,000 Soviet prisoners perished there from starvation, disease, arbitrary shootings, and beatings. With the onset of winter, cannibalism became widespread. Dulag-205 was overrun by the Red Army on 31 January 1943, and the German officers responsible for running the camp were arrested. Over the next eighteen months, the captured Germans were subjected to lengthy interrogations by SMERSH. In October 1944, a Soviet military tribunal found them all guilty of war crimes, and they were executed. For a detailed discussion of Dulag-205 and the fate of the German officers based on the original interrogation files, see Frank Ellis, "Dulag-205: The German Army's Death Camp for Soviet Prisoners at Stalingrad," *Journal of Slavic Military Studies* 19, no. 1 (March 2006): 123–148.

4. Colonel General Viktor Abakumov (1908–1954) was head of the Directorate of NKVD Special Sections from July 1941 until April 1943. From 1943 to 1946, he was in charge of SMERSH. He was arrested in 1951 and shot in 1954.

5. "Spetssoobshchenie 'o politiko-moral'nom sostoianii boitsov 57 armii IUF po materialam voennoi tsenzury' [ne pozdnee 30] aprelia 1942 g.," *Stalingradskaia epopeia,* 141–147. Over the period of 15–31 July 1942, the postal censors attached to the Stalingrad front processed a total of 190,367 documents, of which 105,372 (55.3 percent) were defined as dealing with family matters, 82,395 (43.3 percent) contained positive reports, and 2,600 (1.4 percent) contained negative reports. The three main categories of negative reports were: comments from family and relatives in connection with being evacuated from areas close to the front line (360), complaints from soldiers' families (909), and details of enemy air raids (1,238). "Iz svodki otdeleniia VTs-15 OO NKVD STF o perliustratsii pisem, napravlennykh na front iz sosednikh oblastei' [ne ranee 1] avgusta 1942 g.," *Stalingradskaia epopeia,* 161–163.

6. "Iz dokladnykh zapisok armeiskikh OO i otdelenii VTs v OO NKVD STF o rabote VTs [ne panee 22 sentiabria] 1942 g.," *Stalingradskaia epopeia,* 216–220.

7. "Sluzhebnaia zapiska 2-go spetsotdela NKVD SSSR v UOO NKVD SSSR s vypiskami iz pisem, konfiskovannykh VTs STF 13 noiabria 1942 g.," *Stalingradskaia epopeia,* 267–268.

8. "Dokladnaia zapiska OO NKVD IUZF v UOO NKVD SSSR o vyskazyvaniiakh otdel'nykh voennosluzhashchikh, 5 iiulia 1942 g.," *Stalingradskaia epopeia,* 148–152.

9. *Stalingradskaia epopeia,* 150–151.

10. Ibid., 151.

11. Ibid., 152.

12. Ibid.

13. Ibid.

14. In the early stages of the war, Soviet officialdom considered imposing the sort of harsh punitive measures on German prisoners of war that were designed for the Red Army. In a report to Mekhlis, it was recommended that German prisoners who waged "agitation hostile to the USSR" in prison camps be liable to "the harsh measures of wartime in connection with Soviet laws," which presumably would render German prisoners liable to the ruthless penalties called for in Order № 227. See "Dokladnaia zapiska sotrudnika politicheskogo upravleniia D. Z. Manuil'skogo zamestiteliu narodnogo komissara oborony L. Z. Mekhlisu o rezhime v lageriakh dlia nemetskikh voennoplennykh

i ikh politicheskikh nastroeniiakh, 15 avgusta 1941," V. A. Zolotarev et al., *Russkii Arkhiv: Velikaia Otechestvennaia. Nemetskie voennoplennye v SSSR: Dokumenty i materialy. 1941–1955 gg.* T 24 (13–2) (Moscow: TERRA, 1999), 71–72.

15. *Stalingradskaia epopeia*, 149.

16. "Dokladnaia zapiska OO NKVD DF v UOO NKVD SSSR o reagirovanii voennosluzhashchikh na perspektivy otkrytiia vtorogo fronta i vzaimootnoshenii s soiuznikami posle voiny 4 fevralia 1943 g.," *Stalingradskaia epopeia*, 395–400.

17. "Dokladnaia zapiska OO NKVD STF v UOO NKVD SSSR 'Ob antisovetskikh i porazhencheskikh vyskazyvaniiakh otdel'nykh voennosluzhashchikh 21-y armii,' 6 avgusta 1942 g.," *Stalingradskaia epopeia*, 166–168.

18. *Stalingradskaia epopeia*, 167.

19. Ibid.

20. For an earlier collection of extracts from Red Army soldiers' letters, see Nadezhda Krylova, "Feldpostbriefe von Rotarmisten—den Verteidigern Stalingrads," in Wolfram Wette and Gerd R. Ueberschär, hrsg., *Stalingrad: Mythos und Wirlichkeit einer Schlacht* (Frankfurt-am-Main: Fischer Taschenbuch Verlag, 1992), 102–106. None of the letters cited by Krylova contain any references to deserters, executions, or anti-Soviet remarks.

21. "Spetssvodka OO NKVD STF v UOO NKVD SSSR 'Ob upadnicheskikh nastroeniiakh voennosluzhashchikh i ikh semei Stalingradskogo fronta' (po materialam VTs) 8 avgusta 1942 g.," *Stalingradskaia epopeia*, 175–179.

22. *Stalingradskaia epopeia*, 176.

23. Ibid.

24. Ibid., 177. In a report to Beria dated 1 April 1943 that analyzed, among other things, the behavior of Soviet citizens living under German occupation in parts of Stalingrad, we find no lack of willingness to assist the Germans: "From the very first days of the occupation, the Germans set about the extermination of those persons of Jewish nationality who had remained in the city and carried out harsh measures against communists, members of the Komsomol, and those suspected of engaging in partisan activity. For the most part, the task of uncovering the Jews was done by German military police and the 'Ukrainian Auxiliary Police.' *No small role was played here by traitors from among the local residents. With the aim of searching out and destroying Jews, all apartments, cellars, trenches, and dugouts were checked.* For the most part, the search for communists and members of the Komsomol was conducted by the Secret Field Police with the active participation and assistance of traitors to the motherland in the service of the Germans" (emphasis added). See "Iz dokladnoi zapiski UNKVD SO v NKVD SSSR 'O polozhenii v gorode Stalingrade v period ego chastichnoi okkupatsii i posle izgnaniia okkupantov 1 aprelia 1943 g.," *Stalingradskaia epopeia*, 417–435.

25. *Stalingradskaia epopeia*, 177.

26. Ibid., 175.

27. See Barbara W. Tuchman, *The March of Folly: From Troy to Vietnam* (1984) (London: Abacus, 1994).

28. See "Soobshchenie UOO NKVD SSSR v GPU RKKA o reagirovanii soldat protivnika na upornoe soprotivlenie sovetskikh voisk pod Stalingradom [ne posdnee 15] avgusta 1942 g.," *Stalingradskaia epopeia*, 46–47.

29. Alan Clark, *Barbarossa: The Russian-German Conflict 1941–1945* (Harmondsworth, Middlesex: Penguin, 1966), 165.

30. Only as recently as 1988 was the full text of Stalin's order first published. See "Prikaz Narodnogo komissara oborony Soiuza SSR, № 227, 28 iiulia 1942 g.," *Voenno-istoricheskii zhurnal* 8 (1988): 73–75. As early as the beginning of October 1942, officers at German army headquarters were drafting plans for the creation of so-called *Alarmeinheiten*, emergency or quick-reaction units. According to the order, "The task of the emergency units/quick reaction units is the inculcation of an aggressive spirit in all those formations which are not immediately involved in combat and the strengthening of the bonds between combat troops and those assisting the combat troops, the temporary relief at the front of deployed units, and the additional deployment in critical periods." OKH Org.Abt., 08.10.1942, *Grundlegender Befehl Nr.1 (Hebung der Gefechtsstärke)*, BA-MA, RH 20–6/220/65. On the basis of this order, 100 *Alarmeinheiten* were formed in the 6th Army, with a combined total of 11,131 officers and men. *Alarmeinheiten der dem AOK. 6 unterstellten Divisionen, Korps-, Armee- und Heerestruppen*, BA-MA, RH 20–6/220/47. Though the tasks of these improvised units differ quite fundamentally from those of the NKVD blocking detachments, their formation reflects a growing sense of emergency in the German army.

31. "Prikaz narkoma oborony SSSR," № 227, 28 iiulia 1942 g., *Stalingradskaia epopeia*, 441–445.

32. *Stalingradskaia epopeia*, p. 443. Though not going as far as Stalin, General Pfeiffer, the commander of Gruppe Pfeiffer, nevertheless expressed very similar fears concerning rumors. Passing on his thoughts on various aspects of command, Pfeiffer goes into some detail concerning the effects of rumors on morale: "The less experience soldiers have of war, then the more widespread is rumor-mongering of all kinds. Such rumors, in most cases untrue, distorted, and exaggerated utterances, are to be opposed with the most determined means. Among the troops, they only serve to cause unease. Every soldier must continually be instructed as to the dangers of such rumor-mongering. Disciplinary and judicial measures are to be taken against soldiers who have demonstrably contravened against this ruling. With this in mind, every soldier is to be taught only to pass on or to report further what he personally has seen or what he has been ordered by his superiors." *Gruppe Pfeiffer Kommandeur*, 03.01.1943, BA-MA, RH 20–6/235/139.

33. *Stalingradskaia epopeia*, 443.

34. Ibid., 445.

35. Ibid. A German officer appreciated the dual significance of the introduction of blocking detachments. In a diary that fell into NKVD hands, he noted. "The Russians are taking ever more measures to prevent desertions and soldiers running away from the battlefield. Therefore they have introduced so-called guard companies that have just one task: to prevent by force of arms the withdrawal of their own units. If things have come to that, then all the conclusions about the demoralization of the Red Army are legitimate. However, at the same time, these facts bear witness to the will to resist to the end and with all means." The date of the report indicates that some barrier detachment operations were taking place before the promulgation of Order № 227. See

"Donesenie OO NKVD IUZF v UOO NKVD SSSR s vypiskami iz dnevnika kapitana ver-makhta," 20 iiunia 1942 g., *Stalingradskaia epopeia*, 26–37. In fact, a proposal to form blocking detachments was made by the commander of the Briansk front, Eremenko, soon after the German invasion. See "Direktiva Stavki VGK № 001650 komman-duiushchemu Brianskim frontom A. I. Eremenko, rasreshaiushchaia sozdanie zagradi-tel'nykh otriadov," 5 sentiabria 1941, *Organy Gosudarstvennoi Bezopasnosti SSSR v Velikoi Otechestvennoi voine. Sbornik dokumentov*, tom vtoroi, kniga 2, Nachalo, 1 sentiabria–31 dekabria 1941 (Moscow: Izdatel'stvo "Rus'," 2000), 20; and "Direktiva Stavki VGK № 001919 komanduiushchim voiskami frontov, armiami, komandiram, divizii, gla-vokomanduiushchemu voiskami IUgo-Zapadnogo napravleniia o sozdanii zagradi-tel'nykh otriadov v strel'kovykh diviziiakh," 12 sentiabria 1941, 85–86.

36. "Soobshchenie OO NKVD STF v UOO NKVD SSSR 'O khode realizatsii prikaza № 227 i reagirovanii na nego lichnogo sostava 4-oi tankovoi armii,' 14 avgusta 1942 g.," *Stalingradskaia epopeia*, 180–182.

37. "Dokladnaia zapiska OO NKVD STF v UOO NKVD SSSR 'O reagirovaniyakh lichnogo sostava chastei i soedinenii na prikaz Stavki № 227' 14/15 avgusta 1942 g.," *Stalingradskaia epopeia*, 183–189.

38. "Spetssoobshchenie OO NKVD STF v UOO NKVD SSSR 'Ob otritsatel'nykh vys-kazyvaniiakh otdel'nykh voennosluzhashchikh Stalingradskogo fronta v sviazi s izda-niem prikaza Stavki № 227' 19 avgusta 1942 g.," *Stalingradskaia epopeia*, 190–192.

39. *Stalingradskaia epopeia*, 180.

40. Ibid., 187.

41. Ibid.

42. Ibid., 188.

43. Ibid., 187.

44. Ibid., 191.

45. Ibid.

46. Ibid.

47. Ibid.

48. Ibid., 182. The subtotals add up to 362; the fate of one soldier remains unexplained.

49. Some idea of the escalation can be seen from a report to Beria dated 23 August 1942. It is noted that "over the period 21–22 August in the region of Stalingrad city, the Directorate of the NKVD and the blocking detachments of the NKVD detained 1,077 persons, who included 14 who had escaped from encirclement, 48 deserters, 754 mili-tary personnel detached from their units, and 20 individuals belonging to criminal ele-ments." See "Donesenie UNKVD SO v NKVD SSSR o polozhenii v Stalingradskoi oblasti, 23 avgusta 1942 g.," *Stalingradskaia epopeia*, 193.

50. "Spravka OO NKVD STF v UOO NKVD SSSR o deiatel'nosti zagraditel'nykh otri-adov Stalingradskogo i Donskogo frontov [ne panee 15 oktiabria] 1942 g.," *Stalingrads-kaia epopeia*, 230–232.

51. *Stalingradskaia epopeia*, 230.

52. Ibid.

53. Ibid.

54. Ibid.

55. Evidence to support the arbitrary nature of battlefield executions comes from an activist's letter. The anonymous activist states that "there are many cases when some soldier or other, completely innocent of any wrongdoing, has been unlawfully tried and shot on the spot." See "Pis'mo 'Aktivista' v OO NKVD STF o nedostatkakh v voinskikh chastiakh fronta," 15 dekabria 1942 g., *Stalingradskaia epopeia*, 379–380. Again, just how easily soldiers innocent of any wrongdoing could be shot was revealed to Andrei Zolotov, the editor of *Russia Profile*, by his grandfather, a war veteran: "There was one other story that he, visibly shaken, told more than once, about a soldier who fell asleep in a dugout that was taken by the Germans, and then taken back by the Soviets. The Germans hadn't noticed him. The Russians, having retaken the position, shot him immediately as a traitor. The unfairness of this seemed to have moved my grandfather more than the horrors he witnessed from the enemy." See Andrei Zolotov, "Editorial," *Russia Profile* 2, no. 3 (April 2005): 1.

56. Having lambasted his men for cowardice, the divisional commander of the 64th Rifle Division, according to Antony Beevor, applied the Roman punishment of decimation: "With pistol drawn, he walked along the front rank counting in a loud voice. He shot every tenth man through the face at point-blank range until his magazine was empty." See Beevor, *Stalingrad* (London: Penguin, 1999), 117. Though Beevor provides no source, these executions are all too believable in the atmosphere of the time. We should also question the motives of commanders in carrying out these executions. Were executions primarily carried out to restore discipline, or were they an insurance policy for the commander, who could show that he had, obeying Stalin's orders, "executed cowards on the spot"?

57. Three thousand eighty British soldiers were condemned to death between 1914 and March 1920; 346 (11.23 percent) were executed. Anthony Babington, *For the Sake of Example: Capital Courts Martial, 1914–1920*, with a postscript by Major-General Frank Richardson (London: Leo Cooper/Secker & Warburg, 1983), 189–190.

58. "Dokladnaia zapiska OO NKVD DF v UOO NKVD SSSR 'O rabote osoborganov po bor'be s trusami i panikerami v chastiakh Donskogo fronta za period s 1 oktiabria 1942 goda po 1 fevralia 1943 goda' 17 fevralia 1943 g.," *Stalingradskaia epopeia*, 403–410.

59. *Stalingradskaia epopeia*, 403. An anonymous activist's letter paints an altogether grimmer picture regarding desertions: "Among those remaining troops in the army from the occupied territories, those in the rear, in the units and hospitals, there is just one thought: As soon as they are sent back to the front line, they will desert to the Germans." In a postscript, the activist adds, "Those deserting to the Germans are Ukrainians, Belorussians, and North Caucasians." *Stalingradskaia epopeia*, 380.

60. Kazakevich provides data on the number of executions for the period October–December 1942 in six different armies: the 21st Army (Southwest front); the 24th, 65th, and 66th armies (Don front); and the 62nd and 64th armies (Stalingrad front). Total executions for each army are: 21st Army (18); 24th Army (14); 65th Army (41); 66th Army (24); 62nd Army (130); 64th Army (32). *Stalingradskaia epopeia*, 404. Kazakevich distinguishes between those executed, usually before their units (*rasstreliano pered stroem*), and those condemned to the *vysshaia mera nakazaniia*—the highest measure of punishment—the death penalty. I have assumed that the penalty was carried out, so I

have added this number to those executed in front of their units, thus giving a higher overall figure for executions than that listed by Kazakevich. The number of executions in the 62nd Army for September is given on 403 of *Stalingradskaia epopeia*.

61. According to Kazakevich, no executions are listed for January 1943 because at the time of compiling the report, the data had not arrived. *Stalingradskaia epopeia*, 405.

62. Beevor, *Stalingrad*, 286.

63. In April 1944, Zhukov, believing he had surrounded the German 1st Panzer Army, demanded that the army surrender. This enthusiast for executions and blocking detachments at Stalingrad and elsewhere in the Red Army threatened to have all captured German officers shot before their troops "for having senselessly spilled the blood of soldiers entrusted to them." See Earl F. Ziemke, *Stalingrad to Berlin: The German Defeat in the East* (Washington, DC: Army Historical Series, Center of Military History, U.S. Army, 1968), 282.

64. "Dokladnaia zapiska OO NKVD DF v UOO NKVD SSSR 'O rabote osoborganov po bor'be s trusami i panikerami v chastiakh Donskogo fronta za period s 1 oktiabria 1942 goda po 1 fevralia 1943 goda' 17 fevralia 1943 g.," *Stalingradskaia epopeia*, 403–410.

65. *Stalingradskaia epopeia*, 409. An earlier report mentions the capture of a German female agent: "In connection with the fact that she was wounded, the situation did not permit an interrogation, and Volodina was shot by our people." See "Donesenie OO NKVD STF v NKVD SSSR o khode boev v Stalingrade', 16 sentiabria 1942 g.," *Stalingradskaia epopeia*, 204–207.

66. *Stalingradskaia epopeia*, 405.

67. Ibid., 406.

68. See "Donesenie OO NKVD STF v NKVD SSSR o khode boev v Stalingrade', 16 sentiabria 1942 g.," *Stalingradskaia epopeia*, 207.

69. Ibid., 214; *Stalingradskaia epopeia*, 213–214.

70. There are a number of references to the presence of an NKVD division during the second week of August 1942 in *For a Just Cause*. Grossman notes, "This powerful division with a full complement of men had no combat experience but was well trained and armed and comprised regular soldiers and commanders." Grossman, *Za pravoe delo* (Moscow: Sovetskii pisatel', 1989), 341. The divisional commander is a Colonel Sytin (his surname implies "well fed" in Russian). Sytin is a fictional name used by Grossman. The division was in fact commanded by a Colonel Saraev. The description of the division as being up to strength and well equipped but lacking combat experience at this stage in the war hints at the NKVD's internal security role rather than a task of fighting the Germans. For a detailed assessment of Saraev's division based on some of the surviving files, see Frank Ellis, "10th Rifle Division of Internal Troops NKVD: Profile and Combat Performance at Stalingrad," *Journal of Slavic Military Studies* 19, no. 3 (September 2006): 601–618.

71. Facsimile of a report to Beria, *Stalingradskaia epopeia*, 229.

72. "Donesenie OO STF v UOO NKVD SSSR ob obstanovke v Stalingrade' 21 sentiabria 1942 g.," *Stalingradskaia epopeia*, 213–214. Between 19 and 20 September, it is noted in the same dispatch, the blocking detachments detained 184 people: 21 were executed (7 for espionage, 5 as traitors to the motherland, 2 for self-mutilation, 6 for spreading panic

and cowardice, and 1 as a deserter) and 40 arrested (detention-to-execution ratio 9:1). Among those arrested was the 62nd Army's deputy chief of artillery, Colonel Beliakov. He was arrested for conducting anti-Soviet agitation and on suspicion of espionage (p. 214).

73. Less sinister, perhaps, but no less bitter than the institutional rivalry between the NKVD and the Red Army was that among the generals vying for the laurels of victory. General Gurov, for example, in what amounted to an attempt to downgrade the role played by Rokossovskii, asserted that only the 62nd and 64th armies had the right to consider themselves the defenders of Stalingrad. Within the 62nd Army itself there was a great deal of antipathy on the part of Chuikov and Gurov toward Rodimtsev, commander of the 13th Guards Division, who, much to the annoyance of Chuikov, was promoted as the savior and defender of Stalingrad. Gurov complained to an informer that "all the glory of Stalingrad has been given to Rodimtsev" (p. 415). Another source stated that "Rodimtsev was a general for the papers; he did nothing" (p. 415). See "Iz soobshcheniia 2-go otdela 3-go UNKVD SSSR v UOO NKVD SSSR ob otritsatel'nykh iavleniiakh v chastiakh Donskogo fronta', 5 marta 1943 g.," *Stalingradskaia epopeia*, 414–415.

74. Chuikov, commander of the 62nd Army, writes John Erickson, "dealt out retribution and punishment in a savage enforcement of Order № 227, with 13,500 men reportedly felled by firing squads." See John Erickson, "Red Army Battlefield Performance, 1941–1945: The System and the Soldier," in Paul Addison, and Angus Calder, eds., *Time to Kill: The Soldier's Experience of War in the West 1939–1945* (London: Pimlico, 1997), 244. Antony Beevor, citing Erickson, uses the same figure with a reference to the Institute of Military History, dated 21 January 1993. See Beevor, *Stalingrad*, xiv and 443. Another statistical discrepancy can be identified in the casualty rate for Rodimtsev's 13th Guards Rifle Division. Beevor states that Rodimtsev's division "suffered 30 percent casualties in the first twenty-four hours" (p. 135). Bearing in mind that the division numbered some 10,000 men, this would have been a total of 3,000 killed and wounded. At that rate of attrition, the division would have ceased to exist within three days. A report to Beria and Abakumov dated 16 September 1942 gives the losses on 15 September 1942 as "400 killed and wounded," a casualty rate of 4 percent. See *Stalingradskaia epopeia*, 204. A later German assessment rates Rodimtsev's division as "good." See Anlage 3 zum Feindnachrichtenblatt "Stalingrad Nr. 9," *Gliederung und Kampfwert der Feindverbände vor 6. Armee. Stand 23.9.1942*. BA-MA, RH 20–6/213/84.

75. On the basis of these documents, this relationship is more honestly portrayed in the works of Viktor Astaf'ev, Grigorii Baklanov, Vasil' Bykov, and Vasilii Grossman than in those of officially approved writers such as Vladimir Bogomolov, Mikhail Bubennov, Mikhail Sholokhov, and Ivan Stadniuk.

76. "Dokladnaia zapiska OO NKVD STF UOO NKVD SSSR 'O reagirovaniiakh voennosluzhashchikh chastei fronta po voprosu uprazdneniia instituta komissarov v Krasnoi armii,' 14 oktiabria 1942 g.," *Stalingradskaia epopeia*, 227–229.

77. "Dokladnaia zapiska OO NKVD STF v UOO NKVD SSSR 'O reagirovaniiakh voennosluzhashchikh chastei Stalingradskogo fronta po voprosu uprazdneniia instituta komissarov v Krasnoi Armii,' 16 oktiabria 1942 g.," *Stalingradskaia epopeia*, 233–235.

78. *Stalingradskaia epopeia*, 227.

79. Ibid.

80. Ibid., 235. Comments by Soviet soldiers on the Non-aggression Pact, Churchill's remarks, and the Anglo-Soviet Treaty underscore the dangers of making any kind of statement on political matters, for today's policy is tomorrow's heresy. This is indicated quite clearly in the preamble to a collation of soldiers' attitudes toward the abolition of the institution of commissars. For example, "The majority of responses to the given question bear a positive character, and service personnel correctly understand the government's decision, brought about by the need to introduce unity of command. However, alongside these positive responses in individual cases, negative responses and cases of incorrect interpretations of the decision have been noted." See *Stalingradskaia epopeia*, 227. On 8 October 1942, the day before the decree was promulgated, the correct stance on the question of commissars and dual command would be that dual command was essential and that the party approved it. A day later, this was rendered incorrect, the correct line now being that unity of command was essential. Exactly the same problem was identified by Viktor Kravchenko. Prior to the signing of the Non-aggression Pact, Germany was the target of ferocious "antifascist" propaganda. Official attitudes and consequences for not adhering to them changed dramatically between 23 August 1939 and 22 June 1941, as Kravchenko notes: "Any whisper against Germany, any word of sympathy for Hitler's victims, was treated as a new species of counter-revolution. The French, British, Norwegian 'warmongers' were getting their deserts." See Viktor Kravchenko, *I Chose Freedom: The Personal and Political Life of a Soviet Official* (1946), with a new introduction by Rett R. Ludwikowski (New Brunswick and Oxford: Transaction Publishers, 1989), 335.

81. "Dokladnaia zapiska OO NKVD DF v UOO NKVD SSSR 'O reagirovaniiakh lichnogo sostava Donskogo fronta na Ukaz Prezidiuma Verkhovnogo Soveta ob uprazdnenii instituta komissarov i na prikaz NKO № 307,' 17 oktiabria 1942 g.," *Stalingradskaia epopeia*, 237–239.

82. *Stalingradskaia epopeia*, 239.

83. Ibid.

84. Essential reading is John Erickson's *The Soviet High Command: A Military-Political History, 1918–1941* (London: Macmillan Press, 1962).

85. Carl von Clausewitz, *On War* (1832), ed. and trans. by Michael Howard and Peter Paret (Princeton, NJ: Princeton University Press, 1989), 186.

86. T. E. Lawrence, *Seven Pillars of Wisdom: A Triumph* (1935) (Harmondsworth, Middlesex: Penguin, 1988), 523.

87. The Soviet generals' bleak assessment of their own infantry was shared by the German 6th Army: "His infantry is not up to much," whereas "his armored units show much activity and offensive spirit." *Beurteilung der Lage 6. Armee 7.12.42 vormittags*. BA-MA, RH 20-6/237/113.

88. "Dokladnaia zapiska OO NKVD DF v UOO NKVD SSSR o nastupatel'nykh operatsiiakh 66-i armii,' 30 oktiabria 1942 g.," *Stalingradskaia epopeia*, 251–260. Interestingly, we find the same thoughts expressed by a German soldier in a letter that fell into NKVD hands: "If one thinks about how many of my comrades have been killed who

began their military careers with me in 1939, you are horrified. It is a pity that such valuable human beings perish and the weak and ill survive. What will become of our people!" See "Donesenie OO NKVD STF v UOO NKVD SSSR s vyderzhkami iz pisem nemetskikh soldat i ikh rodnykh', 16 avgusta 1942 g.," *Stalingradskaia epopeia*, 53–56.

89. *Stalingradskaia epopeia*, 253.

90. Ibid., 252.

91. Robert Conquest, *The Great Terror: A Reassessment* (London: Hutchinson, 1990), 429.

92. *Stalingradskaia epopeia*, 253.

93. Ibid., 259. This outcome makes a mockery of an article published in *Pravda* at the start of the battle, "Zabota ob invalidakh otechestvennoi voiny" (Concern for the Invalids of the Patriotic War), 14 September 1942, 1.

94. Soviet casualties at Stalingrad, killed and wounded in both defensive and offensive phases of the battle, were 643,842 and 485,777, respectively, a total of 1,129,619. Colonel General G. F. Krivosheev, ed., *Grif sekretnosti sniat: Poteri Vooruzhennykh sil SSSR v voinakh, boevykh deistviakh i voennykh konfliktakh* (Moscow: Voennoe izdatel'stvo, 1993), 179–182. Published in English as *Soviet Casualties and Combat Losses in the Twentieth Century*, trans. by Christine Barnard (London: Greenhill Books and Mechanicsburg, PA: Stackpole Books, 1997).

95. Clausewitz, *On War*, 231.

96. Isaak Kobylyanskiy argues that patriotism and the interethnic solidarity of the various Soviet nationalities were two important factors in the Soviet victory. Regarding the solidarity of the interethnic groups, he is emphatic. There was, he insists, an "utter absence of interethnic friction among our troops." See "Memories of War, Part 3," *Journal of Slavic Military Studies* 17, no. 2 (2004): 344. A clear distinction needs to be made between purely Russian patriotism, which Grossman sees as the most decisive factor at Stalingrad (and later), and Soviet internationalism, which Kobylyanskiy cites. For example, the apparent ease with which the Germans were able to raise battalions of troops made up of non-Russians and the general scale of disaffection from Soviet power does not offer unqualified support for Kobylyanskiy's view. Nor, indeed, does Stalin's attitude and behavior toward non-Russians. In *Life and Fate*, Grossman offers a far bleaker picture of interethnic relations than Kobylyanskiy, and one that is consistent with the Germans' ability to recruit Soviet citizens of numerous nationalities, especially Slavs, and of course with the whole complex of issues associated with Vlasov. Getmanov, a commissar, bemoans what he regards as the privileged treatment of non-Russian ethnic minorities at the expense of Russians: "Why would we want to set up a synagogue or some chapel in a tank corps? We're all defending Russia. . . . I'll tell you straight, we've had enough of this. Makes you puke! We're always sacrificing Russians in the name of the friendship of nations. These national minorities are barely literate, and we promote them to people's commissars. While our Ivan, even if he's a genius, has to make way for the national minorities! The great Russian people are being turned into some kind of national minority. I'm for the friendship of nations, but not that sort. Enough is enough!" See Grossman, *Zhizn' i sud'ba* (Life and Fate) (Moscow: Sovetskii pisatel', 1990), 164. Again, after Soviet troops have recaptured territory from the Germans, Getmanov's thoughts on Kalmyks suggest deep divisions: "Like day and night—

he said—Russians and Kalmyks. The Kalmyks danced to the Germans' tune. They gave them green uniforms. They wandered round the steppes rounding up our Russians. And just look at what Soviet power gave them! They were just a country of nomads in rags, riddled with syphilis and totally illiterate. There you are, no matter what you feed a wolf, he still looks at the steppe. And during the Civil War, they were practically on the side of the Whites. . . . And how much money has been spent over the decades, on this friendship of nations?" (540).

97. Grossman, *Gody voiny* (Moscow: Pravda, 1989), 368.

98. Ibid., 325–326.

99. Ibid., 354. The soldier Ignat'ev noted in Grossman's diaries may well have inspired the soldier of the same name in *The People Are Immortal*. Grossman almost certainly alludes to Order № 270 in *The People Are Immortal*. For a discussion, see my review essay of Antony Beevor and Luba Vinogradova, ed. and trans., *A Writer at War: Vasiliy Grossman with the Red Army 1941–1945* (London: Harvill Press, 2005), in *Journal of Slavic Military Studies* 20, no. 1 (March 2007): 137–146.

100. Grossman, *Zhizn' i sud'ba*, 295.

101. Order № 270 is, argues Volkogonov, an "example of Stalin's personal, administrative 'creativity'" (p. 44), an order of "despair and cruelty" (p. 45). He notes that Stalin added the names of others, some of whom were not there. See Dmitrii Volkogonov, "Triumf i tragediia: Politicheskii portret I. V. Stalina," *Oktiabr'* 7 (1989): 12–78. Like Order № 227, the full text of Order № 270 was first published in 1988. See "Prikaz Stavki verkhovnogo glavnogo komandovaniia Krasnoi armii,' № 270, 16 avgusta 1941 goda," *Voenno-istoricheskii zhurnal* 9 (1988): 26–28.

102. Grossman, *Za pravoe delo*, 328. Major Berezkin's thoughts on the nature of cowardice are, I suggest, an indirect criticism of Order № 227: "What exactly bravery and cowardice are he was not entirely certain. Once, at the start of the war, Berezkin's superiors had torn him off a strip for his timidity: On his own initiative he had withdrawn his regiment from out of German fire" (*Zhizn' i sud'ba*, 49). Earlier he speculates that timidity and cowardice are something like a cold, something that can be cured.

103. *Novyi mir* 8 (1952): 121.

104. Grossman, *Zhizn' i sud'ba*, 500.

105. The following passage in the journal (chapter 1, part 3), which is flattering of NKVD performance, is omitted from the book edition: "The great weight of the German assault was taken on itself by the NKVD division; one after another its regiments joined the bloody, exhausting battles, first on the northern outskirts of the city and then on the western approach." *Novyi mir* 9 (1952): 63.

106. A recently published collection of press articles and official statements covering the defensive and the offensive phase of the battle creates a very one-dimensional view of the battle. See V. A. Zhilin et al., eds., *Stalingradskaia bitva: Khronika, Fakty, Liudi*, vols. 1 and 2 (Moscow: Olma-Press, 2002).

107. See Hew Strachan, "The Soldier's Experience in Two World Wars: Some Historiographical Comparisons," in Addison and Calder, eds., *Time to Kill*, 369–378. For a counterview, one can cite General Sir John Hackett: "The value of coercion on the battlefield has always seemed to me rather doubtful. Could Alexander really have taken an army

from Africa to the Indus under the whip alone? I doubt it. Was the brutal rigour of Frederick the Great's discipline the only or even the chief secret of his success at Rossbach und Leuthen? Or were the bloody backs of British Redcoats in the eighteenth century the real cause of their performance, say, at Minden? I doubt this." *The Profession of Arms* (London: Sidgwick and Jackson, 1983), 223. General Troshev, one of the senior Russian commanders during both Chechen wars, tends to support Hackett: "At times only by means of their personal example did commanders manage to get the troops to attack. In war there are moments when, confronted with fear, even the harshest orders and threats of tribunals are powerless." See Gennadii Troshev, *Moia voina: Chechenskii dnevnik okopnogo generala* (2001) (Moscow: Vagrius, 2004), 53.

108. This is the view of Major General Zolotarev's team. Readily acknowledging the harsh nature of Order № 227, they argue that "the order played a big role in raising the resilience and military activity and in creating a turning point in the course of military operations." See *Russkii Arkhiv: Velikaia Otechestvennaia*, vol. 17, no. 6, *Glavnye politicheskie organy vooruzhennykh sil SSSR v Velikoi Otechestvennoi voine 1941–1945* (Moscow: TERRA, 1996), 330.

Chapter 7. The Russian War Novel of the 1990s

1. "Voiny u nikh v pamiati netu, Voina u nikh tol'ko v krovi," *Znamia* 5 (1995): 183–199. Those who responded were Petr Aleshkovskii, Tat'iana Bek, IUrii Buida, Mikhail Butov, Petr Vail', Svetlana Vasilenko, Tat'iana Vol'tskaia, Andrei Dmitriev, Denis Dragunskii, Aleksandr Kabakov, Bakhyt Kenzheev, Nikolai Klimontovich, Oleg Pavlov, Viktor Pelevin, Lev Rubinshtein, Ol'ga Sedakova, Aleksandr Terekhov, and Bella Ulanovskaia.

2. "Literatura i voina," *Znamia* 5 (2000): 3–13. Those who responded were Vladimir Berezin, Vasil' Bykov, Georgii Vladimov, Andrei Volos, Aleksandr Kabakov, Mikhail Kuraev, Viktor Sosnora, and Anton Utkin.

3. "Voiny u nikh v pamiati netu," 185.

4. "Literatura i voina," 4

5. Ibid., 11.

6. Ibid., 6.

7. Viktor Kravchenko, *I Chose Freedom: The Personal and Political Life of a Soviet Official* (1946), with a new introduction by Rett R. Ludwikowski (New Brunswick and Oxford: Transaction Publishers, 1989), 402. Solzhenitsyn supports Kravchenko: "The truly historic and universal feat of the Russian people in World War II (and dreadful as it is to ask, will this be the last one in Russia's history?) is one of the enigmas of the Russian character. For millions of people were lacerated by the repressions, lived in a condition of unremitting depression, and were afraid to express their opinion. Indeed, almost half of the population at that time remembered the good life before the revolution and were only too aware of the socialist time of scarcity that came in its place. What was it that attracted the mass of the people to give their lives for such a callous, harsh existence? (Many *zeks* even from the camps applied to get posted to frontline service.) Here, of course, sheer, harsh coercion exerted some effect (one involuntarily ponders Konstantin Leont'ev's assessment that the dignity of our people is won at the price of their

oppressed condition). Here that innate Russian patriotism, still not completely crushed, manifested itself to an enormous degree, but also there is that psychological craving to stand tall even for a brief moment and feel that one is a human being, strong, even heroic, to pass through some deadly battle, which gave one some illusion of freedom." Alexander Solzhenitsyn, *Rossiia v obvale* (Moscow: Russkii put', 1998), 136.

8. Nor is apocalypticism confined to war literature. *The Twelve, We, The Foundation Pit, The Master and Margarita,* and *Doktor Zhivago* are some of the better-known works in Russian literature that exploit elements of the *strashnyi sud,* or Day of Judgment. Film has been highly successful in adapting and blending the apocalyptic and war, obvious contenders being *Cross of Iron* (1977); *Apocalypse Now* (1979); *The Keep* (1983); *Thin Red Line* (1998); *Saving Private Ryan* (1998); and Soviet Russian films such as *Kommisar* (The Commissar, 1967), *Voskhozhdenie* (The Ascent, 1977), *Idi i smotri* (Come and See, 1985), and *Znak bedy* (The Sign of Disaster, 1986). The title *Come and See* is taken directly from Revelation 6, which relates to the opening of the seals and the appearance of the four horsemen of the Apocalypse. As each rider and horse parades before us, we are invited to "come and see" (idi i smotri). For a discussion of the apocalypse theme in Soviet cinema, see Anna Lawton, *Kinoglasnost: Soviet Cinema in Our Time* (Cambridge: Cambridge University Press, 1992), 225–229. For a detailed discussion of the war in Soviet and Russian film, see David Gillespie, *Russian Cinema* (Harlow: Pearson Education Limited, 2003), 124–145.

9. In a footnote to "Golgotha," Sassoon writes, "Written in trenches. The weather beastly wet and the place was like the end of the world." *The War Poems of Siegfried Sassoon* (London: Faber and Faber, 1983), 24.

10. J. F. Hendry, ed., *The New Apocalypse: An Anthology of Criticism, Poems and Stories* (London: The Fortune Press, 1940), 9. A second anthology, J. F. Hendry and Henry Treece, eds., *The White Horseman: Prose and Verse of the New Apocalypse* (London: Routledge, 1941), contains essays explaining the essence of the New Apocalypse: G. S. Fraser, "Apocalypse in Poetry," 3–31; Robert Melville, "Apocalypse in Painting," 135–152; and J. F. Hendry, "Myth and Social Integration," 153–179.

11. See, for example, the early Kievan chronicles in which battles between Russians and Mongols are portrayed as a Russian holy war against nomadic infidels. After the Mongol conquest, this view was no longer tenable, and the Russian chroniclers resorted to what Charles Halperin has called the "ideology of silence." See Charles Halperin, *Russia and the Golden Horde* (Bloomington: Indiana University Press, 1985), 8.

12. For a comprehensive bibliography of Astaf'ev's work, see *Viktor Petrovich Astaf'ev, Zhizn' i Tvorchestvo, Bibliograficheskii ukazatel' proizvedenii pisatelia na russkom i insostrannykh iazykakh,* red. T. Briskman (Moscow: Rossiiskaia gosudarstvennaia biblioteka, 1999).

13. Viktor Astaf'ev, *Prokliaty i ubity* (The Damned and the Dead) (Moscow: Veche, 1994), 12. In the afterword, Astaf'ev laments the fact that contemporary Russians seem to have forgotten everything and "cursed everything holy on earth" (368).

14. On this point, Semen Lipkin records a conversation with Grossman, who argued that the war "would wipe away the Stalinist filth from Russia's face. The holy blood spilled in the war would remove the blood of the innocently dispossessed peasants and of the blood of 1937." Semen Lipkin, *Stalingrad Vasiliia Grossmana* (Ann Arbor, MI: Ardis Publishers, 1986), 15.

15. In an interview given in 1994, Astaf'ev indicated that he was planning a third part to *The Damned and the Dead* under the provisional title *Boliat starye rany* (The Old Wounds Hurt). T. M. Vakhitova, "Narod na voine: Vzgliad V. Astaf'eva iz serediny 90-kh. Roman 'Prokliaty i ubity,'" *Russkaia literatura* 3 (1995): 128.

16. "The most terrible thing were the machine guns, the portable, rapid-firing, 500-round, belt-fed MGs. The guns had been registered well before, and now, as if from the narrow neck of a fire pump, hosed the bank, island, and river with its seething mass of people. The old and the young, the conscious and the unconscious, the volunteers and those called up by the enlistment office, those in penal units, the guardsmen, the Russians and non-Russians—all screamed the same words: "Mother!" "God!" and "Help!" And the machine guns fired and fired, pouring out their multicolored streams. Holding on to one another, the wounded and those untouched by the bullets and shell splinters went under the water in bunches, and the river erupted in mountains of bubbles and red foam." Viktor Astaf'ev, "Prokliaty i ubity," *Novyi mir* 10 (1994): 101.

17. Viktor Astaf'ev, "Prokliaty i ubity," *Novyi mir* 10 (1992): 72.

18. Ibid., 60.

19. James Clavell, *King Rat* (1962), 8th ed. (London: Coronet, 1980), 8.

20. Astaf'ev, "Prokliaty i ubity," *Novyi mir* 10 (1992): 70.

21. Viktor Astaf'ev, "Prokliaty i ubity," *Novyi mir* 12 (1992): 238.

22. The phenomenon of the "goner" has also been observed and commented on by survivors of Nazi camps. See, for example, Bruno Bettelheim, *The Informed Heart: The Human Condition in Mass Society* (London: Paladin, 1970); and Viktor Frankl, *Man's Search for Meaning*, revised and updated (New York: Washington Square Press, 1985). First published in German as *Ein Psycholog erlebt das Konzentrationslager* (1946), Frankl's book became the basis of logotherapy. Even in the camps, men could find a meaning in their suffering and thus survive: "Any attempt to restore a man's inner strength in the camp had first to succeed in showing him some future goal. . . . Woe to him who saw no more sense in his life, no aim, no purpose, and therefore no point in carrying on. He was soon lost" (97–98).

23. Astaf'ev, "Prokliaty i ubity," *Novyi mir* 10 (1992): 84.

24. Ibid., 88.

25. Ibid. Vaskonian, as the storyteller, suggests Platonov in "The Snake Charmer" in Varlam Shalamov's *Kolyma Tales* (Harmondsworth, Middlesex: Penguin, 1994).

26. Astaf'ev, "Prokliaty i ubity," *Novyi mir* 12 (1992): 199.

27. Ibid., 191.

28. Ibid., 199.

29. Astaf'ev, "Prokliaty i ubity," *Novyi mir* 12 (1994): 75.

30. Vakhitova, "Narod na voine," 124.

31. V. Zelenkov, "Komu voina, a komu mat' rodna. Podzagolovok k 'Knigam pamiati'? Zametki frontovika o romane V. Astaf'eva 'Prokliaty i ubity,'" *Nash sovremennik* 9 (1997): 72–73.

32. Ibid., 73.

33. Ibid., 80.

34. Ibid., 82. For another hostile article in the same journal, see Kseniia Mialo, "Mertvykh Prokliat'ia," *Nash sovremennik* 6 (1995): 186–192. For a generally favorable assessment of *The Damned and the Dead*, see Ivan Esaulov, "Sataninskie zvezdy i sviashchennaia voina. Sovremennyi roman v kontekste russkoi dukhovnoi traditsii," *Novyy mir* 4 (1994): 224–239; and Igor' Dedkov, "Ob"iavlenie viny i naznachenie kazni," *Druzhba narodov* 10 (1993): 185–202.

35. This summary is based on Robert Crummey, *The Old Believers and the World of Antichrist: The Vyg Community and the Russian State 1694–1855* (Madison and London: University of Wisconsin Press, 1970).

36. To quote Crummey, "For Old Belief, after 1667, was an indistinguishable blend of opposition to the liturgical reforms, foreign cultural influence, bureaucratic centralism, and social injustice. Antichrist was the symbol of all that was new and oppressive on Muscovite society. His power had to be resisted." Ibid., 16.

37. Ibid., 14.

38. Vitaly Shentalinsky, *The KGB's Literary Archive*, trans. by John Crowfoot (London: Harvill Press, 1995), 208.

39. Quoted in ibid., 200.

40. The *popovtsy* are described as the "collective name of Old Believers who accepted the priesthood, in distinction to the *bespopovtsy*." See S. G. Vurgaft and I. A. Ushakov, *Staroobriadchestvo: Litsa, sobytiia, predmety, simvoly: Opyt entsiklopedicheskogo slovaria* (Moscow: Tserkov, 1996), 230.

41. Astaf'ev, "Prokliaty i ubity," *Novyi mir* 10 (1994): 67.

42. Ibid., 102. Italicized text in this quotation was cut from the edition of *The Damned and the Dead* published by the Moscow-based publishing house Eksmo to mark the sixty-fifth anniversary of the end of the war. See Viktor Astaf'ev, *Prokliaty i ubity* (Moscow: Eksmo, 2010), 393. Other changes can also be noted in this 2010 publication, most of which, essentially supplements to existing plot lines and character development, occur in book 2, "The Beachhead." I can only assume that the initiative for these changes originated with Astaf'ev's wish to add to the first edition of the novel, which was serialized in *Novyi mir* (1992–1994).

43. Astaf'ev, "Prokliaty i ubity," *Novyi mir* 10 (1992): 96.

44. Viktor Astaf'ev, "Prokliaty i ubity," *Novyi mir* 11 (1992): 195.

45. Ibid., 195.

46. D. H. Lawrence, *Apocalypse* (1931) (London: Heinemann, 1972), 77.

47. Astaf'ev, "Prokliaty i ubity," *Novyi mir* 12 (1992): 205.

48. Ibid., 205.

49. Ibid.

50. Ibid., 206.

51. Ibid.

52. Quoted in Shentalinsky, *The KGB's Literary Archive*, 201.

53. Astaf'ev, "Prokliaty i ubity," *Novyi mir* 11 (1992): 196.

54. Astaf'ev, "Prokliaty i ubity," *Novyi mir* 10 (1992): 88.

55. Ibid., 75.

56. Astaf'ev, "Prokliaty i ubity," *Novyi mir* 12 (1992): 206. It should be noted that Osipov was the family name of Stakhii Osipov, an agent of the Vyg Old Believer community. See Crummey, *The Old Believers and the Antichrist*, 163.

57. Viktor Astaf'ev, "Pastukh i Pastushkha" (The Shepherd and the Shepherdess) in *Prokliaty i ubity* (Moscow: Veche, 1994), 500.

58. Astaf'ev, "Prokliaty i ubity," *Novyi mir* 10 (1992): 92. Astaf'ev uses adjectives of light in specific ways. Thus, *svetlyi*, as in "radiant future" (*svetloe budushchee*), implies something secular (*svetskii*), that is, the false promises of paradise on earth, whereas *presvetlyi* ("divine," "saintly," "heavenly," as used in this extract) refers to God's world to come.

59. Bernard McGinn, "The End of the World and the Beginning of Christendom," in Malcolm Bull, ed., *Apocalypse Theory and the Ends of the World* (Oxford: Blackwell, 1995), 60.

60. Vakhitova, "Narod na voine," 129.

61. Ibid., 128.

62. Ibid.

63. See Alan Morris, "Attacks on the Gaullist 'Myth' in French Literature since 1969," in Ian Higgins, ed., *The Second World War in Literature* (London and Edinburgh: Scottish Academic Press, 1986), 76.

64. France raised the Legion Volontaire Française, which served under the control of the SS. Similar national SS legions were raised in other German-occupied states. See chapter 6, "The Foreign Legions," in John Keegan, *Waffen SS: The Asphalt Soldiers*, Purnell's History of the Second World War, book 16 (London: Macdonald and Co., 1970). Guy Sajer, of Franco-German birth, served in the German army on the Russian front. He went on to write a best seller, *Le Soldat Oublié* (The Forgotten Soldier) (London: Orion, 1967).

65. For a Russian perspective on the question of collaboration, see M. I. Semipriaga, *Kollaboratsionizm: Priroda, Tipologiia i Proiavleniia v gody vtoroi mirovoi voiny* (Moscow: ROSSPEN, 2000).

66. Chapters of the novel were first published in *Grani* and *Kontinent*. The full version was first published in Russia in *Znamia* 4–5 (1994). See also Georgii Vladimov, *General i ego armiia* (The General and His Army) (Moscow: Knizhnaia palata, 1997); and *Sobranie sochinenii v 4 tomakh* (Collected Works in Four Volumes) (Moscow: AOZT, NFQ/2Print, 1998). All quotations are from the Knizhnaia palata edition.

67. Catherine Andreyev, *Vlasov and The Russian Liberation Movement: Soviet Reality and Émigré Theories* (London: Cambridge University Press, 1987), 2. Only in January 1945 did the Nazis allow two divisions to be formed. Divisions known as Vooruzhennye Sily Komiteta Osvobozhdeniia Narodov Rossii (VS KONR) are often referred to as the ROA. For further discussion, see Catherine Andreyev's article "General Vlasov i Russkoe Osvoboditel'noe Dvizhenie," *Druzhba narodov* 5 (1991): 170–205.

68. Andreyev, *Vlasov and The Russian Liberation Movement*, 3. One of the first Soviet units to surrender to the Germans was the 436th Infantry Regiment commanded by Major Ivan Kononov on 22 August 1941. See Nikolai Tolstoy, *Victims of Yalta* (London: Hodder and Stoughton, 1978), 40. This book records the fate of forcibly repatriated Soviet soldiers at the end of World War II. See also its chapter 12, "The End of General Vlasov."

69. Viktor Nekrasov, *Stalingrad* (Frankfurt-am-Main: Possev-Verlag, 1981), 447.

70. Vasilii Grossman, *Zhizn' i sud'ba* (Life and Fate) (Moscow: Sovetskii pisatel', 1990), 240.

71. Alexander Solzhenitsyn, *The Gulag Archipelago 1918–1956: An Experiment in Literary Investigation*, vol. 1, trans. by Thomas Witney (New York: HarperCollins, 1991), 253. Kobrisov holds the same view: "Well, he had heard of the factor of surprise, which gave the Germans a temporary advantage, but the greatest surprise was the fact that the greatest military leader of all time and of all the peoples proved to be a half-educated fool and a deserter who for eleven days was absent from his post as commander. How after that could he blame those who removed their badges of rank and tore up documents? Or those who had raised their hands in surrender and then escaped from captivity and made it back to their own side?" Vladimov, *General i ego armiia*, 295.

72. Solzhenitsyn's refusal to come to the aid of a Russian soldier who is being senselessly beaten and tortured by an NKVD sergeant is something he recalls with shame: "This picture will remain etched in my mind forever. This, after all, is almost a symbol of the Archipelago." *The Gulag Archipelago*, vol. 1, 257.

73. Solzhenitsyn returns to the Vlasov theme in *The Russian Question at the End of the Twentieth Century* (London: Harvill Press, 1995): "It is characteristic that even in the very last months (winter 1944–45), when it was clear to all that Hitler had lost the war, Russians who found themselves abroad sought by tens and tens of thousands to join the Russian Liberation Army!—here at last was the voice of the Russian people. . . . General Vlasov is accused of not shrinking, in pursuit of Russian interests, from entering into an ostensible union with an external enemy of the state" (85).

74. Vladimov, *General i ego armiia*, 3.

75. Kobrisov appears to be based, at least in part, on the Soviet general Nikandr Chibisov. Born a Cossack, he served in the tsarist army, eventually joining the Red Army.

76. Aleksandr Solzhenitsyn, *August 1914: The Red Wheel 1: A Narrative in Discrete Periods of Time*, trans. by H. T. Willets (Harmondsworth, Middlesex: Penguin, 1990), p. 100.

77. Vladimov, *General i ego armiia*, 180.

78. Solzhenitsyn, *The Gulag Archipelago*, vol. 1, 256.

79. Vladimov, *General i ego armiia*, 195–196. Figures for those executed in the purges of the Soviet military cited in Stéphane Courtois et al., *The Black Book of Communism: Crimes, Terror, Repression*, trans. by Jonathan Murphy and Mark Kramer (London: Harvard University Press, 1999), are as follows: 3 out of 5 marshals; 13 out of 15 army generals; 8 out of 9 admirals; 50 out of 57 corps generals; 154 out of 186 division generals; 16 out of 16 army commissars; and 25 out of 28 corps commissars (198). "From May 1937 to September 1938, 35,020 officers were arrested or expelled from the army. It is still unclear how many were executed" (198).

80. On 24 September 1943, the 1st, 3rd, and 5th Parachute Regiments were dropped some 25 miles behind the German lines. The airborne assault was not properly coordinated with the 3rd Guards and 40th Armies' offensive. In addition, a lack of boldness on the part of the airborne troops meant that they were rounded up piecemeal. See Philip Ste. Croix, ed., *Airborne Operations: An Illustrated Encyclopedia of the Great Battles of Airborne Forces* (London: Salamander Books, 1978), 158.

81. Solzhenitsyn, *August 1914*, 302. Note too "that intuition shone brightly in the actions of the wayward François, who was probably ignorant of Tolstoy's advice that it makes no sense to stand in the way of people concentrating their whole energy on flight" (310).

82. Vladimov, *General i ego armiia*, 81.

83. Ibid., 198.

84. Ibid.

85. Ibid., 96.

86. Ibid., 299.

87. Ibid., 301.

88. Ibid., 263.

89. Ibid., 21.

90. Ibid., 200.

91. Ibid., 201.

92. Ibid., 202.

93. Ibid., 207.

94. Ibid., 282.

95. Ibid., 273.

96. Vlasov himself has a premonition of his fate. At the very moment when he is about to launch the counterattack that will save Moscow, he recalls the end of a martyr, Andrei Stratilat, who perished with his soldiers. Stratilat suggests the Greek word *strategus* (a general or military leader). Vlasov/Stratilat the martyr also suggests the fate of the Spartans and their king at the pass of Thermopylae. The savage civil war on Corcyra, as noted by Thucydides in books 3 and 4 of *The History of the Peloponnesian War*, has an uncanny resemblance to Stalin's witch hunts.

97. "Prikaz Stavki verkhovnogo glavnogo komandovaniia Krasnoi armii', № 270, 16 avgusta 1941 goda," *Voenno-istoricheskii zhurnal* 9 (1988): 27. In his account of the fighting that took place immediately after the German invasion, Evgenii Dolmatovskii, unlike Grossman, mentions Order № 270 and goes out of his way to highlight the courage and professionalism of Generals Ponedelin and Kirillov, an explicit rejection of Stalin's slanderous attacks. Dolmatovskii stresses Ponedelin's dedication to the Soviet cause and the high esteem he enjoyed in the Red Army. The manner of his capture—he fell into an ambush—is an occupational hazard of war (74–75). The Germans also made attempts to recruit Ponedelin. Again, Dolmatovskii is unequivocal about Ponedelin's behavior: "In the camp, traitors were sent to Ponedelin with the aim of recruiting him for Vlasov's units, but he remained unshakable and calm, and would not listen to any attempts to suborn him" (157). Dolmatovskii's standing up for Ponedelin must be seen as a clear rebuff of Mekhlis and others who saw all Soviet prisoners as traitors: "And one can fight to the death as a prisoner as well" (157). See Evgenii Dolmatovskii, *Zelenaia brama: Dokumental'naia legenda ob odnom iz pervykh srazhenii Velikoi Otechestvennoi voiny* (The Oak Forest: A Documentary Legend about One of the First Battles of the Great Patriotic War) (1983; 2nd ed., Moscow: Politizdat, 1985).

98. Leonid Reshin, "Kollaboratsionisty i zhertvy rezhima," *Znamia* 8 (1994): 158–179. In a study published in 2004, Vlasov is dismissed thus: "He was simply a traitor, guilty of treason, a coward, who by chance rose above his comrades in the second

half of the 1930s. He was a careerist, an average commander and general, who had no combat experience but who was able to talk a lot and quite well 'on behalf of the people.'" See O. Smyslov, *Piataia kolonna Gitlera: Ot Kutepova do Vlasova* (Moscow: Veche, 2004), 6.

99. Mikhail Nekhoroshev, "Generala igraet svita," *Znamia* 9 (1995): 212 (emphasis in the original).

100. Reshin, "Kollaboratsionisty i zhertvy rezhima," 58.

101. Georgii Vladimov, "Novoe sledstvie, prigovor staryi," *Znamia* 8 (1994): 181.

102. Other factors that greatly predisposed Soviet citizens toward abandoning the Stalinist regime were the brutal treatment of workers in factories; the savage penalties imposed for absenteeism, lateness, and sloppy work; and the seven-day work week. One could also presume that ethnic minorities were likely to collaborate with the Germans, and so the Volga Germans—but also Chechens, Ingush, Crimean Tartars, Karachai, Balkars, and Kalmyks were deported with heavy loss of life. "Were likely to collaborate" became indistinguishable from "had collaborated," and punishment was meted out on that basis. Semipriaga defines collaboration as "a variety of Fascism and the practical collaboration of national traitors with Hitler's occupation authorities to the detriment of their people and nation." M. I. Semipriaga, *Kollaboratsionizm: Priroda, tipologiia i proiavleniia v gody vtoroi mirovoi voiny* (Moscow: ROSSPEN, 2000), 21. The author's definition of "Fascism" is limited exclusively to Nazi Germany and its role as an occupying power in Europe in World War II. It is not clear why opposition to Communism during or after World War II should automatically be regarded as a variety of Fascism. To stick with the author's definition of collaboration, the "fascists" after 1945 were the NKVD and the Red Army, who Sovietized the states of Central and Eastern Europe, and the caste of internal, national bureaucrats—the neo-Quislings, we might call them—who collaborated with the Soviet occupation until 1989. As I have noted in my discussion of Bykov's stories, the destruction of religious faith and the organized attacks on religion broke down any link between the party and the people, one factor that made collaboration more likely. The author of a recent study has arrived at a similar conclusion: "In order to understand the psychological nature of collaboration in the Soviet Union, one must bear in mind—and not for the first time—the absence of any such binding link between the people and those in power, which religion had been in earlier times. It was precisely the commonality of faith and the sacred character of power that mobilized the Russian people in the struggle against foreign invaders, who in their eyes were primarily unbelievers. So it was during the Time of Troubles and during the fight against Napoleon's invasion. Betraying the motherland, the main symbol of which was the monarch—God's anointed—was for the simple Russian peasant a terrible sin. The withdrawal from religion by a significant part of the population in the years after the revolution and inability of the new regime to create a complete replacement for it in the form of belief in the communist paradise on earth led to a loss of moral guidance and, under the pressure of corresponding circumstances, worked in favor of making the decision to cooperate with the external enemy. As far as believers were concerned, the new regime lacked for them that sacred power, and in their eyes betraying this regime was not such a sin as betraying the tsar." S. I. Drobiazko, *Pod*

znamemani vraga: Antisovetskie formirovaniia v sostave germanskikh vooruzhennykh sil, 1941-1945 *gg.* (Moscow: Eksmo, 2005), 63.

103. V. Kardin, "Strasti i pristrastiia. K sporam o romane G. Vladimova 'The General and His Army,'" *Znamia* 9 (1995): 200 (emphasis added).

104. Reshin, "Kollaboratsionisty i zhertvy rezhima," 176.

105. In Grossman's *Life and Fate,* Major Ershov organizes a rebellion in a German prisoner-of-war camp. Alarmed at this manifestation of independence, a Soviet commissar ensures that Ershov ends up on a list of prisoners who are to be transferred to death camps. Exactly the same obsession with rooting out heresies can be noted in the prison camps of Vichy France: "Even in the concentration camps, the communists attempted to annihilate their closest rivals by taking advantage of the hierarchies that existed there. . . . The communists often used the concentration-camp system to get rid of their political enemies, deliberately sending them to the hardest sections, even though they themselves were victims of the same Gestapo officers and the same SS divisions." See Stéphane Courtois and Jean-Louis Panné, "The Comintern in Action," in *The Black Book of Communism,* 310. Although, of course, the NKVD relentlessly persecuted any perceived or actual collaboration on the part of Soviet citizens, it made great efforts to recruit senior German officers. In the same way in which the Nazis exploited national Nazi parties in Belgium, Norway, Denmark, and France, the NKVD used national communist parties as a fifth column and also to assist in the process of Sovietization after the Germans had been defeated. German writers in exile in the Soviet Union also aided the Soviet propaganda effort. Especially noteworthy is Johannes Becher's play *Schlacht um Moskau* (Battle for Moscow, 1942), which was written in the Soviet Union.

106. See Esaulov, "Sataninskie zvezdy i sviashchennaia voina," 227.

107. "Paradoxically," writes Catherine Andreyev, "participants in the Russian Liberation Movement have affirmed that they experienced a greater sense of freedom as prisoners of war in the Third Reich than they had as citizens of the Soviet Union. This feeling of intellectual liberty also provided the stimulus for discussions in which political problems were of primary importance." Andreyev, *Vlasov and The Russian Liberation Movement,* 201.

108. Vladimir Bogomolov, "Sram imut i zhivye, i mertvye, i Rossiia . . . ('novoe videnie voiny,' 'novoe osmyslenie,' ili novaia mifologiia?)," *Knizhnoe obozrenie* 19, 9 May 1995, 14-19. The same essay was also published in *Voin* 7 (1995): 64-75. Vladimov countered with "Kogda ia massiroval kompetentsiiu . . . Otvet V. Bogomolovu." See Vladimov, *General i ego armiia,* 407-444. In his discussion of Bogomolov's novel, Lazarev avoids any of the controversial questions—collaboration, Vlasov, the Polish question, and Katyn—concentrating instead on the three SMERSH men and their expertise. See Lazar' Lazarev, *Eto nasha sud'ba. Zametki o literature, posviashchennoi Velikoi Otechestvennoi Voine,* 2nd ed. (Moscow: Sovetskii pisatel', 1983), 330-348.

109. Vladimov, *General i ego armiia,* 408. Exemplifying the high esteem in which *In August 1944* was held by KGB officers during the Cold War (and continues to be held even now among professional Russian intelligence officers) are the warm words in a book published to mark the sixtieth anniversary of SMERSH's founding: "On the operational-investigative work of military counterintelligence, the novel of the Russian

writer Vladimir Bogomolov has been written masterfully, with talent and with absolute documentary precision." See A. G. Bezverkhnii, ed., SMERSH: *Istoricheskie ocherki i arkhivnye dokumenty* (Moscow: Izdatel'stvo Glavarkhiva Moskvy, 2003), 86.

110. "Total war," notes Lev Anninskii, "dictates the rules of conduct which are unthinkable in normal life." See Lev Anninskii, "Bogomolov, Vladimov," *Rodina* 10 (1995): 58.

111. Georgii Vladimov, "Novoe sledstvie, prigovor staryi," in *General i ego armiia*, 397.

112. Bogomolov, "Sram imut i zhivye, i mertvye, i Rossiia," 14.

113. As one example, consider the anonymous letter published in *Rossiiskaia gazeta* (31 January 1995), purporting to have been written by Russian troops serving in Chechnya. The author(s) accused the Russian mass media of "disinforming the population, deliberately exacerbating the political situation in the country, and undermining Russia's authority in the international arena." They argued that it was "a well-planned and -organized information-psychological war against Russia." In Aleksei Simonov, ed., *Zhurnalisty na chechenskoi voine: Fakty, Dokumenty, Svidetel'stva*, noiabr' 1994–dekabr' 1995 (Moscow: Prava cheloveka, 1995), 344–345.

114. Vladimov, *General i ego armiia*, 194. Typical of the leaflets referred to here would be *Boevoi put'*, a Russian-language propaganda paper that was produced by the Wehrmacht for the Red Army. Its headline slogan was "Stalin's death will save Russia"—in the Russian original "*Smert' Stalina spaset Rossiiu*"—an effective play on the Russian acronym SSSR (USSR). The other headline slogan tried to drive a wedge between Stalin and the Russian people: "Bolshevism will perish; the Russian people will live." In fact, the second part comes close to the title of Grossman's first wartime story, *The People Are Immortal*.

115. One suspects that Bogomolov and others hostile to *The General and His Army* were rendered apoplectic by Aleksandr Kabakov's remark: "The last real novel about the last real war was written by Vladimov. Thereafter—silence." "Literatura i voina," 10. Kabakov argues his point at some length: "I think that the key word here—as they say a lot these days—is 'real.' *The General and His Army* is a real novel precisely because, it seems to me, it is dedicated to the *last real war*. And it is not literature that is guilty of the absence of any interest in the wars that followed, right up to the Chechen wars, but life itself. After the Great Patriotic War, if not our conscious then our subconscious refused to consider all later wars as *real* ones. That war was unconditional in terms of its aims, scale, and relation to its participants. That was a War with a capital letter, and not just for that reason was it referred to as the Fatherland War. The people in that war for the greater part did not separate themselves from what was happening, and for that reason it became not only an existential but also, I venture to say, a spiritual-religious experience both for the ordinary participants and for the writers who took it as a theme or merely as a background for their writing. Everyone took part in that war, and everyone carried the guilt for it" (10).

116. Vladimir But, "Orel—reshka" (Heads—Tails), *Druzhba narodov* 55, no. 4 (1995): 23–95.

117. Ibid., 74.

118. Somewhat overshadowed by the publicity and discussion of Astaf'ev's and Vladimov's novels, Grigorii Baklanov's *I togda prikhodiat marodery* (And Then Come the

Marauders, 1995) examines the role of Soviet military tribunals and the NKVD. It is a much harsher work than anything else written by Baklanov. In circumstances similar to those in But's novel, a Soviet amphibious landing is virtually wiped out by the Germans. Denied help, the commander orders a withdrawal. The survivors are interrogated. The commander is executed as a traitor and as an example. In a letter to his brother sent by his former radio operator many years after the war, it turns out that the executed officer was an outstanding and brave commander who was shot because a scapegoat for the operation's failure was required.

119. But, "Orel—reshka," 43.

120. This theme is important for the plot of Konstantin Simonov's *The Living and the Dead*, where the author shows in painstaking detail the consequences for soldiers of losing documents. For a discussion of this theme, see Frank Ellis, *The Living and the Dead*, in *Reference Guide to Russian Literature* (London: Fitzroy Dearborn Publishers, 1998), 742–744.

121. But, "Orel—reshka," 44.

122. Ibid., 46.

123. Solzhenitsyn pays tribute to his commanding officer, who gave him to understand that a letter to a school friend was the cause of his arrest. In an obvious gesture of defiance against the SMERSH officers, he made a point of shaking Solzhenitsyn's hand and wishing him well: "Not only was I no longer a captain, but I had been exposed as an enemy of the people (for among us every person is totally exposed from the moment of arrest). And he had wished happiness to an enemy?" Solzhenitsyn, *The Gulag Archipelago*, vol. 1, 19–20. Joseph Berger's assessment of SMERSH and the NKVD might possibly be shared by former operatives of these organizations but is, as far as I am aware, exceptional among former soldiers and camp inmates, and emphatically not supported by Astaf'ev, Grossman, Solzhenitsyn, Vladimov, Bykov, and But: "There was always tension between the army organization SMERSH, which dealt with military offences, and the NKVD, which dealt with political crimes. I heard many stories of SMERSH protecting soldiers and even getting them back from the NKVD after they had been arrested. Appallingly as the NKVD behaved, they would have been still worse if the army commanders had not fought them." See Joseph Berger, *Shipwreck of a Generation* (London: Harvill Press, 1971), 202–203. Nor is there anything that lends support to Berger's assertion in Bogomolov's SMERSH epic, *In August 1944*.

124. September 2004 saw the start of the series *Shtrafbat* (The Penal Battalion) on Russian television.

125. See Viacheslav Kondrat'ev, "Parii voiny: Strafnye roty v ob"ektive kinokamery," *Literaturnaia gazeta*, 31 January 1990, 8.

126. See "Pis'ma v redaktsiiu: O fil'me *Shtrafniki*," *Literaturnaia gazeta*, 7 March 1990, 8.

127. Viacheslav Kondrat'ev, "Iskupit' krov'iu" (To Pay in Blood), *Znamia* 12 (1991): 33–83.

128. Ibid., 52.

129. Ibid., 39.

130. Carl von Clausewitz, *On War*, ed. and trans. by Michael Howard and Peter Paret (Princeton, NJ: Princeton University Press, 1989), 119.

131. Ibid.

132. But, "Orel—reshka," 26.

133. By a curious coincidence, *The General and His Army*, *The Damned and the Dead*, and *Heads—Tails* share Hollywood's fascination with violently contested amphibious landings in the most successful war films of the 1990s, *The Thin Red Line* (1998) and *Saving Private Ryan* (1998).

134. See, for example, Alan Clark's study of British military bungling in World War I, *The Donkeys* (1961) (London: Pimlico, 1999). The following exchange quoted by Clark reflects the state of mind of Selivanov's superiors: "Sir John French: 'The British Army will give battle on the line of the Condé Canal.' Sir Horace Smith-Dorrien: 'Do you mean take the offensive, or stand on the defensive?' Sir John French: 'Don't ask questions, do as you're told'" (13). For an opposing view of Clark's bleak assessment of British performance in World War I, see Richard Holmes, *Tommy: The British Soldier on the Western Front 1914–1918* (London: HarperCollins, 2004).

135. After the war, Churchill threatened to sue Alan Moorehead if he wrote about the incident. See Nigel Hamilton, *Monty: Master of the Battlefield 1942–1944* (1983), Sceptre edition (London: Hodder and Stoughton, 1987), 580–581.

136. See Neil Sheehan, *A Bright Shining Lie: John Paul Vann and America in Vietnam* (London: Jonathan Cape, 1989). Two recent studies of the planning and execution of the U.S.-led invasion of Iraq highlight the same problem: willful and almost perverse indifference to hard facts on the part of senior military and civilian officials. See, for example, Michael Gordon and General Bernard Trainor, *COBRA II: The Inside Story of the Invasion and Occupation of Iraq* (London: Atlantic Books, 2006); and especially Thomas E. Ricks, *FIASCO: The American Military Adventure in Iraq* (London: Allen Lane/Penguin, 2006).

137. Planning for the Arnhem operation reveals the classic symptoms of the psychology of military incompetence. The intelligence officer (IO) at British 1 Airborne headquarters (HQ) warned General Browning, the commander, that German armor had been identified in the Arnhem area. This was not the sort of intelligence Browning wanted to hear on the eve of the operation. He sent the corps medical officer to see the IO, who was duly told that he was suffering from acute nervous strain and ordered to go on immediate leave. Nine days later, the hapless officer was flown to Brussels, to Browning's HQ, to deal with an outcome that, discharging his professional duty, he had earlier suggested was at least possible. See A. D. Harvey, *Arnhem* (London: Cassell & Co., 2001), 35.

138. See Norman F. Dixon, *On the Psychology of Military Incompetence* (1976) (London: Pimlico, 1994).

139. T. E. Lawrence, *Seven Pillars of Wisdom: A Triumph* (1935) (Harmondsworth, Middlesex: Penguin, 1988), 27.

140. But, "Orel—reshka," 64.

141. Ibid.

142. Ibid. A very powerful defense of Soviet women who were deported from Ukraine to Germany to work as slave laborers has been made by Viktor Astaf'ev in *Oberton* (Overtone, 1995–1996): "You see, they did not abandon the army and the

motherland; was it not the army and motherland that abandoned them to the whims of fate? The foreign occupiers, carrying out their universal evil on the conquered territories, who treated people as they wished. But on the way home, the so-called organs stood like a wall before them. These fine soldiers treated them even more harshly than the thugs of the Gestapo. The girls were stripped of their clothes—for purposes of disinfection and to subject them to a humiliating examination; their possessions were shaken out, the more valuable items taken away; the cheap adornments and knick-knacks were trodden underfoot. . . . And after an inspection, those suffering from venereal diseases were led away somewhere. There were rumors that they were shot." Viktor Astaf'ev, "Oberton," *Povesti, Rasskazy, Esse* (Ekaterinburg: U-Faktoriia, 2000), 215–216.

143. But, "Orel—reshka," 64.

144. Ibid., 62.

145. Ibid.

146. Ibid., 62–63. At a conference in 1988, convened to discuss the Great Patriotic War, Viktor Astaf'ev made the same point about Manstein's success in the Crimea, arguing that even by the end of the war, the Red Army still did know how to wage modern war. In *The Damned and the Dead*, a Soviet officer offers a brutally honest assessment of the way things are done in the Red Army: "Unarmed militia were burned to death around Moscow; combat-ready armies around Voronezh were destroyed. And at Stalingrad, throwing untried, poorly trained troops straight off the trains into battle, we have now suddenly remembered, comprehended that we cannot continue to fight like this. Russia cannot put up with this sort of slaughter and bloodletting for years and years; our motherland is not a bottomless pit." Astaf'ev, "Prokliaty i ubity," *Novyi mir* 12 (1992): 238. But's hostile portrayal of Mekhlis is reflected in an article published in the Wehrmacht's Russian-language propaganda newspaper, *Boevoi put'*. Despite the article's manifest anti-Semitic line—the author refers to Mekhlis as "the Suvorov from Berdichev"—the thrust of the article is essentially correct. Mekhlis played a major role in purging the Red Army of competent commanders during the Great Terror and was himself grotesquely incompetent in military matters. The author of the article highlighted the direct responsibility that Mekhlis bore for the loss of Kerch'. See "Izrail', torzhestvui i vozraduisia!" *Boevoi put'*, no. 39, dekabr' 1942 g. BA-MA/RH 26-384/33.

147. But, "Orel—reshka," 81.

148. Ibid.

149. Ibid., 80.

150. Ibid., 91.

151. Ibid. But's use of "hellish mechanism" may well be an allusion to Bukharin's use of "hellish machine" in his last letter to describe the NKVD and the apparatus of judicial murder established by Stalin. See Robert Conquest, *The Great Terror: A Reassessment* (London: Hutchinson, 1990), 395.

Afterword

1. Grigorii Baklanov, "Die besten Kriegsbücher sind Antikriegsbücher: Gedanken über die Kriegsliteratur," in Irina Antonova and Jörn Merkert, eds., *Berlin-Moskau/*

Moskau-Berlin, 1900–1950: Bildende Kunst, Photographie, Architektur, Theater, Literatur, Musik und Film (Munich: Prestel Verlag, 1995), 467.

2. Thucydides, *History of the Peloponnesian War*, book 1, "The Debate at Sparta and Declaration of War" (Harmondsworth, Middlesex: Penguin, 1972), 80.

3. Ernst Jünger, *In Stahlgewittern, Tagebücher I, Der Erste Weltkrieg*, band 1 (Stuttgart: Klett-Cotta, 2001), 11.

4. See, for example, V. I. Lenin, "Printsipy sotsializma i voina 1914–1915," *Sochineniia*, vol. 21 (Moscow: OGIZ, 1948), 271–307.

5. Reinhard Goering, *Seeschlacht* (1917) (Stuttgart: Philipp Reclam, 1972), 31.

6. Ibid., 58.

7. Viktor Astaf'ev, *Prokliaty i ubity* (The Damned and the Dead) (Moscow: Eksmo, 2010), 569.

8. Erich Maria Remarque, *Im Westen nichts Neues* (1929) (Cologne: Kiepenheuer & Witsch, 1984), 176.

9. Ibid.

10. Baklanov, "Die besten Kriegsbücher sind Antikriegsbücher," 465.

11. Ibid.

12. Ibid.

13. Grigorii Baklanov, "'Ne riskuia vstretit' osuzhdenie," *Vremia sobirat' kamni. Stat'i, portrety, besedy* (Moscow: Novosti Press, 1989), 198–210. The article discussed by Baklanov is William Broyles Jr., "Why Men Love War," *Esquire* (November 1984): 55–65.

14. Broyles, "Why Men Love War," paragraph 3. Paragraphs are used as references because the article was downloaded from www.utk.edu (13 June 2010), and pagination is not the same as in the original published version.

15. Ibid., paragraph 14.

16. Vasilii Grossman, *Zhizn' i sud'ba* (Life and Fate) (Moscow: Sovetskii pisatel', 1990), 118.

17. Ibid., 324.

18. General Makhmut Akhmetovich Gareev, "Pod vidom poiska istoricheskoi pravdy," *Voenno-istoricheskii zhurnal* 12 (2005): 9.

19. Ibid., 10.

20. Ibid.

21. Ibid.

22. Astaf'ev, "Kommentarii," in *Prokliaty i ubity*, 794.

23. Aleksandr Andreevich Svechin, *Trudy komissii po issledovaniiu i ispol'zovanniu opyta voiny 1914–1918 gg.*, 1st ed. (Moscow, 1919), 6. Cited by Gareev, "Pod vidom poiska istoricheskoi pravdy," 15.

24. Milos Stankovic, *Trusted Mole: A Soldier's Journey into Bosnia's Heart of Darkness* (London: HarperCollins, 2000), ix (emphasis in the original).

25. Philip Knightley, *The First Casualty: From the Crimea to Vietnam: The War Correspondent as Hero, Propagandist, and Myth Maker* (New York: Harcourt Brace Jovanovich, 1975); revised edition with a new introduction by John Pilger (London: Prion, 2000).

26. Max Hastings, *Going to the Wars* (London: Macmillan Press, 2000), 140.

GLOSSARY

Auftragstaktik
  Mission-led command in which junior commanders, having been given their missions, were expected to solve tactical problems and show initiative.

Daraufgängertum
  Offensive, aggressive spirit.

dedovshchina
  Bullying and exploitation of recruits by senior soldiers in the Red Army.

degeroisatziia
  The destruction or undermining of the heroic ethos of the Great Patriotic War. This term was often applied to the works, among others, of Grigorii Baklanov, Vasil' Bykov, and Bulat Okudzhava.

divizion
  Artillery battalion.

dokhodiaga
  An inmate of a Soviet camp who has lost the will to live. Literally, a "goner." The word is derived from the Russian verb dokhnut' (to perish, usually used for animals).

fil'tratsiia
  A series of interrogations to which deserters, okruzhentsy (see below), Red Army escapees, and any other suspicious persons were subjected on rejoining the Soviet lines. The process was intended to uncover German agents and spy rings. Until April 1943, this task was the responsibility of the NKVD's Special Sections (see below); thereafter it was handled by SMERSH (see below).

fragging
  The habit of killing officers, often with a fragmentation grenade (hence the term), that occurred in the U.S. Army in Vietnam.

frontovik
  Frontline soldier.

Glasnost
  Literally "openness." A policy adopted by Mikhail Gorbachev that led to the publication of many previously banned and censored works of literature, among them Life and Fate, Doktor Zhivago, and The Gulag Archipelago.

Iazyk
  A prisoner captured for purposes of interrogation (means, among other things, "tongue").

Kessel
  The German word "cauldron" used to refer to the troops surrounded at Stalingrad.

KGB
  Komitet Gosudarstvennoi Bezopasnosti; Committee for State Security.

Kommissarbefehl

An order from Hitler according to which all commissars were to be shot.

Krasnaia zvezda

Red Star; Red Army newspaper.

Kulak

An allegedly wealthy peasant who exploited others.

NKVD

Narodnyi komissariat vnutrennikh del (People's Commissariat of Internal Affairs). Soviet secret police and the precursor of the KGB.

okopnaia pravda

Literally, the "truth of the trenches." The term applied to those writers, among them Vasil' Bykov, Bulat Okudzhava, and Grigorii Baklanov, who did not eschew some of the less glamorous sides of war.

okruzhenie

Literally, "encirclement." Soviet Soldiers who had been encircled by the German army were regarded as potential spies and subjected to lengthy interrogations (*fil'tratsiia*) in order to establish their innocence. A Soviet soldier who had been in a unit encircled by the German army was known as an *okruzhenets*.

Order № 227

This order was issued on 28 July 1942 and was intended to stiffen discipline in the Red Army as the Germans closed in on Stalingrad. The full text was first published in 1988.

Order № 270

Issued on 16 August 1941, this is one of the most brutal orders issued by Stalin. Deserters and commanders deemed to have failed to discharge their duty were liable to summary execution. The full text of this order was first published in 1988.

Osobyi otdel

Special Section(s). The part of the NKVD charged with dealing with desertion, uncovering traitors, and enforcing Orders № 270 and 227.

Osobist

Soviet officer who worked in the Special Section.

pokhodno-polevye zheny

Campaign wives. Female personnel—typically nurses, signalers, and clerks—who cohabited with officers in exchange for better living conditions.

Polizai

The word is derived from the German word "*Polizei*" (police) and refers to collaborators who were recruited by the German occupation forces to assist them in controlling the occupied territories.

povest' or povesti

A short story or tale.

predatel'stvo

Treachery.

Razvedchik

Spy, or in war literature a scout in a reconnaissance patrol.

REMFs

Rear-echelon motherfuckers. A term used in the U.S. Army to refer to soldiers in rear units, such as supply and logistics (see *tylovaia krysa*).

Samostrel

Soldier who shoots and wounds himself in order to avoid or escape frontline service.

sledovatel'

Investigator.

SMERSH

Smert' shpionam (death to spies). SMERSH was a Soviet counterintelligence agency formed in April 1943. One of the organization's primary tasks—and the cause of much injustice and suffering—was the processing (interrogation) of Soviet service personnel and civilians who had been captured by the Germans, had been encircled, or had lived under German occupation. See *fil'tratsiia*.

Spetspereselenets

Special deportee. Those peasants who were dispossessed during collectivization and deported to Siberia and other remote regions of the Soviet Union.

starosta

In the German-occupied territories, these were individuals appointed by the Germans to pass on German orders, to act as intermediaries between the local population and the German occupation forces, and to inform the Germans about, for example, partisan activity in the region. They were regarded as traitors and often killed by partisans.

Terror-Famine

Term used by the British historian Robert Conquest to refer to the genocide in Ukraine and elsewhere in the Soviet Union in the early 1930s, when some 11 million peasants were exterminated as part of the collectivization program.

tylovaia krysa

Literally, a "rear rat." Red Army slang for soldiers in rear echelons behind the frontline (see REMF). A less pejorative, more formal word would be *tylovik*.

Vergangenheitsbewältigung

Coming to terms with the Nazi period, 1933–1945, in post-1945 West Germany.

Volksdeutsche

The concept of the *Volksdeutsche* was formulated in National Socialist Germany. The term applied to the citizens of foreign states who were of German or related blood, who spoke German, and who considered themselves to be part of the German cultural community.

vysshaia mera nakazaniia

The ultimate form of military punishment: execution (*rasstrel*) by firing squad or often a bullet from the commander's sidearm.

zagriaditel'nyi otriad

Blocking or barrier detachment made up of NKVD personnel or Red Army soldiers under control of the Special Sections of the NKVD. Its task was to shoot any Soviet troops who left the battlefield without authorization.

zampolit

 Zamestitel' komandira po politicheskoi chasti; deputy commander for the political unit.

zek

 A slang term for an inmate of a Soviet labor camp. It is derived from the Russian *zakliuchennyi* ("incarcerated").

Zhdanovshchina

 The period from immediately after the end of the war in 1945 until Stalin's death in 1953. Characterized by extreme attacks on Soviet scientists who acknowledged Western contributions to science, especially Darwin, Heisenberg, Einstein, Rutherford, and Wiener. Markedly anti-Semitic, it culminated in the exposure of the so-called Doctors' Plot, in which Jewish doctors were accused of trying to kill Stalin and other Soviet leaders.

BIBLIOGRAPHY

Primary Literature and Sources
Bundesarchiv-Militärarchiv, Freiburg-im-Breisgau

AOK 6. Abt Ia. Lagemeldung. 24.09.1942, BA-MA/RH 20-6/213/120.

Bericht über eine Fahrt nach Stalingrad, 25.09.1942, BA-MA/RH 20-6/213/175.

Dem Herrn Oberbefehlshaber der 6. Armee. 27.9.1942, BA-MA/RH 20-6/214/89.

OKH Org.Abt, 08.10.1942, *Grundlegender Befehl Nr.1 (Hebung der Gefechtsstärke)*, BA-MA, RH 20-6/220/65.

Alarmeinheiten der dem AOK. 6 unterstellten Divisionen, Korps-, Armee- und Heerestruppen, BA-MA, RH 20-6/220/47.

Anlage 3 zum Feindnachrichtenblatt "Stalingrad Nr. 9," *Gliederung und Kampfwert der Feindverbände vor 6. Armee. Stand 23.9.1942.* BA-MA, RH 20-6/213/84.

Gruppe Pfeiffer Kommandeur, 03.01.1943, BA-MA, RH 20-6/235/139.

"Izrail', torzhestvui i vozraduisia!" *Boevoi put'*, no. 39, dekabr' 1942 g. (BA-MA/RH 26-384/33).

Russian-Language Sources

Astaf'ev, Viktor. "Prokliaty i ubity." *Novyi mir* 10 (1992): 60–106; 11 (1992): 188–226; 12 (1992): 168–246; 10 (1994): 62–110; 11 (1994): 37–101; 12 (1994): 57–134.

———. *Prokliaty i ubity.* Moscow: Veche, 1994.

———. *Prokliaty i ubity.* Moscow: Eksmo, 2010.

Baklanov, Grigorii. "Iiul' 41 goda." *Znamia* 1 (1965): 3–41; 2 (1965): 3–71.

———. "I togda prikhodiat marodery." *Znamia* 5 (1995): 3–66.

———. "IUzhnee glavnogo udara," *Voennye povesti.* Moscow: Sovremennik, 1985, 338–444.

———. "Mertvye sramu ne imut." *Znamia* 6 (1961): 18–59.

Bek, Aleksandr. *Volokolamskoe shosse* (1943). Moscow: Voenizdat, 1959.

Bogomolov, Vladimir. *Moment istiny (V avguste sorok chetvertogo . . .).* Moscow: Olma-Press, 2000.

———. "V avguste sorok chetvertogo." *Novyi mir* 10 (1974): 3–109; 11 (1974): 5–95; 12 (1974): 161–232.

———. "V Krigere." *Novyi mir* 8 (1993): 94–114.

Bondarev, IUrii. "Batal'ony prosiat ognia." *Sobranie sochinenii v shesti tomakh, tom 1.* Moscow: Khudozhestvennaia literatura, 1984, 31–218.

———. "Goriachii sneg." *Sobranie sochinenii v shesti tomakh, tom 2.* Moscow: Khudozhestvennaia literatura, 1984, 165–526.

———. "Poslednie zalpy." *Sobranie sochinenii v shesti tomakh, tom 2.* Moscow: Khudozhestvennaia literatura, 1984, 7–162.

But, Vladimir. "Orel—reskha." *Druzhba narodov* 55, no. 4 (1995): 23–95.

Bykov, Vasil'. "Boloto." *Druzhba narodov* 7 (2001): 7–33.

———. "Frontovaia stranitsa." *Oktiabr'* 9 (1963): 67–106.

———. "Kar'er." *Druzhba narodov* 4 (1986): 3–85; 5 (1986): 68–162.

———. "Kruglianskii most." *Novyi mir* 3 (1969): 3–57.

———. "Mertvym ne bol'no." *Novyi mir* 1 (1966): 3–36; 2 (1966): 7–64.

———. "Obelisk." *Novyi mir* 1 (1972): 3–44.

———. *Sobranie sochinenii v chetyrekh tomakh.* Moscow: Molodaia gvardiia, 1985–1986.

———. "Sotnikov." *Novyi mir* 5 (1970): 65–161.

———. "Stuzha." *Znamia* 11 (1993): 7–76.

———. "Volch'ia staia." *Novyi mir* 7 (1974): 5–80.

———. "V tumane." *Druzhba narodov* 7 (1987): 3–61.

———. "Zapadnia" (1964). *Sobranie sochinenii v chetyrekh tomakh, tom 2.* Moscow: Molodaia gvardiia, 1985, 454–493.

———. "Znak bedy." *Sobranie sochinenii v chetyrekh tomakh, tom 4.* Moscow: Molodaia gvardiia, 1986, 6–248.

Dolmatovskii, Evgenii. *Zelenaia brama: Dokumental'naia legenda ob odnom iz pervykh srazhenii Velikoi Otechestvennoi voiny* (1983), 2nd ed. Moscow: Politizdat, 1985.

Grossman, Vasilii. *Gody voiny.* Moscow: OGIZ, 1946.

———. *Gody voiny.* Moscow: Pravda, 1989.

———. *Sobranie sochinenii v 4 tomakh.* Moscow: Agraf, 1998.

———. *Za pravoe delo.* Moscow: Sovetskii pisatel', 1989.

———. *Zhizn' i sud'ba.* Moscow: Sovetskii pisatel', 1990.

Kazakevich, Emmanuil. "Zvezda." *Izbrannye proizvedeniia v 2 tomakh, tom 1.* Moscow: Khudozhestvennaia literatura, 1974, 7–78.

———. "Dvoe v stepi." *Izbrannye proizvedeniia v 2 tomakh, tom 1.* Moscow: Khudozhestvennaia literatura, 1974, 79–132.

Kondrat'ev, Viacheslav. "Iskupit' krov'iu." *Znamia* 12 (1991): 33–83.

Kurochkin, Viktor. "Na voine kak na voine." *Molodaia gvardiia* 8 (1965): 75–194.

———. *Na voine kak na voine. Povesti. Rasskazy.* Leningrad: Leninizdat, 1980.

Kuznetsov, Anatolii. "Babii IAr." *IUnost'* 8 (1966): 7–46; 9 (1966): 15–49; 10 (1966): 23–66.

Nekrasov, Viktor. *Front-line Stalingrad* (1962). Trans. by David Floyd. Glasgow: Fontana/Collins, 1978.

———. *Stalingrad.* Frankfurt-am-Main: Possev-Verlag, 1981.

———. *V okopakh Stalingrada.* Moscow: Gosudarstvennoe izdatel'stvo khudozhestvennoi literatury, 1948.

Okudzhava, Bulat. *Bud' zdorov, shkoliar. Stikhi, vtoroe izdanie.* Frankfurt: Possev-Verlag, 1966.

Pal'kin, Il'ia. "Neizvestnye soldaty." *Zvezda* 5 (1988): 167–179.

Polevoi, Boris. *Do Berlina—896 kilometrov.* Moscow: Sovetskaia Rossiia, 1973.

Shpanov, Nikolai. *Pervyi udar. Povesti i Rasskazy.* Moscow: Sovetskii pisatel', 1939.

Simonov, Konstantin. *Sobranie sochinenii v 6 tomakh.* Moscow: Khudozhestvennaia literatura, 1966–1970.

Stadniuk, Ivan. *Voina, kniga pervaia i kniga vtoraia.* Moscow: Sovremennik, 1977; kniga tret'ia, Moscow: Voenizdat, 1980.

Suvorov, Viktor. *Ledokol. Kto nachal vtoruiu mirovuiu voinu?* Moscow: Novoe vremia, 1993.

Vasil'eva, Tat'iana. "Slezy nevoli." *Zvezda* 5 (1988): 32–76.

Vladimov, Georgii. "General i ego armiia." *Znamia* 4 (1994): 3–71; 5 (1994.): 6–49.

———. *General i ego armiia* (1994). Moscow: Knizhnaia palata, 1997.

———. "Za zemliu, za voliu . . ." *Znamia* 2 (1996): 8–27.

Vorob'ev, Konstantin. "Ubity pod Moskvoi." *Novyi mir* 2 (1963): 46–75.

Secondary Literature

Addison, Paul, and Angus Calder, eds., with a foreword by Len Deighton. *Time to Kill: The Soldier's Experience of War in the West 1939–1945.* London: Pimlico, 1997.

Amel'chenko, V. V., ed. *Stalingrad: K 60-letiiu srazheniia na Volge.* Moscow: Voenizdat, 2002.

Andrew, Christopher, and Vasilii Mitrokhin. *The Mitrokhin Archive: The KGB in Europe and the West.* London: Penguin Books, 1999.

Andreyev, Catherine. "General Vlasov i Russkoe Osvoboditel'noe Dvizhenie." *Druzhba narodov* 5 (1991): 170–205.

———. *Vlasov and The Russian Liberation Movement: Soviet Reality and Émigré Theories.* London: Cambridge University Press, 1987.

Anninskii, Lev. "Bogomolov Vladimov." *Rodina* 10 (1995): 58.

———. "Spasti Rossiiu Tsenoi Rossii . . ." *Novyy mir* 10 (1994): 214–221.

Astaf'ev, Viktor. "Kommentarii," in *Prokliaty i ubity.* Moscow: Eksmo, 2010, 767–794.

Baklanov, Grigorii. "Die besten Kriegsbücher sind Antikriegsbücher: Gedanken über die Kriegsliteratur." In Irina Antonova and Jörn Merkert, eds., *Berlin-Moskau/Moskau-Berlin 1900–1950: Bildende Kunst, Photographie, Architektur, Theater, Literatur, Musik und Film.* Munich: Prestel Verlag, 1995, 465–467.

———. "Ne riskuia vstretit' osuzhdenie." *Vremia sobirat' kamni. Stat'i, portrety, besedy.* Moscow: Novosti Press, 1989, 198–210.

Baranov, Vasilii. "Dnevnik ostarbaitera." *Znamia* 5 (1995): 135–155.

Barnett, Correlli. "A Military Historian's View of the Great War." In Mary Stocks, ed., *Essays by Divers Hands: Being the Transactions of the Royal Society of Literature,* vol. 36. London: Oxford University Press, 1970, 1–18.

Basinskii, Pavel. "Nesluchainyi svidetel'." *Literaturnaia gazeta,* 16–20 January 2002, 3.

Beevor, Antony. *Berlin: The Downfall 1945.* London: Viking Penguin Group, 2002.

———. *Stalingrad.* London: Penguin, 1999.

Besançon, Alain. *The Falsification of the Good: Soloviev and Orwell.* Trans. by Matthew Screech, London: Claridge Press, 1994.

Bettelheim, Bruno. *The Informed Heart: The Human Condition in Mass Society.* London: Paladin, 1970.

Bezverkhnii, A. G., ed. *SMERSH: Istoricheskie ocherki i arkhivnye dokumenty.* Moscow: Izdatel'stvo Glavarkhiva Moskvy, 2003.

Bocharov, Anatolii. *Emmanuil Kazakevich: Ocherk tvorchestva.* Moscow: Sovetskii pisatel', 1965.

———. "Spor prodolzhaetsia i segodnia . . ." *Druzhba narodov* 5 (1966): 282–285.

Bogomolov, Vladimir. "Sram imut i zhivye, i mertvye, i Rossiia . . . ('novoe videnie voiny,' 'novoe osmyslenie,' ili novaia mifologiia?)." *Knizhnoe obozrenie* 19, 9 May 1995, 14–19. The same extract published in *Voin* 7 (1995): 64–75.

Boshyk, Yury, ed., with Roman Waschuk and Andriy Wynnyckyj. *Ukraine during World War II: History and Its Aftermath*. A Symposium, Canadian Institute of Ukrainian Studies. University of Alberta, Edmonton, 1986.

Braithwaite, Rodric. *Moscow 1941: A City and Its People at War*. London: Profile Books, 2006.

Briskman, T., ed. *Viktor Petrovich Astaf'ev, Zhizn' i Tvorchestvo, Bibliograficheskii ukazatel' proizvedenii pisatelia na russkom i inostrannykh iazykakh*. Moscow: Rossiiskaia gosudarstvennaia biblioteka, 1999.

Brock, Peter. *Against the Draft: Essays on Conscientious Objections from the Radical Reformation to the Second World War*. Toronto, Ontario: University of Toronto Press, 2006.

———. *Pacifism in Europe to 1914*. Princeton, NJ: Princeton University Press, 1972.

———. *Twentieth-Century Pacifism*. London: Van Nostrand Reinhold Company, 1970.

Broyles, William, Jr. "Why Men Love War." *Esquire* (November 1984): 55–65.

Bykov, Vasil'. "O pravde voiny i pravde mira." *Druzhba narodov* 11 (1996): 177–178.

———. "'Za rodinu! Za Stalina.' Tsena proshedshikh boev." *Rodina* 5 (1995): 30–37.

Cherushev, N. S. *Udar po svoim: Krasnaia armiia 1938–1941*. Moscow: Veche, 2003.

Chuikov, Vasilii. *The Beginning of the Road*. Trans. by Harold Silver. London: Macgibbon & Kee, 1963.

———. *Nachalo puti, izdanie tret'e, ispravlennoe i dopolnennoe*. Volgograd: Nizhne-Volzhskoe izdatel'stvo, 1967.

Churchill, Winston S. *The Second World War*, vol. 3, *The Grand Alliance*. London: Cassell & Co., 1950.

———. *The Second World War*, vol. 4, *The Hinge of Fate*. London: Cassell & Co., 1951.

———. *The Second World War*, vol. 5, *Closing the Ring*. London: Cassell & Co., 1952.

Ciechanowski, Jan M. *The Warsaw Uprising of 1944*. London: Syndics of the Cambridge University Press, 1974.

Clark, Alan. *Barbarossa: The Russian-German Conflict 1941–1945*. Harmondsworth, Middlesex: Penguin, 1966.

———. *The Donkeys* (1961). London: Pimlico, 1999.

Clausewitz, Carl von. *On War* (1832). Edited and translated by Michael Howard and Peter Paret, Princeton, NJ: Princeton University Press, 1989.

Clavell, James. *King Rat* (1962), 8th ed. London: Coronet, 1980.

Courtois, Stéphane, Nicolas Werth, Jean-Louis Panné, Andrzej Paczkowski, Karel Bartošek, and Jean-Louis Margolin. *The Black Book of Communism: Crimes, Terror, Repression*. Trans. by Jonathan Murphy and Mark Kramer. London: Harvard University Press, 1999.

Craig, William. *Enemy at the Gates: The Battle for Stalingrad*. New York: Reader's Digest Press, 1973.

Crumney, Robert. *The Old Believers and the World of Antichrist: The Vyg Community and the Russian State 1694–1855*. Madison and London: The University of Wisconsin Press, 1970.

Dedkov, Igor'. "Deviatogo maia obiazatel'no vspomniu Vas . . ." *Druzhba narodov* 4 (1995): 172–187.

———. "Ob"iavlenie viny i naznachenie kazni." *Druzhba narodov* 10 (1993): 185–202.

De Jomini, Baron. *The Art of War* (1862), a new edition, with appendices and maps. Trans. by Captain G. H. Mendell and Lieutenant W. P. Craighill. Westport, CT: Greenwood Press, 1975.

Dixon, Norman F. *On the Psychology of Military Incompetence* (1976), with a foreword by Brigadier Shelford Bidwell. London: Pimlico, 1994.

Drobiazko, S. I. *Pod znamemani vraga: Antisovetskie formirovaniia v sostave germanskikh vooruzhennykh sil, 1941–1945 gg.* Moscow: Eksmo, 2005.

Ebert, Jens. *Zwischen Mythos und Wirklichkeit: Die Schlacht um Stalingrad in deutsch-sprachigen authentischen und literarischen Texten*, vols. 1 and 2. Humboldt University, Doctoral dissertation, Berlin, 1989; microfiche, Stanford University, 001904 (x 4).

Ellis, Frank. "Dulag–205: The German Army's Death Camp for Soviet Prisoners at Stalingrad." *Journal of Slavic Military Studies* 19, no. 1 (March 2006): 123–148.

———. "La rivelazione della libertà e gli inizi saggezza in *Vita e Destino* di Vasilij Grossman." In Giovanni Maddelena and Pietro Tosco, eds., *Il Romanzo della libertà: Vasilij Grossman tra i classici del XX secolo*. Soveria Mannelli, Italy: Rubbettino Editore, 2007, 175–198.

———. "10th Rifle Division of Internal Troops NKVD: Profile and Combat Performance at Stalingrad." *Journal of Slavic Military Studies* 19, no. 3 (September 2006): 601–618.

———. *Vasiliy Grossman: The Genesis and Evolution of a Russian Heretic*. Oxford and Providence, RI: Berg, 1994.

Erickson, John. *The Road to Stalingrad*. London: Weidenfeld & Nicolson, 1975 and 1983.

Esaulov, Ivan. "Sataninskie zvezdy i sviashchennaia voina. Sovremennyi roman v kontekste russkoi dukhovnoi traditsii." *Novyi mir* 4 (1994): 224–239.

Falls, Cyril. *War Books: An Annotated Bibliography of Books about the Great War* (1930), with a new introduction by R. J. Wyatt. London: Greenhill Books, 1989.

Fedorov, G. B. "Mera otvetstvennosti." *Novyi mir* 1 (1966): 260–263.

Fel'dman, D. "Do i posle aresta." *Literaturnaia Rossiia* 45, 11 noiabria 1988 g., 16–17.

Ferguson, John, ed. *War and the Creative Arts: An Anthology*. London: Macmillan in association with The Open University Press, 1972.

Fick, Nathaniel. *One Bullet Away: The Making of a Marine Officer*. London: Weidenfeld & Nicolson, 2005.

Frankl, Viktor. *Ein Psycholog erlebt das Konzentrationslager* (1946). Translated as *Man's Search for Meaning*, revised and updated. New York: Washington Square Press, 1985.

Gallagher, Matthew. *The Soviet History of World War II: Myths, Memoirs and Realities*. New York and London: Frederick A. Praeger, 1963.

Gareev, General M. "Pod vidom poiska istoricheskoi pravdy." *Voenno-istoricheskii zhurnal* 12 (2005): 9–15.

Gillespie, David. *Russian Cinema*. Harlow, Essex: Pearson Education Limited, 2003.

Hackett, General Sir John. *The Profession of Arms*. London: Sidgwick and Jackson, 1983.

Halperin, Charles. *Russia and the Golden Horde*. Bloomington: Indiana University Press, 1985.

Hastings, Max. *Armageddon: The Battle for Germany 1944–45*. London: Macmillan Press, 2004.

———. *Going to the Wars*. London: Macmillan Press, 2000.

Hayek, Friedrich. *The Road to Serfdom* (1944). London: Routledge, 1993.

Hendry, J. F., ed., *The New Apocalypse: An Anthology of Criticism, Poems and Stories*, with an introduction by J. F. Hendry. London: The Fortune Press, 1940.

Hendry, J. F., and Henry Treece, eds. *The White Horseman: Prose and Verse of the New Apocalypse*. London: Routledge, 1941.

Higgins, Ian, ed. *The Second World War in Literature*. London and Edinburgh: Scottish Academic Press, 1986.

IAkovlev, A. N., et al., eds. *Katyn: Plenniki neob"iavlennoi voiny*. In the series Demokratiia, Rossiia. XX VEK, Dokumenty. Moscow: Mezhdunarodnyi fond, 1997.

———. *Lubianka: Organy VChk-OGPU-NKVD-NKGB-MGB-KGB 1917–1991 spravochnik*. In the series Demokratiia, Rossiia. XX VEK, Dokumenty. Moscow: Mezhdunarodnyi fond, 2003.

———. *1941 god, v 2-knigakh*. In the series Demokratiia, Rossiia. XX VEK, Dokumenty. Moscow: Mezhdunarodnyi fond, 1998.

Interview with Viktor Astaf'ev. "Nado ne geroicheskuiu voinu pokazyvat', a pugat' eiu—ved' voina otvratitel'na!" *Russkaia mysl'*, 31 October–6 November 2002, 9.

Ivanova, Natal'ia. "Dym otechestva." *Znamia* 7 (1994): 183–193.

Jerrold, Douglas. *The Lie about the War: A Note on Some Contemporary War Books*. London: Faber & Faber, 1930.

Johnson, James Turner. *Just War Tradition and the Restraint of War: A Moral and Historical Inquiry*. Princeton, NJ: Princeton University Press, 1981.

Jordan, David Starr. *War and the Breed: The Relation of War to the Downfall of Nations* (1915), illustrated and abridged by J. W. Jamieson. Washington, DC: Cliveden Press, 1981.

Jünger, Ernst. "Der Kampf als inneres Erlebnis." In *Gesammelte Werke*, band 7, *Betrachtungen zur Zeit*. Stuttgart: Klett-Cotta, 1980, 11–103.

K 50-letiiu. Stalingradskaia bitva (17 iiulia 1942–2 fevralia 1943 g.). Katalog knizhno-illiustrativnoi vystavki. Moscow: Gosudarstvennaia publichnaia istoricheskaia biblioteka, 1992.

Kardin, V. "Strasti i pristrastiia. K sporam o romane G. Vladimova 'General i ego armiia.'" *Znamia* 9 (1995): 199–210.

Kehrig, Manfred. *Stalingrad: Analyse und Dokumentation einer Schlacht*. Beiträge zur Militär- und Kriegsgeshcichte, band 15. Stuttgart: Deutsche Verlags-Anstalt, 1974.

Khorev, Aleksey. "Kak sudili Tukhachevskogo." *Krasnaia zvezda*, 17 April 1991, 4.

Klein, Holger, J. E. Flower, and Eric Homberger, eds. *The Second World War in Fiction*. London and Basingstoke: Macmillan Press, 1984.

Kobylyanskiy, Isaak. "Memories of War, Part 3." *Journal of Slavic Military Studies* 17, no. 2 (2004): 333–344.

Kondrat'ev, Viacheslav. "Parii voiny: Strafnye roty v ob"ektive kinokamery." *Literaturnaia gazeta*, 31 January 1990, 8.

Kravchenko, Viktor. *I Chose Freedom: The Personal and Political Life of a Soviet Official* (1946), with a new introduction by Rett R. Ludwikowski. New Brunswick and Oxford: Transaction Publishers, 1989.

Krivosheev, Colonel General G. F. "Eshche raz o tsene pobedy." *Krasnaia zvezda*, 18 June 1991, 2.

——, ed. *Grif sekretnosti sniat: Poteri Vooruzhennykh sil SSSR v voinakh, boevykh deistviakh i voennykh konfkliktakh.* Moscow: Voennoe izdatel'stvo, 1993.

Kurbatov, Valentin. "Posledniaia pobeda." *Den' i noch'* 1 (1995): 146–150.

Lawrence, D. H. *Apocalypse* (1931), with an introduction by Richard Aldington. London: Heinemann, 1972.

Lawrence, T. E. *Seven Pillars of Wisdom: A Triumph* (1935). Harmondsworth, Middlesex: Penguin, 1988.

Lawton, Anna. *Kinoglasnost: Soviet Cinema in Our Time.* Cambridge: Cambridge University Press, 1992.

Lazarev, Lazar'. *Eto nasha sud'ba: Zametki o literature, posviashchennoi Velikoi Otechestvennoi voine*, 2nd ed. Moscow: Sovetskii pisatel', 1983.

——. "A ikh povybilo zhelezom . . ." *Druzhba narodov* 5 (2000): 216–218.

——. "Na vsiu ostavshuiusia zhizn': Zametki o povesti Vasilia Bykova 'Kar'ep' i nekotorykh problemakh literatury, posviashchennoi Velikoi Otechestvennoi voine." *Novyi mir* 11 (1986): 271–237.

——. *Pamiat' trudnoi godiny: Velikaia Otechestvennaia voina v russkoi literature.* Moscow: Druzhba narodov, 2000.

——. "Shestoi etazh." *Znamia* 6 (1993): 123–179.

"Literatura i voina," *Znamia* 5 (2000): 3–13.

Donald Danemanis, trans. *Marxism-Leninism on War and Army.* Moscow: Progress Publishers, 1972.

Maslov, A. A. "The Death of the Shattered: Soviet Generals Who Perished in Fascist Captivity." *Journal of Slavic Military Studies* 10, no. 4 (1997): 156–184.

——. "Forgiven by Stalin—Soviet Generals Who Returned from German Prisons in 1941–45 and Who Were Rehabilitated." *Journal of Slavic Military Studies* 12, no. 2 (1999): 173–219.

——. "How Were Soviet Blocking Detachments Employed?" *Journal of Slavic Military Studies* 9, no. 2 (1996): 427–435.

——. "Tried for Treason against the Motherland: Soviet Generals Condemned after Release from German Captivity." *Journal of Slavic Military Studies* 13, no. 2 (2000): 86–138.

Materski, Wojciech, ed. KATYN, *Documents of Genocide*. Documents and Materials from the Soviet Archives Turned over to Poland on 14 October 1992, with an introduction by Janusz K. Zawodny, trans. by Jan Kolbowski and Mark Canning. Warsaw: Institute of Political Studies, Polish Academy of Sciences, 1993.

Matrosov, Vadim. "Na pervom rubezhe voiny." *Krasnaia zvezda*, 5 June 1991, 3.

McGinn, Bernard. "The End of the World and the Beginning of Christendom." In Malcolm Bull, ed., *Apocalypse Theory and the Ends of the World.* Oxford: Blackwell, 1995.

Merridale, Catherine. *Ivan's War: The Red Army 1939–45.* London: Faber & Faber, 2005.

Mialo, Kseniia. "Mertvykh Prokliat'ia." *Nash sovremennik* 6 (1995): 186–192.

Nekhoroshev, Mikhail. "Generala igraet svita." *Znamia* 9 (1995): 211–219.

Nekrich, Aleksandr. *1941, 22 iiunia* (1965), izdanie 2-e, dopolnennoe i pererabotannoe. Moscow: Pamiatniki istoricheskoi mysli, 1995.

"Ob uvekovechenii Pobedy sovetskogo naroda v Velikoi Otechestvennoi voine 1941–1945 godov." *Federal'nyi zakon Rossiiskoi Federatsii, priniat 19 aprelia 1995 goda.*

"O nedostatkakh deiatel'nosti zagradotriadov voisk fronta." *Voenno-istoricheskii zhurnal* 8 (1988): 79–80.

Ovcharenko, Aleksandr. "Ot voiny k miru: O tvorchestve IUriia Bondareva." *Nash sovremennik* 5 (1983): 163–178.

Pavlov, V. V. STALINGRAD: *Mify i real'nost'*. Moscow: Olma-Press, 2003.

"Pis'ma v redaktsiiu: O fil'me *Shtrafniki*." *Literaturnaia gazeta*, 7 March 1990, 8.

Pogonii, IA. F i dr. *Stalingradskaia epopeia: Materialy NKVD SSSR i voennoi tsenzury iz Tsentral'nogo arkhiva FSB RF*. Moscow: Zvonnitsa-MG, 2000.

Popov, Aleksei. *NKVD i partizanskoe dvizhenie*. Moscow: Olma-Press, 2003.

"Prikaz Stavki verkhovnogo glavnogo komandovaniia Krasnoi armii," № 270, 16 avgusta 1941 goda'. *Voenno-istoricheskii zhurnal* 9 (1988): 26–28.

"Prikaz narodnogo komissara oborony № 0349, 29 oktiabria 1944." *Voenno-istoricheskii zhurnal* 8 (1988): 80.

Remarque, Erich Maria. *Im Westen nichts Neues* (1929). Cologne: Kiepenheuer & Witsch, 1984.

Reshin, Leonid. "Kollaboratsionisty i zhertvy rezhima." *Znamia* 8 (1994): 158–179.

Roberts, Craig, and Charles W. Sasser. *One Shot, One Kill*. New York: Pocket Books, Simon & Schuster, 1990.

Rutherford, Andrew. *The Literature of War: Five Studies in Heroic Virtue*. Basingstoke and London: Macmillan Press, 1978.

Samsonov, A. M. *Stalingradskaia bitva*, 4th ed. Moscow: Nauka, 1989.

Sassoon, Siegfried. *The War Poems of Siegfried Sassoon*, arranged and introduced by Rupert Hart-Davis. London: Faber & Faber, 1983.

Sella, Amnon. *The Value of Human Life in Soviet Warfare*. London: Routledge, 1992.

Semipriaga, M. I. *Kollaboratsionizm: Priroda, tipologiia i proiavleniia v gody vtoroi mirovoi voiny*. Moscow: ROSSPEN, 2000.

Senich, Peter R. *The German Sniper 1914–1945*. Boulder, CO: Paladin Press, and London and Melbourne: Arms and Armour Press, 1982.

Shentalinsky, Vitaly. *The KGB'S Literary Archive*. Trans. by John Crowfoot, with an introduction by Robert Conquest. London: Harvill Press, 1995.

Shtokman, Igor'. "Chernoe zerkalo." *Moskva* 4 (1993): 187–189.

Shvets, T. P. "Edinstvo protivopolozhnostei. K sravnitel'nomu analizu povesti V. Astaf'eva 'Pastukh i Pastushka' i V. Bykova 'Znak bedy.'" In *Iz istorii sovetskoi literatury: Mezhvuzovskii sbornik nauchnykh trudov*. Perm: Gospedint, 1992, 112–120.

Simonov, Aleksei. *Zhurnalisty na chechenskoi voine: Fakty, Dokumenty, Svidetel'stva, noiabr' 1994–dekabr' 1995*. Moscow: Prava cheloveka, 1995.

Smyslov, O. *Piataia kolonna Gitlera: Ot Kutepova do Vlasova*. Moscow: Veche, 2004.

Solzhenitsyn, Alexander. *August 1914: The Red Wheel 1: A Narrative in Discrete Periods of Time*. Trans. by H. T. Willets. Harmondsworth, Middlesex: Penguin, 1990.

——. *The Gulag Archipelago 1918–1956: An Experiment in Literary Investigation*, vol. 1. Trans. by Thomas Witney. New York: HarperCollins, 1991.

——. *Rossiia v obvale*. Moscow: Russkii put', 1998.

——. *The Russian Question at the End of the Twentieth Century* (1994). Translated by Yermolai Solzhenitsyn. London: Harvill Press, 1995.

——. *Warning to the Western World*. London: Bodley Head and BBC, 1976.

Stadniuk, Ivan. *Ispoved' Stalinista: Vospominatel'naia povest'*. Moscow: Patriot, 1993.

——. "Zametki ob istorizme." *Sobranie sochinenii v chetyrekh tomakh*, vol. 4. Moscow: Molodaia gvardiia, 1985, 380–387.

Stalin, I. "Prikaz Narodnogo komissara oborony Soiuza SSR, № 227, 28 iiulia 1942 g." *Voenno-istoricheskii zhurnal* 8 (1988): 73–75.

Stankovic, Milos. *Trusted Mole: A Soldier's Journey into Bosnia's Heart of Darkness*. London: HarperCollins, 2000.

Ste. Croix, Philip, ed. *Airborne Operations: An Illustrated Encyclopedia of the Great Battles of Airborne Forces*. London: Salamander Books, 1978.

Suvorov, Viktor. "Pochemu Zhukov ne mog navesti poriadok v Germanii?" *Kolokol' (Russkii zhurnal v Londone)* 1 (2002): 55–58.

Thucydides. *History of the Peloponnesian War*. Harmondsworth, Middlesex: Penguin, 1972.

Tkachenko, Petr. "Ne chernukhoi edinoi." *Krasnaia zvezda*, 5 February 1994, 6.

Tolstoy, Nikolai. *Victims of Yalta*. London: Hodder and Stoughton, 1978.

Troshev, Gennadii. *Moia voina: Chechenskii dnevnik okopnogo generala* (2001). Moscow: Vagrius, 2004.

"Tsena pobedy." *Voenno-istoricheskii zhurnal* 3 (1990): 14–16.

Tuchman, Barbara W. *The March of Folly: From Troy to Vietnam* (1984). London: Abacus, 1994.

Tys-Krokhhmaliuk, Yuriy. *UPA Warfare in Ukraine: Strategical, Tactical and Organisational Problems of Ukrainian Resistance in World War II*, with a preface by Ivan Wowchuk. Trans. by Walter Dushnyck. New York: Society of Veterans of Ukrainian Insurgent Army, 1972.

Tzu, Sun. *The Art of War*, edited and with a foreword by James Clavell. New York: Delacorte Press, 1988.

Vakhitova, T. M. "Narod na voine: Vzgliad V. Astaf'eva iz serediny 90-kh. Roman 'Prokliaty i ubity.'" *Russkaia literatura* 3 (1995): 114–129.

Vladimov, Georgiy. "Novoe sledstvie, prigovor staryi," in *General i ego armiia*. Moscow: Knizhnaia palata, 1997, 388–403.

"Voiny u nikh v pamiati netu, voina u nikh tol'ko v krovi." *Znamia* 5 (1995): 183–199.

Volkogonov, Dmitrii. "Triumf i tragediia: Politicheskii portret I.V. Stalina." *Oktiabr'* 7 (1989): 12–78.

——. "22 iiunia 1941 goda." *Znamia* 6 (1991): 3–15.

Volkova, E. V. "Tragicheskaia vina ('Ubity pod Moskvoi' Konstantina Vorob'eva)." *Voprosy filosofii* 11 (2001): 29–39.

Vurgaft, S. G., and I. A. Ushakov. *Staroobriadchestvo: Litsa, sobytiia, predmety, simvoly: Opyt entsiklopedicheskogo slovaria*. Moscow: Tserkov, 1996.

Werth, Alexander. *Russia at War 1941–1945* (1964). London: Pan Books, 1965.

Wette, Wolfram, and Gerd R. Ueberschär, eds. *Stalingrad: Mythos und Wirklichkeit einer Schlacht*. Frankfurt-am-Main: Fischer Taschenbuch Verlag, 1992.

Wright, Quincy. *A Study of War* (1942). Abridged by Louise Leonard Wright. Chicago and London: University of Chicago Press, 1964.

Zaitsev, Vasilii. *Za Volgoi zemli dlia nas ne bylo: Zapiski snaipera*. Moscow: DOSAAF, 1971.

Zelenkov, V. "Komu voina, a komu mat' rodna. Podzagolovok k 'Knigam pamiati'? Zametki frontovika o romane V. Astaf'eva 'Prokliaty i ubity.'" *Nash sovremennik* 9 (1997): 69–82.

Zhilin, V. A. *Stalingradskaia bitva: Khronika, Fakty, Liudi*. 2 vols. Moscow: Olma-Press, 2002.

Ziemke, Earl F. *Stalingrad to Berlin: The German Defeat in the East*. Washington, DC: Army Historical Series, Center of Military History U.S. Army, 1968.

Zolotarev, Major General, ed. *Russkii Arkhiv: Velikaia Otechestvennaia* vol. 17, no. 6, *Glavnye politicheskie organy vooruzhennykh sil SSSR v Velikoi Otechestvennoi Voine 1941–1945*. Moscow: TERRA, 1996.

Zolotov, Andrei. "Editorial." *Russia Profile* 2, no. 3 (April 2005): 1.

INDEX